THE WORK, WEALTH
AND HAPPINESS OF MANKIND

WILLIAM RITTASE.

THE MACHINE AND HUMANITY

POWER and danger in human hands. Along what roads, in what emulations, and to what ends will our great machines be driven?

THE WORK,
WEALTH AND HAPPINESS
OF MANKIND

BY

H. G. WELLS

VOLUME II

ILLUSTRATED

GREENWOOD PRESS, PUBLISHERS
NEW YORK   1968

First Greenwood reprinting, 1968

LIBRARY OF CONGRESS catalogue card number: 69-10170

Printed in the United States of America

CHAPTER THE TENTH

THE RICH, THE POOR, AND THEIR TRADITIONAL ANTAGONISM

CHAPTER THE TENTH

THE RICH, THE POOR, AND THEIR TRADITIONAL ANTAGONISM

§ 1. *Short Studies in the Acquisition or Attempted Acquisition of Wealth*

IN THE preceding chapter we have had to display the financial organization of man's economic life as loose, vague, experimental and extremely dangerous. We have had to show that money is still a most imperfect counter for social service, and that the getting of money, which for the most obvious reasons should be the correlative of productive exertion, becomes in many instances and very easily, a process parasitic upon, rather than contributory to, the progressive development of the economic organization. We have seen how badly the machinery as a whole is working at the present time. We now propose to show how it has worked in recent times in certain individual instances. We are going to put before the reader a selection of individual accumulators for his consideration.

Our studies will be chosen chiefly to illustrate the working of generally accepted property and money ideas and conventions. But one or two of our cases will anticipate certain issues about legislation and administration that we shall deal with in Chapter XII.

The study of individual instances of wealth-getting is a department of social research of growing value and importance. A number of scattered writers* have directed their attention to these enquiries, but so far they have scarcely got beyond the

---

*For example, Richard Lewinsohn with his *A la Conquête de la Richesse, Zaharoff,* and *Histoire de l'Inflation.* A more comprehensive study which Professor Laski recommends is G. Meyer's *History of the Great American Fortunes.*

anecdotal stage. Their studies are not yet numerous enough and searching enough for even a pretense of scientific treatment. The subject is at a stage comparable to that early phase of natural history when the collection of "curios" was preparing the way for the systematic marshalling of specimens in museum galleries.

HETTY GREEN AS AN UNCREATIVE ACCUMULATOR

For our first exhibit, a very wealthy product indeed of the current phase of financial organization, we will take Mrs. Hetty Green, who was born in 1825 at New Bedford and died in New York at the age of eighty-one worth a fortune of certainly over thirteen million pounds and probably of half as much again. She may be described as a pure accumulator. Her life has been written very ably by Boyden Sparks and Samuel Taylor Moore, to whom I make my acknowledgments, and it is essentially the history, as they put it, of a woman with a genius for acquiring and making money and an inability to spend it. She is therefore a very good test of the social value of the money incentive under modern conditions.

Apart from her passion for acquiring and holding money she seems to have been a humorous, industrious woman with a certain personal attractiveness, considerable homely skill in nursing and a taste for domestic drudgery. But she was by nature self-centred and acquisitive, and all the circumstances of her education developed a vindictive persona. Her habits were miserly from the beginning, and they became more so; in her phase of maximum business energy she wore newspapers in winter to avoid buying warm underclothing, and she lived in cheap lodging houses, moving from one to another in order to evade taxation. Her only luxury was hatred. Her self-esteem took the form of revenges of which she was proud. She liked to get equal with people who had thwarted her in her more questionable projects. She was one of those people who nurse grievances and pursue them, and she succeeded in ruining several men and in worrying one unfortunate trustee to death. These were her greater passions. She loved her son—to what extent we shall see—and she gradually dispossessed her husband of his property and separated herself from him on account of his habit of expenditure, in spite of her undeniable affection for him.

She was the daughter of a hard-fisted shipowner and trader, who followed the fashions of New English Puritans in leading a life of successful acquisition; she was at first a bold, handsome girl, whose face hardened quickly; she bullied her mother; perhaps she learnt that from her father; and when she was sent to New York for the winter with $1,200 to spend, she invested a thousand in bonds and went on investing thereafter. If she had the passions and vanities of a girl, she had them well under control. Her hostess in New York, being ashamed of her guest's dowdiness, bought smart and fashionable clothes for her, which Hetty put aside as too valuable to wear. After the death of her mother she lived with an invalid aunt whom also she bullied, making stupendous scenes on the slightest occasion—generally on such scores as the rate of domestic expenditure or the denial of access to her aunt's private papers.

Hetty was heiress both to this aunt and to her father. Her father left her nearly a million dollars as well as other property in trust; her aunt, who died worth about $2,000,000, had covertly made a will devoting about half of this sum to various charitable purposes and giving Hetty only the income for life of the residue. Hetty attempted to set this will aside in order to secure control of her aunt's entire capital, and she seems to have committed forgery, perjury and fraud in her unsuccessful attempts to do this. Then, being married to Mr. E. H. Green, who was also worth at least another million dollars, she set herself single-mindedly to the task of increasing her wealth. The tangle of litigation about the will ended in a compromise that left her with an income of 65,000 dollars a year from tied-up capital, and free cash to the value of about 650,000 dollars. Already before that she had been operating on an original fortune of a million, inherited from her father.

She and her husband lived for a time in Europe to escape the disagreeable atmosphere (and perhaps even the possibility of worse consequences) created by the will case, and in London— from their headquarters at the then most famous and splendid

Langham Hotel—she and her husband engaged in discreet but successful speculative operations. He was an able enough business man, and at first he had considerable influence over her and gave her valuable advice. It is evident from her subsequent history that the choice of that particular hotel was his. He had none of her retentive acquisitiveness. He speculated to spend; he did not know how to hold, and while he consumed what he had and made, Hetty acquired and acquired. In one year she made more than a million and a quarter dollars through the purchase of United States gold bonds. London knew little or nothing of American conditions; there was considerable doubt whether the Washington government might not break faith in regard to these bonds, and at times the uncertainty deepened to panic. There came the sort of opportunity for which Hetty lived.

The Greens returned to America in 1874, by which time the statute of limitations made any further annoyance on account of that will impossible, and they returned in a period of depression when buying cheap was easy.

Sparkes and Moore (*op. cit.*) quote her own explanation of her method:

"I believe in getting in at the bottom and out at the top. I like to buy railroad stock or mortgage bonds. When I see a good thing going cheap because nobody wants it, I buy a lot of it and tuck it away. Then when the time comes they have to hunt me up and pay me a good price for my holdings. I own a lot of city mortgages in crowded sections. They seem to me as good as anything.

"I don't much believe in stocks. I never buy industrials. Railroads and real estate are the things I like. Before deciding on an investment I seek out every kind of information about it. There is no great secret in fortune-making. All you have to do is buy cheap and sell dear, act with thrift and shrewdness and be persistent."

She pursued that system of buying, add our authors, in every transaction in which she engaged, whether she was buying a mortgage, a peck of potatoes, a house or a horse. In the spending of money she might have been compared to an athlete who never broke training. She spent nothing. In Green she possessed a steward who did not charge for his services, who supplied her with food, shelter and clothing, as any husband is required to do. Also in the earlier stages of their married life he gave her some very sound and shrewd counsels. Consequently there was not the slightest drain on her own fortune, and it grew monstrously. A time came when she separated her life and estate from Green's altogether, and he ended his days an elderly, impoverished loafer in a New York club.

She became a grotesque, familiar figure in the financial world of New York, a dingy, alert old woman in a hackney carriage, flitting from bank to bank, with bales and valises of securities. She would invade bank premises with her auriferous litter to save herself the expense of offices; she would borrow clerks and so recoup herself for the charges the banks made for the business they did for her. She would scold and weep and make a terrible fuss if things were not done as she desired.

The reader must go to the biography I have quoted for a fuller account of the habits of this astounding creature, of her gradual effacement of her husband in the conduct of her affairs, and of how she sacrificed the leg of her son, whom she certainly loved very greatly, to her hatred of paying doctors' fees. The leg was injured in a toboggan accident, and failing proper treatment became so bad that at last it had to be amputated. She used to dress herself and her son in their shabbiest clothing in order to get advice and treatment in free clinics. But the doctors knew her. The clinics were warned against her. She grudged the cost of a competent specialist until it was too late. And yet they say she nursed that son, skilfully and devotedly.

Enough has been said here to show the quality of her life. The aspect that most concerns us is that she was able to lead such a life and keep her self-respect. She was proud of herself. Her persona sanctioned these things. The system of ideas in which she was reared, and which prevailed in the world about her, justified her career.

She had grown up in a community which held the getting of money to be the test of a satisfactory life, and where want of money was considered more hideous than any deformity. She was ego-centred, responsive to the standards about her, and capable of great sacrifices, so far as immediate satisfactions were concerned, to the ruling ideas in her mind. In happier circumstances she might have had altogether different ruling ideas; she might have been a fanatic of faith or works; or if money had really been a fair measure of public service, even her avarice might have become an incentive to vigorous efforts for the community. As it was, she became a morbid accumulation and an arrest of spending power. She stimulated no wholesome human activity.

She was misguided. It is the way in which she was misguided that concerns us. She was misguided by our monetary-credit system and by our reliance upon competition in getting as a test of worth. Her significance in this study of human work and wealth lies in her demonstration of the entire ineffectiveness of that money-credit system. The money-credit system should be a system for stimulating and rewarding productive energy. Here we see in the plainest way how its fluctuations can be diverted entirely to unproductive accumulation. That is the fundamental unsoundness of the money motive. We see the surplus profits of the activities of city and railroad converging upward to this sordid, clutching old woman, who desired no progress, imagined no increase in the grace and sweetness of life, opposed any development that touched her monopolies and securities.

Slowly, inevitably, her fortune grew. She was a patient, implacable creditor. Only her death arrested the growth and concentration of her property. An immortal Hetty Green would have become step by step, and in strict accordance with the rules of the money credit game, the owner of an economically arrested world.

And it happened as a further mitigation of her activities that, as her hoard accumulated, money cheapened. She added million to million and became a legendary figure in Wall Street, but all the while something else was happening in the world on a larger scale than any of her operations. New sources of gold had been discovered and were yielding abundantly; cheques quickened and multiplied payments, production increased immensely, and the gross increase of wealth in the world was out of all proportion greater than her individual gettings. In a world of falling prices her strangulating influence would have been a very serious thing, but that abundant later nineteenth century, with its amplifying financial resources, could carry Hetty Green without much discomfort.

THE LANDGRAVE OF HESSE-CASSEL, THE ROTHSCHILDS AND NATIONAL LOANS

Mrs. Hetty Green is a single specimen, a solitary acquisitive individual reacting to the ideas current in her time and circle, of ownership and success. She succeeded, and the world that had made her disliked her. How many minor Hetty Greens, male and female, there are in the world, individual centres of sterilizing ownership, it is impossible to estimate. So it is impossible to estimate their arresting action upon the general economic process. There may be multitudes of minor hoards of the same moral quality.

We will turn now to a larger system of acquisitions, to that great family of money accumulators and operators, the Rothschild family.

The beginning of the story goes far back beyond the beginnings of Hetty Green. It goes back into the period before railways and the gold discoveries of the middle nineteenth century, to the days when the supply of gold was restricted, and almost the only way to wealth and power lay through the acquisition either of land or of the key-metal. Land aggregation, saving and usury, were the older ways in which one grew rich. You saved, you tried to monopolize, you squeezed the needy. The story opens with a territorial prince selling men and lending money, and a Jew trader selling jewels wisely. It brings us into the modern period, when the finance of great industrial undertakings was beginning to overshadow the loans of militant states.

The Rothschilds were shop-keeping Jews in the Frankfort ghetto, general dealers. It was a prosperous but not conspicuously rich family, until the days of Meyer Anselm Rothschild,

in the latter half of the eighteenth century. He was interested
in coins; he became among other things an expert dealer in
medals and jewels, and in those days of small states and diverse
coinages his knowledge and advice were useful to his contemporary, the Count of Hanau-Nunzenburg, who presently became Landgrave of Hesse-Cassel. The landgrave was a seller
of men. Human flesh was one of the chief exports of Hesse-
Cassel. He took his subjects, made soldiers of them, and sold
them by the regiment to various foreign powers, particularly to
the English government, at that time in conflict with its North
American colonies. When any of his men were killed or maimed
he received compensation from the hiring government. There is
no record of the payment being handed on to the wounded men
or the families of those who were killed. He inherited very considerable wealth by the standards of that time, he was insanely
avaricious, and he had marked financial ability. Rothschild, who
had won his confidence steadily, became his "Agent General"
and ally, and in various transactions his partner. Loans were
made to the rulers of Denmark, Hesse-Darmstadt and Baden.
Rothschild was already in possession of a respectable fortune in
the dawn of the Napoleonic age. When the landgrave had to
flee before Napoleon in 1806, Rothschild, in association with
friendly bankers in Frankfort, was able to save the larger part
of his fortune for him.

This Meyer Anselm Rothschild died in 1812, leaving a widow
of vigorous character and five sons. The old general shop still
flourished beside the new and growing bank. The unmarried
daughters, the sons and the daughters-in-law, says Lewinsohn,*
all took a part in the shop; one was cashier; the sons travelled to
deal personally with the more important transactions of the
firm.

A year or so before his death old Meyer Anselm sold his business to his five sons for a sum which he then bequeathed to his
wife and daughters. This was done in accordance with one of the
fundamental principles of Rothschild policy—all money, and the
sole control of the business, must be kept in the family. To this

*A la Conquête de la Richesse.

end he shut out his daughters' husbands from the common interest, and to this end the third and fourth generations intermarried, but without any intensification of the ancestral business
ability.

At the time when their father died the sons had already begun
to spread themselves in Europe. The most talented, Nathan
Meyer Rothschild, had established himself in England, and in
order to facilitate his transactions with the continent had arranged that another brother—James—should settle in Paris.
It was this willingness to adventure themselves in foreign countries, together with their strong family sentiment, which gave
the Rothschilds both their strength and their opportunities.
Through all wars, invasions, blockades and changes of government, they could trust one another in a manner impossible to the
mere groups of banks and merchants who were their rivals.
They could supply one another with the most dangerous and
intimate information, information the collection of which they
organized with the greatest care. Later they instituted a special
system of couriers. In spite of the enormous expense, they found
this worth their while, for they not only secured for their business a privacy which could not be counted upon by any other
firm in Europe, but they left themselves free to send through
the post or in embassy bags any documents which they wanted
the governments of the moment to read. Further, on the basis
of this entire confidence, they were able to let themselves be
absorbed each in the life of his own adopted country, naturalize
himself, and work in the interests of its government, as long,
of course, as it did not threaten Rothschilds in particular or
Jews in general. They knew that, under this scheme, if all the
Rothschilds could not be on the winning side, at least one must
be, and in a position powerfully to assist the others. It is said
moreover, that no one of them ever criticized another's business
policy.

The most dramatic example of this international coöperation
was perhaps the system by which Nathan and James in London and Paris were able to keep Wellington in the Peninsula
supplied with money for his armies. Nathan had already made

a considerable fortune by ordinary trading when he was entrusted, through his father's influence, with the making of some important English investments on behalf of the Elector. This gave him the command, if only for short periods, of large sums of money, and he used them to buy gold and silver and smuggle them across the Channel into France. This in itself was extremely profitable so long as he could be certain that the French would give a passage to his consignments, and to secure consent he arranged that James should go to Paris and interview the authorities. The Continental blockade was in force, but Napoleon had found that he must either allow his allies a certain amount of permitted smuggling into, and out of, England or lose them as allies; and James, by representing that the English were extremely anxious to prevent the precious metals from leaving their country, was able to obtain permission to receive his parcels from Nathan. The English were, in fact, most anxious to get money through to Wellington, and this, James, by using Rothschild connections to buy bills on bankers in the south of Europe, could do with uninterrupted success.

Later England herself ran short of gold, and Nathan was able to make very large profits, first by knowing where to buy gold, which he sold to the English government, and then by undertaking its transport to the troops abroad. He succeeded also in getting across to Holland, where he bought up the French money with which the Continent was flooded, and again through his brother in Paris conveyed it to Spain.

His services to the English were fully recognized by the Chancellor of the Exchequer, and he made use of his new credit to suggest at once that the Rothschilds should be given part of the work of transmitting the British subsidies to Austria. At this time the expenses of handling these subsidies from Britain were very high. Metternich reckoned that what with loss on the exchange, commissions, and bankers' charges, one third of the money—two millions out of six—would disappear before it reached his hands. The British government naturally desired that as much of its money as possible should be spent on the upkeep of the Austrian armies and it was glad to support the advances of the

Rothschilds when they offered to undertake the work without
upsetting the exchanges and to guarantee the money's safe
arrival. But the Austrians at that time preferred to have their
affairs mismanaged by Austrians and Christians rather than
that they should be handled prudently and honestly by foreign
Jews.

In spite of this check, however, the reputation of the firm was
spreading all over Europe. The renown of Nathan in particular was growing, and it assumed a legendary tinge when one
of his agents brought him the news of the victory of Waterloo
a day sooner than the official despatches reached the British
government. It was said that Nathan's information had been
obtained by a special secret pigeon post, and also that he himself
brought it across the Channel through a raging storm, and laid
the foundations of his incredible fortune by utilizing his knowledge on the London Stock Exchange. If, as is highly probable,
he did use his early information in this fashion, he can have made
only a small amount in comparison with the enormous sums he
had already earned. What in fact he did with the news was to
take it at once to the government, which refused to believe it,
and was correspondingly impressed when it was confirmed next
day.

The financial readjustments which followed Waterloo were
the perfect opportunity for the Rothschilds. To begin with, the
war indemnities imposed on France had to be conveyed across a
distracted Europe. To every other agent this meant the physical
moving of cash and bullion in large amounts, with its attendant
risks. The Rothschilds alone were in a position to give an absolute guarantee against losses, for they alone could raise the
money where they wanted it without any movement of cash at
all. They were, in fact, immediately entrusted with the handling
of over £20,000,000; and they received for their successful conduct of the business a commission of 1½ per cent, the warm
thanks of the English Chancellor, and their longed-for opening
in Austria. The government of that country, heavily in debt to
its own bankers, not only now consented to receive its share
of the indemnities from their hands, but also allowed them to

advance large sums on account of future payments. These transactions went off so well that the Emperor—after a good deal of solicitation—granted titles of nobility to all the brothers except Nathan. In fact, so convenient did the Austrian ministers find it to deal with this family, who kept their engagements, who carried through their business with the minimum of disturbance, who took the trouble to have their letters written in a hand which ministers could read, and phrased in a manner which laymen could understand, that in complete reversal of their previous most Catholic attitude, Solomon was invited to set up a branch in Vienna and entrusted with the issue of a lottery loan of 20 million gulden. In the meantime Meyer Anselm (Meyer Anselm II), the eldest brother, who had remained in Frankfort, had lent several millions to Prussia, and the new Viennese branch was soon to finance a loan of £6,000,000 to Russia. All governments at this time needed money even more urgently than usual, and for the Rothschilds it was for a time a question of naming their own terms and picking and choosing among their possible debtors. The nobility of Prussia and Austria were equally in need; so that both the Viennese and Frankfort branches of the firm were also able to build up a lucrative business in making private loans.

The partition of Europe between the brothers was now completed by Metternich, who sent Carl Rothschild to Naples where the Austrians had been crushing a revolution. It was Carl's business to manage the loans forced on the people of Naples by their conquerors and to represent the Austrian interest. A true Rothschild, however, financier rather than partisan, he began to identify himself with the country in which he settled, to oppose the continuance of the Austrian occupation, and to stand out against the more outrageous of the Austrian claims. In order to reëstablish Neapolitan finances he lent the little kingdom very large sums on his own account, and when its rulers proved incapable of prudent administration, he forced them to accept his nominee as Minister of Finance, got their affairs into some sort of order, procured a loan for them from England, and so improved his reputation that he achieved finally the unexpected position of banker to the Pope!

In the meantime James had opened a bank in Paris, where loans were as much in request as everywhere else. It was an immediate success. He soon became, after the King, the richest man in France, and Metternich said to him: "The house of Rothschild plays a much more important rôle in France than any foreign power, with the possible exception of England." The Rothschilds were now the greatest financiers in the world, and for the next twenty years, at least, their fortunes continued to increase.

It is unnecessary, for the purpose of this book, to trace the remainder of their careers in further detail, for they did not alter their policy, the third and fourth generations produced no dominant figures, and on the whole they held aloof from the real business of the new age, the industrialization of Europe. Solomon in Vienna financed Austrian railways indeed, and interested himself in mines and blast-furnaces. But he supported these enterprises solely as a financier—the organization of a great industry, its technical side, made no appeal to him. The French Rothschilds bought oil-fields in Russia, but sold them in 1911 to the Royal Dutch Shell group. First and last the Rothschilds have been dealers in money, with only one other spontaneous interest. If they begged for titles and pushed their way into the social life of the capitals of Europe, it was because that method of approach was forced upon them. Without titles they could not have entered into the personal relations with the nobles who held what was almost a monopoly of offices of state. Old Meyer Anselm had made his way by his knowledge of coins and jewels; his sons patronized the arts in the same spirit—it helped them to obtain what the Americans call "contacts." The head of the firm in Frankfort led a simple bourgeois life—if James in Paris threw money out of his window he did not throw it for the fun of the thing, but as means to an end. Their descendants have acquiesced in wealth—they have never produced a new idea for the handling or spending of it.

They ceased to dominate the finance of Europe, not because

of failure or disaster—they have saved themselves from that with remarkable skill—but because the gold discoveries of the last century, flowing into the new channels provided by the growth of industry, went to build up not only great accumulations but millions of small middle-class fortunes, and thus made possible our joint-stock banking system and its towering structure of credit. There is too much money in the world to-day for the resources of one family to be any longer of dominating importance. The Rothschilds are said, by refusing a loan, to have prevented Metternich from making war upon Belgium. In 1930 ten million small investors would rush to take their place.

To return to the one great unmercenary activity which has been mentioned—the assistance of their fellow-Jews. From the beginning they used both their money and their interest on behalf first of the Frankfort Jews and later of Jewry wherever it may be found. To the present day that tradition holds them. It is easy to set this down to calculation, to say that when they freed their fellow-Jews they freed themselves, and that the money expended came back to them in grateful coöperation. The letters they wrote, the way they went to work, do not give that impression. Racial loyalty seems to have been as much part of the instinctive make-up of these remarkable men as their family solidarity or their persistence in business.

If the Rothschilds had never lived, would the world have been worse or better off? There is no decisive answer to the question. They accumulated enormous fortunes—constellations of enormous fortunes; their rate of profit was extremely high, and the states which harboured them paid dearly for their assistance. On the other hand, they worked very hard for what they earned, and rendered what are called "distinguished services." We may say a great deal against them. They charged too much. Though they turned their coats when governments changed on the whole they supported reaction. They deteriorated under the strain of wealth. They used their wealth and intelligence to set an example of ostentation, and supported no great principle or cause but the grievances of their own race. They were the first to manipulate the Stock Exchange on a large scale. Finally, they were and are, in respect of their own jobs, totally unscientific. In the financial welter which followed the present war, no single Rothschild came forward to unite the enormous fund of information which the family must possess with the theoretic knowledge now at the command of economists. One such man might have saved a thousand blunders and been of incalculable service to the world.

To their credit one must place this—they were honest. To arrive, they made use of the methods of the age, but what they promised they performed. No one had ever been honest before on so large a scale, in respect of transactions passing through so many hands and in such troubled times. They not only honoured their own obligations, they introduced financial integrity and sound financial methods into courts and places where such things had never been seriously thought of. Dishonesty is one of the most wasteful and destructive of anti-social vices, and the prestige the Rothschilds gave to probity in finance was a very great contribution to the economic development of the new time. Whether that contribution could have been made at a lesser cost to the community is now only an historical speculation. All that they did was just and justifiable by contemporary standards.

CORNELIUS VANDERBILT, JAY GOULD AND RAILWAY DEVELOPMENT

We turn now to two men whose money-getting lives are best considered together in contrast and conflict. They lived in the same financial world; they played their games on the same board, but while Gould was essentially a maker of money, Vanderbilt was a man of a more complex intellectual and moral quality. Both were fairly unscrupulous when it came to bribing a legislator or a judge. Neither of them amassed his fortune simply by buying cheap and selling dear and by loans and usuries. They won their gettings by much more active and aggressive proceedings. They played a complicated part in the process of replacing old methods of transport by new—the cardinal fact of human history in the middle of the nineteenth century.

That period saw a very great stimulation of productive industry by the discovery of new supplies of gold in California, Australia and other regions. This meant, as we have already pointed out in our discussion of money and credit, a rise in prices, a fall in the real value of debts, and so a relief of debtors and an unburthening of business. Everywhere enterprise found money easier to obtain, became brisker; in particular, the spread of the new railroads and steamships was quickened.

Material forces and social needs were all on the side of a rapid extension of the new transport over the whole United States. On the other hand, as we have noted in Chapter III, the early disposition was to use railways only for heavy traffic of not very long range, and it was only slowly—and too late to get wide gauges—that men realized the immense possibilities of long-range trains and continental railway transport. Consequently, the story of railway development in America begins with the appearance of a miscellany of petty lines. The linking of these into systems of wider range involved huge operations and bargainings, struggles to "capture" railways and so forth of the most extraordinary sort, made all the more extraordinary by the feeble grip of the legal and police organization, in many of the states, upon bold and resolute men who knew when to employ violent methods. With this linking up of the American network is associated the rise of such names as Morgan, Harriman and others, but it is on Jay Gould and Vanderbilt that we will focus the light for our present study.

Vanderbilt was the older, abler, and greater man but it suits our present purpose better to make Jay Gould the *jeune premier* of our display.

Jay Gould was born in Roxbury, New York State, in 1836. He came of a respectable English family. The Christian names of his forbears included Nathan, Abel and Abraham, and his build and appearance were Hebraic, but according to his biographer, Mr. Robert Irving Warshow,* there is little other evidence of a Jewish origin. His parents were extremely poor, and his health suffered all his life from the privations he en-

---

*Author of *Jay Gould. The Story of a Fortune,* from which many of the facts in this account are taken.

dured as a child. And, for an American millionaire, his religious training seems to have been superficial.

He was obliged to work far too hard on his father's little farm, and when, after only a year's schooling, he got a job in a country store, his hours were from six in the morning until ten at night. He said afterwards that he used to get up at three in order to study mathematics and surveying, and that during this time he arrived at the hard and permanent realization that one must look after oneself and let others do the same. At seventeen he obtained a post as a map-maker, working first for a firm that went bankrupt and then on his own account. He was more or less successful, and local people began to talk of him as a promising young man, but the chief advantage he gained from his surveying work was that it took him from one area of exploitation to another and introduced him to wealthy people. With one of these, a rich retired tanner named Zadoc Pratt, he managed to establish a friendship so close that the old man finally offered to set him up in a tannery. The two were to be equal partners, Gould was to do the work, and Pratt to furnish the capital of $120,000. Gould seized his opportunity, made a success of his tannery, and was soon recognized as an able man of business by the leather merchants in New York. Unfortunately for Pratt, he was also one of those men who find it impossible to be honest. He could not keep his fingers off money, and within a year the old tanner found that his protégé had been falsifying the books. He did not prosecute, but merely told Gould that he must either buy his, Pratt's, share in the business for $60,000 or be bought out himself. Gould went to New York, where he soon found financial backing in a wealthy and respected leather merchant called Leupp, and Pratt retired, having lost $60,000 through his generosity.

Leupp did not live long to regret his bargain. Three years later a wave of depression swept over the country, and in the middle of the business anxieties occasioned by this he discovered that Gould had been using his name to make large purchases with the idea of arranging a corner in hides. Overwhelmed by the fear of disgrace, this second benefactor shot himself, and

Gould was left to struggle with the heirs for the control of the tannery. In the end it came to an actual fight between two bands of armed men. Gould apparently tried to best Leupp's son-in-law over some detail of the negotiations, and both sides tried to secure possession of the tannery by force. Gould's army of fifty men were victors in the battle, but his opponent managed so to tie up the business by litigation that Gould abandoned it and set off for New York with the few thousand dollars he had been able to retain.

In that city he found almost at once another wealthy man to befriend him. This time it was a grocer named Philip Miller, upon whom Gould made so favourable an impression that he was soon accepted as a son-in-law. The marriage seems to have been completely happy, for Gould, it seems, possessed an affectionate and gentle side, which he reserved almost exclusively for domestic use. At that time Miller owned a large block of worthless shares in a derelict railway—the Rutland and Washington—and Gould, who appears to have had no particular occupation, suggested that he might be sent to inspect and report on the line. It ran through country he had covered during one of his surveys; he knew the railway had possibilities and advised his father-in-law to purchase control. This was done, Gould was made president, secretary, treasurer and superintendent, and succeeded within a few months in selling his own share of the railway to a neighbouring line for $130,000.

With the profits from this he purchased control of other small lines, pulled them together, or made a show of doing so, and then sold them to the big railway combinations which were forming at that time. He had a quick eye for the potentialities of these little railways, and in less than a year he had made a profit of $100,000. If in fact he reorganized these lines before he parted with them, it was the last constructive work he ever did. He used his winnings to set up in Wall Street as a partner in a firm of brokers, Smith, Gould & Martin, and from that time forward, whatever he may have said he was doing, he devoted himself to the manipulation of share values.

Little is known about this firm, or about Gould's transactions while a member of it, but neither of his partners came to a good end, and both became his enemies. Martin died bankrupt in an insane asylum, and Smith was ruined by Gould. From the first Gould seems to have worked on his own account rather than in conjunction with the firm, using his connection with it principally to bring himself to the notice of bigger men. The great event of this phase—which covered the period of the Civil War—was that he came into touch with the once notorious Daniel Drew.

Drew was the treasurer and director and virtual controller of the Erie Railroad—the most important of the growing and extending railway systems which connected the Middle West and the Great Lakes with New York. He had got himself on to its board of directors first by spreading rumours about its financial stability at a moment when it needed money, and then himself, for a very high price, lending it the funds required. He was by origin a circus man and cattle drover who had "got religion" and subsequently made a large fortune out of steamships on the river Hudson, and after that another large one on Wall Street. He was now using his position—with an entire disregard for the interests of the shareholders—to cause movements in the price of Erie shares. He could, apparently, make them rise and fall as far and as quickly as he chose, and though the line was a valuable property and doing an excellent business Drew was making more from it on the Stock Exchange than the railway itself made from its total traffic receipts. When he met Gould he was in need of an ally. His hold on the Erie was threatened by New York's greatest financier at that time, Cornelius Vanderbilt, and he felt himself inadequate for a single-handed struggle. Vanderbilt was proposing to rescue the Erie Railroad from Drew's unrighteous hands.

So we bring Cornelius Vanderbilt into the picture. Let us explain who he was and why Drew should have found him too formidable to resist alone. Drew had already had some disagreeable experiences of Vanderbilt. Vanderbilt at this time (1869–70) was over seventy years old. He was born in Port Richmond, Staten Island, and—with his possibly abler son William—he occupied a dominant position in the railway world.

He was essentially an improver of business; Gould essentially a plunderer and wrecker. Throughout his life Vanderbilt had been taking hold of things and making them go better—with very great profit to himself and his family.

His father was a poor farmer, and as a boy of sixteen he left the farm and started a modest ferry-boat service of his own between Staten Island and New York. These ferry-boats then were small sailing boats. It needed little capital to start such an enterprise. By efficiency and ruthless overwork, and by equally ruthless economy at home, he made his service trustworthy and respected. By the time he was twenty-three he had got together three boats and $9,000,—as well as a wife and family. The boats were bringing in a steady income, and most men would have settled down at that in gradually expanding contentment. But steam was now appearing in the world, and he sold out his ferry service and began life again as an employee, as captain on a rackety primitive steamship, in order that he might study and follow up the possibilities of the new power.

At that time the state of New York had granted a monopoly of steamboat traffic to two men, Fulton and Livingston. But this monopoly applied only to the New York landings. The boat Vanderbilt commanded was a "pirate," dodging between the state of New York and the state of New Jersey, and he had not only to secure punctual running with thoroughly unreliable engines, but also he had to protect his boat and his crew from the sabotage and persecution of his competitors and himself evade arrest whenever they stopped within the New York jurisdiction. In spite of the handicap of these conditions, he built up a service, and made it pay so well that to break the competition Fulton and Livingston offered him four times his salary and the command of their largest steamer, if he would abandon his employer and come into their pay. He refused, for he intended to become an owner himself, and to make that possible it was necessary to break the New York monopoly. He remained therefore the manager and inspiration of his original employer in the legal struggle that followed. The details of it may be read in *Commodore Vanderbilt,* by J. A. Howden Smith. In 1824

Chief Justice Marshall, in the Supreme Court of the United States, decided that any shipowner might take his vessels to any landing in the States so long as he possessed a coasting license. So the New York–New Jersey service won its freedom. Steamboat traffic was increasing rapidly on all the American rivers, and Vanderbilt next organized a service for his employer between New York and Philadelphia (25 miles in 22 hours for $3.00), which was the cheapest, fastest, and most comfortable in the country. By 1829 he had $30,000 saved and felt able to set up for himself, move to New York, and build up a fleet of his own.

His driving force, his courage, and the quickness with which he seized upon new developments—such as the water-tube boilers stoked with anthracite which were everywhere displacing the old wood-burning engines—enabled him to cut prices and drive out competitors, and in the years which followed he became a wealthy man, the owner by 1848 not only of some of the finest ships in the country, but also of ironworks and shipyards. At that time Daniel Drew was also running steamships; the two men made friends and together bought the Boston & Stonington Railway, which, with their steamers, gave them a through route from New York to Boston.

It was the Californian gold-rush of 1849 which enabled Vanderbilt to take his next step towards financial greatness. At that time transcontinental railways were undreamt of, and the shortest route to the gold-fields was via Panama. He saw that if he could run boats up the River San Juan—which flows between Nicaragua and Costa Rica—organize a steamship service across Lake Nicaragua and make a canal of a few miles to the Pacific, it would give him a route 500 miles shorter and far less expensive to work than the one in use. He travelled to London to get money for this scheme, but without success, for not only was the San Juan River considered to be unnavigable on account of rapids, but Lake Nicaragua lies so high above sea level that a canal would involve the construction of extremely extensive locks. Not to be discouraged, Vanderbilt went to Nicaragua himself in a small boat with a wooden bottom, determined to steam up the river anyhow. He took command himself, and said afterwards that when they reached the rapids, "I just tied down the safety valve and jumped the damn rocks." He did finally organize his "Transit," taking the passengers as far as the worst rapids in iron-hulled boats "which used to clang merrily as they jumped from rock to rock," and then sending the traveller on by a porterage, another stretch by steamship, and finally a coach service. The scheme succeeded, for the journey was shorter by two days than the Panama route and cost only $300 as against $600. This achievement both made him famous and brought him a fortune; by 1853 he was worth $11,000,000. When he went to Europe again in an immense yacht of his own building, he was received by the Lord Mayor of London at the Mansion House and by the Czar of Russia.

When he got back he found the "Transit" involved in a filibustering war, and he seems for some years rather to have enjoyed taking a vicarious part in it by means of agents, subsidies and political intrigues. But he finally abandoned the enterprise when he sold his ships in 1859. At that time he was running an Atlantic service and was able to compete successfully with other American lines, but taxes placed by Congress on hulls, engines, iron, steel, copper, lead, spars, sails and cordage made it impossible for American boats to hold the sea against the French and British. He decided, therefore, to leave shipping and concentrate on railways.

A large number of railways had already been built in New York State, but they were short, wastefully planned, and overcapitalized, and many of them had gone bankrupt or almost bankrupt in a financial panic which had swept America in 1857. Yet the need of great transcontinental lines, the great future of American railways, was becoming more and more plainly manifest.

And now Cornelius was to find congenial help in his own household for his new creative task. During the Civil War his eldest son William had asked him whether he might be made receiver of a small derelict line in Staten Island. He wanted to try out his administrative ability. He reorganized and reëquipped this line so successfully that in five years its shares had risen from a few dollars to $175. Manifestly, then, this might be worth doing on a larger scale. In 1862 Cornelius began to buy stock of the New York & Harlem Railway, when it stood at $9.00. He got control, gave the line to William to reorganize, and the stock rose to $50. A year later he did the same with the New York & Hudson River. During these operations he was twice assailed by Daniel Drew, and twice defeated him. On the first occasion Drew persuaded the New York Common Council to sell Harlem Railway short, and then break its price by suddenly rescinding an ordinance which gave Vanderbilt permission to run a tramway line in conjunction with the railway. The councillors sold at $100 thousands of shares which they did not possess, only to find that Vanderbilt was the purchaser, and that all the real shares of the company were also in his hands. The bears were ruined, all but Drew, who persuaded Vanderbilt, apparently for the sake of their old association, to let him off for half a million dollars.

The next encounter was of a similar character. Vanderbilt had brought before the State Legislature a bill allowing him to amalgamate the two railways. To do this he was obliged to bribe legislators, and he bought enough promises to get a majority. Drew, however, arriving later at Albany, persuaded the people's representatives that they were missing a chance of making large profits. Hudson Railway shares, he explained, stood at $150; if they sold short and then defeated Vanderbilt's bill they would be able to bring the price down to $50. But again the same thing happened. Vanderbilt, with the support of his friends, was able to buy up all they dared sell, until finally he had bought 27,000 more shares than in fact existed. When delivery became due the price rose to $285—it could as easily have gone to $1,000, but Vanderbilt's friends begged him to settle in order to avoid ruining every broker in Wall Street. Drew, this time, is said to have lost $1,000,000. Even without his bill Vanderbilt was able to effect a practical consolidation of the two lines.

After that he set out to acquire the New York Central, a line running from Buffalo down the Hudson to Albany, where boats or the Hudson Railway carried on to New York. It was not until 1867 that he was able to effect this, and to hand over the line to William Vanderbilt, so that its rails might be relaid, and its engines and cars replaced. In 1869 he secured a Consolidation Bill for all three lines, which now became an efficiently worked and exceedingly valuable property. He was strongly blamed for increasing the stock of the combine from $44,000,000 to $86,000,000, which with a profit in cash of $6,000,000 was said to be an excessive reward. But the service rendered was great, and the shares of the combined enterprise rose ultimately to $200.

And here we take up the story of Jay Gould again, for it was at this point in his career that Cornelius Vanderbilt came into collision with Drew and with Gould his ally, over the control of the Erie. If once he could add that line to the other three his hold over the traffic of New York would be complete. It must have irked his efficient, constructive mind to see a great railway allowed to fall into an almost derelict condition—its rails rusting away, its rolling-stock in shocking disrepair, its service untrustworthy—while men whom he regarded as common thieves gambled with its stock. He announced publicly that he meant to clear out the whole pack of them, and he set confidently to work to secure the election of sufficient of his nominees as directors to control the line. It could not have seemed a difficult undertaking. Drew was not popular with the stockholders; proxies (the power to vote in elections of directors) were usually purchasable, and Vanderbilt must have thought that it would be easy to buy enough of them to enable him to win the forthcoming election, do what he wished about its reorganization, and save himself the expense of actually buying the line.

Daniel Drew was fully aware of his danger, and he invited Gould onto the board in order to strengthen his position. From that moment Gould wielded an increasing influence over the policy of the Erie Railroad. For some time Drew remained as the figurehead, but he was by nature treacherous, and Gould found that his natural ally on the board was not its treasurer, but another director called Fisk, also a protégé of Drew's, and also invited to the board by him in order to defend the railway against the purifying domination of Vanderbilt. These three, Drew, Gould, and Fisk, acted in common throughout the struggle which followed.

It was long and complicated, and its ins and outs are described in a confused but extremely amusing series of articles written at the time by the two brothers, Charles Francis and Henry Adams.* It appeared probable that Vanderbilt's nominees would win the election and get control, and Drew, Gould and Fisk decided to provide for this contingency. Drew, by arrangement with them, went to Vanderbilt and offered to cease certain of his market operations, and in particular to send Erie shares up instead of down, in return for an agreement that if he were defeated he should be reinstated on the board after the election and sit there in the Vanderbilt interest.

There is really no reasonable explanation of the fact that Vanderbilt accepted. He knew Drew, he knew the man was incapable of an honest intention, much less straightforward conduct, and yet, after the election had resulted in a victory for Vanderbilt's side, he replaced his old enemy on the board. Then he began to draw up plans for an amalgamation of all four railways.

This was the last thing Drew wanted, for it would have put an end to his manipulation of Erie stock. Quietly, therefore, behind Vanderbilt's back, he began to agitate against the proposed amalgamation. Its actual terms when they were stated gave him an excuse. Vanderbilt intended to divide the profits of the new pool between all four lines in such a way that Erie, which earned more than half of the total, would receive only one third. The Erie directors joined together to refuse this, and Vanderbilt found himself defeated.

There was no doubt that he had been betrayed by Drew, and he was extremely angry. In addition, he had been made a fool of in public. He announced, therefore, that he intended to buy

---

*Reprinted 1929 and published as *High Finance in the Sixties*, Yale University Press.

up the line and ordered his brokers to purchase enough Erie stock to give him and his friends control.

At that time there was in existence about $86,000,000 worth of shares. A large amount of this was held in England by persons not favourable to Drew, the whereabouts of the rest was pretty well known, and Vanderbilt felt confident of his ability to carry out his purpose. Only one danger seemed to him serious, and that was that the Drew party might issue more fresh stock than he could buy. Once before Drew had sold short of Erie and then produced, at the last moment, 58,000 fresh share certificates printed to meet the occasion. Now again Drew's game was trending in the same direction. Under a statute of the state of New York, a railway company might create and issue its own stock in exchange for the stock of any line which was under lease to it, and Drew and his friends had recently bought and leased to the Erie a little railway called the Buffalo, Bradford & Pittsburgh. By creating and issuing new Erie stock in exchange for the Buffalo, Bradford & Pittsburgh stock, the Erie gang could greatly increase the load of stock Vanderbilt would have to buy.

To prevent this manœuvre Vanderbilt decided to litigate. His lawyers applied to the Supreme Court of New York, and, on the strength of some of Drew's past transactions, asked for a series of legal injunctions which would suspend Drew from his office of treasurer, order him to return to the Erie Railroad 68,000 shares of its stock said to be improperly held by him, and debar the directors from adding in any way to the amount of the company's stock then in existence. These injunctions were granted by the judge—a certain Judge Barnard, who was destined to be turned off the bench at a later date for his activities on behalf of Gould and Fisk—and their effect should have been to lessen the amount of stock which Vanderbilt would have to buy by one fourth of the whole amount.

Drew, Fisk and Gould, who were all selling short, seemed to be heading for ruin. Nevertheless, they continued to carry on business and to sell to Vanderbilt, day after day, stock which they did not hold. As for the injunctions, they went to another judge who, under the American legal system, had coördinate authority in New York State with the first, and from him they obtained another injunction suspending one of the directors who was a friend of Vanderbilt's and his channel of information, and staying all proceedings in the suit commenced before Judge Barnard. Vanderbilt replied by getting the latter to forbid any meeting of the Erie Board or the transaction of any work by them, unless his director was at liberty to participate. The Drew, Gould and Fisk group thereupon applied to yet a third judge, before whom they accused Judge Barnard of having entered into a conspiracy to speculate in Erie stock and of using the process of the court in order to aid his speculations. Thereupon this third judge issued an injunction restraining all parties from committing any acts "in furtherance of said conspiracy," and ordering the Erie directors, other than Vanderbilt's nominee, to continue in their duties and in particular not to desist from converting bonds into stock. In the meantime Judge Barnard was "issuing half a dozen injunctions a day," but being now commanded by the law both to do and not to do everything possible Gould, Drew and Fisk left the judges to fight it out while they perfected their preparations for their final struggle with Vanderbilt.

Before the first injunction they had held a meeting of the directors which authorized an issue of convertible bonds for $10,000,000 for "completing, finishing and altering the road." They said that it was to be spent in replacing the company's worn-out rails with steel rails and in laying a third rail which would enable trains of standard gauge to run over the Erie's permanent way. Ten minutes after the meeting closed they had a second secret meeting and agreed to sell these bonds to Drew and his friends at 72½ per cent. Half of these bonds were at once converted into stock and sent to Drew's brokers. As for the rails, Drew gave orders that the old rails were to be relaid inside out, so as to present their unworn edges to the wheels; of the third rail nothing more was heard.

Then the first injunction came into action, and the price of Erie rose, for the public seems to have imagined that the Erie directors would be deterred by it from adding to the amount of stock on the market. They did not know their men, for the vice-president of the company immediately signed fresh share certificates for the whole of the remaining $5,000,000 worth, stating that he did so "in case a modification of the injunction could be obtained." The secretary then told a messenger to take the books containing these signed certificates and lock them in the safe. A few minutes later the messenger returned, saying that Mr. Fisk had met him, taken the books away from him, and carried them off. That meant that, unknown to Vanderbilt, another $5,000,-000 was interposed between him and the control of Erie.

On the day after that, these new shares were placed upon the market. At first Vanderbilt's brokers and friends continued to buy, and the price of Erie continued to rise. Then somebody noticed the dates on the new certificates. It was realized that the Erie directors had disregarded the injunction, but nobody could tell to what extent. The price fell from 80 to 70. Vanderbilt went on buying, but when night fell it was clear that he had failed to obtain the control he desired.

On the contrary, the Erie directors had obtained $7,000,000 in return for practically worthless stock, at least $4,000,000 of which came from Vanderbilt. This $7,000,000 had been obtained in despite of injunctions, and the Erie gang was subject to all sorts of pains and penalties in the sovereign state of New York. But before warrants for contempt of court could be issued the offenders were over the Jersey ferry, safe in the sovereign state of New Jersey.

In Jersey City these financiers took up their quarters in a hotel, surrounded themselves with an armed bodyguard, mounted three 12-pounder guns on the waterfront, filled patrol boats with riflemen, and announced that Vanderbilt and Judge Barnard were trying to have them kidnapped. They were said to have taken with them in a cab $6,000,000 in notes; at any rate, they had with them enough money to secure the passing of a bill by the New Jersey legislature in two hours, making the Erie Railroad a corporation of New Jersey. Then they set on foot a newspaper campaign against railway monopolies, reduced the

Erie rates and fares in order to embarrass Vanderbilt still further, and squabbled over the division of the spoils. For a while they were safe, and as arrests could not take place in New York on the Sabbath Day, they could even visit their friends from time to time.

But they wanted to go back to New York for good, and Gould drew up a bill which he proposed to pass through the legislature of New York State, legalizing the recent transactions and making it impossible for the Erie Railroad to be absorbed into Vanderbilt's group. The first time it was introduced the bill failed to pass, and Gould was obliged to take the risk of going himself to Albany where the New York State legislature has its seat, in order to interview members of the legislature. He was arrested, but succeeded first in getting bail and then in giving his custodian the slip. He had taken with him $250,000 of the money recently acquired, and Vanderbilt's papers soon began to bring against him charges of corruption. He was never prosecuted, but subsequent inquiry proved that while in Albany he signed a large number of cheques for large amounts and distributed them among senators without—according to his own statement—being able to remember why he paid them or what he did with them. In any case, he spent enough in the town, in whatever manner and for whatever reason, to make Vanderbilt feel that opposition would be likely to fail. Vanderbilt at this moment was not in a happy position. The carrying off of the $6,000,000 had brought about a monetary stringency and forced down the prices of all stocks, and he was loaded with Erie shares whose price he was only just able to maintain. The price of the legislators at Albany on the other hand was high, and when Senators disembarked from the special trains which it had seemed worth hiring for such an occasion, they found that Vanderbilt's agents were not in the lobby to buy them. Their disappointment and spite were such that they passed not only the Erie bill, but two other railway bills which they hoped might prove harassing to the Vanderbilt railroads.

Soon after this Drew opened secret negotiations with Vanderbilt, hoping no doubt to make something for himself at the expense of Fisk and Gould. But his partners got wind of it, appeared themselves at the rendezvous, and insisted that any settlement must include Drew's retirement from the Erie Board. Terms were arranged. As Vanderbilt said, he could buy up the Erie Railroad, but not the bond printing press. It was agreed that all suits were to be dismissed and offenses condoned; Vanderbilt got $4,000,000 back in return for Erie shares, various of his friends got money—the property of the railway—Drew retired with a certain amount of plunder, and Gould and Fisk got the line.

This settlement cost the Erie treasury $9,000,000 and left the company burdened with 150,000 additional shares. Gould and Fisk held themselves out as exceedingly indignant—"thunderstruck and dumbfounded" was the way Fisk put it—and stated that in their opinion the line was likely to go bankrupt. But it was all they could get, and they proceeded to make the most of it. They turned all but their own friends off the Board and brought on instead Tweed and Sweeny, the bosses of Tammany. Tweed had been an ally of Vanderbilt, but he had been rewarded for his services to that financier with Erie stock, and he therefore thought it better to go over to Gould, taking with him control of the politics of New York City and the services of certain of her judges. Among them was Judge Barnard, and from that moment his injunctions were as freely at Gould's disposal as they had been at Vanderbilt's.

Thus protected, Fisk and Gould started once more to manipulate Erie stock. In the course of the next few months they manufactured another 250,000 shares, broke the price from 80 to 40, and then—when they had bought all they wanted and desired to force a rise—obtained from Judge Barnard a ruling authorizing the railway to buy the new stock back at par. This ruling directly contravened a law forbidding railway companies to traffic in their own stock, and it led to the bringing of various legal actions. At one time no less than six judges were issuing contrary injunctions in different courts on behalf of different parties, and no less than three different receivers and a referee were judicially appointed to control of the railway on behalf of different applicants. But Gould and Fisk were not, in the end, dislodged. Gould stated in evidence before one committee of enquiry that he thought himself entitled to issue as much stock as he wanted when elections were pending, in order to keep the railway out of Vanderbilt's hands, and this argument is said to have made a favourable impression on the committee. In any case, they came to another agreement with Vanderbilt, by which he was to have a bill he wanted to consolidate the lines he owned already, and they were to have a bill allowing them to issue as much stock as they pleased, and be subject to reëlection only once in five years instead of every year. After that they were the undisputed masters of Erie.

One more brush with Vanderbilt took place before hostilities between the two parties ceased. The rate for a carload of cattle from Buffalo to New York was at that time $125. Vanderbilt cut his rate on the New York Central to $100. Gould reduced his to $75; Vanderbilt went down to $50. Gould retaliated by offering to carry at $25 the carload, and Vanderbilt went down to $1.00. Gould, apparently, was beaten, and the whole of the cattle-carrying trade went to the New York Central. In the meantime, however, Gould had been buying all the cattle west of Buffalo, and he now made a very large profit out of what was practically free carriage to New York. It is said that when Vanderbilt heard that he was carrying Gould's cattle for a dollar a load he resolved never to try conclusions with him again.

All the same, the two men, from policy and conviction rather than from personal feeling, were usually to be found on opposite sides on Wall Street. Vanderbilt worked for prosperity, he took control of enterprises in order to make them flourish; Gould's method was to manufacture disaster in order that he might pick up shares cheap. When Gould and Fisk in 1868 and 1869 respectively, cornered bank notes and attempted to corner gold, it was Vanderbilt who steadied the market and saved numerous firms from ruin. In those days it was easy to corner bank notes. The supply was inadequate to the needs of an expanding commerce, in the autumn when crops were being moved there was always a shortage, and the banks were obliged to keep a cash reserve of 25 per cent against their advances. When Gould and Fisk, together with Drew, managed to raise $14,000,000 and turn it into notes, which they then withdrew, the banks were obliged to call in loans to the extent of $56,000,000. There was an acute crisis; prices fell, shares slumped heavily; the confederates who had been selling short for months made enormous profits, and numbers of innocent people were ruined.

Of the unsuccessful attempt of Fisk and Gould to buy up and corner gold we will not tell here. By a treacherous manœuvre Gould managed to sell most of his holding to Fisk, while Fisk, under an agreement with him, was continuing to buy at top prices, and harmony was only restored between them later after Gould had assisted in an ingenious plan for shifting the liabilities Fisk had incurred, to a man of straw. In the later days of their association Gould and Fisk established themselves very sumptuously in New York. They had an office in the buildings of the Grand Opera Company, and Fisk had made for himself a private banqueting hall and a private passageway connecting his apartment with the stage. The troupe of the opera kept him supplied not only with mistresses but with a permanent attraction for his business associates. He is said to have remarked of them: "I travel on my shape, and I like these scarlet women: they're approachable!" Gould took no part in such activities, he stuck to the office, he preferred in the intervals of his piracies to cultivate flowers and lead a peaceful domestic life. His preference was wise—Fisk was murdered later on by the lover of one of his mistresses; but in the meantime the two men worked very well together.

To Gould the murder of Fisk was a great loss. He had been liked by the shareholders and the railway employees, and was useful when it came to a rough-and-tumble. After his death the English shareholders—of whom there had always been a surprisingly large number—decided to get rid of Gould. They organized an opposition on the Board, and when he refused a directors' meeting the English party held one, marched to the Opera House, broke through its guard, held their meeting in the face of an assortment of warrants, and elected a new Board.

Their hands were strengthened by Gould's old partner Martin. He had been brought near to ruin by one of Gould's corners, and now he offered his enemies the firm's old books, knowing that they contained evidence which would have sent the great financier to prison. For once Gould could do nothing, and he retired from the Erie followed by a suit on behalf of the company for nearly $13,000,000 and various criminal charges. He was again arrested, but even out of that he made money. By stating that he intended to make restitution, he sent up the price of Erie stock; by denying it, he brought the price down again. When he had done this two or three times he had got rid of all his shares and made enough to indemnify himself against pretty nearly anything that might happen. In the end he did actually hand over a number of securities with a par value of $6,000,000 in return for a withdrawal of the criminal charges, but these papers were found later to be worth practically nothing.

Gould left the Erie Railroad with $86,000,000 of stock and funded debt as against the $22,000,000 it had carried when he joined the Board. Not one dollar of the increase represented any real improvement. Erie, like all Gould's lines in his later life, remained notorious for its mismanagement, inefficiency and dangerous state of neglect. It did a magnificent business, but it was a long time before it emerged from the receiver's hands, and nineteen years after Gould left it before it was able to pay a dividend.

We will not deal in detail with any of Gould's other enterprises. Our story is already too long. A consolidation of the various "elevated" lines in New York brought him fresh unpopularity. Part was due to his having acquired control of the Manhattan by a bear campaign in the course of which, speaking as one of its directors, he made a sworn statement that the line was "hopelessly and irretrievably insolvent." Shortly afterwards it became known that he had been purchasing a majority of its stock, and as soon as this was done the price returned to the point from which he had depressed it. Further, by posing as a friend, he deliberately ruined Cyrus Field, one of his associates in the transaction, for suggesting that the Elevated Railways ought to be a public service.

From that time forward he became less active. In 1884 there was a Wall Street panic in which he is said to have lost very nearly $20,000,000. Whatever his losses he was able to leave to his descendants one of the largest fortunes in America. He was not and had never been a man who gave to charity. By this time his health was failing—although he could not bear to admit the fact, he had developed tuberculosis. In 1892 he died. When the news of his death reached Wall Street, all the securities in which he was known to have large holdings went up.

The nomad, the pirate, was written all over the life of Jay Gould. He played a rôle in the spreading American community parallel to that of the early nomad raider towards the early agriculturalists in the alluvial plains of the Old World. He plundered and he devastated. Were he taken as the test instance for freedom of private enterprise and the contemporary cash and credit system, they would stand condemned for having produced and tolerated him. In the conflict between the State in the person of Judge Barnard, for example, and this anti-social individual, the latter seems to be given all the power and freedom, and the former is a mere weak bribable piece in the game. But the Vanderbilt story throws its light on our problems from a different angle. This is even more the case with the Rockefeller history to which we shall next proceed. We find Vanderbilt and Rockefeller the instruments of very broad economic reconstructions, which it is hard to imagine achieved in any other fashion. Reactionary and conservative-minded thinkers would argue that Jay Gould was an unavoidable evil, that he was the shadow of the freedoms in which alone progress could occur. But progressive and socialist would dispute this. They would maintain that all the good and little of the evil of the Vanderbilt-Rockefeller type could be released in quite a different fashion.

J. D. ROCKEFELLER AND THE ORGANIZATION OF OIL PRODUCTION

In our second chapter (§§6, 7, and 8), we have described the amazing increase in available substances and the development of new sources of power that are making over man's world anew. Each extensive exploitation of new substances, and each new utilization of power since the onset of this period of science and invention, has had for its correlative the development of great fortunes. We may take as the typical story of this species of wealth the history of oil and the Rockefeller fortune.

While Vanderbilt was extending his railways, J. D. Rockefeller was building up that "Mother of Trusts," the Standard Oil Company, and amassing what many people believe to be the greatest single fortune in the world. The life history of Rockefeller is the history of his trust; he made it, and equally it has made him; he has grown and adapted himself to it as it grew, so that apart from its story it seems hardly necessary to detail his personal life in chronological order.

A fact outside his business life on which hostile critics have laid stress is that he is unquestionably a sincere Baptist, that he attended his church every Sunday until age forbade, and brought up his family as believing Christians. They found that inconsistent with many of his business acts. There is, for example, legal proof, in judgments and accepted evidence, for the statements that his business methods have included lying, perjury, the bearing of false witness against his neighbours, widespread bribery, the corruption of other men's servants and of public officials, the use of threats, and the obtaining of illegal drawbacks and rebates. His whole career indeed has displayed a very complete disregard for the rights or interests of anyone opposed to himself and his projects. "The little revolutions" he has stirred up in Mexico and South America have cost many lives, and he has ruined by the thousand not only the fortunes of his fellow-citizens, but what—if we are to hold to the precise teachings of his sect—he should regard as their immortal souls. But while doing all this, he has been accustomed to collect money for his church with great energy and ability. He also gave abundantly and freely; and he has certainly always been a charitable man. Such apparent inconsistencies of doctrine and method may be due to nothing more than intense preoccupation with his main concern. A man concentrated upon an accumulative effort that rapidly developed vast creative possibilities may have had no time to turn back on his upbringing and scrutinize the precise formulæ of his faith. And there is a sort of constructive excitement, an intensity of conviction, that can make men extraordinarily ruthless and unscrupulous in their dealings with antagonists and obstacles. Theologically J. D. Rockefeller has remained what he was as a boy; in substance and effort he has changed with his times, his successes and his opportunities.

All his life he has given generously. It is estimated that his benefactions must by now have amounted to £600,000,000. And they have been made—we have had occasion to note it already in this work—with distinguished wisdom and ability. They have left a perceptible mark on the advancement of science. A "perplexing psychological dichotomy," say some observers, a man whose right hand is abnormally unaware of what his left hand is doing. But before we dismiss the personal make-up of J. D. Rockefeller in this way, as a monstrosity, we have to bear in mind the standards of honesty and enterprise, the legal and political unscrupulousness, the ready resort to violence, prevalent in the American community at the time of his ascent. He bore false witness perhaps in a crisis, but what was the tangle he was pushing through? He stirred up revolutions in little states, but what had the governments of those little states done to him? We have already had a sample of those standards in our study of Jay Gould as a money-maker.

The importance of J. D. Rockefeller in the development of modern economic conditions is very great. Two great achievements are his. In the first place, he organized the collection and marketing of mineral oil and the comparative stabilization of its price throughout the world. In the second, he inaugurated, by his immense success, the era of Big Business.

Even now it amazes that from his first entry into the oil business it was under ten years before he attained virtual control of the entire industry—before he was in such a position that he alone could fix the prices of both crude and refined oils. When he went to the oil-fields, an unknown man of no particular wealth, he found that every section of the trade was suffering from overproduction, wasteful methods and confusion. The getting of the oil to the surface was carried on by that type of greedy, emotional, optimistic pioneer which is attracted by risky enterprises promising enormous profits. These men were in many cases able and ingenious, but one fact always defeated them—the fact that if a man refrained from drilling for his own oil it might be drained away from under his land by the drilling of his neighbour. The "oil men" were never able to overcome the suspicions to which this gave rise and combine to restrict their output when some hitch occurred in transport or marketing. Only once did they stop the drills and for only a few months. They would let the oil run to waste on the ground rather than not drill. Any accident, therefore, might break the price of oil, and with production continually pressing upon storage capacity, new oil-fields being discovered and old wells running dry, prices fluctuated from dollars to cents, and individuals alternated between wealth and ruin.

The refining section of the industry was run by ordinary business men, but as in the early days it had been impossible to get their machinery and materials to the wells, the stills had been started wherever transport conditions made it feasible. As the railways built branches to the actual oil-fields, these refineries found themselves being undercut by new enterprises starting at the mouth of the wells. As for the railways—the four roads in question were in a state of what almost amounted to open warfare. As will be evident from the section on Gould, they were precluded by the personnel of their governing bodies, and the fraud, violence and treachery which had characterized their relations, from entering into any durable or trustworthy agreements. Their officials, though probably less corrupt than their directorates, seem to have been incapable of refusing bribes, and various oil refineries had already found it practicable to extort illegal rebates on their cargoes. And all these causes of difficulty and uncertainty were accentuated by the activities of speculators.

It was the refining section of the industry which Rockefeller entered when he turned from a mixed transport and commission business to deal with oil. Within three or four years, through sheer ability, he had become the largest refiner in the country, only to find himself faced with falling prices due to reckless overproduction on the fields. He had every reason to desire that some sort of order might be introduced and some attempt made to limit production and to stabilize prices, and the plan he produced was always stated by him to have been drawn up solely for the good of the industry. There is no reason why we should not take his word for it. For good or evil, had the plan remained secret it must have succeeded. First he persuaded the leading firms of the Cleveland district to enter a common company and allow him to arrange for their buying and selling. This made him by far the railroad's largest customer. Next he used this position to bully and bribe the railways and extort from them concessions which would involve the ruin of his competitors. The scheme took some time to arrange, for he had to convince the railway chiefs (or so they swore) that his company intended to take in all the existing refiners, but in the end he secured three things: a heavy rebate on all his own oil, a cash payment for every barrel of oil carried for a firm outside the company, and a promise of the fullest and earliest information of any moves on the part of his competitors. Armed with this agreement, he was able to go to the refiners who had not already joined his company, and make it clear to them that if they would not sell out to him at what he considered a reasonable price, they would have to go out of business.

As far as the refineries were concerned, his plan succeeded— he was able to buy up on very advantageous terms all the remaining stills in the district. He shut down the less efficient and less favourably placed, and limited the production of the others; he introduced improved methods and took over the buying and selling for the industry. In fact, he rationalized the industry on the refinery side.

For a time, however, as far as the producers were concerned, his scheme failed. His secret leaked out, and when they found their transport charges being raised, the oil men organized to attack him. The story of this struggle is extremely interesting and very valuable to anyone who wishes to understand the social behaviour of human beings, but there is neither space nor need to tell it here. With the rest of the early story of Standard Oil it may be found in Ida Tarbell's well known indictment *The History of the Standard Oil Company*. It is enough to say that the organized oil men so far won that they got Rockefeller's company condemned in the courts as an illegal conspiracy in restraint of trade, forced him to dissolve it, and made him sign an undertaking to take no more rebates from the railway companies. For some months they boycotted him, and they succeeded in rousing a great deal of sympathy. In fact, they won the first engagement in that prolonged fight between the Standard and public agitations which was to continue until the Great War. By then, on the one hand, Mr. Rockefeller's benefactions had for more than a decade maintained their exculpatory flow, and on the other, the importance of a steady, efficient production of petrol to mechanized armies and navies had placed the great oil companies under the protection of their governments and beyond the reach of newspaper criticism.

This initial check, however, did not frighten Rockefeller in the least, or succeed in changing even the details of his procedure. By this time he had made up his mind to obtain, through control of transport, effective control of the whole industry, and he did it. He bribed his way through the boycott, bought up some of his chief enemies, and had concluded a fresh arrangement for railway rebates some days before the date on which he had promised to forswear them forever. It was his pull with the railways which made it impossible to defeat him. He kept to himself the names of all the firms he had bought or brought in —he could tell every railway in turn that he would withdraw all freight if they dared to disoblige him, and none of them knew that he was, in fact, dividing it between them all. As long as cars were the only means of moving oil, he could undercut everyone else on account of his rebates, and if that did not force his competitors to sell, he could either see that they were refused cars or storage, or he could tamper with their supplies of raw material. Whenever the producers organized against him he had only to wait, choking their outlets, until they could hold up oil no longer, or at worst to buy enough men among them to defeat the others. When judgments were given against him in the courts, ordering him to dissolve his trust, he pretended to obey them, changed a name or two, and went on conducting his affairs in all other respects precisely as he had before. When he was personally indicted for conspiracy, he contrived to get the suits withdrawn at the cost of a bargain which he did not keep.

The railways themselves were able to do nothing against him. When one of them, the Pennsylvania, dared to resist his demands in order to protect the rights of the last considerable group of independent refiners, an all too manifestly arranged strike broke out on their line which crippled its working, and a drop took place in the price of oil which forced the refiners to sell out.

When it became clear that the pipe line would supersede the railroads as carriers of oil, Rockefeller extended to pipe lines the methods he had adopted with refineries. When the producers attempted to construct a line of their own to do what was supposed to be impossible—to pump crude oil over the Alleghany Mountains to the sea—he obstructed them at every step. His newspapers attacked the characters of the chiefs of the enterprise in order to damage its credit. His agents frightened the farmers over whose lands the pipes must pass, by stories of poisonous leakages and unquenchable fires, and gangs of railway employees attacked the workmen laying the pipes.

The first attempt to get a free pipe line past him was killed by this sort of opposition. A second succeeded, only for it to appear that a third of the company's shares were in Rockefeller's hands, and that his nominees were so strongly entrenched in its councils that he was able to impose a working alliance upon it.

As he monopolized the pipe lines, he also reorganized them. That is a very important point on his credit side. He did not monopolize to extort and stagnate. In his hands the pipe-line organization became a service of extreme efficiency. When in 1878 a new oil field was discovered, in three years United Pipe Lines created a whole new system of pipes to carry this fresh oil. But the cost of this extraordinary achievement was recovered from the men in possession of the fields by Rockefeller forcing down the price of crude oil while he kept up the price of refined. It was complained that at one time he was eating up the whole of their profits by his charges for transport and storage. Perhaps it is truer to say almost all. They could do nothing effective against him because he was the only carrier and also the only purchaser for their oil.

While he was completing his control inside the industry, he was carrying on a tremendous campaign for markets, not only throughout the United States, but in every country in the world. As always, his method was to make his own enterprise extremely efficient, to insist on the highest skill and integrity among his own people, and to take every possible advantage of the timidity, greed or dishonesty of everyone else. By the end of the century he had built up in his own country a system of espionage and corruption so complete that he was said to receive information about every movement of every barrel of independent oil. If a peddler hawking paraffin on a barrow purchased a gallon from an outsider, he was confronted by a Standard agent and bought up or intimidated or systematically undersold.

Standard Oil was also engaged throughout this period in fighting anti-trust legislation, as well as the private bills by which the dwindling number of independents sought to secure way leaves or charters. Rockefeller was said to have bought a seat in the Senate of the United States for the uncle of Standard's treasurer, and his agents were familiar figures in the lobbies of all lesser legislatures.

Gradually the knowledge of these methods leaked out. It did not simply leak out, it came out presently in a blaze of denunciation—perhaps of exaggeration. Whenever, as happened frequently, a suit was brought against the Standard Oil Company—and it was a rich corporation to bring suits against—the evidence given would be published as loudly as possible in the press and more than once it roused—or was used to rouse—a great popular campaign against trusts. At every step in his career Rockefeller had engendered envy and resentment, and every corner grocer by now was feeling that although he was living in the land of the free, the Standard would break him if he did not knuckle under to its regulations. In those prosperous days there seemed to be enough wealth for all—men might easily believe that only wanton rapacity could spread far-reaching frustration in order to organize a trade. And in fact the success of his methods had been so great and manifest that nobody felt safe; small men in every industry wondered when they went to bed whether they might not wake to find their independent livelihoods menaced by such another frustrator, and the ordinary consumer was induced to believe that the Standard kept up the price of oil systematically, except when it was undercutting to ruin someone. A campaign against the trusts became a leading issue of party politics; there was a burst of legislation, and in 1907, at the end of a tremendous lawsuit, the Standard were ordered once again to be dissolved and to pay $29,000,000 in costs and penalties to the State. Rockefeller is said to have received this news while he was playing golf, to have paused, observed: "It will be some time before that judgment is carried out," and to have gone on with his game.

In fact, the fine was never paid, nor was the judgment ever made effective. In 1911 there was a show of dissolution, but nobody supposed for a moment that either the direction or the policy of the Standard would be changed. It was rumoured that Rockefeller had made another fortune on the Stock Exchange by anticipating movements in his shares. Nor did anyone credit his statement that he had retired from control of the Standard in 1895—when the first dissolution was supposed to be taking place—and was living now as a private citizen concerned only with his family and his charities. In fact such was the public state of mind that nobody believed a word to which the Standard officials swore unless it served to condemn them. When on one occasion a man brought to trial for tapping one of the Standard's pipe lines admitted that he had stolen a considerable quantity of their oil, the jury acquitted him forthwith.

The hatred that was felt for Rockefeller seems to have died down. That may be due in part to his age and in part to his

liberality. But much more is it due to changing views of the
utility of his achievement. In the days of his ascent the social
ideal in America was a mosaic of small independent, prosperous
undertakings. It was a jostling conflict in which no doubt many
failed, but wherein also with a certain smartness but with no
steadfast wickedness, and with loud protestations of "live and
let live" and "give everyone a chance," everyone might expect
to do as well as his neighbour—and perhaps a little better. The
reality to which this ideal led was a clumsy, socially wasteful
life of petty competition, keen rivalries and mean triumphs.
Politics were profoundly corrupt, the law courts untrustworthy,
the press blatant and unscrupulous. There was no living spirit
of public service, no "sense of the State," no coöperative end.
It was an Individualist's heaven, Babbitt land. That was the
world into which J. D. Rockefeller was born, with a relative
steadfastness of purpose and a power of organization greater
than he knew. In a muddle-headed and unscrupulous scramble
he was clear-headed, creative and unscrupulous. He did not
play a much wickeder game than everyone about him was playing, but he certainly played that wicked game better. And so
the world about him was filled with the resentment of the defeated and the protests of besters out-bested. Most of the literature against him is saturated with the paradoxical implication
that in a competitive world one should not compete too much.

No one who understands anything of the conditions out of
which he arose can believe that this organization of business
on a new scale, the elevation of a private business to the dimensions of a world power, could have been achieved by generosity
or scrupulous fairness. Generosity in his dealings would have
been exploited and fairness misunderstood. He competed after
the patterns of competition all about him, and so—to the great
economic advantage of mankind—he killed competition. If his
success was a scandal, then the competitive system in business is
responsible for the scandal. He is the supreme individualist
working out individualism to its logical end in monopolization.
And of all the base criticisms his career has evoked, the charge
that his magnificently intelligent endowments have been planned

to buy off criticism or save his soul from the slow but sure vindictiveness of his Baptist God is surely the most absurd. It is made a grievance against him that, unlike most of the successful financiers and industrial adventurers of our time, he has not bought yachts and palaces and women, run theatres, gambled, been a "good feller," and bred a family of spendthrift sons. His worst enemy cannot accuse him of a trace of the normal snobbery of the *nouveau riche*. He has deposed and bought legislatures, but that was because they were not for public service but for private sale. Manifestly he has grown and broadened at every stage of his career. He has changed as he has lived. The young man born into conceptions of Protestant virtue and self-help, saving his few dollars weekly and gripping every opportunity with all his strength, developed consistently into the great business chief whose thoughts and influence have spread out from the organization of pipe lines to the organization, with the same unsentimental thoroughness, of scientific research.

We are trying here to state the facts about this extraordinary man. He is put here for the reader's consideration and judgment. It has been urged against him that he debased business standards in America, and certainly that is unforgivable. But did he do so? He was living in the world of Jay Gould and Hetty Green. He did not raise standards as the Rothschilds did, but did he lower them? Something in the nature of J. D. Rockefeller had to occur in America, and it is all to the good of the world that he was tight-lipped, consistent, and amazingly free from vulgar vanity, sensuality and quarrelsomeness. His cold persistence and ruthlessness may arouse something like horror, but for all that he was a forward-moving force, a constructive power. Like begets like, and he did not so much seek to found a family as to create a great research organization and devote his family to it.

THOMAS ALVA EDISON

Except perhaps George Stephenson, who invented the locomotive, no human being can have created more wealth than Edison, for his was certainly the most ingenious mind that has

ever devoted itself to the commercial application of science. He
was born in 1847 at Milan, Ohio, and his formal education was
limited to three months in the common school of Port Huron,
Michigan. Reading and writing he had learnt at home. The rest
of his finally immense scientific equipment, he got for himself,
driven by an indefatigable curiosity. His first patent was a
device which nobody wanted to use—an instrument for enabling
an assembly to vote by pressing buttons and for registering and
counting the votes. It worked very well, but was refused by
Congress on the ground that it counted the votes too accurately.
That refusal made a deep impression on the young inventor.
He resolved that henceforth he would produce what people
wanted instead of what he thought they ought to want. The
fruits of his resolution were to build up half-a-dozen new industries, to provide employment for millions, to extend the
reach of civilization, and to enlarge the life of almost everyone
who lives within it. Henry Ford says of him that he doubled the
efficiency of modern industry—that it is due to Edison that
America is the most prosperous country in the world.*

The list of his inventions is too long to give—he took out
1,500 patents. They astonish by their variety as much as by
their importance. Edison made the telephone possible and turned
the telegraph into a general means of communication. He invented the first electric lamp that would give the amount of
illumination needed in a building—the incandescent lamp—and
in order to make it useful he worked out an entire system for the
generation and distribution of current. He himself says: "It was
necessary to think out everything: dynamos, regulators, meters,
switches, fuses, fixtures, underground conductors and a host of
other detailed parts, down to the insulating tape. Everything
was new and unique. The only relevant item in the world at that
time was copper wire, and even that was not properly insulated."

Existing dynamos were only 40 per cent efficient: Edison's
dynamo gave an efficiency of 90 per cent. This made possible
the line of advance which emancipated industry from the belt

---

*Henry Ford: *My Friend Mr. Edison.* See also Dyer and Martin: *Edison, His
Life and Inventions.*

and shaft and led to modern high-speed tools. He made the typewriter into a practicable instrument and contributed to the development of the storage battery. He invented the microphone, the phonograph and the kinetograph, which was the beginning of the cinema. The first electric cars were made possible by his work, and he also constructed an electric railway—though there the Germans had been before him. He devised methods for making and handling cement which brought it into the field as a material for building construction, and a technique for separating and smelting the iron which is found in sand. He introduced paraffin paper and the mimeograph, which multiplies copies of letters. During the war he worked out thirty-nine inventions for the Navy Department of the United States, but although his country had already recognized him as one of the greatest men alive, he was forced to complain that the Navy Department paid little attention to what he offered them.

This is a formidable list, even though in almost every case the theory of the subject had been worked out and the first practical applications made by others. The principle of the telephone, for instance, had been established seventeen years before by Reis of Frankfort. Professor Bell, of Boston, succeeded in producing a system which would carry for twenty or thirty miles; it was Edison who turned it from a brilliant experiment into a commercial success. In the same way with his incandescent lamp. When he began to work on that, the now obsolete arc lamp, with its sizzling carbons and fluctuating glare, white with occasional violet blushes, held the field; the incandescent thread of imperfect conductivity, the metal thread that would glare or fuse, was known, but not the carbon filament which glared but did not fuse. The task of Edison was to find a filament which was reliable and would burn for long periods, and a lamp which could be handled by the public and would be cheap both to produce and to maintain. His chief original invention was the phonograph, which he was inclined for some time to consider as a toy. The principle of the kinetograph—that successive images superimposed upon the retina at more than a certain rate of speed produce an illusion of movement—had been known for nearly two centuries. The invention of the celluloid film by Eastman synchronized with his own work on the subject, but he was never sufficiently interested to join the host of experimenters who were trying to find a way of projecting the images on a screen and who did ultimately produce the cinema world.

In the beginning, it was accident which directed his attention to electricity—the branch of science which seemed especially waiting for a man with just his gifts. His first interest was chemistry. As a boy he was continually starting fresh enterprises in order to earn the money he needed for books and materials for experiment—he liked to read everything that had been written on each point and to work out every experiment for himself. For he found that he was able to learn more from the actual sight of them than had been gathered, or at any rate recorded, by their originators.

This was an expensive way of working, and his parents were poor. His father dealt in grain and wood; his mother had been a schoolmistress. He disliked school—she gave him the elementary training which enabled him afterwards to teach himself. At twelve he took a job as newsboy on the Grand Trunk Railway which runs between Port Huron and Detroit, and he added to this occupation a number of others initiated by himself. He opened stores in Port Huron, he employed other boys to sell vegetables in Detroit and provisions to emigrants in passing trains. He published a newspaper of his own which he printed on the train itself in a laboratory installed in a baggage car. He would have made a success of it if he had not set fire to the car with some phosphorus and so been deprived of his laboratory and turned off the train.

After this setback he became a telegraph operator—he was one of those men who seem able to learn anything they choose and become expert at everything they learn. As a skilled telegraphist he could get a job wherever he liked, and for some years he wandered about in Canada and the northeastern states, either on railway telegraphs or reporting the proceedings of Congress —work which included filling in the gaps in the speeches caused by the faulty apparatus of those days. As he went he seems to have left a trail of small inventions behind him, but none brought him in any money, and one at least got him into serious trouble.

He was engaged to send signals at intervals through the night from the station where he was working to the next along the line, and he invented an automatic which would do it for him. One night an unusual call was made. He did not reply, so a party went to look for him and found him asleep in comfort beside his apparatus.

It was in New York that he got his first real chance. He had gone there from Boston—where he had invented the vote recorder—in order to sell an idea for a telegraph cable which could be used for two messages at once in opposite directions. The Pacific Telegraph Company adopted it, and are said to have made a great deal of money by it, but to have refused to pay the inventor anything. Certainly he was almost stranded when he noticed one day a noisy crowd outside an office. There had been a breakdown on the Stock Exchange telegraph, and the crowd believed that the apparatus had been wrecked by speculators who wished to prevent the arrival of news. Edison walked in at once and offered to repair the damage in an hour. He carried out his promise, and received in reward the post of technical director of the Gold Reporting Company with a salary of $800 a month.

It was his first good position; he not only saved money there, but met men who were impressed by him and afterwards became his clients. He was soon able to start a small company, "Pope, Edison & Co.," and set up a workshop where he could spend most of his time experimenting. There he devised an improvement in the Stock Exchange ticker which he was able to sell for $40,000, and from that moment the flow of his inventions never ceased.

At first he seems to have had great difficulty in getting paid for them. For our present purposes that is a very interesting point to press. We have been studying money-getters hitherto. But here we have something else, a creator who was forced into money-getting. It is not only that this man did his work from quite other motives than the money motive, but that he was impeded in doing it by money-getters. They bested him, time after time. There are stories about an English company who bought some automatic telephone apparatus and never paid for it at all, and about American companies who involved him in litigation and paid him reluctantly and on a niggardly scale. But he had become well enough known for telegraph companies to bring him their problems for solution, and in four years he managed to save nearly half a million dollars. It was then that he built the laboratory, workshops, library and houses at Menlo Park which were afterwards to become world-famous.

From that time his course was fixed. He had already married, and though afterwards he moved from one set of buildings into another and made occasional voyages to Europe to introduce inventions or receive homage, his real life was spent in the laboratory, among his workers and collaborators. There he took most of his meals, received his guests, and in his spare time held singsongs with his men. His methods of work were still extremely thorough—to start from the beginning, have everything read, worked out, noted up and tried. But he knew how to surround himself with able men and how to coöperate with other minds. He himself could work for days and nights on end if he wanted to, and sleep when he had finished. Time meant nothing—the clock in his laboratory had no hands to its face. He expected his staff to work in the same heroic fashion, and such is the appetite of human beings for interesting work of any sort, their passion for machinery and their capacity for hero-worship, that most of them seem to have enjoyed the life and accepted the régime. If anybody, thinking himself indispensable, tried to impose conditions, Edison would do a little inventing and work out a method which got rid of him.

For his work the man grudged nothing as too costly. He would experiment for years and get deeply into debt in order to try out every possible combination. He recently examined more than 15,000 plants in order to find one which would grow in the United States and assure her supply of rubber in case of war. He spent $40,000 on his electric-light experiments before he got his first crude carbon filament. It burned for 45 hours and was made out of a piece of suitably treated sewing thread. On the other hand, he gathered in great pecuniary rewards. He manufactured many of his inventions himself instead of selling the rights, and he became under necessity a good man of business. In order to popularize his lamp he contracted to sell at first for 40 cents, although it was costing him 125 cents to make. For three years he lost money—the cost of manufacture was coming down, but sales were increasing rapidly. In the fourth year the cost was down to 37 cents, and he made good all his losses. Finally he invented machines which made a lamp for 22 cents, and then he sold the business.

Edison was manifestly not a man who cared for money for its own sake. Why should he? The acquisitive instinct is plainly something quite different from such gifts as his, and the delights offered by the luxury trades must have seemed extraordinarily stupid and simple to an inventor of his calibre. He had no time to waste in spending and no need to surround himself with visible reminders of his success. All he asked for was the money he wanted to carry out his work—work which has opened to mankind inexhaustible possibilities of wealth. Not all of his inventions have been developed—as the world is organized to-day it does not follow that the man who buys a patent will make the best, or indeed any, use of it. A firm may think it worth its while to suppress a novelty rather than to produce it or to compete against it. It would pay a World State over and over again to buy, not the inventions of men like Edison, but the men themselves—to allow them whatever they want to carry out their experiments, give them the freedom of the planet, and then make the results as they came available to the world at large. That is manifest. Also, as we shall show plainly in our studies of government (Chapter XII) and education (Chapter XV), it is at present manifestly impossible.

HENRY FORD

Ford, like Edison, is clearly a man of higher moral calibre than the examples we have taken before them. His, too, is a mind dominated by constructive motives, by the desire to invent, and to invent in such a way as to lessen human labour. He was born on a farm, and he says himself: "My earliest recollection was that, considering the results, there was too much work on the place. That is the way I still feel about farming. . . . That is what took me into mechanics."

As a matter of fact, though this may have been his conscious excuse for withstanding his father's wishes, he was instinctively and from the first a lover of machines. His toys were all tools; he says: "The biggest event of those early days was meeting with a road engine. . . . The second biggest event was getting a watch." These three impressions are quoted because they determined the course of all his future energies. He is a born engineer, and that stands as the root of his success. In his workshops the technician is king, and as Mr. Ford happens also to be a great organizer, his shops get ahead of those whose owners are less interested in the work being done than in the profits to be made from it.

To this main purpose of saving toil he has added another— that of using his enormous undertaking to build up prosperity where he wants customers. The acquisition of a personal fortune really seems to count for nothing. He puts his money back into the business, where he spends it in improving his factories, raising his wages and lowering the price of his products. His business, to him, is "almost sacred." He has devoted his life to it, and it is the axis of the philosophy which he expounds in his books. In this doctrine, too, he believes with the faith of a man who has started life with a few simple ideas, carried them out, and found that they made of him the world-famous head of a great industry.

His mechanical training he began himself, with the help of the watch. By the time he was thirteen he could take it to pieces and put it together again so that it would keep time. At seventeen he persuaded his father to let him become an apprentice in a machine shop, and in his evenings he worked with a watchmaker. There he decided that, as watches are not universal necessities, he would not devote himself to making thirty-cent watches, but would invent a mechanical tractor which would do all the hardest work of a farm and especially ploughing. To this end he took a job with the Westinghouse Company, where he would have a chance of working on road engines, and in his spare time, in a little workshop at home, he endeavoured to build a steam car that would run. He built it, and it did run, but he soon realized that steam vehicles, to be safe, must be far too heavy for the existing country roads, and too expensive for any but the richest farmers. Moreover, the public showed no interest in agricultural machinery—it was only through the success of the motor-car that the farmers came to see its possibilities. So he turned his attention to road cars and began his search for something light, something cheap, something that could be used by everyone. The Westinghouse Company could not help him with this, so he left them and "looked around for another sort of motive power."

The single cylinder petrol engine had already been developed in England, and in 1885 Ford was given one to repair. He then built one for himself, to make certain that he understood it, and began to experiment on double cylinders. He moved to Detroit, took a job with the Detroit Electric Company and worked half the day and all night long on Saturdays at bringing out a car of his own. His main difficulty was that though he knew that other people were working on horseless carriages he could not know what they were doing. His main support was: "That my wife was even more confident than I was." In 1893, when he was thirty years old, this first car "ran to my satisfaction." It was built of bits and scraps, its wheels were bicycle wheels, and it was not cooled at all, but he drove it a thousand miles and then sold it for $200.

About this time he met Edison—an important meeting partly because it influenced the trend of his ideas, partly because he received encouragement on the subject of his car. He even refused the position of general manager to the Edison Company in Detroit because it was coupled with the proviso that his car must be abandoned. By 1899 he felt that he could do something with his car; he threw up his other job and "went into the automobile business." He had saved money, but he was not in a position to finance a whole undertaking by himself, so he formed the Detroit Automobile Company in which he was chief engineer but holder of only a minority of the stock. This arrangement was not successful. The creative man and the financier were almost immediately in conflict. Ford wanted to make better cars as a step towards a wider market, the company wanted to make immediate profits. To the man obsessed by his idea, the man of nearly forty who had given up his life to the solitary accomplishment of his task, this attitude was shocking. Nor was it financially successful. He resigned in 1902, "determined never again to put myself under orders." From that day to this he has been unable to tolerate either the ideals or the methods of financiers. He is, indeed, one of our most striking witnesses against the value of the money motive.

In 1903 he founded the Ford Motor Company. First he built a car fast enough to win in a race against the track champion of America; then he founded the company on the advertisement this gave him. In the new concern he was vice-president, designer, master mechanic, superintendent, general manager and owner of 25½ per cent of the capital of $100,000. Only $28,000 of this was ever paid, and this $28,000 is the only money the company has ever received from other than sales of cars. From that time, he says, he was never short of money. In 1906 he brought his holdings up to 51 per cent; a little later he was able to increase this to 58½ per cent. In 1919 his son, Edsel Ford, bought up the rest of the stock at a price of $12,500 for each $100 share. This seems to have been done in order to reaffirm once again Ford's dislike of sleeping partners in business. He has no use for the investing public, and that, in view of what we have said in Chapter IX, § 10, is very interesting to us. The other stockholders had brought an action against him, in which they demanded that a larger proportion of the profits should be distributed in dividends instead of being put back into the business. Ford won his case by convincing the court that the best possible use had been made of the shareholders' money, but he did not care for a fiduciary position when that meant running his business to profit other people instead of to justify the creative drive in himself, and he solved his difficulty by getting rid of them.

The only outside shareholders now are understood to be those of his own workpeople who have bought shares offered under a special scheme.

From the beginning he ran this new company on his own lines. As what he wanted to produce was not a luxury but an article for general use, he determined to "concentrate on the best selling product," to produce the smallest number of models at the lowest possible price, to make them as light as possible, foolproof and perfectly reliable. He announced that what he was selling was not a machine but a guaranteed amount of service, and that if anything went wrong it was up to the company to see that the purchaser suffered as little as possible. This brought him customers in large numbers at a time when buying a car was considered to be a rich man's gamble, since it might be expected to break down at any moment, and there were no arrangements of any kind for service or repair.

In 1909 he carried this policy to its logical conclusion and decided to sell only one model, Model T, of which he said: "Any customer can have a car painted any colour that he wants so long as it is black." But though only one model was on sale at any given moment, the car itself was always changing, continually having put into it, the maker claims, better workmanship, better material, and better design. That model ended, for instance, by using twenty-four different types of steel.

When he had decided on the form of this model he turned to build up his marketing. That in itself must have been an undertaking sufficient for the ambition of most business men. Ford's idea was to sell through a network of agencies which were to cover the United States. Every agent was to have clean, attractive premises, carry a complete stock of spare parts, be able to offer a reliable repair service, and know every potential customer in his district. When this was on its way to accomplishment, he turned back to improving the efficiency of his system of production.

This system of production has received as much criticism as the car; it has been as successful. Its master idea is the elimination of waste. Not an inch of factory space is to be wasted, not a moment of time, not a fragment of scrap, not an ounce of physical strength nor of mental effort. Ford has built an electric motor into every machine in the engineering shops in order that their alignment might not be restricted by the possibilities of pulleys and shafts and belts. It is wasteful to employ engineers simply as pedestrians and carriers, so the work, with all necessary tools and materials, is everywhere carried by machinery to the hands of the men. He will not have a man obliged even to shift his feet if it can be avoided. . . . It is wasteful for able-bodied men to do work which can be carried on by disabled men, and he therefore employs considerable numbers of blind, deaf and crippled men. They are paid the usual rate of wages, and he says that they are worth more to him than normal men, for they are glad of the work, and not so worried by its monotonous or trivial nature as men who look about and hear outside noises would be.

It is wasteful to spend human labour hewing and hauling coal when we all, in the course of our ordinary lives, produce combustible refuse without devoting any particular time or thought to it. He therefore, where refuse is available, builds power plants which are able to consume it—his new Dagenham works will be run largely upon the rubbish of London. . . . It is wasteful to ship cars (and pay import duties on them) when parts can be packed more compactly and more conveniently handled. He therefore ships parts and has them assembled wherever in the world they are needed for sale. This involves the complete interchangeability of every part, and that means that many of them must be accurate to $\frac{1}{10000}$ of an inch. To control this the gauges, themselves ten times as accurate, must be tested to something like a millionth of an inch. In order to achieve this degree of accuracy Ford became himself a manufacturer of gauges.

But his greatest struggle has been devoted to the saving of time. When he started mass production it took him twelve hours and twenty-four minutes to assemble a chassis. By subdividing every operation and studying every movement he cut that down to one hour, thirty-three minutes. Dies, again, required seven hours to make and could only be used about 40,000 times. He devised a method which would produce in two minutes a die which can shape from 80,000 to 100,000 pieces. The same story has been, and is, going on at every point in his factories. He never ceases his search for machines which will carry out a process faster or with less human labour. By the time he had exploited to the full the process of subdivision, the invention of the turret enabled him to build machines each one of which performs several operations on a part before returning it to the worker. When electric welding became practicable on a large scale, he decided to dispense with all casting as fast as his staff could invent machines to do each particular job by welding instead. So he gained in strength, lightness and simplicity, in the elimination of faulty castings and in the supersession of that machining which all finished castings require. In fact, Ford's principle is that while every operation is standardized for the time being, no single operation, material or product is ever standardized in the sense that it is considered incapable of improvement.

To obtain the incentive for this unceasing, relentless pursuit of economy, Mr. Ford relies on his basic principle of constantly raising wages and lowering prices. He believes in the theory that it is the function of industry to create the prosperity which will enable the public to buy its products. If these are to be sold all over the world, money must be distributed as widely as possible. More than once he has cut prices and raised wages, not because it was justified by the figures of his actual business, but on the promise of the increased sales which he anticipated as a result of this procedure. When, on one occasion, the new sales did not mount quickly enough to prevent a loss, instead of putting back the old price he made a further cut, and this brought him the result he wanted. His own explanation is that the whip laid to the backs of the staff by increased charges resulted every time in new economies which more than counterbalanced the new burdens. The whole thing happened, however, at a time when there was a sharp deflation going on in the United States, so that in real value his new price was very little smaller than his old one. The remarkable thing about the transaction is that he should have been able to cut his price enough to maintain what amounted to a substantial increase in the real value of his wages—a feat which the rest of the world seems now to be finding impossible.

The Ford rate of wages is now, in America, a minimum of six dollars a day. Sixty per cent of his men earn more than this under a system of rewards for efficient work. His foreign wage scales are worked out to produce an equivalent real wage in the currency of the country concerned, and he states that the cost per minute per man in different countries works out exactly in inverse ratio to the level of wages paid. In the nineteen years during which it was producing the famous Model T, the Ford Company paid out wages and salaries to the amount of almost two thousand million dollars. If the rewards of agents and outside workers in garages and repair shops generally are added, the total comes to nearly five and a half thousand million dollars. This does not include the pay of the workers on his railway, oil-fields or rubber plantations or in his mines. The sums distributed by the company in purchases fall little short of five thousand million dollars. He may well claim that this is a substantial contribution to international prosperity.

It is in pursuit of this prosperity, as well as to save the heavy costs of transport, that he has placed his factories and assembly shops all over the world. He likes to balance the drain of money into the funds of the company by the provision of work and a corresponding outflow of wages and salaries. But he goes further. He thinks that work should be so planned as to provide the best possible life for the worker. The great industrial cities he regards as evils—the normal life seems to him one which allows a man to work on the land in summer and come into the shelter and light of the factory in winter time. He has several factories of this type established in the United States. In Kentucky and Virginia he is said to be taking factories to the mouth of his mines so that the miners may be able to spend only half their working hours below ground and for the rest of their time earn their living as machinists.

While all the work of carrying out this system was being done, Ford was extending his business. During the war he added to the manufacture of Model T that of farm tractors for the English government, and many smaller products for the government of his own country. These tractors realize a very early ambition. They are designed to lessen the heavy work as well as the cost of farming—each is in reality not only a tractor but a light and portable power plant. Since the war he has scrapped Model T—of which 15,000,000 had been sold—and substituted a car built on more modern lines; he has also undertaken the manufacture of a luxury car—the Lincoln. In addition, stoppages in his supplies of raw material, some due to accident, others to business operators, have forced him to buy a railway (which paid for the first time after he took it over), mines, rubber plantations and oil-fields and to manufacture for himself glass, cloth and several other materials needed for the manufacture of his car.

He is now, in fact, by himself a gigantic "vertical" combine.

It does not fall within the scope of this book to discuss Mr. Ford as a pacifist, as a denigrator of Jews and bankers, as an admirer of the arts who presented the "homey" Detroit patriotic poet, Mr. Guest, with a Ford car every year for several years, or as the nature lover who has had his garden fitted with birds' nests suspended on flexible steel springs so that his wrens may use them undisturbed by sparrows. It is more to the point that he has created and maintains a large model hospital specially organized to check the professional failings of doctors, and that he runs schools for boys in which the pupils are trained in several skilled crafts and earn from the first a good rate of wages. He has given the world these, and a car and a tractor which have reduced labour for millions. He has given it also his great business, a heavy item to the credit of the individualist capitalist system. This is what that system can do—run at its best, with the spirit of greed eliminated and a real desire to help mankind put in its place. Even so, his productive organization has been attacked—bitterly attacked—on the score that it is a despotism, that it is harsh and that it wears out its men.

A despotism it is—that is what makes of it so illuminating an example. As for the other charges—that sort of thing is a question of more or less which cannot be weighed here. The figures he gives of average length of service make it clear that they are not physically worn out. The criticism seems to boil down to this—that they are completely absorbed, capable away from work of only the crudest recreations and unable to play any extra part as useful citizens. That is a criticism which can truthfully be made of whole classes and communities of business men in every country, and it leads us again to the connected problems of education and the use of leisure.

In summing up Mr. Ford's work and its rewards the question of desert seems hardly relevant. However much he has, and whether he deserves it or not, his is a mind which can be trusted with money. Let him make as much as he can—it will be used for important purposes and in a stimulating and individual way.

ALFRED LOWENSTEIN

We now turn back again from these processes of wealth accumulation by creation, to the more purely acquisitive type of accumulators. While the great forces of invention and accelerated communication embody themselves in such great industrial forms as Standard Oil, Imperial Chemical Industries, United States Steel and so on, there runs by the side of these huge organizing processes a great multitude of people intent merely on getting rich by virtue of the opportunities they afford. We have studied old-fashioned forms of accumulation in the cases of Mrs. Hetty Green and the Rothschilds. Essentially such types are "wealth-grabbers." The wealth was there, anyhow, and they did nothing to increase it. They merely accumulated it. Let us see now how wealth-grabbing can be practised under more recent conditions, with the aëroplane to replace Nathan Meyer Rothschild's corner in fishing boats, and with all the bold precedents of the railway and oil kings to follow. Alfred Lowenstein, whose life was ended accidentally or deliberately by a fall out of an aëroplane while crossing the English Channel, can be taken as the crowning instance of the modern financial adventurer who neither evokes wealth nor buys existing wealth, but who seizes upon it as it struggles into being.

There remains an element of mystery about his end. A preliminary enquiry returned a verdict of accidental death, but his body was recovered a week or so later and Dr. Paul, the French pathologist, examined the body and reported the presence of "toxic matter." Lowenstein seems to have been in the midst of very extensive financial operations in which he was losing considerably, and there is no very clear account of his actual position at the time of his death. He may have been mortified and tormented by his situation at that time, but he was certainly not a ruined man. Very naturally, the tragedy was followed by a slump in the securities in which he was interested, but the mere fact of his death while the market was in a nervous state would be sufficient to account for that. Here is a man who appeared suddenly in our financial skies, buying and selling on a scale of romantic enormity.

He was, it seems, the son of a small banker in Belgium; he was born in 1874, and when his father went bankrupt with 1,800 (pre-war) francs of debt in 1892, the son reconstructed the firm, accepted his father's obligations, and became a broker in Brussels. For some years he worked in partnership and without any great distinction. He was a propagandist of the geographical distribution of investments and showed himself skilful in guiding the investing public to new fields of risk. His first considerable opportunity came in 1906, when he was able to raise capital for the Rio de Janeiro Light and Power Company. Investments in Brazil were not well known at that time, and he earned his money by a very vigorous pushing of the new securities. He proceeded to other South American flotations. His methods did not pass without hostile criticism. He was already a multi-millionaire (in francs) before the war. The war perhaps retarded his development for a time; he joined up and served his country in England (where he bought remounts for the Belgian cavalry), and in America, but he still found opportunities for profit. The relative value of railways, tramways, power companies and so forth in South America increased with the destruction and exhaustion in Europe; the French and Belgian francs staggered at the end of the war and every ordinary investor was assailed by doubts and fears. Wealth offered itself to the alert, and Alfred Lowenstein was one of the alertest men alive.

It was after the war that his phase of conspicuous magnificence began. Then he became a speculator on a vast scale, interesting himself chiefly in hydro-electric undertakings and the new great industry of artificial silk. He clambered to the position of the third richest man alive. But all he did was to "find money" for these enterprises, and he found it in the most expensive way for both the enterprises and the primary investors. It is hard to avoid the conclusion that even at the best phase of his career he was only in a very limited sense an operating organ of the economic body. Possibly he irritated a too sluggish banking world which was retarding new developments into greater activity. That is very doubtful. Essentially he was a boil on the face of business, and a very conspicuous and dangerous boil.

Privat* gives some glimpses of his life in its brilliant phase. He moved between a suite of rooms he possessed at Claridge's in London and a suite he took by the year at the Ritz in Paris; he had a palace in Brussels, a great estate at Melton Mowbray, where he entertained the Prince of Wales, and a great villa at Biarritz. He was surrounded by an army of secretaries and stenographers. He had private aëroplanes for the use of himself and his special messengers at Croydon, Le Bourget, Brussels and elsewhere. When the Belgian and French franc went through a period of rapid devaluation in 1925 he offered, upon certain conditions, a loan to these governments at 2 per cent sufficient in amount for an immediate stabilization. It was refused. His ambitions were boundless. He seems to have aimed at a control of the entire electric supply of the world. He was caught by a sudden restriction of his credit through the concerted action of a powerful group of banks, and shorn of a

*La vie et la mort d'Alfred Lowenstein.

considerable part of his incredible fortune. He tried to regain what he had lost, too hastily and rashly; his operations were ill-judged and unsound, and he was certainly in the grip of a second shearing operation at the time of his death. How far he was a mere gambler and "operator" it is hard to determine. His anticipation of the future of electric-power enterprises and of artificial silk was certainly intelligent. Privat says he consulted fortune-tellers and was guided in some of his decisions by communications made to him through various "mediums" by a spirit "Phlogiston." By the scale of payment of ordinary human activities, the wealth he came to handle was fantastically vast. It was somewhere in the region of twenty million pounds or so. In 1928 the 430,000 shares of his International Holdings Company stood at £31,000,000 and receded to £18,500,000. On the news of his death in July this fell further to £12,500,000.

It is very remarkable how poorly documented all such careers seem to be. There is nothing about Alfred Lowenstein in the New Encyclopædia Britannica and nothing about him in the 1928 Who's Who. I have quoted already from an able little book about him by Maurice Privat, but it is improbable that his life will ever be exhaustively studied. While the poor little affairs of obscure, industrious men of letters are made the subject of intensive research, and while every scrap of their entirely unimportant private correspondence commands the money of eager collectors, the far more romantic, thrilling and illuminating documents that must be scattered abundantly through the world, about these seekers and makers of great fortunes, are neither gathered nor cherished. When at last the scientific historian of the economic processes of our times sits down to his task, he will have small reason for thanking the collectors of letters, diaries, private account books and personal memoranda. Beautifully preserved First Editions, autographs, and the self-conscious love letters of a thousand insignificant scribblers will leap to his hand, while hardly a scrap of early Harmsworthiana or Zaharoffiana or Lowensteiniana will be forthcoming.

MEN WHO HAVE GONE BEYOND THE PERMITTED LIMITS

If, however, we descend to the next lowest grade of wealth-seekers, we come immediately to a soundly documented record, because we have the reports of their trials. These are the quite illegal wealth-seekers, the men who did not restrain their ac-quisitive effort within the limits of the law. They were too impatient or too clumsy or not lucky enough to avail them-selves successfully of the permitted ways of acquiring large sums suddenly. They blundered into tight corners, and then, by the rules of the game, they cheated, or else they set out to cheat from the outset. Such "operations" as those of Jabez Balfour with his Liberator Society, which flourished in appearance for fifteen years after it was bankrupt, or the London and Globe Company frauds of Whitaker Wright, may serve as classical instances of financial affairs below the threshold of permis-sible enterprise, and from such cases we pass down to a con-sideration of such simpler abuses of confidence as the creation— the forgery, to be more exact—of fictitious shares. This has been occurring periodically on a large scale throughout the last hundred years, and it has taxed the economic process to the extent of many millions. The recent Hatry crash in London may serve as the type case; it is the last of a long series, ex-ceptional only in its boldness. These cruder frauds are due simply to bad checking in the business machine, and so of course is plain embezzlement, which also recurs with a certain regularity and is a calculable and insurable risk. Many cashiers, many bank managers, many bankers, many chairmen of boards get a feeling that no one is watching them closely, and under various stresses a certain proportion succumb to this appearance of opportunity. It is often a very justifiable feeling, and some perhaps go undetected. They snatch a profit somewhere and put the money back in time and cover their traces. The embezzler, the criminal operator, the bold but just tolerated operator, the brilliant and accepted operator, the pushing and promising young "giant" in the City, the admired financial magnate, and the triumphant amasser of wealth can be brought all together into our picture because they have this in common —they are possible through the general defectiveness of our methods of accounting in the distribution of purchasing power. They are produced by the imperfections of an evolved and still tentative system of defining economic relationships. It is not acquisitive, speculative or dishonest individuals, therefore, but a system of uncertain values that has finally to be arraigned if anything has to be arraigned.

But the best plan for mankind is to arraign nobody, declare a general amnesty and get on with the task of so reorganizing our methods of direction and payment that all this juggling in the counting-house of human affairs, to the detriment of worker and consumer alike, may become impossible.

§ 2. *The Contemporary Rich*

We have shown how arbitrarily purchasing power is distributed in relation to productive activity because of the extraordinary looseness of the world's financial machinery. Wealth to-day has become largely financial. It is no longer mainly a directive ownership of actual property but a monetary claim upon production. The owner-producer, after the fashion of Henry Ford, is the exception, not the rule. The majority of the rich belong to the investing public. They are the upper stratum of the investing public.

We have shown by some typical instances how the financial system works. For the real creators of wealth, finance is an embarrassment; but it is the normal way to wealth, nevertheless. The intervention of a highly speculative and adventurous stratum of financiers and business operators of various sorts between the producing and consuming activities of the community, diverts and intercepts a large amount of the world's production from what an increasing number of people consider its only legitimate destinations. They hold that the gross product of our collective activities, or rather the power to purchase that product, should be the reward for definite services rendered and for contributions to the collective welfare. There is this interception and concentration of purchasing power. A considerable section of the "well-off" and rich classes in the community represents this intercepted purchasing power in action. Dominant purchasing power means the right to "call the tune" for social life, and not only the way in which this intercepted purchasing power is accumulated, but the way in which it is expended, is a matter of primary importance in a comprehensive study of economics.

The way of living and spending of these financially successful people, the new rich, must affect the general operation of demand and supply in the community very profoundly, but whether their purchasing power is dominant and whether they are really "calling the tune" is a very different matter. If they spend variously and discursively they may not in the aggregate make much of a demand in any special direction.

All rich people, be it noted, are not to be regarded as the result of the interception of purchasing power by speculative operations. The big new wealth is largely that, but it is only one of the possible types of wealth. There are old fortunes as well as the *nouveau riche*. There are social types of an older tradition who share the privilege of irresponsible spending with these comparative newcomers. Such are the recipients of the exaggerated rents due to modern urban developments, of the royalties upon coal and other mineral wealth discovered underneath landed estates, and the like. And for the purposes of this economic analysis we must also include the British, Dutch and Scandinavian royal families—almost the only royal groups which have had the good sense to abstain from those stock-exchange adventures which send kings into exile. Akin to this special rich type is the mediæval wealth of the protected princes in India and various other Oriental rulers. Such relatively unacquisitive rich people trail a picturesque tradition of honour, titles and precedences into the world of modern wealth. They give it a dignity it would otherwise lack, and in a partial traditional way they give it a direction. They supply the framework of a social organization, a discipline, an aspiration towards social solidarity, that would otherwise be wanting, to the great accumulators of the present time.

The proportion of new wealth to old in the modern community is probably very large. There are no exact figures. The question is discussed very interestingly by Sir Josiah Stamp in *Some Economic Factors in Modern Life* under "Inheritance." In the past a vast part of the wealth in the world was inherited, and there was a permanent wealthy *class* with a rôle and tradition of its own. But wealth is not the same thing in the modern community as wealth in the eighteenth century. Its dispositions are different; its reactions are different; it is altogether less stable.

In the wealthier life of most European communities there is evident, or at least there is still traceable, a seasonal social routine, typically or originally centring on the movements of a court or the assembly of a legislature, and deriving many of its observances from the pre-railway era. Its observances still preserve a faint association with current political and social functions. Because it was, in fact, once functional and responsible. Even in the United States of America there is a certain limited movement of wealthy people to and from Washington, but the life of the rich in America is far less centralized and far more highly individualized than in Europe. There is not the same association with social and political responsibilities. American wealth, throughout the continent, is almost entirely modern wealth of the modern type, arising without any tradition of political or social responsibility whatever, out of the financial and industrial events of the last hundred years. There is no such rendezvous of political, intellectual and artistic life as the London "Season" used to be, and still to some extent is. There is nothing to equal the desertion of Paris in July and the return to Paris in October. But even in the countries of old established routines, these routines are manifestly undergoing a process of effacement. The convergence upon court, Ascot, and Goodwood, is less and less obligatory and general, and the rich tend now to follow their own devices as they were never disposed to do before. In other words, their solidarity is disappearing. They are free and individualized beyond all precedent.

We have already dealt in a general fashion with "How Mankind is Fed" and "How Mankind is Clothed and Housed." We can but glance here at the way in which the rich are fed, clothed, housed—and amused. The conjunction of leisure and great purchasing power involves a very vigorous demand for amusement on their part. Perhaps it will be best to begin with housing. The story of the household of the contemporary rich, takes up from the household of the rich family of the old régime possessing at least one great country estate, almost self-supporting, and a big town house. To these were added shooting estates, houses in hunting country, stud farms, with a very numerous staff of servants and estate men. The new wealthy were at first disposed to fall into this pattern. Many of the earlier *nouveaux riches* were indeed completely absorbed into traditional "society," and their descendants are among the most conservative of those who continue the country-house tradition.

The country house, however, even when it is still in the hands of the old type of rich people, is, under the stress of new facilities for provisioning, becoming less and less autonomous, and with this departure from actuality there is an increasing development of toy farms and dairies and the like, a playing at utility after the fashion of the Petit Trianon. A sort of "out-of-town" house has gradually replaced the great house, the château of the old order; it is smaller, more luxurious, better fitted to save labour and trouble, less and less a centre of local life and more and more dependent on exterior supplies. There has been a tendency to go abroad, to the French and Italian Rivieras, for example, in the case of British, Germans and Americans, and there to build and occupy beautiful toy villas and garden villas, inhabited only for a part of the year. Now such pleasant houses spring up in South Africa, Florida, California and wherever there is any exceptional charm of climate. The rich become more and more delocalized and cosmopolitan.

The country house, in the homeland where it is still used, is no longer central and self-sufficient socially. There is a golf club or a country club at hand for informal social mingling. The country house is not, as it used to be, a centre of continuous living. Parties gather for the week-end and vanish again. The "letting" of both town and country houses has increased; they are, generally speaking, less personal than they were, or else in exceptional cases they are much more personal, the "creations" of their owners, intensely individualized. Most of us have heard and seen something of these latter very personal houses in America and Europe. They are what a Cockney would call "fancy" houses—on the analogy of "fancy ladies." But the distinctive habitat of new wealth is now not a house possessed, but a great hired house, the pleasure villa without any tributary "estate" or with merely sporting "grounds" attached, or it is the hotel de luxe. The new wealth does not settle; it goes now here, now there. It does not root locally as the old wealth did; it produces no type of home of its own; it seems to be conscious of its own impermanence.

Here we need give no detailed account of the modern life de luxe in all its irresponsible glitter. The contemporary society papers, the large illustrated advertisement-carrying weeklies give and renew a constantly changing picture of these activities. Marvellously dressed people stand about in groups. They do not seem to be up to very much and in fact they are not up to very much. They do not appear to be actively oppressing mankind or to be doing anything active at all to avert a possible catastrophe from the system that has produced them. They do not know how they were produced, and they do not understand what threatens them. A large part of the energy of the new spending goes into a search of pleasure, sensuous pleasure, or it seeks the mere gratification of vanity or the stimulus of personal danger. Many of the new rich, if they employ fewer servants, have, nevertheless, larger retinues than the older kind. It would need a little band of novelists to describe many of these retinues. The extremely rich have actual courts. Service passes on the one hand into friendly help and on the other into actual prostitution. So far as published letters, law reports, scandal and the contemporary novel admit the student to this side of life, the adventuress appears to be playing a larger rôle in an increasing number of personal dramas than ever before, and the satellite systems of flatterers and illegitimate dependents of every type develop thickly and readily about almost all holders of preëminent purchasing power. These satellites again collectively furnish employment for a large class of purveyors of their own.

The beauty specialist and the parasitic doctor of the rich merit the attention of the modern playwright. The parasitic doctor is a convenient dealer in the stimulants and drugs his professional qualification enable him to supply. To be a patronizable artist, writer or critic supplying intellectual and æsthetic reassurance, supplying drugs for the mind, or a religious teacher, supplying drugs for the soul, is now also a métier, and at a slightly different level comes the exclusive dressmaker.

From these intimacies we pass to the rich man's architect and decorator, the rich man's landscape gardener and the builder of the rich man's automobile. Here to a large extent we pass beyond the range of prostitution. We find an increasing factor of technical ability and technical conscientiousness. And this applies also to the household and estate servants of the rich man. "Things have to be right," so far as these people are concerned, and the seductions of flattery and self-abasement are no longer of primary importance. They retain their backbones. In the hotel de luxe and the great restaurant which have to cater not only for the very rich but for the merely rich, this is even more so. The standard of performance in all such places has to be a very high one and their control must be in the hands of able, if cynical, men. There is a continual unpremeditated struggle between the rare and fickle rich and the vast and calculable multitude of people with mediocre fortunes, for the services of this type of organizer and director. And the same struggle occurs in the continual development of new and more agreeable forms of de luxe travel and its rapid cheapening down to middle-class requirements, less lavish but more certain.

Few of the rich, and very few indeed of the new adventurous rich, are content to be merely sensuous and flattered. They want to go on happening. They come out—and particularly their young people come out—of their securities to flirt with danger, danger de luxe, in aëroplanes and hydroplanes, in travel in unsettled countries, in destroying such big game as survives in the world, in riding to hounds across cultivated land, in the desperate driving of powerful cars. Still more of them, as patrons, spectators and backers, taste the delights of dangerous exploits and athleticism at second hand. Others, returning to tease the risks that might once have ended them, gamble frankly. Gambling is socially much more mischievous in the rich than in the poor, but our laws seem to be based on the reverse idea. There is nothing to prevent the active entrepreneur, on whose stability some great enterprise and the employment of thousands of people may depend, from hazarding the welfare of the whole organization upon the chances of the tables. Just as there is nothing to prevent him from gambling as desperately upon the Stock Exchange. Abruptly his business may have to be transferred to other hands, sold up possibly to his former competitors, managed by some inexpert trustee, or closed down altogether.

An account of rich leisure would not be complete without a glance at the worlds of sport and gambling. The Turf survives from antiquity. In Great Britain it is part of the traditional monarchy, and the king by right divine still goes to Ascot and Epsom very much as the Son of Heaven used to go to the great Temple in Pekin to sacrifice and inaugurate the seasons. The race meeting is a very ancient function in the life of man. It was once a really vital social function, a parade of the entire community. There were seasonal races at Stonehenge before the beginnings of history. I do not know if Newmarket derives from some East Anglian Stonehenge or Woodhenge, through an unbroken tradition, or if it was a Stuart revival. Horse Show week in Dublin seems more certainly the survival of an ancient gathering.

It would be an interesting thing if in our still unrealized encyclopædia of Work and Wealth we could have a history and social description of the Turf—for the non-sportsman. Had we the time and resources available, we would go into the racing stables and consider the code of honour prevalent there. We would discuss the science of form. We would gather our material for a psychology of betting. Here too the initiatives of the rich spread their influence far and wide throughout human affairs.

There is a little world of people whose way of living is to bet. Many there are who "do quite well by it." They live in not unpleasant places, their days are passed in a pattern of sunshine under trees, white rails, green turf, amidst holiday crowds, to the accompaniment of the swift, thudding crescendo of the racing horses. Wealth flows into this bright little world from the casual betting of the outsider and from the deliberate spending of the sporting rich. Our present economic system can carry it, just as it can carry the innumerable thousands of grave quartettes who are at this moment playing auction or contract bridge. No one has ever attempted to measure the proportion of human intelligence and energy absorbed by betting. There are great offices, beautifully organized, with polite clerks and managers and small regiments of typists working upon this quite sterile activity.

The outward radiation of the mentality and example of the contemporary rich calls for a very close scrutiny. Their concentration of purchasing power is by no means all-powerful in economic life. It is not even all-powerful in evoking styles and fashions. Its prestige is very great, but not so great relatively as was the prestige of the nobility and gentry of France and England and the small royalties and princes of Germany and Italy in the eighteenth century. They constituted an organized system, and modern wealth does not do so. Modern plutocracy is an indeterminate pressure of purchasing power, it sets perhaps certain standards of smartness, it may give a direction to gambling and many of the more expensive sports; its individuals can bribe enormously, can subscribe to pay the debts of reckless "statesmen" in difficulties, or splash about ignorantly and mischievously in public and international affairs; but in regard to commodities in general I doubt if the new rich have anything like the directive purchasing power of the middling mass of people, whether these people be rentier, in business or employed.

Except for the rentier section which may be, and probably is, shrewdly discriminating in its expenditure, this class of middling people, this great main mass of the modern community—so far as purchasing power goes—though it has neither the leisure nor the breadth of experience to buy with acute directive force, has broad essential requirements that must be respected and obeyed. Its want of discriminatory leisure is supplemented by the modern development of the advertiser. It has to be flattered and tempted and induced to spend by the advertiser. The advertiser has to explore the mind which the class as a whole has not the freedom to make up. The advertiser studies and guesses, and the nearest guess, the one that crystallizes the unformed wishes of the prosperous mediocrities, wins. It is certainly this middlingly prosperous class and not the rich which sustains most of our theatres, evokes such things as broadcasting and the cinema, suffers the modern press, accepts and is the medium for the propaganda of the less expensive sports like lawn tennis and golf, and tolerates the contemporary café and restaurant and ordinary travel conditions.

I am inclined to think that it is increasingly the advertising producer who determines changes and fashions in the consumption of people of middling fortune, and that the mere snobbish imitativeness and life at second hand which formerly prevailed in this mass are becoming relatively unimportant. In the past the middle class had no patterns for social behaviour except the ways and equipment of royalty and the nobility and gentry. The nobility and gentry indeed played the rôle of an advertisement system then for purveyors. In London the Royal Arms over a shop, and the words "By Appointment," were of immense value to shopkeepers. I doubt if they are now. The modern rich by comparison have neither the uniformity, the prestige nor the desire to impose their standards. They do not want to lead and dominate morally; they have no sense of responsibility for the general behaviour; they want rather to be free and uncriticized or admired and conspicuously different. They are not so much a class now as a number of miscellaneous experimenting fortunate individuals. They arouse envy rather than emulation, and the immense publicity given to some of their more remarkable feats of expenditure probably evokes not merely curiosity and admiration in the ordinary beholder, magically inhibited from anything of the sort, but personal humiliation and envious hostility.

The very rich are now a criticized phenomenon in the social scheme. They are stared at like strange large wonderful animals, but they are not loved. There is no element of affectionate ownership in the feeling of the public for any of them, except (in Britain and the Scandinavian countries) for royalty. And even the prestige of royalty is difficult to measure. It collapsed very suddenly in Russia and Spain. Setting royalty aside, few people, outside the parasite systems the very rich have collected about themselves, would move a hand to save them from extinction. They are easy to tax. Income tax, super tax, surtax, death duties deflate their accumulations, and they seem unable to prevent it, while the steadying of productive enterprise by changes in company law and the spreading exactitudes of the statistician, may presently limit the scale of new speculative gains and check the appearance of fresh great fortunes. If we are right in our supposition that the loosely investing public is a transitory phenomenon in economic development, we are probably still more right in anticipating the passing of these large wild fortunes which now move so portentously, so like the hurrying tail of a belated carnival procession at nightfall, across the accumulating uneasiness of the contemporary scene.

§ 3. *The Alleged Social Advantages of a Rich Class*

There can be little question that the existence of this irresponsible rich class, so conspicuous in contemporary life, involves a very considerable waste of human resources, a vulgarization of youthful imaginations, and a widespread demoralization of potential producers. Moreover, it carries with it the possibility of powerful, irrational interventions in the political and general mental life of the community.

But that is only one side of the case for and against the "idle rich," and our survey will be a very inadequate one if it does not take the other side into account. We have to consider very carefully what case for the defense can be offered on behalf of the free spending and the free initiatives these great fortunes afford.

It can be urged that although a very large part of the spending of the contemporary rich is, in a word, waste, that is not true of all of it. Some of it produces things that are vitally important, things which as yet we do not seem able to produce in any other way.

We have already foreshadowed this line of defense in the treatment in Book II of the development of Science and the release of Invention. There it will have been shown how the intellectual emancipation of mankind has been sustained through all its phases of vigour by the existence of people with leisure and liberty of movement, people we may best describe as independent gentlemen. In the gratification primarily of their own curiosities, such men lit that lamp of Science which now illuminates the whole present and future of mankind. Movements of searching criticism and ideological reformation have, it is true, come mainly from the dissentient priestly type, but the positive establishment of these new idea systems and the accumulation of new facts have generally demanded a greater freedom and purchasing power than the intellectual rebel has had at his command. Roger Bacon, in an impoverished world without any rich leisure class, cried out and was extinguished, but the Academies of independent gentlemen in the easier circumstances of the Renascence experimented and printed and distributed their observations and made the modern world possible.

In this survey of human economics we have classified the royal and noble as an older section of the rich, and it is inconceivable how the earlier phases of the scientific movement could have occurred without the patronage and endowment of these stabler rich people in the past. Right down to the present, it is to the free rich that men of originality have had to turn to realize a great multitude of projects that would otherwise have lain dormant; explorations, great laboratories, bold innovations in apparatus, which made no appeal to the common voter or the political boss. The enormous debt of the world to Mr. J. D.

Rockefeller alone, is a powerful argument against any too hasty conclusion that the great lumps of riches in the social organism are essentially or even mainly morbid growths. We must take the Rockefeller endowments in one hand, weigh them very carefully against the extravagances of other families as fortunate but less intelligent. The name of Rockefeller is not alone. There are a score of conspicuous names which stand like pillars to sustain the work of modern research. Wealth is not always reactionary; often it is not even self-protective.

It is not simply in the field of science that the rich have a reasonable claim to functional value. They have also played an as yet quite unassessed part in the development of the arts and the protection of intellectual freedoms. The free rich have been the informal protectors of free speech. A very considerable proportion of the more influential and less popular organs of critical and philosophical discussion are still subsidized by relatively rich people, and it is difficult to imagine how their practical independence could be sustained in any other way.

People of smaller means, it may be urged, might form societies and subscribe small sums that will be effective in the aggregate. But the really rich man of understanding and leisure can see that he gets what he pays for, and that is exactly what a crowd of well-off but busy people putting up guineas and five-pound notes never does. They fall a prey to secretaries and such like "organizers," and once a society has given itself over to a secretary it is usually very difficult to come together to call him to account. The waste of money through the impotent subscriptions of people of moderate fortunes, runs parallel to their haphazard investments and is due to the same reasons. They are attempting things outside their scope of direction and control, they are attempting often vitally important things for which they have insufficient time and specialization. A middle-class association is a very inferior substitute for a single intelligent rich patron.

It is even more difficult to imagine politicians directing public money carefully and intelligently into a channel which is as likely as not to repay them with corrosive comment, and will certainly never repay them by a vote. The bad side of rich leisure, the side of luxury and waste, we must remember is its most conspicuous side. There are, collectively, a very considerable number of less obtrusive rich people going about businesses that are necessary to the progress of mankind. Just exactly what proportion these redeeming functions bear to the pure waste and social mischief of free wealth nowadays it is impossible to say. There, beyond all denial, are these redeeming instances, these salvagers of spendng power.*

Here, at any rate, is a considerable justification for the existence of a relatively rich class in modern life, but it does not follow that there is any justification for the sort of rich class that has been produced by the financial confusedness of economic life during the past hundred years. But why presently should there not be a different sort of rich class? There might easily be a rich class with more responsibility and less vulgarity. Much of the life de luxe which flaunts itself before the worker is a very vulgar and wasteful life indeed.

But since, as we have seen, wealth can change its character in a couple of hundred years, from concrete possessions to entries in share lists and bank credit, why should it not go on to still more abstract and much more controllable reservations and allocations of spending power?

All the good and less of the evil of free spending may be obtainable, we would suggest, by some other class of free spenders, not yet clearly defined. There is, for instance, no reason why great royalties and public grants should not still be paid to inventors and artists and men of conspicuous creative ability. True, that creative ability is not always associated with organizing and directive ability. But a world of vigorous productivity, with a high standard of general comfort and behaviour, will not only be able to afford experimental-minded and intellectually active rich people, but it will realize the need for them. It may even choose and appoint men and women to spend great sums of money as they think fit. It is amusing to think of a rich class, rich

---

*But for a criticism of rich man endowments see Professor Harold Laski's *Dangers of Obedience,* Chap. VI.

by achievement, election and appointment, and not through acquisitive concentration—people whose wealth has been given to them and not grabbed by them.

A sort of foreshadowing of the kind of thing that might be done more extensively in the future, is to be found in the recently established "Pilgrim Trust" which has assigned to five men (Mr. Baldwin, the Rt. Hon. Hugh Macmillan, Sir James Irvine, Sir Josiah Stamp and Mr. John Buchan) a practically unrestricted freedom to spend two million pounds in any way they think proper for the benefit of English people. The donor in this interesting experiment with wealth is Mr. Harkness of New York. His modesty makes him doubt his ability to spend his money to the best advantage, and so he has decided to delegate the task to these others. He washes his hands of the money. He insists on the freedom of his trustees. But manifestly a rich world in the future could play the rôle of Mr. Harkness and give a popular man or a group of competent people the free disposal of large sums of money.

§ 4. *The Ideal of Equal Pay for All*

The Communist ideal that everyone in the community should have equal pay has recently been widely popularized by Shaw in his *Intelligent Woman's Guide to Socialism and Capitalism.*

Everybody has heard of that idea now, even if there has been little or no discussion. It is an idea that was always in the background of nineteenth-century Socialist thought; it is the idea of Ruskin's *Unto These Last,* and it seems to have been the idea of Jesus in that parable of the Workers in the Vineyard to which Ruskin's pamphlet owed its title. It is the ideal, if not the reality, of Russian social administration. It is the statement of a moral attitude, and not a biological or economic conclusion.

There is a marked strain of unresolved mysticism in the naturally very clear and critical mind of Shaw. It is an essentially scientific type of mind that has never undergone any mental discipline, it is a scientific mind that was found and brought up by musicians and artists, and it has been greatly depraved by his irresistible sense of fun and his unsurpassed genius for platform effect. His is a fine intelligence which is always going off on the spree. No men can be mentally energetic all round, something everyone must take for granted, and Shaw is no exception to this rule. His indolence is about fundamentals. He betrays an unwillingness to scrutinize the springs of his opinions, and these springs arise, more directly than is usual among minds of his calibre, from personal attachments and reactions. He has never freed himself from the dispositions of nineteenth-century radicalism and equalitarianism. Equal pay for all, equal purchasing power for all, is really the logical extension into the sphere of material things of the pretensions of nineteenth-century democracy. Equal pay—so soon as the immediate personal needs of a human being are satisfied—means an equal share in the direction of the world's productive activities. For that end, the present mental equipment of a normal man is at least as insufficient as it is for the exercise of political controls.

It has already been pointed out in this survey how deeply the socialism of Marx was coloured by democratic obsessions, and how, in the presence of modern conceptions of economic organization, this quality in his doctrines has given a curious double face to the great experiment of Soviet Russia. The consequence in Russia is, and the consequence in any attempt to realize the proposal of Shaw would be, to make a fraternal communism of the extremest kind the common profession of faith, while at the same time—under the pressure of modern inventiveness and large-scale production which demands skilful direction—vesting practical direction in a highly concentrated body, holding power in some questionable manner, claiming to work for the "general good" and restraining all criticism and divergent initiatives. The practical realization of "Equal pay for all" can work out only as a dictatorship giving the individual citizens, in roughly equal amounts, what it considers to be good for them. The loss of variety, liberty and above all, initiative, involved by this equalitarianism, may easily be too high a price to pay even for the elimination of the luxurious and wasteful rich from the social process.

We must insist here that it is unsound to assume that wealth is the *cause* of poverty. That is, we hold, one of the popular delusions of our time. The position to which our studies in this book bring us, is that both irresponsible wealth and poverty are produced by a faulty, inaccurate economic mechanism, as smoke, noise, dirt and delay are produced by a badly adjusted motor-car. But the noise does not produce the stoppages, or vice versa, and one may be eliminated without the other.

Equally unsound is it to assume, as the "equal pay" idea implies, that any economic organization will grind out the same amount of wealth, and that it is only a question of the equal or unequal division of a fixed total product. The sterilization of wealth by the Hetty Green type of accumulator does far more mischief to production than would be represented by the deprivation of millions of workers of a contribution merely equivalent in the aggregate to her accumulation. The Hetty Green type holds up creative exploitation; it not only makes off with wealth but it misdirects wealth and obstructs the creation of fresh wealth. Hetty Green is only one case of the immobilization of natural resources and economic possibilities under uncontrolled private ownership. It is an unscientific theory of property that is to blame. Restrictive property is only one form of "riches." "Operations" of the Jay Gould type, again, work like bombs thrown into the engine room. But such operations are preventable. Riches can be evoked as well as acquired. The enrichment of Ford and Edison enriches everybody.

Is it impossible to readjust affairs so that service may become a necessary associate of enrichment? The trend of the facts we have accumulated and arranged in this and the preceding chapters is towards an affirmative. It is manifestly childish to suppose that either an efficient monetary or an efficient credit system has yet been worked out, much less tried out. The world has hardly begun to think intelligently about money. Our classifications of property and our legal control of its use are infantile. The science of social motive has barely dawned. The problem of leaving freedom of initiative in an organized world remains untouched. Much thought and trial, dispute and disappointment lie ahead. We are faced with periods if not ages of conflict and confusion in which the victory of constructive forces is by no means assured. It is the purest fantasy to imagine that we can leap at one bound from all the complexities of the contemporary system to an equalitarian Utopia. Even if anything of the sort is socially or biologically desirable.

§ 5. *Do the Modern Rich Want the Poor to Be Kept Poor?*

Here it will be interesting to discuss a paragraph in a recently published book on monetary questions, Professor Soddy's *Money Versus Man.* It is a very significant sign of the times to find so distinguished a figure in physical science as the Nobel laureate for 1921 drawn by the urgencies of the subject into a scrutiny of finance. His approach is extraordinarily fresh and vigorous. He has already published *Cartesian Economics* (1922), *Wealth, Virtual Wealth and Debt* (1926), and *The Wrecking of a Scientific Age,* and he has declared himself in Who's Who to be "interested in Postdiluvian Economics." He is certainly a welcome leader in the attempt to put orthodox political economy into the palæontological museum. There is an inspiring riotousness in his style of attack. He is not a solitary phenomenon. He is a pioneer. The banker's parlour, the stockbroker's office and the board room are going to be invaded by an increasing number of highly intelligent and highly sceptical enquirers, resenting bluff and mystery, using unflattering words like "antediluvian" and "dishonest old fumblers" and suchlike phrases with a startling readiness, and very resolutely "wanting to know."

We can represent Professor Soddy as saying on behalf of physical science: "We men of science have abolished toil and people are still toiling; we have created plenty, and everywhere there is want. What has got between us and them?" And then sharply: *"What the devil are you money-fakers up to?"* These are not his words, but that is his manifest temper.

Here, however, we are not dealing with his temper, but with a very vital issue he raises. He raises it as a side issue, but it is indeed a fundamental issue. What he says in the particular matter we now want to discuss, follows. It is a bold assertion of the malevolence of successful humanity. He says in effect that most energetic men live for power and to triumph over their fellow creatures. Here is the passage:

"Now it is one thing for science to make some relatively much richer than others, and quite another, without even a by-your-leave, for science so insidiously to undermine the established order of human society as to put all beyond the persuasive influence of want. There are many neither unimportant nor over-scrupulous people, if not the majority of the most forceful and successful people in the community, who would probably quite openly side with no civilization at all rather than a, to them, so thoroughly uninteresting and objectionable one. Some have, in fact, already scented the danger. It used to be only the genuine artists and æsthetes who railed, quite ineffectively, at the growing mechanization of the age. But when the tide turns, and science by making the poor richer makes the rich relatively poorer, the movement to break up the machines and revert to hand and serf labour is likely to receive some very unexpected and effective recruits."

In fact, he would add to our three main groups of personas, the peasants, the nomads and the educated types, a fourth, the modern money manipulator, a new type whose primary delight is domination and oppression through relative gain.

How does that square with the psychological analysis of social and economic relationship we have been making in this work?

I think we shall have to recognize that there is nothing in the story of the development of the current economic financial system as we have unfolded it, to rule the plain accusation of Professor Soddy out of court. The old system, before the industrial and mechanical revolutions, was quite frankly repressive. It had the excellent excuse that human society could not exist unless people were kept down. The priest kept himself down, helped to keep the peasant down, and all the surplus of good things in life, the pride and the glory, fell to the gentleman, the aristocrat, and the prince, the successors of the nomad conqueror. These upper-class people had the colour and high places of life, and to them fell such women as they desired. It is impossible to ignore the rôle of women throughout the past of mankind as prizes, incentives and rewards. They have always fallen into that rôle with extreme readiness, accepted the jewels and dresses and played the hostess queen to the triumphant robber. Through the long ages of insufficiency, women have always been the demure receivers of the captured joys and displays of life. And the society these ladies adorned, the young they educated, understood quite clearly that the toiler had to be kept under—there was no need for anyone to stipulate that the poor should be kept poor, for that followed as a matter of course. The priest went about the human battlefield mediating between the parties, persuading the rich to be charitable and the poor to be grateful and resigned, and doing his best (the more intelligent of him and when Statutes of Mortmain and the like did not prevent him) to get what he could of productive property out of private hands.

The development of modern industrialism, subtly associated with mechanical invention and following on the mental releases of the Reformation period, changed a world of insufficiency to a world of potential universal plenty, but it found no ideology ready for such a state of affairs. So it went on with the old. The personas of the people engaged in it arose out of the long established main types. The "educated" personas were creating opportunity but did not themselves exploit opportunity. The scene for the new act in the human drama opened therefore with getting and grabbing. It need not have opened in that fashion, but it did. The industrial entrepreneur was essentially the child of the grasping, hoarding, economizing, close-working peasant type; the financial adventurer was essentially predatory. The two intermingled with each other to become the New Rich as we have studied them in §1, and to associate themselves with, and largely buy up, the Old Rich, so far as prestige and claims to essential dignity were concerned. They were New Rich in Old Rich traditions. The elements of triumph, display, the buying of splendour for women, the buying of feminine adoration, contempt for the generality and a certain jealousy of any competition, rivalry and comparison on the part of the generality—they took over all these things as a matter of course and found them very congenial. What fills our fashion papers to-day, amidst the pages and pages of luxury advertisements, but the photographs of successful people displaying their triumph for the admiration and envy of mankind and, more particularly, for the incitement of womankind?

That the modern rich generally do not feel any strong desire for the poor to be less poor—so long as their poverty does not make them dangerous—is manifestly true. So far we go with Professor Soddy. They are evidently prepared to endure the sufferings of others with smiling courage, and even to repay envy with a certain exhibitionism that rouses its interest even more vividly than its resentment. But is it true that there is any strength of will behind these naïve products of our present clumsy financial mechanism? That is where we part from Professor Soddy. Let us admit that the modern rich cannot be expected to help in the monetary and financial reconstruction of human affairs. Let us recognize that they will even encumber and hinder. They will appear, they do appear, lumpishly auxiliary in all sorts of reactionary and obstructive movements. They will be supporting romantic monarchy here and patriotism and religious intolerance there, if only for the sake of the titles and reassurance they can get, the coronations they can attend, the patronage they may exercise. All that much is true. They cannot be expected to be very much more than a stupidly consuming and resistant mass. But what is an altogether different matter: are they likely *in any effective and organized form* to put up a fight against the steady development of one genuinely conceived economic state in the world?

Now there it is we have to join issue with Professor Soddy—and others. His clear and vigorous mind is irritated at the dragging distresses, the baseness and injustices of our world when he has the sure knowledge that it might be energetic and happy; he assumes social good-will as a duty, and then very naturally he hits out and hits round in an ecstasy of indignation. But there are things about life that so far he ignores; his biology, his psychology and his philosophy of living are, if we may say so, not as serene as his physical science. To him the world is an exasperating spectacle of reasonable creatures behaving unreasonably and wickedly. But the fact is they are not yet very reasonable creatures. And they do not admit that social goodwill is a duty. They do not pretend it is. They have not the idea of service in their personas. Let him look at the spectacle again and look at it whole, as we are trying to do in this work; let him look at it as a species of about nineteen hundred million individuals, descended from rather ferocious, ego-centred, ape-like ancestors, not very greatly modified yet, and modifying very slowly, and only very slowly muddling their way to knowledge, reason and efficient coöperation. He can never see the absurdities of the situation better than he does now, but he will find then that he has a better grasp upon the obstacles he is up against and the nature of the remedial processes in which we have to put our trust.

He will become less impatient and more constructive. He will give us more explicit plans and fewer scornful witticisms at the expense of—everybody. He denounces a burthen and embarrassment of rich people who live, not only idly and luxuriously, but obstructively, on the exaggerated debts they have imposed upon the community. He denounces our banking system. So far as these are indications for reconstruction they are of immense value. But he finds much more deliberate plotting by the rich against the poor than our survey has revealed. He finds plots where we find instincts and traditions. He thinks entrepreneurs and bankers are anti-social men, and we have found reason to suppose that they are becoming, and likely to become, less and less anti-social. He does not concede that many of them are routinists who can be turned into different routines, and that a certain leaven among them is as anxious to achieve what he wants as he himself. He does not envisage the possibility that the present enormous and preposterous debt charge of mankind, like the almost universal preëmption of natural resources by private owners, may constitute as inevitable a phase in human development as slavery or the primitive taboos, and that it may already be at its maximum and be quite easily amenable to a tremendous reduction and writing off. He thinks, for example, that the present struggle to arrest the hopeful expansion of human affairs for the sake of the gold standard is due to a conspiracy of powerful, aggressive, able men. We think that it is due to a blind convergence of fear, habit and traditional stupidity. He cannot wait for the steadfast unfolding of our release from tradition. He turns, in his passion, to governments to take this, that and the other profit-making privileges out of the bankers' hands— now. But even as he turns to governments he remembers what they are. He turns to "democracy," and the thought of the daily newspaper rises hideously between him and that ideal rescuer. Crowd action is no remedy. And then he shows his bad temper. It is, we find, a most sympathetic bad temper he displays. But it is no use for constructive purposes; it has to be controlled.

That is why it is so interesting to quote him here. In response to his indignant outcries we are enabled to underline the more deliberate impression our survey evokes. We do not believe that any large proportion of bankers are plotting to keep the world poor. There is a number of honestly perplexed men among them, men who are dismayed and distressed by the turn things are taking. They are often business men unaccustomed as yet to the scientific method of thought, but they are picking it up steadily.

And, further, as to the rich generally. There are only a minority of rich people, we suggest, who clearly and definitely want the poor to be kept poor, and they are not among the "forceful and successful" types. Progress is encumbered by the relative barbarism of women, but even among women education is spreading. The people who really change things are not the luxurious receivers in "society," not the men who want outstanding power and triumph—they are men like Edison and Ford. Professor Soddy, in the passage we have picked out to make the text for this section, seems to forget men of the Edison-Ford type, just as he forgets the existence of men like himself. Where did *he* get his social passion? Whence comes his indignation? Why is he not on the other side?

He is actually writing book after book to change men's ideas

—that is to say, their minds and their personas about these things—and yet, all the while, he does not seem to take into his reckoning the great and growing body of other excited and disinterested men engaged in unorthodox extra-mural educational activity; nor does he show any sustaining disposition to co-operate with other workers in the same field.

The way to the new world economy, when everyone will be prosperous, is likely to be hard, difficult and dangerous. But the best brains will be on our side. They will not be against us. We may have to wade through morasses of foolishness and fight stampedes of boorish plutocrats, but that plotting of a "majority of the most forceful and successful people in the community" against progress, is a nightmare of Professor Soddy's bad hours. It is a nightmare to be exorcised, because such things rankle in the brain and make us violent and bitter, just when, if we are to be of any real service to mankind, we should be most careful in our adjustments and accusations.

If Professor Soddy is right and the interpretation of current fact in this book is wrong; if it is true that the majority of able spirits among the contemporary rich are, for the sake of power and preëminence, deliberately impoverishing a community, which need not be impoverished, then the conception pervading this book of the progressive construction of a universally prosperous economic world community out of the current social order, is unsound. There is nothing to be hoped for along that line. There is nothing for it but, as the Marxists teach, a class war against the rich and the able, social insurrection, the breaking-up of the whole contemporary organization of mankind in wrath and disgust, and beginning again upon a different ground plan, with whatever hope is left to us, amidst the ruins.

§ 6. The Poor

Abandoning for once any resort to our encyclopædic *Science of Work and Wealth* or our imaginary museum collections, we have, by merely flapping at the reader the familiar smart illustrated periodicals, *Vogue,* the *Graphic,* the *Sketch, Punch, La*

Vie Parisienne and their kin, added the Turf and sport generally, the gambler in the Casino, the brilliant crowd at a levee, the smart prostitute, the hotel chef, the fashions and the palace, to our enumeration of human life methods; and we have linked all this brilliant swarm and their motives and what they are doing and why they are doing it with the worker in the factory, the miner in the seam, the peasant among his vines, the shepherd on the mountain side and the spray-wet fisherman hauling in his nets from the heaving sea. We have shown the strands of this relationship running through mint, bank, office and stock exchange. This futile, expensive existence of the rich is a surplus product of the economic machine.

By the time these rich people have been brought in, our spectacle of activities will have extended to more than a thousand million living souls, each conducting itself according to a persona of its own, each with its own idea system and its separate vision of the world about it, and yet all reacting mutually in one economic ensemble. But still something very grave and essential remains to be explained and considered. There is a deep shadow into which we have now to go, a gathering multitude which can neither work contentedly nor play happily, the unemployed without purchasing power, those who mingle want with a joyless leisure, the apparently superfluous poor.

How do they stand in regard to the rich? We have already pointed out that the one mass is not directly and quantitatively dependent on the other, that it is unsound to assume that if there were no rich there would be no poor. It is too hastily believed that the poor are poor *because* the rich have taken something away from them. That is not the truth of the case. The relationship is much more subtle and complicated.

The very variegated class of rich leisure is held together by the common characteristic of a purchasing power enormously exaggerated by traditional conventions about property, or by the loose working of the financial parts of the economic machine. Now in contrast we have to consider a great, and it would seem a growing, mass of nonproductive or insufficiently productive people whose purchasing power is either slight or nonexistent.

Certainly the machine gives here and deprives there. But that is not by any means the same thing as taking from one and giving to the other. It is not a process that can be remedied by selling up the rich man and giving all that he had to the poor. The faults of the machine are by no means so simple as that.

Always in the world there have been the poor. Poverty is not a thing confined to the species *Homo sapiens;* it is a phenomenon throughout all the orders, classes and kingdoms of life. It may strike some readers as an odd phrase, but it is true that most animals and plants live in extreme poverty. They have no reserves, that is to say, they live from hand to mouth. *Homo sapiens* is alone among living creatures in the possibility that he may abolish *want,* for himself and perhaps for many plants and beasts. All other species exist in almost continuous contact with a margin of starvation. If by some splendour of fortunate chance a species is lifted into abundance for a time, straightway it increases and multiplies until the margin of hunger is once more attained. The only qualification of that law is when some other hungry creature, great or small, hunter or parasite, preys upon a species abundantly enough to bring the increase of that creature below the resources of its food supply. A living species must be devoured, or it will multiply until there is an internecine struggle for food, with famine destroying the defeated. A species must live in constant danger, or in constant need. Hunger or the hunter is the common alternative of life. We win the hearts of nearly all inferior creatures and persuade them to subdue their instincts and belie their natures, by feeding them.

"The poor ye have always with you." That has been accepted too readily as a divine assurance that the prevention of poverty is impossible. But there can be no denial that hitherto want has always dogged the footsteps of life. The life of the ordinary savage and the ordinary barbarian is an extreme poverty. Savages will abandon the infirm and put an end to "useless mouths" with a brutality that outdoes Napoleon. And this they do in the midst of potential wealth the nearness of which they do not suspect, and which they have no means of exploiting.

A short history of destitution through the ages would make

a grim and painful book. It is hard to get an idea of the proportion of the population at various periods of the world's history which died of starvation, or through the weakening of resistance to other diseases by undernourishment or exposure. I am inclined to think it was a very considerable proportion indeed. Few districts of the world in past times got through threescore and ten years without actual famine, and up to the middle of the nineteenth century people still wandered about the cities of western Europe in actual immediate need of bread. There is real starvation happening now in China, India and Russia. The state of affairs in such countries as England, France and the United States—the rarity of extreme hunger—is abnormal and altogether modern.

The growth of the sense that the existence of poverty is discreditable to the rich and the ruler, and that they ought to do something about it, is comparatively recent. I believe that up to the beginning of the nineteenth century the general feeling was that the poor were very much to blame. One threw them crusts and gave them old clothes and permitted them to sleep in outhouses, insisting relentlessly on "gratitude." One did that as a virtuous exercise with very little sense of any converse obligation. The Elizabethan poor law was a law in restraint of wanderers; a device for maintaining social order; it was not primarily to abate distress. The charities at the convent gates of pre-Reformation times accepted the perennial fact of restitution unquestioningly.

But through the ages there has also been an undertow of protest. In Egypt, long before the Hebrew prophets, there was a literature denouncing the exactions of the rich and complaining of debts and labour conditions. That seems, however, to have been a protest against types and individuals rather than against the system. The bad rich man ground the faces of the poor, but the riches of the good rich man (how rare he was!) and the existence of the poor were hardly challenged.

It was only, I believe, with the radiation of humanitarian ideas and feelings in the middle and late nineteenth century that the protection, not only of human beings, but of the larger beasts, from starvation and even from conspicuous undernourishment, came to be considered a public duty. A skinny foreigner, a quaint beggar in rags, a miserable horse, were fair fun for the caricaturists until less than a hundred years ago. Since then there has been a steady development of the organized mitigation of want. There has been a sustained and increasing effort in all civilized countries to make deaths from exposure and under-nourishment impossible, to rescue and reinstate people who have fallen into destitution, and to assist those who are slipping down towards that state. Unemployment, which was formerly re-garded as a marginal condition necessary for the proper work-ing of the wages system, is now considered an evil not merely to be alleviated, but to be fought and overcome.

The *Science of Work and Wealth* when it comes to be assem-bled in its encyclopædic form, will have to review contemporary methods of dealing with this stratum of uncertain, diminishing or nonexistent spending power. It will have to give a general vision of the life of the underproductive. It must amplify its description by photographs to show how the poor live, not only in the dismal back streets of America and Europe, but in the poor quarters of Chinese and Indian cities, and it must give pic-tures of famine relief work and sanitary missions invading kraals and tents and hut villages. It will have to go far beyond mere industrial unemployment; it must give a panorama of poverty throughout the world. Then it will show us more par-ticularly the Labour Exchange, the Workhouse, and the Casual Ward of the more highly organized cummunities. It will explain the regulations of Old Age Pensions and Unemployment Pay. It will note the varieties of poor-law method following the vari-able temperaments and economic ideology of typical states.

The broad fact underlying the whole spectacle of the allevia-tion of distress that we glance at in this fashion is that the modern community has been gradually recognizing and accept-ing the responsibility for the maintenance of every one of its citizens at a certain low minimum standard of shelter, food and clothing, irrespective of the productive activities of the particu-lar individuals concerned. It does not compel them to work in return. It does not even afford the opportunity to work in return. That is the worst aspect of this sort of relief. What the community offers is dull, dreary, and undignified, no doubt—"pauperization," to give it its proper name—but, nevertheless, life and continuation. This is an absolutely unprecedented state of affairs. It is a biological revolution. In all the rest of the kingdoms of life defeat, whether through defect or ill luck, has meant death. So hitherto life has been driven up the scale of efficiency. *Now,* what does defeat mean in the modern community? Stagnation. A dingy and unhappy stagnation.

The immense increase in the total of human productivity under modern conditions renders this possible. There can be little doubt that a few hundred million economically active people could now feed, clothe and house all the rest of the race—as nonproductive paupers, that is—at a base, dullish but endurable level of existence, and still have a surplus for a fairly pleasant type of successful life. And it is plain that the stratum of intermittently productive, insufficiently productive and nonproductive people is under the present conditions of concentrated production and of maintenance for the unemployed, increasing in proportion to the whole community. More and more people are coming out of employment, are being superseded; the modern organization has no jobs for them and no use for them. As industrialization spreads over the world, the supersession of the small producer and the diminution of hands needed for any given product go on. Nothing like the possible ratio of inactive dependents has yet been reached. This relative stagnant mass can go on growing. There has been much exaggerated writing about the Rapid Multiplication of the Unfit, for it does not follow necessarily that the people who are coming out of employment are inferior in quality to many who remain at work, or that their superfluousness is a consequence of relative breeding rather than a supersession; but the fact nevertheless confronts us that this perplexed and perplexing lower stratum to the economic edifice may continue to expand, and probably will continue to expand for some time, relatively to the whole human population.

The economic world machine is rapidly coming to resemble an unhealthy overgrown body which is accumulating two sorts of unwanted secretion. On the one hand, it has been accumulating the new, generally functionless rich, the Consuming Unemployed, a sort of plethora, and on the other it is developing a morbid mass, a huge tumour now growing very rapidly, of Penniless Unemployed. These two developments are so independent that it might be quite possible to eliminate one and still leave the other increasing formidably. We have already pointed to possible processes that may lead to the resorption of the irresponsible rich. The graver riddle is certainly this New Poor, this menace of the unemployable expropriated.

What is humanity doing about it, and what is it doing for humanity?

§ 7. *The Paradox of Overproduction and Want. Community Buying*

Let us turn this business about and look at it from another direction. It is not a simple matter, and its problems do not admit of simple solutions. Several processes are at work concurrently, and any single simple solution will be true only of its own process. The poor are not a class, but a miscellany with scarcely anything in common but deficient purchasing power.

First there is the product of the immemorial comprehensive process of the struggle for existence: the real failures. These are people definitely and manifestly below the average. They have inherently feeble bodies or minds. Biologically it is bad that they should survive and reproduce. Our world is wealthy enough for them to live out their lives as pleasantly as they are capable of living them, but the persuasion spreads steadily that by birth control in some form, by humane sterilization—now a proven possibility—such strains should be brought to an end. The problem is not quite so simple as those unfamiliar with genetic science may suppose, but for all its complexities, there is no reason to doubt its ultimate solution. It seems that a progressive extension of genetic knowledge, medical science and organization and hygienic control, will suffice to meet this biological aspect of the problem of the poor.

And then, always since society began there has been the correlative of the man who grabbed the lion's share; there has always been the opposition of the "have's and have-not's." There are the poor of the old social inequality. They too are commonly of the weaker sort. They have been living their distinctive lives in contact with their "betters" for many generations. They are hereditary inferiors. Tradition mixes with heredity perhaps in many of those who fall into this class. They were poor because there was not enough to go round. They came late or they had been pushed aside. They were the outsiders of the crowd round the rice bowl.

But there is a third sort of poor to-day. There are the poor by sheer chance, the poor with as good heredity as any other class of people. It is difficult to maintain that the majority of the people one meets, inadequately employed or out of a job, or that the populations of impoverished regions beyond the more highly civilized areas, are all individually inferior to the people who are busy and prosperous in the more active parts of the economic system. There are defectives in the crowd and poor creatures in the crowd, but they are only ingredients in the crowd and not the whole of it. The others have been born at a disadvantage, in a declining district or a shrinking industry; they have been involved in the misgovernment of some reactionary State; their parents or grandparents were sufficiently prosperous at home not to emigrate to some new land of hope, which presently gave their defeated and departed neighbours all the opportunity that was receding from their own native country. The incidence of education is still the most uncertain element in life; here a fine family may live in a reactionary district that will not suffer an efficient school or a modern factory; there the best of teaching, training and employment may be forced on every mediocrity. That this man in a modern community is illiterate, limited in his outlook, inapt for any new job, badly nourished, angry, resentful and unwilling, and that man, well informed, hopeful, readily useful, may have nothing whatever to do with their inherent quality. The forces that have determined their fates are too wholesale and remote to have tested it. Very exceptional individuals are known to have triumphed over the most desperately discouraging circumstances, but generally they have done so at a price, and their careers are no disproof of our general proposition that the main, mediocre mass of mankind is in no way being sifted and selected by the relative increase in unemployment throughout the world. This second sort of poor —the poor of economic fluctuations—is being deprived of purchasing power not as individuals but as units in a group. There is no selection at all among them.

And very plainly one cause—though not the only cause—is that production is being run primarily for the profit of entrepreneurs and their financiers, and not for the good of the mediocre mass. The profit side has the first call on economies. Every economy in production which diminishes the amount of work needed generally diminishes in the same proportion the amount of wages paid relative to the total output. But if profit was not a primary end and things could be so adjusted, by a reduction of hours of work per day, or weeks of work per year, or years of work per lifetime, there need be no such ejection of workers as occurs from the employment in question. The industry would continue to create as much dispersed purchasing power in the community as it did before, instead of skimming more of it off in a concentrated form for the financier and entrepreneur.

Since concentrated wealth is apt to run into special channels of luxury and waste, there is a wide and well founded feeling in the world that it is less desirable socially than a more diffused spending power. In the end economy of production that leads to restricted employment must be bad for industry itself, because in the case of anything but a commodity de luxe it means producing more for a community less able to buy. We are faced indeed with the spectacle of industry, through sheer progressive efficiency, producing more and more, and killing the demand for its product as it does so. That seems indeed to be the essential fact of current economic troubles. There is too much wheat,

steel, coal, copper, rubber, oil in the world, too many motor-
cars, too many gramophones, sewing-machines, and radios, and
there is a gathering multitude of people, not defectives, not
intrinsically inferior people, but people at a quite chance disadvantage, who cannot buy this accumulation of unsold commodities.

Prices fall, production declines; that does not solve the problem, because it only increases the multitude which cannot buy.
Economists tell us that if by a miracle everyone alive could wake
up the recipient of sound bonus shares worth £100 a year, the
whole world would be transformed for a time at least into a
busy hive of well paid production. Our present anæmia, our las-
situde, would vanish. The problem of restoring purchasing
power to this new poor, these modern poor evoked by the
economic fluctuation, is exercising a great number of extremely
ingenious minds. Their findings lack unanimity and assurance, but
their general idea is the same.

One school assures us that production for profit is at the root
of the evil. Among other things it is. That is the central idea
of the Socialist. But the abolition of production for profit is not
to be done in the twinkling of an eye. The whole modern
economic process has grown up on production for profit, and
the redoubtable attempts of Soviet Russia to produce an industrialism upon different lines in one swift revolutionary change
merely expose the complex difficulties of the task. The peasant
persona with its diverse modifications, which is still the prevalent
persona in our species, is all against it. The less abundant but
more energetic and influential adventurer type is equally against
it. We have shown how the gradual subjugation of business
finance to scientific control, may mitigate many of the wilder
fluctuations of business enterprise, but that is a comparatively
slow and intricate subjugation which gives us more hope for the
next fifty years than for to-morrow. Meanwhile the squeezing
out of fresh unemployed goes on.

Restriction of hours of employment, the relief of the labour
market at either end by giving old-age pensions and raising the
school-leaving age, the deliberate raising of wages *à la* Ford

above competitive rates, are admirable palliatives—and something more than palliatives. The workers still in employment may develop new wants as their standard of living rises, and this may attract a certain proportion of the out-of-works into new industries and make buyers of them again, and so again increase demand. But such measures alone will not arrest the secular restriction of organized and rationalized industries to a dwindling staff of increasingly efficient and no doubt increasingly better paid workers. And, moreover, against the vigorous application of such measures to shorten hours and take the young and the old off the labour market, fights the traditional spirit of international competition. "This will put us at a disadvantage against the foreign producer" is a deadly objection. The British workers have a limit set to their progress by Indian, Egyptian and Chinese workers. There is no world authority yet to handle labour conditions as one single world-wide problem.

Another school of thought lays greater stress upon what is practically a distribution of buying power to the unemployed in the disguise of public works. The prosperous classes are to be taxed either directly or by the indirect method of currency inflation, to provide the means for a comprehensive rehousing of the community, a replanning of town and countryside, new roads, bridges, harbours, parks, schools, hospitals. There will be no attempt to secure a bookkeeping profit on the transaction. The profit will be social. Since admittedly the modern community has to support its poor at some level of comfort, it may just as well, it is argued, give as large a proportion of them as possible, work and active buying power, by such great public undertakings. Instead of just carrying on, it will stimulate. The gross wealth of the community will be increased. Concurrently with the restoration of purchasing power to the people thus actively employed by the State, there will be a restoration of general industrial activity. As employment increases the State will slacken its operations; as it falls, it will put new energy into its public works and adornments. This is the "Plan" of Foster and Catchings in their *Road to Plenty* published by the American Pollak Foundation. All these proposals will shock the minds of such

Victorian individualists as still survive, those fundamentalists of economics, profoundly, but they will be accepted as a matter of course by the new types of scientifically educated business, banking and public officials, who seem to be ousting slowly but steadily the crudely acquisitive business men of the old régime from the control of our economic destinies.*

How far our world has gone already in the free distribution of food and services to producers out of action, how far it has gone in the distribution of purchasing power in doles and pensions, and how far it is committed to public enterprises to take up the slack of unemployment we cannot yet tell in detail. The facts have still to be gathered together and put in order. The total already attained is likely to be a surprise to many. And we have to remember that if there is anything whatever to be said in defense of armaments, it is that they distribute a very large amount of purchasing power to skilled workers and trained and fit men who might otherwise stand out of employment. A sudden world-wide disarmament, unless it was accompanied by colossal housing and transport schemes and the vigorous reëquipment of civil life, might enormously increase the world's economic difficulties. The thought of this possibility is one of the obscurer obstacles in the way to the abolition of war. It is one of the many reasons why merely negative pacifism is futile. Men will not be able to give up war preparation *until there is something else to do in the place of it.*

A colossal increase of public or quasi-public constructive works throughout the world seems therefore a necessary condition for both the establishment of world peace and the control and reduction of unemployment and poverty. It is not that man *may* plan and make a new world for himself; he *has* to do so or be overwhelmed by his own undisciplined devices and impulses. Work and wealth or disaster are the alternatives of his destiny. The present system has to pass on to this phase of organized collective enterprise or break down. This is no dogma; it is

---

*The reader interested here can expand this section further by looking up the publications of the Pollak Foundation (Newton 58, Mass., U. S. A.). Another book he may find stimulating and suggestive is F. Henderson's *The Economic Consequences of Power Production.*

the plain and inevitable conclusion to the considerations we have put before the reader.

A prominent American business man recently put the ideas we are suggesting here into a phrase that is capable of considerable enrichment in its interpretation. He was discussing the paradox of overproduction. He said that while this current system, the profit-motive system, our so-called capitalist system, had been able to evolve the most efficient mass production, it had still to solve the secret of "mass consumption." In itself the phrase has scarcely more in it than "rationalization" when it was used by the late Lord Melchett as a counter catchword to nationalization, but if we confer upon it the cognate idea of the "community-buying" of peace-time material as well as of war material, we find it at once germinating in a very suggestive and profitable manner. We shall see later how the community-buying of armaments was forced up during the last half century by armament salesmanship, and there is no apparent reason why a similar procedure on a larger scale on the part of architectural and transport salesmen, should not presently come to the relief of the present paradoxical deadlock in economic life. The cathedral building of the Middle Ages was, as we have noted, a form of community-buying. Not only the remaking of roads (already going on in Great Britain, for example) and the comprehensive replanning of the entire transport system, but the deliberate rebuilding of entire towns with modernized sanitation and public services, the continual modernization of our rationalized industrial plant and the entire reconstruction of the layout of the countryside for production, health and pleasure, may be made collective communal enterprises. If we can build magnificent jails and asylums out of our common resources, why should we not build great housing quarters for common people to prevent their becoming recalcitrant and criminal? If punitive comfort, why not preventive comfort?

There need be no violent revolutionary transition to such a new economic phase. The idea of collective buying has indeed been tried already to assist distressed producers. It is not a new idea. Brazilian coffee, for example, and Canadian wheat have been dealt with in this fashion. The risk of loss, the actual loss in an overstocked market, is thrown upon the public credit. These are instances, and not very successful ones, of collective buying for resale, but there can be also collective buying for communal use. Then there need be no risk of loss. Existing methods of buying and distribution are in fact extremely plastic, and amenable to unlimited progressive adjustment. But such adjustment demands for its achievement a very considerable change in the spirit of financial and industrial enterprise, and a general rise in the intelligence and understanding of the community. It involves almost necessarily certain measures of currency inflation. Inflation is dangerous to all but very well informed and well disciplined communities. We are brought back to what has been said already about grades of organization (in Chapter VII, § 9), and to the fundamental importance of educational level, in all these matters.

Let not the reader unfamiliar with modern economic discussion, imagine that there is anything novel or indeed anything unorthodox in this suggestion of collective employment in rebuilding cities and the like great undertakings. I turn over *Some Economic Factors in Modern Life,* by Sir Josiah Stamp, and I find him quoting Professor Lethaby with approval as saying: "Except for a hundred or two buildings, London needs to be rebuilt from end to end. No writer on Economics has yet told us what are the limits to expenditure on public arts, whether a beautiful city is an investment or an extravagance." I turn from Sir Josiah's luminous page to my newspaper, and I read of two million unemployed in Great Britain, most of whom are being paid a dole for very miserably doing nothing. Then comes a communication from Professor Miles Walker, F. R. S. He is a professor of electrical engineering and an inventor of distinction, and he and a few friends have drawn up a scheme—a perfectly reasonable scheme, if we disregard the psychology of a profit-seeking community—for setting the unemployed to work to supply the needs of the unemployed. Nobody is going to dismiss the controller of the London, Midland & Scottish Railway, or a Nobel laureate in physics, or Professor Miles Walker, as dreamy Utopians or impracticable propagandists, and yet this is how they are thinking. These are men of the facty sort; men who can count. That unemployment and every form of poverty are avoidable is for these authorities not a mere opinion: it is a straightforward statement of fact. It would seem impossible to them for any review of human activities to omit that statement.

§ 8. *The Attempt of Soviet Russia to Abolish Rich and Poor Together**

At present the readjustment of distribution to modern methods of production is being attempted on a quite heroic scale in Soviet Russia. We have already discussed certain aspects of this great forward effort in human affairs. For indisputably it is an effort to go forward. An ultra-modern ideology involving a grade of organization higher and more elaborate than any that has yet existed in the world is being imposed, with how much success it is still impossible to say, on a great region of the earth where the normal culture remains in essence mediæval and where many vitally essential industrial organizations are still undeveloped—and this in the face of the hostility of foreign governments and world-wide distrust. At every stage in the process, the difficulty of insufficient understanding by the public and inadequate directive power have had to be faced by the adventurous fanatics who seized upon Russia after the exhaustion and social disorganization caused by the Great War of 1914–18.

In Chapter IV, § 5 we have considered the Russian attempt to pass at one stride from peasant cultivation to agricultural

---

*G. T. Grinko's *The Five Year Plan of the Soviet Union* is authoritative and more or less official. Michael Farbman's *Piatiletka, Russia's Five Year Plan,* is like all his work, clear, scientifically impartial and illuminating, and another very sound book is H. R. Knickerbocker's *The Soviet Five Year Plan.* For a vivid picture of human life during the phases of this monstrous experiment in social reconstruction, the general reader cannot do better than read the books of Maurice Hindus, *Broken Earth, Humanity Uprooted* and *Red Bread.* There are many other very competent and interesting books, and a veritable flood of superficial and inferior productions upon the Russian effort. We make no attempt here to adjudicate upon them, but we can certify to the excellence of those we have named because we have made a liberal use of them.

production upon big estates, but so far we have had very little to say about the industrial development of Soviet Russia. But there many of the things that we have been suggesting as probable developments of contemporary business conditions in the Atlantic world have already been anticipated. It is hard to decide whether Soviet Russia is rather desperate, inspired and heroic or presumptuous and headstrong. Her forward thrust is unprecedented in history. With political institutions of the most provisional sort, without even the skeleton of an efficient civil service, without freedom of criticism and suggestion, using indeed to this day terroristic methods of the crudest and bloodiest sort, she has attempted to evoke an exhaustively planned economic organization of more than a hundred million people which shall buy and sell as one merchant. She has attempted to eliminate that individual buying which is still the general practice of contemporary civilization for all but war material, high-roads, educational appliances, and a few other common needs. Her Communist professions, as Knickerbocker points out, are absurd. Her system is an ultra-modern State Capitalism.* She has made the State the universal buyer and seller, she buys machinery and staple imports collectively, and whatever the outcome of her effort, it is impossible not to believe that the most valuable lessons, examples and warnings are to be found in her expedients. Towards the ends her government seeks so passionately, hastily, bitterly and clumsily, the economic order of the whole world is moving slowly but surely, if only on account of the economic paradox between increased output and diminished consuming power that evolves from capitalism. It is rather the luck than the merit of the Atlantic systems that they may go more circumspectly and comfortably towards the common goal of a planned and measured reorganization of economic life, in which the motive of profit will be replaced almost altogether by the motive of service, and goods be distributed as common needs rather than as industrial and financial prizes.

Chief among the difficulties of Soviet Russia is the fact that her economic development was conceived as a world system a

---

*See also Gide and Rist: *Histoire des Doctrines Economiques* (1922).

score of years in advance of any general recognition of the necessity for developing economic life on planetary lines. It was conceived rather than planned, and her painful history is largely a record of convulsive improvisations as this or that vast unanticipated obstruction has become apparent in her path. With an educational standard far too low for effective working, and in a state of extreme industrial underdevelopment, she has from the beginning found herself out of step with the rest of the industrialized world, and in unconcealed antagonism to all other governments. This has necessitated, among other intricate extra, arrangements, the building of a wall between her internal currency and that of the world outside. Internally she has inflated, and it is hard to see how any increase of State or individual production can be managed without inflation. The elements of modernity in her experiment are mingled with an impatient dogmatism. Hence her perpetual trouble about social and political propaganda abroad through her attempts to bring some classes at least in the populations of the world outside her into sympathy with her leading ideas. It is reasonable that she should persist in propaganda; her very existence is a propagandist demonstration; and it is logical that the separatist national and imperial governments her effort threatens by example and precept alike, should resist her implacably. She is premature. She is progress entangled with a pronunciamento. She crushes recalcitrant workers and shoots disingenuous or inefficient officials. The immense tragic sufferings and sacrifices of her people, the blunderings, harshness, obduracy and cruelties of her overworked administration, the internecine angers and tyrannies of her dictatorship, must not blind us to the greatness of many of her efforts and achievements. Dogmatic, resentful and struggling sorely, crazy with suspicion and persecution mania, ruled by a permanent Terror, Russia nevertheless upholds the tattered banner of world-collectivity and remains something splendid and hopeful in the spectacle of mankind.

A complication of the Russian situation is the present rapid increase of her population. She is now, if we may rely upon her official statistics, adding about three and three quarter millions

annually to the population of the world. Although her birth rate
has fallen from 46.8 per thousand (pre-war) to 40, her death
rate has come down from 30.5 to 17.4. So that her effective rate
of increase has risen from 16.3 to 22.6. The significance of
these figures will be perhaps better appreciated after the reader
has gone through Chapter XIII, but it is foolish to ignore the
advance in the quality of domestic life they imply.

In our review of human activities these scores of millions of
perplexed peasants in Russia, and the ill fed and badly housed
workers in her impoverished towns—150,000,000 altogether of
peasants and workers—are an extraordinarily important item.
However ill fed and badly housed they now are, the vital
statistics we have just given show that they are cleaner and better cared for than in Tzarist times. Our survey must not ignore
these millions of babies.

And it must display also the peasant with his highly individualized fences broken down to make the great fields of the
Kolkhozy, and his family, its most intimate ties broken, entering
a community house. Moreover, we must picture the workers in
the newly erected factory, all bought complete in America to be
set up in Russia, listening to the exhortations of some revivalist
from the Communist party sent to keep up their spirits. They
are poor. They are inept at this new job. They blunder humil-
iatingly and are reproached ferociously and punished without
pity. They go short of clothing and they feed badly. Poverty
still broods over all things Russian. Nevertheless, they are busy;
they are not expropriated and defeated and aimless like the
gathering accumulating unemployed of the Atlantic civilizations.
They are sustained by a flickering enthusiasm that can be blown
up at times into passionate hope.

Our more intricate Western world may solve piecemeal and
day by day the complex riddle of industrial stagnation in the
midst of wealth that confronts it now. It may have its local
political and social troubles and convulsions, and yet never pass
formally through the social revolution foretold by the prophet
Marx. But self-sufficiency in response to Russian self-sufficiency
will hamper our Western world enormously in its systematic re-

construction. Russia is in sore need of coöperation with, and understanding from, the Western world, but the Western world has also much to learn from Russia, and much to unlearn also of its prejudices through the sacrifices of Russia. We can learn much of how enthusiasm can be raised and of what it can do. We can also get some idea of what enthusiasm cannot do, without an educated, self-disciplined service of creditors, officials and industrial officers.

We have described in Chapter IV, § 5, the violent reconstruction of Russian agriculture. We have noted the difficulty of mechanizing farming, with a population untrained in large-scale production and the handling of machinery. This difficulty reappears in a magnified form in the attempts of that super-individual, the Soviet State, to create, out of the earth, so to speak, with a minimum of imported machinery, great modern industrial plants. The Moscow correspondent of the *Manchester Guardian* (May 23, 1931) draws an impressive picture of the state of affairs at the huge new attempt to out-Ford Ford in the production of tractors at Stalingrad. He tells of the clumsy handling of the machine tools, of six thousand breakages to three thousand machines in ten months. The output has not yet reached a twelfth of its maximum possibility. He quotes Ordzonikidze, the head of the Supreme Economic Council, who visited Stalingrad to find out why the Five Year Plan was not producing its promised results there, and why only 3,000 not very good tractors were forthcoming instead of an estimated 37,000. There is a reassuring frankness about many of these Russian reports, and this is what Ordzonikidze discovered, among other troubles:

". . . complete absence of accounting; factory buildings filled with waste products and the courtyard piled with filth and damaged products; complete absence of control over the coming to work of the workers; foremen and engineers not at their posts; uncontrolled starting and stopping of conveyors, absence of suitable care for equipment, an absence of persons responsible for the correct course of production in individual departments." . . .

These are the words of one of Stalin's most intimate and trusted helpers. When presently our survey brings in the organization of government and administration in the modern State, we shall be the better able to understand how inevitable were these wastes and confusions in the Russian improvisation.

But the frank admission of difficulty and disappointment is not the only virtue of the Bolshevik. There is also great boldness and courage in changing methods directly they disappoint. On June 23, 1931, Stalin addressed a conference of economists in Moscow and announced a new phase in this great experiment. He said that progress had been hampered by the cessation of the voluntary flow of peasant labour into industry, particularly into the timber, coal, building, transport, and iron industries. The countryside, therefore, must be constrained to deliver to industry sufficient supplies of labour based on a system of contracts between the economic organizations and the collective farms. He rebuked those economists who "sigh for the good old times when labour came voluntarily," and admonished them to recognize the new conditions requiring new methods. But economists, he continued, must realize that the conscription of labourers was not the whole task. Labourers must be bound to enterprises to which they were indentured and "labour flux" combated by a system of differential wages to increase productivity. Hitherto there had been hardly any difference between the earnings of skilled and unskilled workers and therefore the unskilled had no incentive to improve their qualifications. That evil could no longer be tolerated. The Soviet State required from the workers hard work, discipline, and mutual emulation. A system of payment according to the worker's need could not be allowed, and workers must be paid strictly according to the amount and the quality of the work they performed. One of the most important tasks would be the creation of a new "productive, technical *intelligentsia.*"

The economists, Stalin declared, must not be afraid to face the truth, and should openly admit that the system of an uninterrupted three-shift day had not everywhere been justified. Many enterprises had introduced the uninterrupted day on paper without enough preparation. Those enterprises must boldly throw away their paper reforms and return temporarily to the one-shift day, as the tractor works at Stalingrad had already done, and cease the practice of "charming away difficulties" by high-sounding phrases and heroic resolutions which accomplished nothing. Further, the one-man system of management must be established everywhere. Unwieldy combines must split up into smaller units. Instead of a board of directors one single director must be charged in each small combine with full personal responsibility for the conduct of affairs. . . .

So much for the internal difficulties of the Russian experiment. Let us now consider how the difference in phase with the rest of the world affects its external relations.

In every country where trading with the Soviet Republic is permitted, this gigantic super-individual is represented by a buying organization, such, for example, as the American "Amtorg." This negotiates credit, gives orders, sells produce, it is the commercial representative of Russia Unlimited.

Russia Unlimited has one single purse against the foreigner. Its internal monetary system is protected by elaborate barriers against confluence with that of the external world. But it has a continual need of foreign money to buy vitally necessary imports. Its efforts to get something to sell for that money are amazing. William C. White (one of the first scholars to be sent by an American university, the University of Pennsylvania, to study Russia at first hand) describes the intensive effort to produce salable exports to meet Russia's needs of machinery. There are "drives" to collect waste—old rubber, for instance, and scrap iron. "A municipal order in Moscow," he says, stated "that deposits would not be paid on empty vodka bottles unless the original cork was returned with them"—a foreign market had been found for second-hand corks. "Prizes are offered, which included at one time that most desired of all premiums, a trip abroad, for those who were able to suggest new products for export." There are expeditions exploring the White Sea for iodine-producing seaweed; the Caucasus is experimenting in tea-growing to cut down the Chinese import; Turkestan cotton ousts

American. In order to keep up his payments abroad, the super-individual tightens his belt, exports goods—wheat and even manufactured cotton goods that are badly needed by his people at home. The Russians suffer amidst hope and exhortation, and the limit of their endurance is unknown.

Every "capitalist" country is divided within itself about dealing with this super-individual. There are the trades which sell to Russia and the trades which Russian produce undersells. The former are naturally pro-Soviet, and the latter are all for the prohibition of trading. The super-individual is making a remarkable fight for it. He betrays many signs of intense strain, but he keeps on. If his factory organization lags, his agricultural production is exceeding expectation. If he wins through, as he hopes to do, Russia will become an exporting country, underselling the produce of profit-seeking agriculture and industrialism, with a rising standard of internal comfort and no unemployed. That is the goal of the Russian effort, and even if it is not completely achieved, its partial realization is bound to compel very great readjustments in the economic organization of the rest of the world. These readjustments are bound to be also in the direction of comprehensive planning, and that again must involve either a voluntary or an imposed directive control. The enterprising individual must become more coöperative or he must be made more coöperative. And so we come back again here to the need for a high educational level in the community to make the large coöperations of a new age possible.*

§ 9. *The Race between Readjustment, Disorder and Social Revolution*

Let us consider now how far we have come towards a comprehensive review of human activities. The panorama we have evoked up to this point is world-wide but still incomplete. We have as yet given no direct attention to the governments of

---

*In *Stalin,* by Isaac Don Levine (1931) the reader will find a vivid account of the current phase of the Five Year Plan and of the strange personality behind that plan.

mankind, or to the education of mankind, and very little stress has been laid as yet on the differences of the masculine and feminine rôle in economic life. We have disregarded race and rank and many ancient pieties and loyalties. Our spectacle, thus simplified, exhibits a great confused variety and mingling of world production, distribution and consumption, plantations, mines, factories, transport, commodity markets, stores, shops, stock markets, banks, full of busy human beings, guided each one of them by a complex of motives, which, for most of the ordinary acts of economic life, are symbolized and presented in terms of money. It is as if society said to the individual: "Do this and you get so much." We have spoken of money therefore as the blood, the vital fluid in this contemporary economic body. The financial world, the banking system, mints, treasuries, play the rôle of the glands and nerves that control, increase, or restrain and purify the animating flood. And further we have traced how loosely that circulatory system and its controls are working, so that chief among our distresses we have on the one hand an excessive concentration, a congestion of wealth in the hands of an unhelpful and even obstructive minority, who have got it and who grip it, and on the other a morbid increase of undernourished and encumbering multitudes of human beings. We cannot therefore compare the economic life of the 1,900,-000,000 human beings now alive to that of a healthy animal body. It is a sick body if it is to be considered as any organized body at all. It is indeed more like a body struggling to come into being and failing in strength and determination. It is manifestly in need of treatment, possibly of very drastic treatment. It may be in need of surgery.

We began this work as a survey of productive activities. It was only as our study became closer and more searching that this contrast of the rich who have got the money and the poor who have not, came, almost in spite of our design, athwart the spectacle. Gradually we have been forced to recognize that in the course of twenty-five centuries or so, the ancient rules, servitudes and tyrannies of mankind have given place, step by step, by the substitution of money for other methods of compulsion,

THE RUSSIAN WORKER

TIGHTENING bolts preliminary to permanent riveting on one of the water distributors of the Dnieper Dam. The distributor is in the substructure of the power house and will be the largest in the world. According to present plans, the dam, with nine such distributors, will be completed in 1933.

M. ROSENFELD, FROM WORLD PETROLEUM

OIL TO-DAY

OIL storage at Bayonne, New Jersey. In the foreground are distribution pipes leading to a great variety of stills and tanks.

to the rule of wealth. The latter steps in this transition, made in the past three centuries, have been the most rapid, so that now the cash nexus reaches from the jungles to the mountain tops, and the rich are the potential, the inadvertent rulers of mankind. The pen (with a cheque book) is mightier than the sword. A sense of price is the secret of power. The rich man may not actually rule the world, but outside Soviet Russia no rule seems possible without him.

We find ourselves therefore describing not the working of a world-machine, planned and efficient, protecting and expanding human life, but a fortuitous concurrence of unplanned, unforeseen economic interactions, which has developed very rapidly and wonderfully in the past century, but which now betrays an alarming and quite unprecedented instability. It is not, we find, an economic order we are dealing with; it is an arithmetical crisis in the affairs of the human species. What promised to become a world-wide economic order is threatened by disaster in the counting house. Our work is inspired by the hope and belief that our world will yet develop into a real economic order, but we can give no certain assurance for that hope and belief.

Our analysis, in the preceding chapters, of social motives and of the money-credit system of the world enables us now to state the main factors in the present world crisis in elementary terms. There has been a stupendous increase in human power and productive ability during the last hundred years, and such an "abolition of distance" as to bring all mankind into close and rapid interaction. But there has been no sufficient corresponding adjustment of the monetary system and the system of ownership, so that humanity is entangled at every turn by obsolescent barriers, burthened with a constantly appreciating load of debt, and debarred from access to land and natural resources generally. The production and distribution of real wealth on anything like the scale of scientific possibilities is prevented by the concentration of financial wealth in the hands of a restricted, miscellaneous class of acquisitive and retentive people, the modern rich, enterprising only in acquisition, a class which has, so far, shown no signs of realizing either the possibilities or the dangers of the present unstable and unsatisfied state of mankind.

In Chapter VIII we ventured upon a broad and what we believe to be a very serviceable classification of human personas. There we made it clear that the ideology of the rich and influential, as we know them to-day, is very largely a mélange of ideas and dispositions derived from peasant and predatory types of mentality. With some exceptions the rich have done little to create the wealth they control. They have acquired it. Whenever business magnates or financial leaders are gathered together, there the boor and the brigand appear. The idea of creative service is there too, no doubt—and in increasing measure—but we have to remember always that the conduct of human affairs, when it is disinterested, is disinterested in spite of great inherent internal resistances. Every step towards a clear-headed, clearly understood control of economic life in the general interest of the race is made against the resistances of these baser factors present not only in the dominating rich but in ourselves and in everyone concerned. It is generally made, therefore, clumsily, ambiguously and slowly, and the present situation seems now too urgent for slow, clumsy or ambiguous measures.

The rapid accumulation of a great mass of superfluous poor people in our Western profit-organized civilization is now a continuous process; the ratio of that mass to the general population rises steadily, and there is all too great a possibility of effectual obstruction to any scientific alleviation of its stresses. A conflict develops steadily between the needs of this mass and the less intelligent and creative of the rich. The boor element in the wealthy and influential stratum is disposed to resist all attempts to alleviate the lot of these unemployed, to resist the giving of doles and any assistance in kind, and also any shortening of the working week, any increased superannuation of workers, any restrictions upon the employment of the young, of women or of old people, that might reabsorb many of those out of work. The masses in Russia, we are assured by most observers, *hope*. The supreme ambition of the boorish element among the modern rich seems to be to destroy hope. And this boorish spirit above will also appeal to patriotism, to that international competition which is based on the sweating of a working class, as an excuse for the unmerited privations and repressions it will want irrationally and instinctively to thrust upon its inferiors. This resistance of the casually and adventurously rich to scientific readjustment and to the scientific amelioration of change, will go on in the sight and knowledge of the expropriated and will deepen the natural antagonism of the have's and have-not's. The cinema, the popular press, the ever increasing *visibility* of modern realities, all tend to bring inequalities of fortune more and more vividly before the minds of the have-not's. The delusion of a fated subjugation to the wealthy nobility and gentry is continually more difficult to maintain. Yet the stupider elements among the modern rich are doing their utmost to sustain it. We have here the necessary elements for an intensifying class war.

Can the insurrectionary side in a class conflict between rich and poor supply the directive will and intelligence needed by the modern economic complex? Faced with an imminent class conflict, this question becomes imperative.

It is surely too much to expect people who have been deprived by the boorish element among their rulers from adequate knowledge and education, and who have no experience whatever of the directive side of economic life, to understand or sympathize with the constructive forces in a modern State. The poor, the "proletariat" in particular, as we have shown (Chapter VIII, § 2), also inherit their own distinctive modifications of the narrow peasant psychology, and their reaction is likely to be in the main not so much an effort to readjust as an unintelligent resentment not only against the rich, but against the methods and machinery of modern production, against social discipline and direction. They can hardly be expected to revise and improve what they have never been permitted to understand. That would be too difficult. Their education, such as it is, has been deprived of any constructive and directive ideas by the reactionaries above. So they are likely to show themselves much more disposed

to hamper and break up the contemporary organization altogether than to reconstruct it. They are living shabby, anxious,
undignified lives on the margin of subsistence. By that they
judge the system. "Anything," they will say, "is better than
this"—ignoring the fact that much might be worse.

If Soviet Russia succeeds and begins to prosper, or even if
it can survive and make a fair appearance of success, this
inevitable insurrectionary tension in the Atlantic populations
will increase, and the resistance of the property-owning classes
may be hardened by incipient panic. It may be. Or it may be
mitigated by an intelligent realization on the part of some of
their number of the need for extensive economic readjustments
and sacrifices. How far rich and influential people will consent
to learn and lead, and how far they will merely resist and suppress, is only to be known after the event, but on that depends
the whole issue of progress or disaster. Some resistance to
adjustment there will certainly be. We have no statistics to show
us how far the modern rich man belongs to the educated class
and how far he is a boor. So far as he is a boor, he will simply
hold tight and resist and provoke the multitudinous boor below.
We can count with some certainty, therefore, for some decades
ahead, on the presence of very active, chaotic, revolutionary
stresses in the world outside the Russian experiment. The boor
above, afraid for his gettings, will be disposed to use to the
extremest limit whatever advantage he may have with the legal,
police and military organizations of the community in defense
of his mean accumulations. He will be using all his influence
for suppression and more suppression, and when he finds the
spirit of the public services and the legitimate political system
too fair, reasonable and temperate for his purposes, the brigand
who is also in his composition will come to the surface and resort
to illegal violence. He will seek a "strong man" to seize on
power, lead the *Jeunesse dorée,* and keep the resentful and
threatening multitude in order. The boors of good fortune above
are no more likely to show compunction than the millions below
in smashing up the slow-won methods of order and law. Reasonable and constructive-minded men will find themselves in a cross

fire of misunderstandings, suspicions, panic and class hatred. That cross fire will be the atmosphere in which the building up of the modern world state must be achieved. Even though we dismiss Professor Soddy's suggestion that able men are generally wicked, we are still left face to face with the fact that many rich and powerful adventurers are as stupid and incurably dangerous as the departed Romanoffs.

The possibility of an arrest and even a retrogression of material civilization outside Bolshevik Russia, as grave or graver than the indisputable setback that occurred between 1914 and 1918, has to be faced. Confidence in public justice, faith in the law, is a slow and sensitive growth. When it is destroyed, human affairs sink to a lower level. When the law does not command respect, the lawbreaker becomes a hero. When the law does not give assurance of well-being, everyone drifts towards lawbreaking. The day of the sentimental gangster who robs only the rich dawns, and the epoch of dictatorships and popular "saviours" arrives. The gangster of the hired bravo type is confronted by the gangster of the Robin Hood type. Gangster and politician assimilate. It becomes more and more difficult to sustain firm and balanced government and to preserve the general liberty of discussion and initiative.

In various parts of the world we have, already, a number of more or less illegal dictatorships made possible by this antagonism of the ignorant and base-spirited rich above and the ignorant and base-spirited masses below. Usually it is the rich and privileged of the old and new types who have saddled themselves and their country with a military dictatorship. In Russia only has it gone the other way about, and the "proletarian" (or Stalin in the name of that mystical being) has become autocrat. In many cases the dictatorship is more or less controlled and steadied by an organization, the Fascisti in Italy, the Communist party in Russia; in others it is more frankly a brigand dictatorship. The persistent weeding out of his rivals and critics by Stalin is rapidly reducing the party control of Russia to a personal absolutism. In China an organization, the Kuomintang, with its variants and derivatives, struggles to keep its mind clear and maintain a constructive nationalist ideology against brigand adventurers and ruthless foreign exploitation.

Besides these broader displays of illegality, these seizures of whole nations and provinces, there is manifest throughout the world a widespread change in the popular attitude towards criminality, based on the deepening distrust of the expropriated masses in the spirit and intention of the existing legal order. This is due not to any intensified unfairness in the law, but to an acuter, less acquiescent criticism by the ordinary man. Indeed, the law has not gone back; it is more enlightened than it was, but it has not kept pace with the increase of scepticism and impatience. Its developments have not been sustained by public opinion because there is no general understanding of, or participation in, its modifications. The law does not advertise its modernity. It should. It should get out of sham Gothic buildings and sham dignity, antiquated wigs and fancy dress, and demonstrate its beneficent workings in the light of day. It should associate itself with modern concepts of society and bring its problems into line with everyday discussion. It is absurd that the only legal proceedings that are made interesting to the contemporary public are in the criminal courts.

The masses are losing any belief they ever had that the social organization embodied in the law is on their side. They are also losing faith in the value of money, the honesty of banking, and the security of any savings and investments. They are, in brief, being disillusioned about the social system to which they have hitherto submitted. The immediate loss of confidence, the diminution of confiding honest living caused by recent displays of monetary and credit instability, has been enormous. Fluctuations in money values leave the masses with an impression that governments can and will cheat. Then everyone, to the best of his courage and ability, begins to cheat and snatch also. The idea spreads that one is a fool to be conscientious. Concealment of all sorts increases. Economic morale is destroyed.

Across our broad picture of the world's expanding social and economic life we have to bring these shadows and symptoms of social disintegration. We add to our representation of the rather foolish and incoherent spending and waste of the modern rich, a multitude of mines and factories closing down, fields and plantations relapsing from cultivation, and gatherings of more and more unemployed workers, listless and dissatisfied, at the street corners. They trusted the property owners to keep things going, and the property owners have let them down. Criminal gangs multiply, and the forces of order lose energy and confidence. These are the outward and visible signs that profound changes are going on inside hundreds of millions of brains. There is manifestly a fading sense of obligation, loss of faith in the "honest" life, a growing sense of undeserved frustration, an increasing disposition to snatch pleasures and satisfactions while they are still within snatching range. These may not be all or most of the change that has occurred, but they are the changes that produce the most disquieting symptoms. There has been a world-wide seeping away of the beliefs, assurances and confidence on which the steady working of the traditional social organization has depended, and by which it has been able to carry on. We have therefore to balance this current degeneration of social morale under the stresses of our economic monetary and financial maladjustments, against the huge constructive achievements of the last hundred years.

What is happening may be a necessary parturition before the birth of unpredictable mental harmonies. These millions of brains, perplexed, anxious, greedy, planning, angry, resentful, vindictive, aspiring, this teeming ocean of gray matter, may be traversed by currents and stirred by tides whose movements we scarcely begin as yet to apprehend, much less to measure. The printing press, the cinema, the radio, stand ready to be used by anyone with the power and courage to use them upon this reservoir of will. We have all the means—and we have now the ideas and knowledge—needed to orient all these hundreds of millions of minds towards the undeveloped abundance, the clear and splendid possibilities of life at hand. We can set that tide going. We are surely in the dawn of an age when human motives and wills mingle and modify and combine, with a power and perhaps a violence they have never known before.

In our penultimate chapter we shall study the educational processes of the modern community, and we shall then be better able to weigh the factors in this crisis in social morale. We may then form a better conception than we can now of the profounder readjustments demanded by the present situation. We may realize how immense and rapid, under modern conditions, may be the readjustments in those hundreds of millions of brains.

Before we come to that, however, we have to consider two other systems of mental disturbance, the very great changes that are going on in the relations of women to men and of women to the community, and the tragic complication of all these problems we have opened up, by the impact of material progress upon the political and racial divisions of mankind. Then our outline will be completed. Throughout all these aspects of human life, as we pass from one to the other, runs one common theme, the theme of unforeseen and uncoördinated expansions of human power and possibility, and the consequent conflict of crude and novel opportunities and dangers with things outgrown. Things come out of the past and change in their nature under our eyes. The ancient antagonism of the rich and poor resembles the present antagonism of the rich and poor, but nevertheless, it is not the same antagonism. The old-world rich were real masters; the old-world poor were real slaves and serfs. The old-world civilization was only possible with that dominance and that subjugation. That order of things seemed inevitable. But the new-world rich are no longer essential to the productive scheme, they have become curiously detached from its administration, and their relations to the poor are indirect and complex. Possibilities of release and liberation open before our species, undreamt of before the Conquest of Power and Substances began.

CHAPTER THE ELEVENTH

THE RÔLE OF WOMEN IN THE WORLD'S WORK

§ 1. *How Far Sex Need Be Considered in This Survey.*

§ 2. *Women as Workers and as Competitors with Men. The Keeping of Wives and Families by Men in Relation to Feminine Employment. Social Neuters.*

§ 3. *The Inherent Difference of Physical and Mental Quality between Men and Women.*

§ 4. *Motherhood and the Dependence of Women because of Motherhood.*

§ 5. *Some Moral Consequences of the Traditional Inferiority and Disadvantage of Women. Feminine Acquiescence and Disingenuousness. Prostitution. The White Slave Trade. The Gigolo.*

§ 6. *The Power of Women through Reassurance and Instigation. Woman's Rôle in Determining Expenditure.*

§ 7. *Is a Special Type of Adult Education for Women Needed?*

§ 8. *Possibilities of Distinctive Work for Women in the Modern Community.*

CHAPTER THE ELEVENTH

THE RÔLE OF WOMEN IN THE WORLD'S WORK

§ 1. *How Far Sex Need Be Considered in This Survey*

WE HAVE now brought our survey of human activities to a fairly comprehensive stage; we have got the whole ant-hill working, we have shown the workers busy and we have studied their motives and incentives. But still the spectacle is an extremely simplified one. Governments and politicians remain to be considered. No national flags have appeared. We have not yet brought the custom house and the barrack yard into the picture; we have indeed set aside the whole complex of national rivalry and war. The numbers of this human multitude and the increase of populations have yet to be studied; we have not mentioned crime and prison, and though we have alluded constantly to education, nevertheless the schools, colleges, instruction books of the world have still to be displayed.

And not a paragraph has been given yet to that intimate human activity, the relations of the sexes. That we will now take up.

While we have noted the progressive supersession of the autonomous home by collective services, we have refrained from considering how this has changed the mutual relations of man and woman in the ménage. Even in Chapter VIII when we set out the broad types of persona as the basis of our study of social interactions, we did not trouble ourselves with the fact that there are a feminine peasant and feminine nomad and (less important hitherto but not necessarily less important now) a feminine educated type. We would justify that simplification by saying that, roughly speaking, for the broad social ends of that chapter, the woman goes with the man of her class, that the peasant's woman shares his outlook on the world and has the feminine to his persona, and that the nomadic autocratic woman agrees also in all its main essentials with the ideology of her male.

"Roughly speaking," I write. But now let us try and speak and think a little less roughly, and take into consideration that every human affair is two-sided, that from the hut of the savage to the palace of the king or multi-millionaire the woman is thinking and acting with certain differences—perhaps ineradicable differences—of her own. Hitherto we have considered the net result, the common denominator, economically and socially, of male and female. Now we are admitting that this human drama may have been played, and may always have to be played, by two series of non-interchangeable actors. Each may have a kind of rôle which is inseparable from the drama. Through the looms of our world of work and wealth may be running two systems of lives, about nine hundred and fifty million individuals in each, having different dispositions and different ends.

We write "may be" and not "is." We are posing a question here. By way of reply we offer the suggestion: that there are indeed such differences of disposition and end, but that they are the slight differences of essentially similar as well as kindred beings. They are coöperative and not antagonistic differences. They can point to a common destiny. To the end of time there are things that will be better done and rôles that will be better played by women than men, there are things women will think more desirable than men do, and *vice versa,* and a large part, if not the larger part, of human operations are, and will remain, definitely assignable as men's jobs or women's jobs.

But let us ask first, how far does sex extend into the being of a man or woman? Are we male or female to our finger tips? Many creatures are sexed, so to speak, only as far as reproduction goes. A herring has a soft roe or a hard roe, and that is as much sex as a herring seems to have. Nor is there anything particularly virile or ladylike about the male or female ostrich. It is only when incubation or suckling and the care of the

young come into the life cycle of a species that we remark any
wide structural or temperamental divergences. All these divergences are related to the reproductive specialization of the
female. The Hominidæ do not present as much sexual divergence
as most varieties of cattle; there is with them neither an all-
round mental nor physical ascendency of either sex; while, for
example, a man is able to hit harder, run harder and toil more
heavily than a woman, she seems to swim better, is quicker to
learn the balance of a bicycle, and has more endurance for
continuous low-pressure work. There seem to be very small
odds against her when it comes to the handling of an automobile
or aëroplane. The conquest of Power, the abolition of toil, is
relieving woman of many economic disadvantages. The light
machine has put her upon terms of equal competition with men
in many once masculine trades. The progressive socialization of
the household is detaching her more and more from traditional
household drudgery, and birth control minimizes her ancient
specialization as the reproductive sex. Our species, never very
highly differentiated sexually, is now, it would seem, undergoing
a diminution of sexual differentiation.

§ 2. *Women as Workers and as Competitors with Men. The Keeping of Wives and Families by Men in Relation to Feminine Employment. Social Neuters*

Let us now review very briefly the work of women, and
particularly woman as an industrial worker, side by side and in
competition with man.

Before the war there was a polite pretence, maintained by at
least the middle and upper classes of the Western world, that
women were incapable of doing ordinary industrial work. They
could work in the household, but they could not "work for a
living." Cooks, for example, were supposed to lack the intelligence needed for minding a machine; and housemaids, "up and
downstairs all day," the strength required for climbing the steps
of tramcars. When, during the war, women appeared doing these
things quite successfully, everybody expressed astonishment and

admiration. Women themselves seemed to be as astonished as anybody. The newspapers were full of it. People wrote books about it. And yet in Great Britain alone, before the war, nearly five million females were working outside their homes for wages and over one hundred thousand of them were in the metal trades.

It is this sort of mass illusion and mass convention about women that makes it difficult either to estimate what they can do or to find out what they are actually doing. Nobody seems able to think about them without feeling strongly in the matter and being moved to pretenses and concealments. Everything undergoes a conventional dramatization. Women themselves dramatize their behaviour in one way and men dramatize it for them in another. Cold, clear statements of fact are rare—we have only partial information, and statistics so incomplete that they cannot be compared one with another.

The industrial life of women goes on against the opposition of these conventions. In no period have men approved of their women working for money. To do so reflected upon the social position of the head of the family and implied a threat to his authority. The rich, from a mixture of good and bad motives, do not like their women to work at all. Even the poor resent their working away from home. It was only when engineering became coloured with patriotism, so that women in the factories became a credit to their country instead of being vaguely shameful, that the average citizen was prepared to realize what they could do there. And now that the war is over and its glamour gone, we are again at a stage when nobody seems to know or to want to know, fully and exactly, to what extent women are employed in industry, what they are doing, what they are being paid or the conditions under which they are working.

Women, as far as their work goes, may be divided into two main sections: those who work in and about homes, and those whose employment takes them into the outer world. The first group is engaged all over the planet in domestic tasks and crafts and agriculture. It is the huge majority of womankind. It includes, indeed, the American housewife with her heating from the main, her electric refrigerators and her country club, but also the savage wife—who, besides cooking and taking care of her children, builds huts, cultivates the ground, spins, weaves and makes baskets and pottery—and the whole multitude of domestic slaves and servants. It includes nearly all the women of India. Among these are scores of millions of Hindu wives, married before they are nubile, slaves not merely of their husbands and mothers-in-law, but of a rigid system of custom and superstitions, that makes the cardinal phases of life horrors of helplessness and uncleanness. Millions may never leave the homes and are thrust into solitary huts to bear their children. Most of these domesticated women workers are not paid in money, though money may be given them; where they are paid they are not paid very much. And in spite of the vacuum cleaners and gas cookers of the Western world, the bulk of this work is still done under conditions and by methods which are centuries out of date. The work is monotonous, lonely and imprisoning; it is set about with class distinctions; the performers have often no taste for it and have not been trained to do it, and they leave it whenever they get the chance. Woman may be a domesticated animal, but she certainly has not a domesticated soul. She loves toil and restraint no more than man. Housekeepers buy bread and send the wash to a laundry; the cook's daughter takes a job in a tea shop, and the intellectual young school teacher refuses to marry at all. In Russia, the Bolshevik authorities tell us, it is the women who take eagerly to the collective farms, who vote for "going collective" in village after village. What are supposed to be their deepest instincts disappear promptly when the chance of getting away from housework appears. According to the official figures there were over 13½ million Russian women working on collective farms in March, 1931, and the figure was then said to be increasing. The proportion of domesticated women seems to be falling, all over the world.

Manifestly there must be a corresponding increase of non-domestic women. One group of non-domestic feminine employees, however, is almost certainly shrinking. These are the mere poor drudges, the sweated, the exploited women, in

corners or on the fringes of the industrial world, toiling at work
so badly paid and disagreeable that men refuse to do it. Factory
acts and laws dealing with public health are abolishing this type
of employment in civilized countries. Filthy jobs like gut-
scraping have been cleansed and disinfected; the beer-bottling
and rag-sorting that used to be carried on in insanitary cellars
are now performed in dry and properly ventilated workshops,
often with the help of machinery. In the opinion of a high
official in the Factory Department of the English Home Office
real driving and oppression of women, so far as the modern communities are concerned, are now only to be found in domestic
service, where in rare instances a little slavey has not spirit
enough to leave a tyrannical mistress. As industrialism spreads
into backward countries where there are no trade unions or
restrictive laws, exploitation reappears for a time. Dame
Adelaide Anderson's report on the employment of children in
Egyptian industry describes cotton-ginning sheds filled with
irritating dust where boys and girls of seven are kept at their
work by whips. Women still coal ships in Japan. But international control in these matters is increasing, and unless there
is some sort of world collapse, our great-grandchildren may very
well live in a world completely cleansed from the barbarous
industrial consumption of women drudges.

But the bulk of non-domesticated women now, the real modern
women workers, are the product of education acts, trade union-
ism, and the light machine. It may be a lathe or a typewriter,
but where a machine can be made light and easy they are drawn
to it to perform, generally speaking, the less responsible kinds
of work of which it is capable. In comparison with men they
take down letters but do not dictate them, they mind machines
but they do not set, mend, improve or invent them. And they
receive, as a rule, from rather over half to two-thirds of what
a man would get for doing a similar if not identical job. They
are young (Sir Josiah Stamp has estimated that half the women
in industry in Great Britain are under twenty-three), and they
are badly organized.

A want of organization of women workers is a world-wide

WILLIAM RITTASE

ON THE SUNNY SIDE OF THE BALANCE

WE CANNOT do justice to modern civilization until we bring its vast developments of holiday play and open-air exercise into the reckoning.

WILLIAM RITTASE.

WOMAN IN INDUSTRY
A DELICATE step in the making of radio tubes.

phenomenon. In Japan, where the number of men and women in the factories is almost equal—rather over a million of each—there are three men in the unions for every woman. In England 32 per cent of the "gainfully occupied males," as the census returns call our men workers, are organized, and only 15 per cent of the smaller total of gainfully occupied females. The cause of this abstention does not seem to be hostility towards trade unions, but low wages and adolescent amateurism. The younger women regard their time in the factories as an interlude preceding marriage, and they want every penny either to collect a dowry or to pay for the clothes and outings which ensure a wider choice of husbands. When women's wages rose during the war and marriage seemed less certain, they flocked into the unions: since then they have lapsed into their old indifference to industrial organization.

It is claimed that the influx of girls into industry has had on the whole a civilizing influence upon working conditions. It was probably their appeal as unprotected minors to Victorian sentiment which passed the first factory acts, and when under pressure of foreign competition that sentiment hardened, its place was taken by a growing biological conscience. The presence of women in the factories seems to have raised the standards of cleanliness, decency and comfort there. And as soon as their working conditions ceased to be hopelessly degrading, their greater desire for colour in life, pleasantness, romance, their views on the subject of manners and conduct, have had a decisive influence on the industrial atmosphere. Filth and brutality have retreated before them. The general amelioration of life in the past half century may have had its share in these improvements, but the industrialization of women was the main progressive force.

What is the present outlook for women in industry? They seem likely to remain an important industrial factor—possibly in increasing numbers—but not as life workers. That girls should have somewhere to go between leaving school and entering into marriage is under contemporary conditions an obvious social convenience. But whether they will ever occupy more than the lowlier positions in industry is another question. Apparently, as a sex, they lack both a man's ambition and his disinterested mental curiosity. They do not mean to remain àt the work and they are not willing—except in a few trades here and there like the Lancashire cotton trade—to train for skilled or responsible positions. Moreover, employers, because of the possible transitoriness of their engagements, are unwilling to train even those girls who ask for the chance to qualify themselves for higher posts. It is difficult, therefore, to estimate the force and soundness of their disposition to take and use such a chance. The matter is further complicated by the fact that in the factories of Great Britain, trade-union regulations shut women out from entire industries and from the cream of the skilled jobs in most of the rest. In America the wages for unskilled labour have been so good relatively that it has been difficult to induce even men to train for the best positions, which to a surprising extent therefore are filled by skilled craftsmen from Europe. In Russia, where there are now no such barriers, 150,000 women, we are told, are being specially trained for skilled work, but it is too soon to say whether they will prove as valuable as men. In Latin countries an exceptional woman may be found doing anything—but she remains exceptional. At present, indeed, it is only in Scandinavia that women as a sex seem to be demonstrating any aptitude for the more skilled branches of technical work, and obtain employment to any perceptible extent on equal terms with men.

THE KEEPING OF WIVES AND FAMILIES BY MEN IN RELATION TO FEMININE EMPLOYMENT

The industrialization of women on anything like equal terms with men goes on not only against trade-union bars and the distracting competition of the marriage market, but also against the long established prejudices of our race. The belief in woman's inferiority as a worker still prevails. This inferiority is not proven up to the hilt, because the handicap of the bars and distractions we have noted prevents a fair try-out, but it remains the established impression. Without bars and handicaps it is felt that she would still be inferior. This persuasion may be due partly to the fact that she is paid lower wages even on work she is better able to do than a man. To get 60 per cent of a man's wage means in effect only 60 per cent of his food, freedoms and self-assurance, and girls, from the first day they go to work, are accustomed to this attitude of inferiority to their brothers and accept it without demur. And because they accept it they are now being employed in many types of work instead of men. They have not actually driven men out of men's own jobs—they are generally prevented from doing that by trade-union agreements—but either they have followed domestic trades, such as sewing, cooking and laundry work, out from the home into the factories where they are now very largely carried on, or a skilled trade carried on by men is changed into a trade where the skill goes into machines which can be managed by young women—though this very possibly would not have been done if it were not for the woman's lower wage. This question of relative wage rates is likely to become more acute in the future. At present both working men and working women seem to accept the proposition that man, as woman's superior and as the potential keeper of a woman, is entitled to be paid more for what he does. The man protects his standard of living not by forbidding the woman to undersell him, but by shutting her out completely from this or that particular pool of work. The result is that new trades—such as electrical work for wireless apparatus —get very largely handed over to women, and there is a constant inducement to break up skilled jobs in this or that part of an old trade and get the rearranged operations classed as women's work. An intensification of this might at any time cause the present discrepancy in rates to be felt as intolerable, and men might then insist upon a uniform rate of pay for both sexes. That might check the increasing relative employment of young women for some time, though it might ultimately increase the proportion of skilled women who meant to make their jobs their life work.

At the back of the disposition to underpay women relatively to men is the old tradition that the man has to "keep a family."

This is what the trade unions are defending when they bar women from the better paid types of employment. Modern industrialism knows nothing and can know nothing of marriage so far as its pay sheets go. If a factory were obliged to discriminate between married and single, put up the pay of each worker whenever he chose to marry, and give him a rise whenever his wife presented him with a baby, it is plain that in this world of competition it would have to restrict its employment to guaranteed bachelors or go into an early bankruptcy. The present state of affairs is a rough adjustment to social conditions under which young men leaving home and going into employment are strongly impelled to marry. The normal state of mind of the adult male in a trade union is that of an actual or potential family man. He does whatever he can through his union to prevent the girl underselling him by her unskilled labour, or getting beyond his reach by winning her way to skilled employment on equal terms. She does the former, but so far she has shown very little energy in doing the latter. And he tries to keep his wages up to a level at which he can "keep a wife."

It has frequently been asserted in the British press that a serious factor in unemployment is that women are driving men out of work. That is not true. Certainly, while the number of men employed has increased, the increase of employed women has been sensibly greater. But it has not been enormously greater. The gross difference between 1923 and 1930 shows a steady increase in the number of women employed in the industries covered by the British unemployment insurance, from a little under three million to three million and a half. If the pre-war rates of employment held to-day there would be about a hundred thousand more men and about a hundred thousand less women industrially employed. That is all. A large part of the increased industrial employment of women has nothing to do with the unemployment of men; it is a transfer of women from domestic to industrial life, because work that was formerly done in the home, laundry work, sewing, baking, urban lunch and tea service, is now supplied outside. Also the nursery has fewer children and needs fewer nursemaids. There were a quarter of a million fewer domestic servants in 1921 in Great Britain than in 1911. Nor, so far as Great Britain goes, is feminine employment responsible for male unemployment, which is greatest in the heavy industries where women do not compete with men.*

We may therefore dismiss this suggestion that the industrialization of women is to any considerable extent the cause of masculine unemployment. It is the ancient tradition for a woman to look to a man to keep her, and that in effect is what ninety-nine women out of the hundred, even in most "advanced" circles, still do. The modern woman likes to keep free and own herself, but she finds it as a rule more practicable still to do so at the expense of someone else. What is of far more importance in a study of womanhood under modern conditions, is the vast masses of unemployed men which are now appearing in every modernized community, who have little or no earning power at all. Instinct and tradition conspire to make nearly all of them want to "keep a wife," but a vast proportion realize that they will be quite unable to keep children. An increasing proportion of men workers, workers of the black-coated class as well as manual workers, must marry women with a certain apologetic air therefore and with the agreed intention of evading offspring. There is a steady increase in the number of childless ménages. A new sort of marriage and a new sort of home have come into existence unobtrusively but surely; a marriage which does not ensue in a brawl of children. It ensues, however, in a dreadfully unoccupied woman, whose leisure becomes a grave problem to the community. She lives a life of small economies. She feels her uselessness in the measure of her intelligence. At the side of that fruitless type of ménage there is also an increase of "bachelor women" on the one hand, maintaining themselves on their pay, and on the other, an increasing number of men at a level of pay and employment below the possibilities of even keeping one woman.

---

*The British health insurance figures show 70.5 per cent men to women in 1912 and 68.2 per cent in 1928. The percentage of males in the British Civil Service was 88.6 in 1913 and 77.6 in 1929.

SOCIAL NEUTERS

Deliberately sterile ways of living have existed for a long time. In France, for example, it has long been customary in a great number of bourgeois households to employ man and wife, often quite young people, on the distinct and carefully observed condition that they have no children. Such callings as that of the shop assistant, having gone on for a hundred years or more, imposing a practical celibacy upon the majority of those who followed them. But the self-subsisting woman is—as anything but a social exception—practically new, and what is more significant is the rapid increase and wide dispersal of these hitherto exceptional types of life, which have no reproductive value in the community. In Roman times the proletary was that impoverished section of the community which contributed nothing but children to the commonweal. These new types constitute a sort of negative proletary which contribute few or no children at all.

Our mechanized civilization is thus producing, in increasing quantities, individuals whose sexual life is of no social importance whatever. That does not mean that they are not making love and leading a very full emotional and physical sexual life; many of them are. But this part of their existence produces no results that justify any sort of control of the sexual life by the community. From the biological point of view they are as neuter as the worker bees.

In Chapter XIII we shall deal with the main facts of the population question and then the high probability that this mass of neuters in our species will increase will become very plainly apparent. The time may be quite close at hand when only a half or a third of the adults in our world will be producing offspring.

The social and economic utilization of the women of this neutralized mass is a much more serious problem than that of the men, because of the greater relative importance the reproductive (and not simply the sexual) side of life has had for womankind. At present this problem of feminine frustration and lack of rôle outside domesticity is overshadowed by the far more serious economic and political difficulties in which our world is entangled. But whenever those difficulties are cleared away this problem will emerge to primary importance. So far from the relative increase of feminine to masculine employment being a serious and threatening phenomenon at the present time, the much more serious fact is that so few women relative to the numbers who are now unproductively dependent are striking out for a social and economic independence of their own.

§ 3. *The Inherent Difference of Physical and Mental Quality between Men and Women*

It was only after the writer had set himself seriously to summarize the differences of man and woman that he realized how vague, vaporous, and useless is the enormous literature of the subject. It is like a wide, warm, damp, haze-filled gulley between science and literature, choked with a weedy jungle of pretentious writing. One has not so much to summarize as to mow down and clear away, thousands of volumes that in the guise of general discussions express merely personal prejudices and aspirations. The substantial matter of even profoundly "scientific" works is not so much a record of controlled observations as a series of casual remarks.

No really definite attempt has yet been made to discount the enormous subjective factor that enters into thought about the business, or to make allowances for the variations in the amount and nature of that subjective factor at various stages in the sexual cycle of the observer's life. Inherent and imposed qualities are recklessly jumbled by everyone. No clear recognition is made of the varieties of human type and race. No account is taken of age phases. A Bengali woman, a Patagonian woman, a Norwegian fisher-girl or a Hottentot woman, has each a definite difference from her associated male. She has an innate difference and an acquired difference. There are an innate difference and an acquired difference in Bengal, and they are not at all the same differences as those in Norway. And the woman passes from phase to phase in her life orbit—as her man does also—according to her type.

But in nearly all this sex literature these differences are assumed to be, if not the same, at least of the same nature. People write of "virile" and "feminine," of what men and women are and will do, regardless of pattern or phase. So far as one can generalize about these "studies," by "man" is meant a male of middling class and some education in one of the European or American communities, round about the age of forty, and by "woman," a female in the same social stratum, of from twenty to thirty-five. About whom the pens scribble uncontrollably.

Our task here is not to swell this already overwhelming literature of provocation, excitation and complaint. We have to state the material facts of the case as compactly and clearly as we can for the purposes of our spectacle. The rest matters no more to us now than—love poetry.

We may add a few observations upon the question of physical difference already posed. In all varieties of *Homo sapiens,* over and beyond the differences of the actual reproductive organs, we note that the female pelvis is relatively more capacious than the male, the upper parts of the legs are set differently, the breathing is more costal and less abdominal, the whole build is lighter, softer and finer. The difference is not so marked in some races as in others, but it is always a difference in the same direction. As with the other Primates, the fully developed human male is heavier than the fully developed female. On these points there can be little or no dispute. The relative fineness and lightness of the female extends to the head, neck and brain. The differentiation is obviously less wide in man than in the gorilla. And all these differences seem liable to great exaggeration through custom and social condition.

As Metchnikoff pointed out long ago in his *Nature of Man,* natural human life is full of incongruities. The human female is capable of sexual intercourse and excitation ten years before she reaches the age when she can bear children to the best advantage; she can have sexual intercourse forced upon her against her will as very few female animals can; she cannot resist as effectually; and in many savage, barbaric, and even civilized societies, the complete development of a large proportion of

women seems to be greatly retarded by their premature subjugation to sex. They do not really grow up. Presently their stock
of vitality is put under contribution for child-bearing. Or if they
do not marry young they do not marry at all, and so go on to
what may perhaps be considered another type of underdevelopment. The sexual life of the human male seems to be more passionate and violent but more transitory and incidental than that
of the female. The storm passes, and he is quit of the urgency
for a time. He returns to the work he was doing. He gets a
better chance therefore of maturing according to his innate and
individual possibilities.

These essential differences and these natural disadvantages
have been greatly masked, distorted and exaggerated by custom
and tradition in all human societies. We do not know, with any
certitude, anything that we can call the "natural" sexual disposition of either man or woman at any stage of development. So
great has been the masking that in Britain and North America,
for example, it was commonly assumed until a few years ago
that the majority of women were, as the phrase goes, "cold"—
devoid, that is, of strong sexual appetites—and that the minority
who sought pleasure in sex were abnormal and reprehensible.
This assumption prevailed during a period of repression, and
it was only an intensification of an almost world-wide mental
disposition. But it was no more than a convention. Now, simply
through the annulment of various prohibitions and the lifting
of a veil of secrecy, this assumption of feminine frigidity is no
longer accepted. Now, it would seem, a great multitude of
women are as sensuous and excitable, if not more sensuous and
excitable, sexually than men. There is a difference in the tempo
rather than the quality of their desires.

These again may not be permanently valid observations; we
may be witnessing only the release and sur-excitation of feminine
desire through the lifting of old repressions and the realization
of new opportunities and novel systems of suggestion. Yet it is
plain that until we have more definite knowledge in this field
we are unable to decide upon almost fundamental issues in
social life—such as our treatment of prostitutes—or in educa-

tion. Our estimate of good or bad conduct must remain in many respects provisional.

It seems at least clear that women are more selective in their sexual conduct and more easily subdued to self-control. Sex in the normal male is more resentful of control and more forcible in achieving its ends. Yet here again, while the male is more disposed for open rebellion against prohibitions and lapses easily into a rude, clumsy, aggressive, mean pursuit of reliefs and satisfactions, the subconscious urgencies of the female may in the end be a slower but more effective drive. He can be more easily put off with crude gratifications than she. It has always been possible to separate parenthood from sexual relationships in thought, and it is becoming possible to do so in practice. Traditional morality sets its face against such a separation, but modern ideas are changing that. It is asserted by many now, asserted but not proved, that through the larger part of adult life, physical and mental health is only possible while the stir and satisfactions of sexual relationships are going on, and that parenthood need not be involved in that emotional system. The sexual life of a woman earning a living for herself, if it is conducted in this spirit, approximates very closely to the sexual life of a man living under the same conditions. She is more in conflict with tradition, but beyond that there is no other important difference between the two.

On all such questions the physiological and psychological sciences give us as yet scarcely any clear, assured and measured information. They ought to do so, and presently, no doubt, they will. But as it is we are left rather to the immediate and superficial appearances of the case, and to guesses and intuitions. It is manifest that in the relations of men and women we are dealing with plastic mental material which can be moulded into a great variety of fashions by suggestion, law, custom and accident, but we are still incapable of stating the limits and conditions of that plasticity.

On the whole there seems to be a rapid and considerable assimilation of qualities and conditions going on, women are gaining freedoms, enlarging their scope, and men are losing privileges, authority and personal prestige, but it does not follow that that assimilation will go on indefinitely until we return to the herring's immunity from all secondary sexual characters. Men and women may readjust to new and progressive conditions, retaining and even intensifying certain male and female characteristics. And we may find that there will be a definition and recognition of many more rôles than the traditional two, between various sexual types. The private sexual life is not our concern here, but we are concerned with all varieties of sexual rôle that affect the general social and economic process.

§ 4. *Motherhood and the Dependence of Women Because of Motherhood*

The life of the ordinary mammal, up to and including the more primitive human types, is almost entirely taken up by growth, sleep or basking, the search for food and reproduction. That fills the year. Up to our own times that was as true for human beings in the mass as for their humbler relations. They worked, they paired, they brought up a family. There was little margin to their days and by the time the family was completed and launched life was nearly consumed.

Men and women were pressed forward by custom and daily necessity from the cradle to the grave. Since the number of female births is roughly equal to the male, the normal state of affairs has been monogamy, with a certain amount of polygamy superimposed whenever exceptional men as chiefs and so forth got a chance of monopolizing more than their share of the supply of women. This was balanced against the greater liability of males to violent death, and the lesser resisting power of the male to many forms of illness. (The proportion of females to males is somewhere about 21 to 20 in western Europe.)

A certain obvious division of labour established itself therefore (with a variety of interpretations and minor variations) throughout the world. The frequent pregnancy of the female, and the young children's need of protection, made it natural and proper that the male should do the more heavy, active and adventurous part of the food-hunt or food-production, and that she should keep house and cook and stay with her offspring. Upon the basis of these necessities (which are necessities no longer) the whole tradition of feminine dependence was established.

But the business of parentage is as much the male's concern as the female's. It is as much the business of life for one as the other. The natural social man, as we find him expressing himself in the peasant persona, is benevolent and responsible, but tyrannous and possessive, towards his woman and his children. He is the captain of the home, and she is the mate. All mammals and all incubating birds make great sacrifices of personal freedom to the production and welfare of their young; man makes greater and more prolonged sacrifices because his young need protection for so long, and woman has made even greater sacrifices than man. Throughout the ages she has been obliged to concede leadership. If it is not in her nature to concede leadership it is woven now almost inextricably into her persona by the power of tradition.

This convention, the thrusting upon her of rather more than a fair half of the toil of the household, premature conception, the worries of children, have used up the majority of women rather faster than their men. In the past women *aged,* and where old-fashioned conditions prevail women still age, sooner than man. The man, when he has had the power and authority to do it, has therefore tended always to supplement his first mating and bring in younger wives. For many thousands of years there has been the urge towards the possessive polygamy of energetic and powerful men, either imposing itself openly as in black Africa and much of the Orient, or working beneath the conventional arrangements of society, against the necessary habitual monogamy of average men and women. Polyandry, on the contrary, is a Tibetan rarity, and is rather a fraternal shareholding of women than any equivalent to the possessive polygamy of the influential male. Where women have had great power and opportunity—the Empress Catherine the Second of Russia, for example—it is true that they have shown themselves as polyg-

amous as men, but such occasions have been rare. Of prostitution
we will speak later. None of these exceptions does very much to
alter the fact that motherhood has been so great a disadvantage
to women as to impose upon them a dependence and defenseless-
ness that are almost inextricably woven into our social tradition.

But now very rapidly, in the countries affected by the Atlantic
civilizations, a conspiracy of circumstances has been changing
and destroying all the foundation facts upon which that tradition
was based. The chief elements in this conspiracy have been, first,
the restriction of births and such a hygienic prevention of infant
mortality that physical motherhood becomes a mere phase of a
few years in a woman's life; secondly, the socialization of education and of most domestic services; and thirdly, the supersession of any protective function on the part of the male by the
law and the police. Woman is left almost abruptly released and
exposed. But the tradition of countless generations of disadvantage and real dependence clings about her.

§ 5. *Some Consequences of the Traditional Inferiority and Disadvantage of Women. Feminine Acquiescence and Dis-ingenuousness. Prostitution. The White Slave Trade. The Gigolo*

The quality of the life of women throughout our changing
world to-day is determined by two main factors. First there is
the mechanical factor in economic progress; the supersession
of toil, particularly of heavy toil, and the socialization of many
of the more important tasks that were once distinctively feminine. This mechanical factor makes for an equalization of economic importance and a release of women from the implication
of inferiority. The only remaining physical differences between
man and woman are becoming horizontal, i. e., differences between individuals in the same class, and not vertical differences,
in which all women are put below all men, or vice versa.

But secondly there is a huge mass of tradition still operative
by which the man is incited to take the overmastering and responsible rôle, and the woman tempted to accept and make the

most of the old-time subservience, instead of insisting upon the logical consequences of the new conditions. She finds she can get most of the traditional advantages and concessions, won for her by her past devotion to maternity and domesticity, while being in fact relieved of most of the burthen of that devotion. She finds this the more easy and excusable because the pride of the men with whom she has to deal in business or professional life is easily roused against her; it makes things difficult for her as an equal or antagonist; it makes it harder to play a man-like rôle than if (all other things remaining equal) her sex were male. On the other hand, it wins her unjustifiable "chivalrous" concessions.

Ancient tradition makes it seem right and proper to a man—even if he is an economically incompetent man—that he should have a woman of his own, under his control. The feeling is very widespread that every man should have a woman of his own, and there is plainly a sex consciousness like a class consciousness in the matter. There is sex solidarity. There is a widespread psychological resistance on the part of both men and women against the economic equalization that material changes are bringing about. A woman working on her own behalf does not get a fair deal from either men or women. Municipal authorities in Great Britain usually dismiss their women doctors on marriage, even when they are running maternity clinics. But a male doctor may marry, and marry again after the briefest widowerhood, and no municipal authority will take cognizance of the matter.

There is more here than an envious prejudice against seeing two incomes flow into one home. Nobody minds how many incomes a man earns, inherits and marries. What almost nobody really believes is that a grown-up woman has a right to manage her personal life as freely as a man. Not only is she expected to live more timidly, but large sections of the population feel that they have a right to compel her to do so. And the forbidding of outside work to married women, the shutting of them up in their homes, is bad for the home, where it produces a combination of restlessness and mental stuffiness, and bad for the reputa-

tion of women as workers. They are accused of emotional instability, of "bringing their feelings into their work," of lacking ambition, breadth of mind and human understanding. The
traditional influences of which we have been speaking are powerfully reinforced by financial factors. Under all the talk about
women's emancipation, and in spite of the considerable steps
that have been taken towards legal freedom, there remains
the fact that the overwhelming majority of women in the world
are economically dependent—have no money of their own at all.
Hundreds of millions of them are not allowed to own money
or any property but personal jewelry. Over most of the world
the husband has control of his wife's property: we find this state
of affairs not only in backward countries, but in France, Switzerland, Belgium, Spain, the State of Florida and the Province of
Quebec. Where they may own it, custom—and the sincerely held
belief that a man needs money more than a woman—diverts the
flow of inheritance into male hands. Where money is left to
women it is, more often than not, tied up so that they are not
free to use the capital. We have already seen that as wage-
earners they earn less for the same work than would be paid
to a man. As a sex, when it comes to money of their own, they
are poor.

The effects of this comparative poverty are so far-reaching
that it is difficult to determine where they end. For one thing,
it means that women on the whole are not educated to deal
with any aspect of money but spending. They do not realize,
imaginatively, its industrial and financial functions. They are
urged by every magazine and paper they pick up, by the implications of almost every book, to regard themselves as spenders,
as elegant or beautiful, or, at the worst, subtle creatures, for
the maintenance of whose elegance, beauty and subtlety an
immense mass of spending is necessary and justified. We have
already seen in our section on Cosmetics how this works out in
detail. So when money falls unfettered and in large quantities
into the hands of a woman, she is likely to be someone with no
ideas about money but that it can be spent in amplifying and
decorating her personal life—with a certain minor flow towards

charity and the support of art and music—and she will receive far more admiration, gratitude and press publicity for doing that with it than for using it in any fruitful or constructive manner.

As for the women who have no money—or less money than the corresponding men of their class—they are hampered at every turn. It is not worth while spending so much on their education as on that of boys, because they cannot be expected to earn so much. The ordinary English parents may be as willing to make sacrifices for their daughters as they are for their sons, but if one or the other must be preferred, it is only common sense to invest in the boys. Then there is the question of capital—women, because of their customary poverty, cannot buy practices and partnerships or stock or premises; they have to remain as employees, assistants, secretaries. Even in a profession newly opened to women, like medicine, we find groups of doctors joining together to run a practice and taking in a fully qualified woman, not as a partner, but as a mere salaried assistant, to do the work they most dislike. And in such positions—partly because they are paid less, partly because there is the risk, if they are young, of losing their services on marriage—they are generally regarded as less valuable than men. This may not be true of the individual employer, who will readily admit that the women in his own office do their work as well as men would do it. But that does not prevent him from considering them inferior, as a whole, to the same sort of men.

The result of all this is that while the conventional relations between men and women are weakened, the much advertised new relations which are arising to replace them do not correspond to economic fact. Marriage and dependence still provide the most dazzling social and monetary prizes for women. Except for those born rich, prettiness, suitable clothes and pleasing manners are far more likely to lead to success in life than ambition, knowledge and intelligence. Women want children, homes, love-making, and on the other hand travel, entertainment and ornamental backgrounds. Men alone can give them these, and men prefer as a rule to give them only for personal and emotional reasons. "Emancipated" women at the present time are therefore likely to be inconsistent. They value freedom, and they claim equality, but unless they are prepared to give up every other side of life to these, they must not behave as equals except after they have got what they want. This may be as unfair to the man involved as the original predicament was unfair to the woman—it is not surprising that there is a great deal of talk about the relations between the sexes and a good deal of open hostility. But that does not mean that there is more sexual unhappiness. On the contrary, it seems likely that there has never been a time when there was so little.

Economic inferiority—not of actual gross earnings, perhaps (on account of the number of women who cease to earn after marriage), but of status and opportunity—will probably diminish. It is more difficult to see what will relieve the almost complete dependence of the married woman. Increasingly, parents are unwilling to provide dowries even in countries where they are under considerable social pressure to do so. The system which is proposed in lieu of them is that of endowment of motherhood or children's allowances. There are several ways of securing such payments—they may come from the State, or from the industry in which the husband is employed. But they presuppose a high degree of national organization. They would benefit women—there would be a considerable transfer of wealth direct from men to women—the mother would no longer be wholly dependent on her husband, the unmarried woman worker would find it less difficult to establish the principle of equal wages for equal work. On the other hand, they would almost certainly involve the lowering of the wages of single men, and in most of their forms they extend the dangerous principle of distributing public money whose expenditure is not subject to control.

In the meantime the majority of women are not yet insisting with serenity and steadfastness upon their legitimate autonomy. It takes a Hetty Green, for example, to keep a woman's fortune from the exploitation of her man. Few women with property have as free an enjoyment of their property as men have, the law and sentiment notwithstanding. They give way. They cannot, as they say, "endure a row." Nor do women insist as plainly as men do on their own tastes and desires. They have to "get round" the man. This is the story the modern novel and play have to tell over and over and over again in thousands of forms, the story of a compeller and an outwitter.

The testimony of contemporary literature seems to be that on the whole the outwitting defeats the compulsion. But it may be that the dominance of the male decision gives us neither plot nor drama, and yet in reality is the more widely prevalent state of affairs. A struggle for the "upper hand," as Samuel Butler describes it in *The Way of All Flesh*, occurs in a great number of pairings. In the past probably a greater proportion of women lost that struggle than at the present time, and it may have occurred more generally. A more intelligent education of children for adult life and sexual relationship, the progressive alleviation of mutual pressure in a broadening social life, and greater facilities to escape from marriage, may go far to eliminate any need for such a painful and intimate struggle in the future.

In a complete summary of human activities it is necessary to bring into the picture that ineradicable class of women, the oldest profession in the world, the prostitutes. The peculiar conventions of the pre-war age required writers to mention this trade only in terms of exaggerated horror. It flourished everywhere, and everywhere there was a pretense that it did not exist. It was outcast, unspeakable, untouchable. Moreover, in all ages the peculiar circumstances of these women have subjected them to legal extortions and illegal exploitation, and in default of the normal male husband-protector, they have had to resort to a variety of illegal defenses. A type of man has been evoked to organize and profit by their necessities. And they have been less able to escape their special disadvantages because within, in their own minds, they were trained and prepared to acquiesce in the traditional standards of feminine conduct.

Let us consider dispassionately what a prostitute is. A prostitute hitherto has usually been a woman, though, as we shall note in a moment, this is not necessarily the case. And her rôle through the ages has been to sell feminine companionship to men who were in urgent need of it for limited periods. Excited moralists have been prone to exaggerate the purely physical side of her existence; those who are better acquainted with the realities of life know that the common prostitute has no particular skill or charm in her caresses, and that the element of sensuous gratification is of hardly more importance to her intermittent relationships than it is to permanent wifehood. If one notes the districts which prostitutes frequent, the social aspect of prostitution becomes apparent. Such women have abounded in seaports since the beginning of time; they walk near railway termini; they are in evidence wherever business brings men up from the country for a stay at some commercial centre; they hover where unmarried men are gathered. Loneliness, loose intervals of time in a friendless place, these call for the prostitute quite as much as gross desire. Prostitutes not only go with these lonely, comfortless men, but they hear their talk, they flatter and console them, they give and receive real friendship and affection. They do not in their normal rôle minister simply to lust; what they sell and give into the bargain is much more than that. It is womanhood. They witness in fact to the inherent dependence of the male mind upon women, of one sex upon the other. They are temporary wives.

But our world has never accommodated itself to this institution of temporary wives, much less has it made any effort to protect them, and so this type of relationship—so inevitable that never in any part of the world has it been stamped out altogether—has been subjected to every possible type of degradation. These women are tolerated and assumed to be intolerable, they are exploited both legally and illegally, prosecuted and persecuted; they are forced down into a festering obscurity where the thief, the bully, the blackmailer and the cruel coward, make life horrible for them. They take a colour from their surroundings, they succumb to the suggestion of their shamefulness; dissatisfied by a perpetual truncation of their friendships, they evoke vile male dependents, and often they themselves become mentally distorted. And across the disorder of their lives is drawn the threat and darkness of those contagious diseases lust transmits. The stigma upon them is so widely appreciated, their dangers are so great, that very few girls or women take to the life voluntarily. They fall into it. So that there has always been a calling, a trade, quasi-illegal, the White Slave Trade, to provoke and tempt and cheat young inexperienced women into it, and to find out, help and exploit those who have offended the established code of good behaviour and so are ripe for enlistment. And naturally the White Slave Trader is active wherever underpaid and insecure feminine labour is to be found.

In our interminable encyclopædia of work and wealth there would be space to discuss in detail the treatment of this persistent social element throughout the ages and in various parts of the world at the present time. It would be an intricate story of confused aims, general muddle-headedness, intolerance, jealousy and cruelty. Almost all its uglier and viler aspects would be directly traceable to the tradition of feminine subjection, and the necessary dependence of women upon some powerful protector. It is possible that in the future, as the equality of men and women ceases to be a mere sentiment and establishes itself in usage and law, there may be a relaxation of interference with the private sexual life of women, and the harsher and socially more injurious aspects of intermittent sexual associations will disappear.

Prostitution in the past has been chiefly feminine. That is not due apparently to any inherent sexual difference. It is a difference in rôle which puts men more in need of casual women. In the past women have stayed at home more than men and have been more firmly kept at home. It is the man, especially the man as traveller, sailor, merchant, soldier or student, who has been driven by the stresses of loneliness and boredom that lie at the base of this business, and who has had the freedom to solace himself. His womankind were driven to obscurer consolation or none at all. But now that types of free and prosperous women are developing, who can travel and get away from the observation and moral support of their own community, the parallel need evokes the parallel supply. The dissipated middle-aged woman is becoming almost as common as the dissipated middle-aged man. In the pleasure resorts of Europe and North Africa one meets now the wealthy lonely American wife or widow, looking for the consolations of masculine intimacy and picking up the "gigolo," the dancing partner, as a protégé, a companion and often a venal lover. She is almost as abundant as the Americans who visit Europe to get drunk. But the drifting, prosperous women are by no means all Americans. The gigolo is entirely the equivalent of the prostitute adventuress at the same social level, but because of the difference in his sexual tradition, no one has yet set about pursuing him with a *police des mœurs*, segregating him in brothels, banishing him from ordinary life and legislating against him. He does not seem in need of protection from Geneva, and the White Slave-Trader finds him an unsuitable commodity.

But if he can take care of himself, surely the ordinary adult woman, if she were given proper treatment as a citizen like any other citizen, could do likewise. The difference in the world's treatment of male and female prostitutes is a very interesting and significant consequence of the age-long traditional disadvantage of women. And of a changing attitude towards the personal sexual life. In that saner, better instructed and franker world to which we seem to be moving, when women will be able to fend for themselves, and will be as free to come and go and do this and that as men are, the peculiar needs, tensions, shames and distresses that have maintained the prostitutes' quarter, the red-lamp district, the Yoshiwara, throughout the ages, may be at last alleviated, and prostitution as a special and necessary aspect of social life, that enduring scar upon the mutual kindliness of the sexes, may be superseded and disappear altogether.

§ 6. *The Power of Women through Reassurance and Instigation. Women's Rôle in Determining Expenditures*

Let us turn now to another aspect of the contemporary relations of men to women which is also of very great economic im-

portance. We have dealt hitherto with the disadvantages of
women in relation to men. We have now to consider their very
real power over men.

It is not exact to say men and women have a need for each
other. They have all sorts of needs for each other. It has already
been suggested that men resort even to prostitutes for much
more than mere sexual gratification. They have a strong need for
a general association with women. Their imaginations require
that, perhaps more than the feminine imagination calls for the
companionship of men. In many cases that desire may change
over to repulsion and misogyny, but hardly any men are indifferent to women. Normally they want to be approved of and liked
by women; they want their acts and successes to be sanctioned
by women; women are the custodians of their self-respect.
Women will observe men and attend to the demands of their
personas, keep them in heart, keep them in countenance, in a
way no man will do.

We write "normally." We are dealing here with the average
commonplace human being, who makes up the body and substance of the economic process. There are exceptional instances,
there are perhaps exceptional races, where the man will watch
and sustain the woman's idea of herself and so determine her
actions in a manner entirely feminine. And many women nowadays woo and flatter other women. But the general situation
is that the woman throws the qualities of bravery, brilliance,
cleverness, generosity, dullness, stupidity, elegance or inelegance,
meanness, baseness or foulness over the various acts of the man.
She owns the moral box of paints. The determination of the
values of an extraordinary number of things rests with women.
Even when they are slaves they are appraising slaves.

This appraising function of women, their power over masculine self-esteem, combines with their real practical ability to
control his social and physical comfort to give them an economic
importance out of all proportion to their legal ownership of
purchasing power. The greater part of the wealth of the world
is still in masculine hands, but a very considerable proportion
of that spending power is controlled by or actually delegated

to women. What, outside actual business needs, purchase of stock, material, premises, general investments and so forth, do men buy? They buy, one may say, railroads, war material, shipping, aëroplanes, public buildings. They buy their own clothes and their sporting outfits. But even when it comes to the railway and steamship, was it the male or the female demand that evoked the train or cabin de luxe? That we will leave an open question. But so soon as we come to actual living conditions, the woman's influence appears. Men may buy the sports car, but the comfort of the ordinary car is the woman's affair. In domestic architecture it is mainly her taste and needs, her consideration for herself and her consideration for her domestic servants, that have to be respected, and still more is this the case when it is a question of furniture. Household equipment and material, all food and her own steadily increasing wardrobe, are almost entirely in her hands. According to some rather sketchy statistics from America, 80 per cent of the shoppers in a large city are women.

This means that women, and especially the women of the more freely spending classes, exercise a great and perhaps a predominant directive influence on productive industry. They call the tune for most perishable goods. Textiles, furniture, building material, catering, are all manufactured and marketed with a view mainly to their satisfaction. They rule the tea shop, they now invade and change the spirit of the restaurant, and in America, where custom closed the drinking saloon to them, they voted and shut it down. The colours and fabrics, the tones and tastes of daily life and who men may meet outside their business and their clubs, and what shall be permitted in social life, are in our Western communities dependent upon their decisions.

So far women have exercised their enormous influence over the quality of daily life, with very little sense of any collective responsibility. It has been done individually with no perception of an aggregate effect. They have set about making homes and making up personalities, and have not thought that they were thereby making a world. Even with regard to their children, they have directed attention almost entirely to their present happiness and personal well-being, and disregarded as entirely the way in which social life as a whole would be affected by their upbringing. I think, if educationists were consulted, they would say that in spite of the immense debt of educational progress to particular women, the general influence of the ordinary mother is often tiresome and rarely directive. Her ideas are limited to immediate things; she notices health, feeding and good manners. The rest she leaves uncritically to the school.

She leaves it uncritically to the school because she has never been taught to ask what the school is for.

This is directly due to the fact that a great majority of women of the spending class are relatively uneducated. They have not learnt to ask what anything is for. So far, the ordinary girl of the more prosperous classes has not been educated as well as her brother, she has not had the stimulus of a professional career, and her instruction has been sooner discontinued. The men and women of the labour classes of the Western world are now fairly on a level in the matter of education, and have for the most part what we have termed in this work a peasant persona or an urbanized or industrialized peasant persona. But when we consider the class which prolongs its education beyond the elementary school stage, we get a much greater number of males who are educated to the level of what we have styled variously the "service" or "clerical" or public-spirited persona. There are more men infected with ideas of service, of professional and class honour than there are women. The woman's persona in the middle and upper classes still falls in most cases into the more primitive classes of peasant or predatory or a mixture of both. The woman of a good social position is peasant-predatory much more often than the man, and she sets the pattern for the main mass of women. Probably we are not dealing with innate sexual differences here, but only with a wide divergence of tradition and a long lag in woman's education. The experiences of the Catholic Church would seem to show that women can be educated to a service ideology as completely as men.

This lag in feminine education which leaves a dominating

majority at the peasant-predatory level, is manifested most strikingly at the milliner's, the costumier's, the jeweller's, and the beauty specialist's. The tradition of service, the process of "impersonalization" through education in the Western world, has made men deliberately inaggressive in their costume, made them at least ostensibly public-spirited, and more and more amenable to official and business and creative preoccupations. This is not a natural thing: it is the result of formal and informal educational influences. The illiterate ancestors of these same preoccupied and creative Western men were more gaudy and splendid in their costume than their contemporary women; they wore conspicuous jewels, dyed their hair and beards, and had little sense of loyalty to anything but a person, prince, king or other leader. Their women had neither the same opportunities for a show or the same chances of getting the stuff. To-day a great proportion of Oriental men retain that disposition of mind, and most Western women are still, as a sex, at the same barbaric stage. Quiet clothes and unobtrusive uniforms are to be endured only under protest, as acts of extreme self-mortification. And as a consequence, if the Western world were all men and the only buyers in the world, the pearl diver and the pearl imitator might now cease from their labours altogether, the dealers in jewelry and precious stones shut up shop, the trapper and hunter wear their furs themselves or go out of business (leaving a happy remnant of fur- and feather-bearing creatures to survive), and the whole great industry of cosmetics and all the costumiers and milliners would tumble into bankruptcy. The sale of splendid furniture for display and of architecture for great gatherings would also cease almost altogether. A few court officials and professional soldiers might still betray a craving for furs, decorations and cosmetics, the secret indulgence of the gorgeous dressing-gown and the vivid pyjamas might intensify, but these demands would be too infinitesimal to sustain all that multitude of workers and arrest the ruin that the disappearance of Western femininity would entail.

And although there is no possibility of Western women disappearing, there is a very strong probability of their standard

of education rising to the masculine level and of a general wes-
ternization of their world. This opens a prospect of women more
gravely dressed and more gravely occupied than at present.
Women may presently want to outshine other women as little
as contemporary men do, and that conception of jewelled,
painted and triumphant gorgeousness which rules our own social
life now only so far as women are concerned, but which still
rules the lives of men and women alike in the courts of most
Oriental princes, will disappear altogether.

Yet to think of gorgeousness disappearing altogether from
social intercourse is almost as painful as anticipating the extinction of humming-birds. Men, under the influence of science,
puritanism and practical convenience, have taken to costumes
as undistinguished almost as modern service uniforms, but those
dressing-gowns and pyjama suits in their outfitters' windows
betray how near to the surface the craving for gorgeousness
remains. The popularity with them of "fancy-dress" balls and
entertainments and of "dressing-up" parties confirms this testimony. Academic costume, the nodding plumes of the deputy
lieutenant and the insignia of various American "orders of
chivalry"—voluntary and unsolicited chivalry—give it further
support. Perhaps the typical modern professional woman already
approaches a quasi-masculine compromise, dressing with the
greatest severity during business hours, and upon occasion expanding magnificently into an evening costume. But these half
private and occasional relaxations into splendour of serious
men and women involve preparations and purchases of a much
more incidental sort than does that sedulous, untiring hunt for
elegance of the essentially barbaric women of to-day.

It has been asserted that a man's conception of his importance
to himself and others seems to be more in his *doing* something
than in his *being* anything; while on the contrary the form in
which women seem to see themselves lies rather in being something than in getting anything done. There is a certain truth in
this if we may judge by the famous figures of our world. The
famous men of our time have done this or that; the famous
women are "personalities." They are ends in themselves; they

exhibit, and it carries nothing forward. If anything is done by them it is a display stunt. They do something a man has done before—charmingly, I admit. These are persons released to some vigour of expression. In ordinary life both man and woman must live under the restraints of common usage, but there is sound reason for assuming that famous people are, in all things except their especial distinction, just ordinary folk let loose. They are fair samples of what most men and women would be and do if they had the same opportunity.

But this difference of doing and being between men and women as it is displayed to-day may not be a real difference between men and women at all; it is much more probably another aspect of the difference between the barbaric and the educated disposition. If that is right, then the reactions between men and women must be undergoing a change now. If woman is to become less of a gaudy incentive to man and more of a companion and collaborator, then her particular rôle of scrutiny, appraisal, encouragement and reassurance is likely to be played far more subtly and penetratingly than ever before. As she becomes less of a prize in a competition, she will become more of a judge of effort. She will have a different influence upon spending and the spirit of spending, and that means she will exert an increasing influence upon getting and methods of getting.

In our study of the working of contemporary financial arrangements we have shown by a concrete instance or so the immense mischief caused by the financial adventurer. Most of our readers know well enough, if only by repute, the sort of individual who flounders through the world of finance to bankruptcy or the jail, leaving ruin in his track. What is the vision that justifies his risks and toil? Essentially it is success in a world of vulgar display, a world ruled by peasant-predatory standards in which the approval of women and power over women play a large part. For them he becomes a divinity distributing the coveted means by which gorgeousness becomes possible. And that woman-made apotheosis enables him to dismiss all compunction about the method by which he has filched, sneaked or bullied his way to wealth. If he has arrived at divinity, he can afford to forget that the means of arrival were in no sense divine. An extensive infiltration of womankind by educated types would make much of the successful adventurer's gorgeousness seem tawdry and its methods of attainment unclean. Such women would bring a new set of social values to bear upon their estimate of personal quality. They would regard the successful peasant-robber not as a hero who had stormed the golden gates of opportunity, but as a greedy and extraordinarily tiresome and destructive parasite upon economic life. They would reveal his affinities to the gangster, pure and simple. All the money in the world in that colder light would not suffice to make him anything better than Clever Alec, the spoiler of things. They would tilt the balance of his self-esteem against him.

§7. *Is a Special Type of Adult Education for Women Needed?*

It may be that the pattern of man's education has been followed too closely in the planning of the feminine equivalent. Because men can be most conveniently trained and educated continuously and progressively from five to twenty-five or so onward, it does not follow that women can be educated in the same continuous fashion. Their phases of maximum educability may occur at different periods of their life history.

Since this idea arises naturally out of a comparison of the masculine with the feminine quality and life cycle, we may perhaps anticipate our Chapter on Education and discuss the implication of this particular suggestion here. The suggestion is that it may prove a better arrangement to have a resumption of definite study by women and the taking on of new tasks and new responsibilities by them round about the ages between thirty-five and fifty. A girl should, of course, be educated from the beginning to look beyond the romantic phase of life, to regard that phase as partial and terminable, to consider the concluding years of life not as a process of growing old—growing out of things, but as a going on to a new system of activities. The loss of youth should not be the tragic thing it is for women; it should

at most be no more tragic for them than it is for men. But it is
a less gradual change in one case than in the other, and their
transition to the really adult phase needs to be more definitely
recognized and made than is done at the present time.

Even where women are not constrained by custom to the
premature acceptance of a sexual rôle, the emergence of sex
seems to affect their lives in the opening phase of adult life much
more fundamentally than it affects the lives of men. It is hardly
too much to say that in the alert and curious-minded girl, possibly more eager for knowledge than a boy of her age, a new
personality is born at adolescence. The change is greater and
more revolutionary than it is with the ripening male. Its onset is
relatively catastrophic. The new personality that emerges may
be domestic, maternal, erotic, or religious, or a mixture of any
of these—the choice will be determined partly by type and
partly by circumstances—but it will be typically an acutely self-
conscious personality and given to dramatizing its performances.
In the course of two or three years this new-born personality
seizes upon its rôle. In the average woman we may go so far
as to say that the new system of interests and emotions for a
time takes charge of her life altogether, thrusting the wider
interests of a human being aside, or rather, making of them a
mere background to this intensified individual personal life.

It may be biologically desirable that women should for a phase
lose touch with broader interests and take themselves thus seriously and intensely as persons, both as lovers and the recipients
of love, as wives and then as mothers; it may be altogether good
that their minds should undergo this narrowing down to and
concentration upon the personal life. In all these intimate rôles
more is required of them to-day than has ever been asked before,
and more still will be required as the level of civilization advances. The mothers of young children, at any rate in the more
forward races, are generally aware of the new responsibilities
placed upon them by modern advances in infant management,
general hygiene, child psychology and educational practice. They
are genuinely anxious to improve themselves. All over England
and America there are circles of women, from the poorest wives

of agricultural and casual labourers upward, who are studying these subjects and finding them enthralling. In fact, this seems to be the most important result so far achieved by the spread of education among women. Whatever else may be said in this chapter on their technical and professional performances compared with those of men, there can be no doubt that their mental emancipation has resulted in happier and healthier nurseries. The little children of 1931, class for class, are better grown, better looking, more scientifically fed and clothed, than children have ever been before, and their minds develop more freely. Let any reader whose memory goes back to the parks of one of our great cities thirty years ago, compare the uncouth and ragged hordes which poured into them when the schools of the poor closed for their holidays, with the friendly and intelligent little creatures who appear to-day. The change is startling; it is due, of course, to many factors, but it could not have taken place without the devoted efforts of the mothers of these children.

What we are now considering, however, is not the children but the mothers. The management of a nursery has never been such a highly skilled job as it is to-day, but it does not go on being a job for nearly as long. In almost all families the girls as well as the boys now go to school—the family itself seldom exceeds four—and by about thirty or thirty-five the modern mother is more or less out of work. The personal life has called her, and the urgent demands of her personal life have been satisfied. And now what is she going to do with the rest of her life, the thirty or forty years which remain?

The answer to this question is naturally dependent upon economic circumstances. If times are hard she will be obliged to dismiss the maid and do her own work, and even though this may leave her with time on her hands, there will be no money for books or fares or subscriptions; she will not be able to get about as one must get about if one is to fill any function outside the home. But if her circumstances are prosperous, then there are two possible roads before her. The majority of middle-aged wives can be carried by the community as parasites or semi-parasites, for the most part either sunk into nonentities or "developing their personalities" by spending as much money as they dare and snatching at their diminishing chances of sensation, or, on the other hand, some rôle, some sort of useful part can be found for them.

At present there is no such rôle for most of these women in the forties and fifties. Their old jobs, if they had jobs before marriage, do not want them back, and there are not nearly enough fresh openings. Individuals of an original turn strike out for themselves and take to charity, religion or politics, but no one who meets large numbers of middle-aged women can doubt that such occupations fail to absorb more than a few of this surplus. Some months ago a leisured woman wrote to the "Home Page" of a London evening paper and asked its readers: "Is there, after forty, any alternative to bridge?" They replied in large numbers, but the only alternatives they could offer were that she should feel ashamed of herself, or count her blessings, or find some blind neighbour to whom she could read aloud.

The instance sounds trivial, but the problem is profoundly important in the developing social life of the world. These millions of underoccupied citizens have votes, control expenditure and exercise great influence on the general body of opinion. If they are to be left to themselves because they are uninteresting, left to a narrow and frivolous personal life, the world is creating for itself a force of ignorance, prejudice and self-satisfaction, an atmosphere of mental stuffiness and sluttishness, which will impede all efforts to clear and widen thought and to build the future upon a controlled and courageous use of knowledge.

Here, it seems, a new development of our educational system is demanded. Here is a remediable waste. Here are great numbers of citizens, emerging from a score or less of vivid years of intense personal preoccupation, anxious to find new systems of interests, desirous as a rule both to be of use and to improve themselves, but failing for the most part to satisfy these wishes. A considerable proportion of these released women, released to complete triviality and ineffectiveness, are extremely unhappy. The widespread nature of their need is indicated by the existence of Women's Institutes of Canada and Great Britain and the

Women's Clubs of the United States. These give some social relief. But there is need for something more systematic and scientific. It should be possible for a middle-aged woman, without feeling that she is not wanted, or making herself ridiculous, or getting in the way of young people, to reëducate herself. She may wish to take up again interests which she has neglected since her marriage. She may wish to extend her range—probably in the direction of some science dealing with human life—politics, economics, education, psychology, hygiene or history—or she may simply want to have some sort of interest taken in her by somebody, to find other people who feel as she does, to be shown how to use her leisure. Even at that, she constitutes an opportunity, she is unused raw material for social organization. She is a citizen, and there is work to be got out of her. She needs, as the automobile people say, "reconditioning" so that she can return to the open road of life afresh.

In the next section we will discuss the possibilities of distinctive work that present themselves to women in the continually more intricate weaving of the modern community, and in our Chapter on Education the nature of the moral and intellectual effort towards a more scientific organization of human society will be examined. In Chapter VIII we have defined what we call the educated persona. As our survey of the mental life of our world develops, the reasons will become more and more manifest why women should regard the highly sexualized and personal years that follow their adolescence as only a phase in their development, and find, in the later acquisition of the educated persona and disinterested work, an escape from this living death so many of them lead now as mere waste products of the social body.

§ 8. Possibilities of Distinctive Work for Women in the Modern Community

In the excited days of feminine emancipation at the close of the last century there was much talk of the changes and marvels that would happen when this ceased to be a "man-made" world.

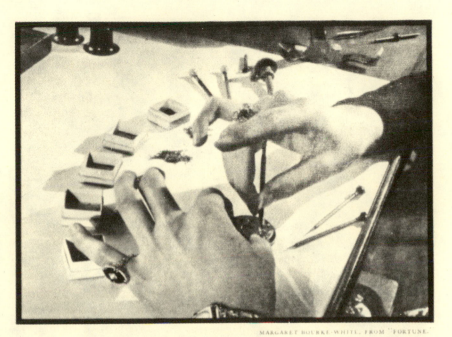

THE HANDS OF THE MODERN WATCHMAKER

THEY are the hands of a woman. In the past they would have been the hands of a man.

WILLIAM RITTASE

A MODERN SILK MILL

THE operator is engaged in one step in the manufacture of stockings. In the background are the weaving frames.

Women were to come into their own, and all things would be the better for it. As a matter of fact, the enfranchisement of women, the opening of every possible profession to them, such legislation as the British Sex Disqualification (Removal) Act of 1919 meant that women were not coming to anything of their own, they were merely giving up their own—or, if you will, escaping from it. And now sufficient time has elapsed for everyone to see quite plainly that women had been not so much emancipated to a new and wonderful distinctiveness as—*despecialized*.

Certain distinctive types of work for woman remain. Everything that cannot be socialized of motherhood; certain forms of work such as nursing, where there is authority without initiative, remain especially hers. She has her distinctive beauty and that power of exploiting the elements of personality which reaches its climax in the great actress. These things are forever hers. For the rest, she is free now to do what she can and find her level. She writes novels and plays, and when she restricts herself to the subtleties of social behaviour and domestic relationship she does better than any man. She pilots aëroplanes and hunts big game with due assistance. She does scientific work; she practises medicine, pleads in the law courts, owns and runs businesses, farms, and the like; there are very few things she does not attempt. A woman captain of a Soviet ship recently came into the port of London. The level of feminine achievement is often high, higher than that of second-rate men, but in none of the open fields, except domestic fiction, can it be claimed that any women have yet displayed qualities and initiatives to put them on a level with the best men in any such department of activity. Outstanding women may presently emerge, but they have not yet emerged. In literature, in art, in the scientific laboratory, they have had a fair field and considerable favour. They suffer under no handicap. But so far none has displayed structural power or breadth, depth and steadfastness of conception, to compare with the best work of men. They have produced no illuminating scientific generalizations. The most successful feminine criticism so far has consisted of temperamental responses and brilliant flashes of personal comment.

It seems fairly certain that women are not going to outstrip men or even to equal them, in the fields in which men are certainly successful. Is there any chance that they may make a special contribution in those directions in which men have so far fallen short of their own feats of mechanical invention and creation—the social fields, politics, administration, education, where interest is concentrated on human life and personality rather than on machinery or abstract thought? *Prima facie*, these are the matters in which one would expect women to display distinctive aptitude. They may have an instinct for management, and their curiosity seems to be naturally inclined towards the practical problems of life rather than mechanisms. Where they exercise political power—as opposed to personal influence over politicians—legislatures have found themselves obliged to take a greater interest in social questions. On governing bodies—in spite of the fact that women are hardly yet placed in such positions for their own sake, but only too often because they are the wives or daughters of some influential man—their work is admittedly of weight. Even if their share in the world movement for peace (see Devere Allen's excellent *Fight for Peace*, 1931) has proved a feeble one, there can be little doubt that Prohibition (with its still unfolding consequences) followed in the order of cause and effect upon their enfranchisement. In politics, as in factory life, they seem disposed to make things cleaner and to throw their weight in favour of open and decent conduct.

Nevertheless, it is only in one country that they seem to be rising to the most responsible type of position, and that is a country where conditions are unusual—Russia. Nearly all facts as to Russia are disputed, but there does seem to be a consensus of opinion that under the stimuli provided there—if the reader pleases he may regard them as monstrous and abnormal stimuli—women are losing some of the characteristics which lessen their usefulness in other countries. They are said, there, to display an intellectual curiosity, a mental energy, as great as that of men. Nobody shrinks from appointing a woman to any position for fear that as a woman she will be timid, personal, unscientific, limited in her outlook. Between the young women and the young men there is said to be no difference in these respects. Women are as free as men to choose what they will do, and they are, in fact, entering everywhere into the administration of the country. In the villages the peasant women sit on the local soviets and, as we have said, serve on the coöperative farms. In the towns they are largely employed as inspectors, welfare supervisors, and assessors and collectors of taxes. There are numbers of them in the army—a few are actually there as soldiers, but the majority either teach the men or are responsible for their health and their living conditions. And they are reported to do this sort of work not only as well as, but on the whole better than, men, showing themselves in this particular range of activities more conscientious and sympathetic and less liable to corruption than male officials. And this in a country where the pre-war percentage of illiteracy among women was 65 per cent.

It is interesting to note that even here, where sex is actually no longer a bar to any occupation whatever, more women than men are studying administration and pedagogy, more men than women, technical subjects, such as engineering.

Yet it has to be noted, in spite of all this, that not one single outstanding figure in the direction of Russian affairs since the Revolution has been a woman. No women leaders have resisted the degenerative processes that have reduced the government of Russia from a group control to the harsh autocracy of Stalin. The opposition of Lenin's widow to Stalin was easily swept aside. No other women rallied to her. For all the releases and exposedness of women in Russia, the Soviet world remains a man-made, man-ruled world.

The change which is said to have taken place in the mentality of women in Russia may be exaggerated. Even if that is so, or even if, though real, it is a sort of adaptive coloration, it will still be interesting to consider the conditions which have produced it.

What are the operative factors?

In the first place, and as a key to the entire explanation, the women of Soviet Russia have to do without comfort. And it is in their homes that discomfort reaches its highest point. The overcrowding is appalling; all attempts at private cosiness are doomed to failure. Everything hopeful, stimulating or interesting is part of corporate life, attaching to the schools, the factories, the workmen's clubs, the communal farms. If you do not come out and mix and share, you have nothing to do but rot. Secondly, it is a time of intense intellectual excitement. Not only is the air full of new ideas, but at any moment some or any of them may be acted upon. In England we have come to rely upon a comfortable time-lag of fifty years or a century intervening between the perception that something ought to be done and a serious attempt to do it. Even in America they have time to think things over if they want to. Russia is obliged to think and act almost from day to day—it is important for a woman to know something of what is being thought, because at any moment it may be upon her, twisting the whole fabric of her life. Lastly, in Russia women are legally equal, and they are really free. They have as many opportunities as men, and as much money; they are mistresses of their own bodies, and very great efforts are being made by means of crèches, nursery-schools and so forth, to enable them to shorten the periods during which economic dependence through maternity is inevitable. Above all, they cannot sell their sex—in Russia it simply is not possible to obtain a life of ease by physical attraction plus a little lying and a great deal of flattery. Or even by steadfast affection, personal loyalty and devotion to home duties. It is not possible, indeed, to obtain a life of ease in any way whatever. What is obtainable is a share in some of the most exciting work the world can offer. There is a whole nation to be taught—9,000,000 women are now taking the special classes for "the liquidation of illiteracy" —healed, organized, inoculated with the new doctrines. Bodily life in Russia may be sordid by Western standards, but the life of the mind seems to be extraordinarily dramatic and stimulating. Moreover, all this woman's work is manifestly wanted. That alone, for many women, must alter the colour of life.

It would be wrong to draw any conclusion from the Russian experiment except that women are adaptable—that in certain circumstances they can shake off that mental sloth and that intense concentration upon their personal lives which obtain in most other countries. It may be that in their hearts they are longing to slip back, that if, at length, the Communist State achieves material prosperity, its women will return with relief to reading fiction and following the fashions. Probably not. For all over the world even though women may not be scaling the higher peaks of achievement, the steady and continuing release of their spirits and the steady and continuing rise in the general quality of their work are indisputable.

It may be that they have latent in them a coöperative steadiness denied to the normally less stable, less calculable, less tractable male. The rôle women have played in assistance, reassurance and instigation has already been discussed in § 6. We return to the suggestions of that discussion here. The future unfolds a prospect of increasing teamwork in which women may have to play a steadying, harmonizing and sustaining rôle. In the past there have been countries and cultures where the support of women has defended religious observances and organizations against disintegration. Women have played the part of a social mortar. They seem able to accept more readily and with a greater simplicity, and they conserve more faithfully. In the more subtly moralized, highly educated and scientifically ruled world-society of the future, that world-society which is the sole alternative to human disaster, such a matrix function will be even more vitally necessary. That, rather than the star parts in the future, may be the general destiny of women. They will continue to mother, nurse, assist, protect, comfort, reward and hold mankind together.

Hitherto the rôle of woman has been decorative or ancillary. And to-day it seems to be still decorative or ancillary. Less frankly decorative, perhaps, and more honourably and willingly ancillary. Her recent gains in freedom have widened her choice of what she shall adorn or serve, but they have released no new initiatives in human affairs. This may not be pleasing to the enthusiastic feminist of the late *fin de siècle* school, but the facts are so. In a world in which the motive of service seems destined to become the dominant social motive, there is nothing in what we have brought forward here that any woman need deplore.

CHAPTER THE TWELFTH

The Governments of Mankind and Their Economic and Military Warfare

§ 1. *Political Organizations.*

§ 2. *A Short Study of the British Government at Work.*

§ 3. *The Permanent Official.*

§ 4. *A Collection of Governments.*

§ 5. *Assent.*

§ 6. *Frontiers and the Official Intercommunication of Governments.*

§ 7. *The Custom House.*

§ 8. *War Preparation as an Industry.*

§ 9. *The Rôle of the Armament Industry in Fostering Belligerence. Sir Basil Zaharoff. Alfred Krupp.*

§ 10. *Spying and Spy Hunting.*

§ 11. *The Service Mentality. Police.*

§ 12. *Passive Pacificism.*

§ 13. *The League of Nations and Other Experiments in Internationalism.*

§ 14. *Projects for Cosmopolitan Synthesis; Necessity Drives Us towards World Controls.*

CHAPTER THE TWELFTH

THE GOVERNMENTS OF MANKIND AND THEIR ECONOMIC AND MILITARY WARFARE

§ 1. *Political Organizations*

HITHERTO, as far as possible, our survey of the human community has ignored political machinery. But we have now reached a point where we must take up the activities of governments and show how this world-wide plexus of work and acquisition and spending that we have spread before our readers is directed and controlled.

We shall still avoid politics so far as advocating measures, taking sides or discussing parties or policies go, but we must ask the reader to keep it clear in his mind that a description of political machinery is no more "politics" than a description of the stage is "drama" or a description of the human nervous system and its working, ethical exhortation. We are telling how things are. If at points they appear ridiculous, the fault is not in the description but in the facts.

And here we come to the broadest reality of the human situation to-day, which is this: that while the material forces man has evoked make, with an air of inevitability, for the unification of mankind into one world system of exchange and mutual service, the direction and control of his affairs is subdivided into a patchwork of over seventy* sovereign states, each theoretically independent of the others, free to go its own way and shape or misshape its destinies as though there existed no foreigners in the world. We have been brought already to recognize the profound evil of this divided control, in the matter of money and credit.

*Counting the United States as one but the British Empire and its Dominions, so far as they are separately represented at Geneva, apart.

Later in this chapter we shall trace the way in which the net of frontiers strangles economic life and keeps the world in constant imminent danger of a war catastrophe. But first, before we go on to this geographical fragmentation of human politics, let us examine some of these seventy-odd governments now in operation and, disregarding the question of frontiers and foreigners for a section or so altogether, consider the efficiency of these centres of management side by side, as it were, with the contemporary aëroplane, dynamo, biological laboratory or steel foundry.

By political organization we mean all the authorized activities that protect, direct, permit or prevent, in the name of the community. The State, in its various ramifications, is the political organ. Political life is the control, or the attempt to control, direct or influence State activities; it comprehends the minister in his bureau, the autocrat, the politician in opposition, the agitator at the street corner, and the conspirator in or out of jail. It is ostensibly if not actually the centralizing process of the community.

§ 2. *A Short Study of the British Government at Work**

Let us approach our first study of an existing government, that of Great Britain, by asking what it has to do, and what sort of arrangements would be made to house and organize it, if we entrusted the task to some intelligent specialist in the layout of industrial plants or the like. For the purposes of our present enquiry we may accept the existing ingredients: the monarch, an "upper" assembly of irremovable legislators, and a "lower" but more powerful body of elected representatives. (No one has ever yet attempted to run a business with an upper and a lower board of directors.) We will also assume the party system and cabinet government as they exist. We shall have a word or two to say about the number of these representatives and the method of their election, but beyond that we will merely consider the

---

*For a more respectful account see Sir Erskine May's *Law, Privileges, Proceedings and Usage of Parliament.*

most expeditious and fruitful way of organizing the energies of
all these factors.

The monarch we may, according to the best English precedents, leave out of our speculations. He is a constitutional
monarch whose responsibility has been taken over entirely by his
ministers. He is a ceremonial figure, the "golden link" of empire. He may not dispute about himself, and so, by an obvious
courtesy, he is above criticism. He is tradition made inert like
the Mace upon the table of the House of Commons.   He—or
rather "the crown"—is a time-honoured symbol of authority,
and there is no reason whatever why a crown should not remain
forever the emblem of authority in the commonweal. That, at
any rate, is the accepted theory and for many reasons we will
refrain from any reflections upon that accepted theory. We will
discuss the processes of British government without the faintest
flavour of lèse-majesté.

Now, first this government must be housed. Our expert would
insist, of course, upon a building of the very newest type. No
great business combine would dream to-day of carrying on its
operations in a building a hundred years old. It would have the
soundest, best equipped structure conceivable, with every possible device and convenience to ensure the well-being and facilitate the operations of its directors. Each of these select and
elected persons would have at least one private room, well lit
and fitted with telephone, special information and news tickers,
properly encased in soundproof covers, works of reference and
so forth. There would be stenographers and dactylographers
swiftly available, and there would be a big, efficiently organized
library with a large and competent staff present day and night to
help and supply information. Airy and pleasant dining rooms,
newspaper rooms and conference rooms go without saying, and
the whole building would be linked by lifts and passages planned
elaborately to economize time and trouble. The administrations
of the various ministries of the State would no doubt be housed
in separate buildings of their own, but each would be represented in the parliament house by a group of offices constituting
the bureau of the responsible minister. The prime minister would

be the chairman of the cabinet, the board of final decisions which would meet in a convenient chamber near his bureau, whenever final decisions were necessary.

The primary function of the elected members of the lower house is to watch and question the proceedings of the ministries and the cabinet. They mediate between the section of the community they represent (and collectively for the community as a whole) and the administration of the ministries. They have also to function in legislation, that is to say, in modifying the functions of the ministries. They would naturally be continually forming and reforming groups for those ends, for the enforcement of protests and suggestions and the drafting of legislative extensions and amendments.

At intervals the upper and lower houses would meet to discuss and decide upon these matters, and for this our government building would have to have debating chambers. Every session in the debating chambers would be convoked for a specific end, *coram populo,* to repudiate a minister or a line of action or to pass a law; it might adjourn, but it would not disperse until it had got its business done. And the need for such debates would determine the number of legislators in either house. There is a minimum below which the various interests of the realm would not be represented; there is a maximum beyond which an assembly begins to take on the lax, vaguely emotional quality, the fluctuations of excitement, and the boredom of a public meeting. These maxima and minima have never been worked out properly, but probably the best size for a businesslike deliberate assembly is somewhere between two hundred and fifty and three hundred and fifty persons. It is no good whatever to encumber government with more members than are needful. The elected house would represent the constituent element of the community, and in a world where distance has been abolished it is obvious that territorial constituencies, except upon a provincial scale, are out of date. . . .

But there is no reason why we should go on with this simple business statement of what is needed for the proper management and direction of Great Britain limited. The reader approaching this subject through museum avenues of business appliances, industrial layout, and rationalization expedients, will be in a position to imagine all the necessary efficiency. Let us, since our concern is not with what men might do but what they do now, turn rather to the actual working mechanism of British government in a period of dire stress and danger for all the world.

Our first intimation of incongruity comes when we contemplate the buildings, the Houses of Parliament, in which this great business is carried on. They do not look in the least businesslike. Nor do they make up in dignity or splendour of feeling what they lack in mechanical efficiency. They look as if a late Gothic cathedral had had an illegitimate child by a Flemish town hall. Even as an exhibition of the Victorian Gothic temperament, the building is less entertaining than (say) the London Law Courts or the Tower Bridge over the Thames.

A closer acquaintance suggests that the architects first designed the exterior and then rather inattentively fitted in an interior. There are the legislative chambers themselves with their lobbies, presidential throne, bilateral arrangement of seats for the "Ins" and the "Outs" in the struggle for office, galleries for admirers, and so forth, and beyond these there are a network of passages and staircases into which open various offices and chapel-like committee rooms devoid of any modern business convenience. The legislative chamber, in the case of the elected representatives, has seats for rather less than half the total number of members. But, of course, since forty-odd hours of oratory per week is more than any but the hardiest can bear to listen to, most of its seats are ordinarily empty. Scattered about the building are a few crypt-like apartments, capable of accommodating perhaps five per cent of the legislators, in which they can work individually with their secretaries. There are, literally, miles of corridors, but only one lift to serve the four floors used by members. Only ministers and under-ministers have rooms of their own. A large proportion of these are of the kind which would be set apart for the use of servants in Victorian dwelling-houses—ill-lit and ill-ventilated. And as the building dates from

Victorian times and lends itself but poorly to modernization, many of them are still fitted with a sacristy containing an ewer and basin for ablution. The ordinary members have only small lockers of the kind allotted to schoolboys in Victorian seminaries for their private books or papers. Every member has a hook all to himself in the cloakroom, and to this hook a loop of pink tape (renewed every session) is tied, in which he can hang his sword! Interviews with visitors from outside must be carried on either in corridors or in one or two underground tea or smoking rooms. There is no modern system of communication between the various parts of the building. As in primitive Africa, human porterage is relied upon as the means of conveying messages, and an hour may easily elapse between a visitor's arrival and the unearthing of the member he wishes to see. What this method lacks in speed, however, it makes up in dignity, the messengers being large and slow-moving men, wearing evening dress even in daylight, and ornamented with large gilt chains and badges after the manner of provincial mayors. Kitchens are interspersed among committee rooms, and for a considerable period every evening favoured regions of the building are pervaded by the sounds and the odours of good, old-fashioned English cooking. These, however, are not the only odours which are distributed by the ventilation. In some mysterious manner the drainage in the Thames contributes an intermittent miasma to a perennial stuffiness. Yet surely, for such important business as is done here, it would be better to drench the workers in super-oxygenated air of the utmost purity. Everywhere, even in the case of kitchens, lockers, smoking rooms and lavatories, an elaborate imitation Gothic scheme of decoration prevails. In his utmost privacy the member of parliament still crouches in a niche.

The building is of a type of limestone exceptionally sensitive to the acids of the London atmosphere, and a touch of eventfulness is given to its façades by the occasional fall of lumps of the decaying stuff. This is most felt upon the celebrated Terrace, a long narrow passage between the building and the river. Here teas are served to members and their friends and constituents, heedless of the occasional avalanches. Here social influence is brought to bear up the legislator, as the student may learn from the still sufficiently contemporary novels of Mrs. Humphry Ward.

The enquiring stranger will naturally wish to be shown the library and the organization for prompt information. He will find three or four rooms lined chiefly with files of State papers and with collections of books on British birds and field sports— dating from the times when the majority of elected members were country gentlemen. True, a selection of the customary reference books to be found in clubs and hotels, and a few recently published political biographies, along with a small shelf of current books from a circulating library, indicate a faint recognition of modern requirements. But no effort is made, even from such pathetically inadequate material as this library comprises, to assemble for the use of members from time to time such books or papers as bear on subjects under discussion in the legislative chamber. There are no research workers, preparing synopses or abstracts of information: no effort, indeed, at all to relate the library, as such, to the specific needs of those who might use it.*

For obscure tactical reasons in the Party Game, the House of Commons consists of 615 members, a crowd too great for free deliberation and too small for mass meeting treatment. When most of them are present, a number must stand and cluster. There are about 760 peers in the House of Lords, about 28 are minors at the time of writing, and most of the others stay away, so that there is not the same congestion. At the risk of seeming farcical to the uninitiated it may be worth while to give some particulars of the way in which the business of a great empire is conducted in this ill-equipped, ill-ventilated and totally unsuitable building.

Every legislative measure must go through several stages of debate in the elected assembly—second reading,† committee, financial resolution (when money has to be found), report, third

---

*No "wireless" is permitted anywhere in the Houses of Parliament.

†First reading has, surprisingly, been abbreviated to a mere formality occupying only a few seconds.

reading—before being sent to the hereditary chamber for further consideration and discussion there. It is the nominal aim of the Ins to keep the debates on each of these stages as short as possible, in order that the promises they have made to the electors may be redeemed at an early date. The ordinary members on their side of the House are accordingly expected to remain silent, leaving it to their leaders to make explanatory statements and reply to the criticisms of the Outs. These latter, on the other hand, since the basic article of their creed is that everything proposed by the Ins is bad, and since furthermore they will, in the ordinary course of events, be outvoted anyhow, aim at lengthening out and delaying the debates as much as possible in order to hinder the Ins from carrying through their legislative programme. The business of talking is on their side, accordingly, not confined to the leaders, but is enthusiastically carried on by as many of their supporters as can contrive to speak for half-an-hour or more without too often repeating what has already been said several times, and without making too apparent their lack of knowledge of—and often indeed, lack of interest in—the subject under discussion. This kind of debating sometimes goes on into the small hours of the morning, sometimes right through the night, the Outs hoping that sheer physical fatigue may force the Ins upon "the rack," to make concessions. The Ins may retaliate by moving and carrying the closure of a debate, but they do this at the peril of being represented (by the Outs) to every elector in the country as enemies of freedom of debate, betrayers of democracy, etc. And although every elector knows that the voting which ultimately decides every question is carried out on strict party lines, and knows, too, that most members do not listen to the debates, he has been trained to the belief that this freedom of debate is a highly important thing, in the vein of Magna Carta and the Bill of Rights.

Recently a small group of members (including Sir Oswald Mosley and Mr. Maxton) became convinced that the economic situation demanded certain urgent remedies, and they did their

A GOVERNMENT BUILDING
IN THE BEST HISTORICAL STYLE

The Capitol Building at Washington, which recalls, by its name and architecture alike, the political traditions of Rome.

THE CROWD REJOICES

THE reception to Colonel Lindbergh in New York City. The air is white with rolls of ticker tape, torn up telephone books and infinite bits of torn paper. One of the principal ways in which New York shows its appreciation of a distinguished visitor is to shower tons of paper upon him.

best to work out how long these urgent measures would take. After the most careful enquiry and computation, they came to the conclusion that the measures immediately needed would take at least ten years of parliamentary time to put through.

This normal routine of parliamentary procedure may not strike the outside observer as an altogether dignified way of giving effect to the national will. But that is because he does not realize with what solemnity and formality it is carried on. There are certain honoured quaintnesses even in the discussion. All speeches must be addressed to "Mr. Speaker," the chairman of the assembly, and other members may only be alluded to by an elaborately circumlocutory form of address. For the convention of addressing the Speaker there is something to be said. It keeps debate impersonal; it prevents wrangling duels and direct insults "as man to man." But the other circumlocutions are a great strain. Ministers and ex-ministers are "right honourable gentlemen"; ordinary members "honourable gentlemen"; members with military or naval posts "honourable and gallant gentlemen"; and members who are also lawyers "honourable and learned gentlemen." Their surnames must never be used, but only the name of their constituencies. Plain Mr. X thus becomes "the honourable and learned gentleman, the member for ———." A similar rule forbids any direct mention of the hereditary chamber, the House of Lords, which can only be referred to as "another place." Furthermore, the proceedings are in costume. On his entry into the chamber Mr. Speaker, who is always attired in eighteenth-century court dress, plus a wig and gown, is attended by another functionary, the Sergeant-at-Arms (wearing a sword to justify his title), who carries the Mace, symbol of the Speaker's authority. This is deposited upon the table of the House, and it is removed as ceremoniously, and placed on two hooks under the table, when the assembly sits "in committee" and Mr. Speaker's place is taken by the Chairman of Ways and Means. There is no rule forbidding general conversation while someone is addressing the assembly; but there are strict rules against a member speaking with his hat on, though he may wear it while sitting.* And although members may walk in and out of the chamber as often as they please, whether anyone is speaking or not, they must always bow to Mr. Speaker or his deputy on entering or leaving. No member may stand in the chamber unless he is speaking, except on a certain marked-off area of the floor which is deemed to be outside the House. If a member's toe protrude across the line of tape (called "the Bar") marking the boundary of this area, he is guilty of a grave breach of decorum, and all those members in the chamber who have witnessed it are expected to chant, "Bar! Bar! Bar!" until the intruding toe is withdrawn. So too, if in the excitement of speech-making he chances to step away from his seat and set his foot in the gangway.

The debates are occasionally interrupted by a message from "another place" demanding Mr. Speaker's presence in the hereditary chamber to hear some message from the King, or to witness the Royal Assent being given (in archaic French—"*le Roy le veult*") to certain measures. The hereditary chamber thus asserts its superiority by compelling the attendance of representatives of the Lower House within its own precincts, while the latter saves its dignity by ceremoniously closing its door in the face of the peers' messenger and obliging him to knock and then knock again and then knock, three times altogether, before he is admitted. He then enters and delivers his invitation, and the Speaker, after repeating in full the invitation which everyone has just heard, heads a procession of members to the "other place." He and they cluster just outside the doorway and remain dutifully standing while the King's message is read. The procession then returns to the elected chamber, and the Speaker reads out the message in full once more.

The method of taking a vote of the members is as deliberate

---

*He must also put it on—or borrow someone else's to put on—if he wishes to rise to a point of order after a vote has been called. Otherwise, hatless, Mr. Speaker would not "see" him. There is much innocent fun when a large-headed member is thus forced to use a small-headed member's hat, or vice versa. The presence of women members has now brought in an added touch of humour when, for example, an eager hatless man finds nothing but a bonnet available to restore him to technical visibility.

as the rest of the procedure. It is processional. (Edison invented a method of voting and counting all the votes in a minute or so without a member leaving his place, half a century ago. In Texas a mechanical voter is actually in use, and the result is recorded in twenty seconds.) Every member must leave his seat in the chamber and walk in queue through the fair way of one or other of two lobbies, the "Ayes" or the "Noes," passing through a sort of wicket, where he gives his name to a clerk, and then through a door where he is counted by two tellers. And so round the course home. When all have been counted, the tellers advance to the table of the House and, after bowing twice, read out their figures. This arrangement occupies from ten minutes to a quarter of an hour, and can even be made to last longer by the adoption of dilatory methods if either side is intent on hindering the course of the debates. Sometimes during the committee stage of a measure, votes on several amendments are taken in quick succession, members spend from two to three hours in a single evening filing through the lobbies.

This registering of his vote is, of course, the most important part of an ordinary member's duties. His efficiency, or other-wise, as a legislator is rated by his constituents according to the number of divisions in which he votes. Since he is seldom in the chamber when a vote is called, Whips appointed by his party are stationed at the door to tell him which lobby to enter and, if he is of the curious, troublesome type, what the voting is about. Apart from voting, his chief opportunity for individual participation in the business of legislation comes during question-time, when, during the first fifty minutes of each day's proceed-ings, he may put questions to Ministers on any matters of public importance. Questions in the main fall into three groups: those put down by the Outs with the aim of embarrassing the govern-ment by compelling them to make a definite statement on some issue about which the government prefers to be indefinite; those referring to matters of local constituency interest, put down by members to advertise to their constituents the fact of their pres-ence in Parliament; and those which genuinely seek information on some point of policy or administration or aim at securing publicity for some genuine grievance.

But the student must not imagine that the private member may ask any questions he pleases. There are intricate rules and regulations about what he may or may not ask and about the form in which his question may be put. You would imagine that somewhere among the pillars and vaults and masonry a small bureau would have been established to which members would take their questions and have them put into acceptable form and passed, but that is not the Westminster way. The Member of Parliament must hand his questions, while debating is in progress around him, to the "Clerk at the Table" who sits immediately in front of the Speaker. He must then stand meekly by, like a schoolboy at the head master's desk, while the official ponders his question and discovers breaches of the rules in it. Having been instructed to alter it, but not daring to ask for any explanation lest he be called to order for brawling under the Speaker's very nose, he goes out and writes out another form of words. And so on, and so on—until the master is satisfied. A sufficiently lucid code of regulations as to the correct phrasing of questions could probably be drawn up in ten minutes and printed on a postcard. But apparently no one at Westminster has thought of this.

If he fails to obtain what he considers a satisfactory answer, our questioning member may announce his intention of raising the matter on the adjournment of the House, that is, after the business of the day is over, late at night, when both he and the Minister concerned are usually too tired to take more than a perfunctory interest in anything, and when, incidentally, it is too late to get any notice in the press of the matter. Or, if he feels acutely about the subject and desires some publicity for it, he may get himself suspended (i. e., expelled from the sittings of the chamber for a week or longer) by refusing to obey Mr. Speaker's order to him to sit down after his question has been dealt with. Then there is a "scene" in the House, which gets duly reported in the newspapers.

Often, when the question is inconvenient to the government,

the member will get no open reply at all. He will be asked to wait while enquiries are made. Unless he is obstinately persistent he may hear no more about the subject. A special report from the department concerned may even be placed quietly in the library at some later date, but he will not necessarily be informed of this, and the information may lie safely hidden on a top shelf or in an obscure cupboard. This, of course, can happen very easily indeed to questions on foreign or colonial subjects, where some time must elapse before replies from the territory concerned can be obtained.

During certain parts of every session one day, sometimes two, in a week are set apart for the discussion of private members' motions or bills (which of them are thus discussed is decided by ballot). But as there is practically no likelihood of these debates influencing the course of legislation already decided upon by the government, they may be regarded as academic exercises, of use only to those members who desire practise in the art of speechmaking.

We have noted the phases through which a bill must pass before it goes to "another place." That is only half its career. After the Commons it must go through similar stages in the House of Lords. But here business is expedited somewhat, and their lordships rarely sit longer than from tea-time to dinnertime.* (Voting is carried out in the same way as in the Commons, except that the lords, instead of being divided into "Ayes" and "Noes," declare themselves "Contents" or "Not Contents.") If a bill is passed by the lords it needs only the Royal Assent to become an Act of Parliament. In the event of the lords rejecting a bill, the commons may pass it again, this time with a minimum of formality and discussion; and if they repeat this procedure a year later, and again a year after that (which assumes that the Ins have not become Outs in the meantime), the bill becomes law without the consent of the lords.

The parliamentary session has a variable length, but is never less than a year (about eight months of actual sitting). It is

---

*They have, of course, no budget or estimates to deal with, entire control of finance being vested in the Commons.

opened by a King's Speech, written, of course, by ministers, which outlines in brief the programme of forthcoming legislation. This speech is read by the monarch himself to the assembled lords and commons, and the occasion is marked by a large amount of pageantry, with Gold-Sticks-in-Waiting and Gentlemen of the Household greatly in evidence.

At the end of the session all incomplete bills are dropped entirely. This is called the "Massacre of the Innocents" by "old parliamentary hands." Every scrap of work done upon these frustrated measures is absolutely wasted. Everything must begin again at the next session—the same stages, the same speeches, the same arguments, the same indignation—all over again.

For traditional reasons of a complex type, the government is regarded as a solid body of inseparables. If the members want to get rid of an incompetent minister of finance, they cannot do so without turning out the entire government and breaking off every other ministerial activity in progress. A prime minister, defeated or in a bad temper, may decide to advise the King to dissolve parliament, and then back go the affairs of the nation, in all their complexity and incompletenesses to the general population, under conditions we will consider a little more closely in our section on Assent.

Such are the machinery and working of the supreme government of what is still the greatest empire the world has ever seen. Our most effective comment is to turn our eyes for a mere instant back to Mr. Ford making motor cars, or to the mechanisms described at the end of Chapter IV.

The fact that the British Parliament is ceasing to be an efficient instrument for the government of a modern community has become so patent and painful to the more intelligent among politicians themselves that we find both Mr. Winston Churchill —who has sat in both Conservative and Liberal Cabinets—and Mrs. Sidney Webb—the wife of a Labour Cabinet Minister— putting forward schemes for its reform. Their plans have something in common: both start by pointing out that whereas the problems which confronted our ancestors were conceived in political terms, those that concern us to-day are mostly economic in character. And neither writer is able to regard our present House of Commons and House of Lords as suitable assemblies for the discovery or expression of economic truths. Mr. Churchill in his pamphlet "Parliamentary Government and the Economic Problem" states the position succinctly. What the peoples demand to-day, he says, is more prosperity. They ask to be delivered from "the new punishment—the Curse of Plenty"—a state in which they find themselves starving in the midst of world-wide "over-production." But the remedy he proposes for this is not particularly drastic. He wishes to set up an Economic Sub-Parliament, subordinate to Parliament, appointed by the party leaders in proportion to the number of their followers in the House of Commons. These appointed members are to be possessed of "high technical qualifications"—that is, they are to consist of "40 members of the House of Commons experienced in economic subjects, and 80 business men, Trade Union representatives or economic authorities" among whom should be "not less than 20 members of the House of Lords." And the work he wishes them to do is to take over, with the consent of the House, bills which have passed their second reading, or any other bill or clause which they may be asked to consider, and debate them with fearless detachment from public opinion —and, one imagines, though he does not say so, equally fearless detachment from the opinion of the party leaders by whom they are appointed.

To this scheme one might put forward the objection that what is wanted is no mere discussion of bills after their principles have been settled, but a wider general knowledge of economics. The Macmillan Committee was a committee of experts of great brilliance and the highest standing. It was asked to advise on the financial policy of the country during the present crisis. In July, 1931, it reported that it is absolutely vital that a policy should be adopted which will tend to raise world-prices and increase consumption. In August, 1931, a National Government was formed in order to carry out a policy of checking consumption and forcing prices down still further. As we write efforts are being made to carry this out with the minimum of Parliamentary voting or discussion. In such a vortex what would happen to the straw of Mr. Churchill's economic parliamentary sub-committee?

But the main objection to his scheme, as our readers will have told themselves, is that economic problems are international. What is necessary is not that Trade Unionists and business men and members of the House of Lords shall have still another opportunity of stating their opinions, but that governments themselves shall consider their economic measures from a world point of view. The time to take expert advice is before the principles of bills are decided, the advice that is needed is that of real experts, and the danger to be overcome is that the present rules of the British democracy are too ignorant of finance and economics to be able to either understand or to criticize their pronouncements.

Mrs. Webb's scheme goes further towards meeting the first of these objections. She would have the range of questions which are generally called social removed from Parliament altogether and handed over to an elected National Assembly together with the government departments concerned with their administration. This would have great advantages. It would relieve the pressure on Parliamentary time. It would mean that there was a far greater chance of bills being voted upon by people with some interest in their contents—the division into social questions on the one hand and foreign affairs, defense and imperial questions on the other does correspond to two different types of politician. It would revive cabinet government, which is made impossible at present by the sheer amount of work to be done. The weak link of the scheme is finance, which Mrs. Webb would leave in the main to the old Parliament after handing over certain sources of revenue to her National Assembly. Finance nowadays, as we are being sharply reminded, is more than the mere spending and raising of taxes. It is impossible to decide on wages or hours or unemployment insurance without reference to international money questions. And an assembly which had no responsibility for foreign affairs might tend to be even more insular than the existing Parliament. The parliaments of the future, if the world is not to relapse into chaos, must regard themselves as the local organs of the world state, and reforms which do not envisage this must fail at an essential point.*

§ 3. *The Permanent Official*

But does so clumsy, antiquated and slow an administrative machine really govern? The answer is that, except in a very broad and qualified sense, it does not. It has been partially superseded, just as the monarch has been almost entirely superseded, by other agencies. The King parades on public occasions as the head of the State. The members of the government parade as his responsible advisers. But what does not parade, and what is altogether less obvious to public observation, is the organization of departmental officials. A large and increasing share in government falls to this stratum of active workers, and it becomes necessary, therefore, that we should consider the rôle of administering and interpreting the law that falls to them.

Under all governments there has been this class, since civilized communities began. They were scribes, they were viziers, they were chamberlains and chancellors, they appear in endless variety, beside and behind the throne and spreading out over the administered country. A history of the Civil Service in Egypt throughout the dynasties has not yet been written. Probably Professor J. H. Breasted could tell us as much about it as anyone. There are studies still to be made of the Civil Service of the empires of Mesopotamia also, and we know far too little of what is to be known of the Civil Service of the Roman Empire. The thousands—generation after generation; I suppose it amounts altogether to millions—of men in these services, whose names are now for the most part forgotten, have held the machinery of civilization together and kept it going through-

---

*For a fuller development of the matter in this section see the chapter on Political Institutions in Laski's *Grammar of Politics*.

out the ages. Civilization could no more have existed without them than a human body without a nervous system. I would suggest that one of the chief contributing causes of the collapse of the great Mongol empire of the early thirteenth century and of the Arab empire of the eighth, so that they were blown out and burst like paper bags, was largely due to their inability to develop any effective civil service over the vast areas of their conquests in time to consolidate them. Some historians dwell upon the political incapacity of Mongol and Arab—perhaps unjustly. When the Mongol came upon an established machine of government in China, when the Arab found the same thing in Persia and Egypt, and the Turk in Byzantium, they founded enduring empires. Or rather, they took them over—and were taken over. A time may come when history, grown more penetrating, will have more to tell about clerks and less about conquerors.

In our analysis of the motivation of the human community in Chapter VIII, we gave some broad indications of the development and variation of the priestly persona. The departmental official, far more even than the teacher and the man of science, is in that tradition of honour and devotion. He has definitely put adventures in gain behind him. He is far more restricted in that respect than the official in any public utility or industrial enterprise run for profit. The latter type does for many reasons tend to assimilate to him as the scale of business enlarges, but the private official is generally more enterprising and bolder in accepting responsibility. The chief accusation against the public functionary throughout the ages has also been the chief grievances against priesthoods, conservatism; he is overdisposed, it is said, to follow precedents and refuse risks.

In the last two or three paragraphs suggestions have been thrown out for at least three enormous books. It is the privilege of a work like the present one to make such demands. Let us now ask for yet another great volume, with appendices and all complete, which shall be a full and careful study of the history, working and psychology of the British Civil Service for the last hundred years. It would be a most valuable and directive addition to the political science of the whole world. It would analyze problems at the very core of an organized world state.*

Great Britain, struggling with the unprecedented problems of an expanding industrialism at home and a spreading empire about the world, made its first break with patronage in 1856 and introduced a method of open competition for entrance to Hailey-bury College, leading on to the Indian Civil Service, which was further developed into a system of open competition for most home Civil Service appointments in 1870. There had been qualifying examinations for Haileybury since 1813, but not open competition. Open competition was really a primarily important innovation in administrative structure, and the outcome of a long and sustained discussion that had been going on for half a century. To Jeremy Bentham (1748–1832) we must ascribe the launching of this idea. His *Official Aptitude Maximised and Expense Minimised,* which was part of his great incomplete *Constitutional Code,* was a scheme for competitive examination for official appointments. The idea was supported vigorously by Sir Charles Trevelyan and Lord Macaulay. The speech of the latter upon the Indian Civil Service Charter Act in 1833 was a masterly statement of the case for the new method. The Indian Civil Service Charter Act in the days of Company rule in India was renewed every twenty years, and when it came up again in 1853 this great innovation was applied to India. A committee, Sir Charles Trevelyan's committee, sat from 1849 onward to bear fruit at last twenty-one years later. So the first modern civil service was born. The method of selection by open competition, hitherto unheard of in the Western world, has created a civil service, with a body of upper officials of a new and better type, singularly free from personal and party ties, exceptionally intelligent and intellectually enterprising. It lets in the "rank outsider" of ability and energy: that is its supreme merit.

No doubt the system of examination is open to very great

---

*Dr. Finer, of the London School of Economics, has published various studies. An excellent, clear book, not too long, and full not only of fact but suggestion, is his *British Civil Service.*

improvement. The "subjects" to which marks were and are most heavily assigned in the competition are subjects remote from the realities with which the competitors will have to deal. It is possible for a Treasury clerk, for instance, to be blandly ignorant of economics, social and administrative science and psychology; he learns his business from the files of his department and is all too apt to absorb the shibboleths and habits of thought of the City financiers with whom his duties bring him into contact. He has not the assurance and strength of scientific knowledge, and the City he should dominate, assimilates him. Good as the official by competitive examination is, an insistence on the social and political sciences as of dominant importance in his success would certainly make him better.

This new civil service presently revealed a spirit of enquiry into the objectives of government such as no other civil service had ever before displayed. It produced a novel ideology. Fabian Socialism is essentially a product of the British Civil Service. Both Sidney Webb (now Lord Passfield) and Sydney Olivier (now Lord Olivier) were among the chief creators of that school of nonrevolutionary administrative socialism, socialism by evolution. They were both civil servants, and it would be difficult to estimate how far the ideology of social reformers and public servants throughout the world at the present time has been affected by this remarkable initiative. Closely associated in its beginnings with the Fabian Society and with the activities of Webb and his brilliant wife, is the London School of Economics, still the most vigorous and efficient centre of modern social, political and economic thought in the world. These initiatives are, we say, in a large measure by-products of the new British Civil Service; the expression of its bolder and more innovating spirits. They are cited here as evidence of what is possible and not of what is general as yet in the new type of civil servant. But each sweep of the competitive scythe brings in with the rest, a contingent of original minds. The majority of British permanent officials have proved less lucid and outspoken than these outstanding figures. They have done the tasks put before them without any overt excursions into general political suggestion, but their circumstances must dispose them to a very similar way of thinking.

Behind the antiquated and sometimes almost farcical forms and procedures of the British monarchy and parliament there now stands this stable organization of experienced and competent permanent officials, protected from the attacks of powerful and influential persons and legally excluded from party politics.

From top to bottom there are now almost 310,000 national civil servants in Great Britain; twenty times the number at the beginning of the nineteenth century. In addition there are 120,000 state industrial workers. Side by side with these there are the independently recruited local government officials (of the county councils, etc.) amounting to about the same total, to whom the principle of competitive examination has been as yet only partially applied. That 310,000, we must note, includes a multitude of postmen and suchlike subordinates with hardly any directive influence whatever. It is in the upper division chiefly that the vital and directive minds are to be found, a few hundreds (*circa* 1200) of them in all, but hundreds of extraordinary importance in the working of the governmental machine.* The politicians manœuvre against each other, fight their party battles in the country, repeat their catchwords, make their vast absurd promises and win their way to office. There they find themselves in the presence of complex administrative problems for which they have neither the necessary knowledge nor the aptitude. They find themselves nominally heads of departments but in reality intermediaries between departments they cannot handle and the enquiring private member. The newly appointed minister says unto this man go, and he goeth—but the minister never finds out how he manages to go; and to another come, and he cometh —with a dossier of documents sufficient to dismay the stoutest politician that ever shouted on a platform. The legislator can-

*There are four grades of British civil servant, responsible for taking decisions under a minister, with the following approximate membership: 1,150 administrative, 4,350 executive, 6,500 technical and scientific and an inspectorate of 2,150.

not legislate without the help and instruction of his departmental staff. Between procedure on the one hand and the departmental official on the other the Member of Parliament and even the Minister is a sorely baffled man. He came to exercise power, and he finds himself not so much carrying on as being carried on.

It is impossible to overstress the significance of this modern type of civil service, which is neither elected from below nor appointed from above, but which emerges by a system of examination from the educational organization of the country. Elected, it would be, like the politician, merely a reflection and an exploitation of the self-pushing peasant type; appointed, it would be servile to the masterful predatory adventurer. It must be evident that in no section of the community is a modern ideology and a creative disposition of mind of greater importance and effectiveness than among these permanent officials. As the world of scientific workers emerges from the clerical traditions of the past, so also is the "trained" and "expert" official likely to emerge. They will be kindred types of similar origin.

We are still, so to speak, only in the first generation of the competitive civil service type, and already it is clear that it has a mind of its own. That distinctive mind is likely to develop to quite formidable proportions in the years ahead and to modify our conceptions of government and governmental possibility profoundly. And, though this is anticipating certain ideas we shall develop rather more fully later, it may be extraordinarily helpful to international coöperation in the future, if the meetings and interchanges of civil servants of different countries could be facilitated and multiplied. The meetings of the "great statesmen" of various nations at Geneva are apt to be rather like the casual meetings of Guys in the London streets on the Fifth of November. The things flap about with their great eyes goggling at the photographers and reporters. The General Election bonfire will come sooner or later, and the next meeting may be of quite another pair of Guys. But the permanent official remains and returns and grows in significance.

§4. *A Collection of Governments*[*]

It was rather amusing in § 2, even though it may have seemed a little irreverent to some of our readers, to survey the sacred procedures of the British Parliament in the light of modern rationalization. Manifestly we were dealing in this instance with a very old-established and intensely self-satisfied body. It has muddled along in the sunshine of British good luck for so long that it is still saturated with the idea that the sunshine is the outcome of its own peculiar virtues. It palavers, it plays its little slow game of processions and ceremonial, it rejoices in its leaders and "characters," it delays and obstructs human progress—with an unsullied conscience. Since the social machine does in a manner get along from day to day, and since the permanent official is relatively invisible, the public shares this delusion of the politician's essential importance. And there is no fundamental difference in quality, though there may be differences in degree, when we turn from the British government to other contemporary sovereign powers.

We find, for example, the government of the United States aloof from all the vital centres of American life in the District of Columbia. Washington has the better of Westminster at least in the possession of a comprehensive and admirably administered library. But the contact of the individual Congressman with the executive ministries is even more remote than that of the British Member of Parliament, because neither the President nor the Ministers he has selected sit in the House of Representatives. There is, therefore, no question time at Washington. The President may or may not assemble his Ministers after the fashion of the British Cabinet. There are 435 members of the House of Representatives; they sit for two years and legislate or serve on various standing committees which communicate with parallel committees of the Senate and with the ministries (de-

*A very readable, good little book on the subject of this section is *Parliament* (*History, Constitution and Practice*), by Sir Courtenay Ilbert. It is a pre-war book now brought up to date (1929). A more extensive study will be Dr. H. Finer's *Theory and Practice of Modern Government,* still in the press as this is being written.

partments). The individual Congressman may be even more ineffective and evanescent than the British Member of Parliament. He may feel even more like an uninvited stray dog in an unfamiliar house. Unless he is *in* with the party bosses, the rules of procedure paralyze him completely.

The Washington Senate is, however, a very different sort of body from the Assembly. There are ninety-six Senators at Washington, two for each state, who sit for six years, thirty-two are replaced or reëlected biennially, and the Senate is therefore, quite apart from its constitutional powers, a more permanent, homogeneous and effective body than the Lower House.

The framers of the Constitution contrived a complicated system of interlocking vetoes to prevent any possibility of convulsive political acts. The President may veto legislation, the Senate must endorse by a *two-thirds* majority every treaty with a foreign power. All save the minor processes and undertakings of American representatives abroad therefore are provisional and conditional upon the assent of the Senate. This has provided some stupendous surprises for the European mind, as, for example, the repudiation of the League of Nations by the Senate, after nearly every chief avenue in the European capitals had been rechristened Avenue Wilson. From first to last a European Foreign Office is never quite clear about what it is dealing with in America. Behind this formal government again move those great shadowy monsters, the Democratic and Republican party organizations. They become incarnate in Conventions; incarnate, they are seen to be creatures of frenzy and unreason. They produce "platforms" which straddle and evade every real issue, they menace, they make, and they break all the actors upon the Washington scene. They developed mainly between 1830 and 1840, they underwent great transformations through the Civil War, and they have ever since controlled the Washington government. They are in effect now as much the real government of the United States as Mussolini is at the time of writing the uncrowned King of Italy. The President is first and foremost a party man. He has been for a hundred years. He does not stand in the shoes of George Washington. He stands on one of his shoes. Moreover, this government at Washington is a government whose powers are strictly limited and defined. It has no concern over such (now) world-wide concerns as labour legislation, marriage, divorce and general morals, public health, mineral resources, water power, company law, bankruptcy, insurance and education. These are affairs for the eight-and-forty sovereign governments constituent of the Union.

Senate, House and President are elected at different times for different periods. Hence a President, for a part or the whole of his term, may be confronted by a hostile Assembly.

At Washington and in each of the eight-and-forty state capitals, just as at Westminster, there centres a civil service organization. On the whole, the American Civil Service is not so stable and competent as the British equivalent. It varies in quality from state to state. The Federal Civil Service developed late in American history, and to its delayed and hampered development many weaknesses of the American government are to be ascribed. A hundred years ago the party machines, those two great party organizations behind the ostensible government, which actually dominate American politics, laid hold of Civil Service appointments and used them boldly as party bribes and rewards. No qualifications were exacted from the candidates for office, their salaries were taxed to contribute to the party funds, and, subject to the Four Years' Tenure of Office Act of 1820, they went in and out with their party.

This unfortunate arrangement has not only hampered the development of a great modern civil service in America, but it has introduced a perverted realism and a criminal bitterness into American party politics unknown in the British world. The gangster has stood close to the politician for a century. President Garfield, for example, was assassinated by a disappointed political gangster, and under one administration, a revenue service, appointed on this "spoils system," robbed the federal government of $75,000,000. After fifty years of ineffectual discontent, and following upon the shock of President Garfield's murder, the public rebelled, and the Federal Civil Service Act of 1883 (followed speedily by similar acts in the states of New York and Massachusetts), laid the foundations of a civil service in America adequate to the needs of a great modern community. Other states, however, still clung to gangster party officials, and only after 1905 did a new wave of purification sweep Wisconsin, Illinois, and several other states onward towards civilized civil services. And there at present things remain. The rest of the states have not been swept.

The Federal Civil Service Act itself was not altogether comprehensive; it excluded a number of appointments, higher grades of postmastership, collectorship of customs and inland revenue and other administrative offices, which remain to this day party jobs subject to both appointment by the President and confirmation by the Senate. (If the President makes an appointment in defiance of party feelings, the Senate may not confirm. He must parley and choose again. Generally the President does not make these appointments at all, but leaves it to the interested Senator or party boss.) Because of this exclusion from the Acts there still remain in the United States about 17,000 federal officials of no particular competence, subordinating their proper duties to party intrigue. But the bulk of the Federal services (about 700,000 posts) is now carried on by permanent officials.

The struggle of the United States to establish and maintain scientific standards in these matters is by no means ended. The Senate clings obstinately to its patronage. The examination for even the higher grade appointments of the Federal service, says Graham Wallas, are not nearly so severe as the British, and for that and other reasons, they do not attract as good a type of man from the universities. It is a specialist's examination; it does not test general education and intelligence. In that respect the British conditions err on the other side. The pay in relation to the prevailing standard of life is low, and there is no effective superannuation. There is not the same career for an able man. The civil servant is not respected. He may be treated with great popular ingratitude. Citizens lack respect for the administration, and over great areas lawlessness prevails because the public services do not command respect.

And yet nowhere is this lawlessness absolute. In human affairs nothing is ever as good as it ought to be and nothing is ever as bad as it might be. Men may be crookedly appointed and still feel a sense of duty. There may be party politicians who may believe they are supporting the right thing—if a trifle subtly and indirectly—and at times they may even be roused to see that they get the right thing. Everywhere men value good report. In spite of every adverse force, the American nation is developing, slowly but surely, and in its own fashion, that essential organ for a modern state, a powerful and efficient civil service. Political entanglements notwithstanding, there are points upon which American public organization already compares favourably with any European parallels. The technicians, the economists, medical men, architects, chemists, draughtsmen and so forth, seem to be more severely chosen and chosen more definitely in relation to what they have to do. The prevalent hard thinking about efficiency methods permeates governmental work. There is not the same gap in sympathy between business procedure and public functionaries that we find in Great Britain. Professional organizations (of engineers, accountants, architects, e. g.) seem bolder and more vigorous and influential in America than in Europe, and make themselves better felt in the direction of public affairs.

When we turn to France we find a fine civil service (with which, in contrast to the British and American instances, the educational organization is combined), still rather disheartened and demoralized by an extensive reduction of salaries and prestige through the revaluation of the franc. The same thing has happened in Germany. Before the war the German bureaucracy was a very powerful body, appointed from above and responsible, says Finer, to no one but its conscience. It was appointed only after the most thorough education, selection, and probation—a system with two hundred years of history. It had public prestige of the highest degree, and a high tradition of efficiency, service, and liberal reform. It was sometimes overbearing, but just and clean. It was the state-conserving element in the Revolution of 1918 and the reaction of 1923. In spite of the temptations and tactics of political parties, it still preserves its professional dignity and capacity and becomes now more conscious than ever that it is the essential institution without which Germany must fail.

But we cannot embark here upon even the most elementary description of the working of the French or German governmental machinery. Or of any other governments. Treatise beyond treatise would arise. It was Aristotle, the Father of Systematic Knowledge, who made the first collection of governments (158 of them) as a supplement to his *Politics*. (Of this collection only the *Constitution of Athens* survives.) In that vast encyclopædic museum which overshadows our book there would be a complete display of the constitutions and methods of legislation and administration of mankind, it would be the list of Aristotle brought up to date. There the student would contemplate the housing and organization of the inkpot-throwing parliaments of eastern Europe (the members of the Mother of Parliaments have no inkpots handy), the highly disciplined Fascist legislature, to which Fascists only may be elected, the new parliamentary or pseudo-parliamentary organizations of China and Persia and Turkey, and those mass meetings which figure as parliaments in Soviet Russia.

I visited the Russian Duma in 1914; it conducted its deliberations in Potemkin's old riding school under a colossal portrait of the Tzar, enormously booted, and was otherwise a very good imitation of a modernized Western parliament, with priests and women among its members; and I visited and addressed the Soviet of the Commune of the North in Leningrad in 1920. That was a vast meeting of a couple of thousand people or more, a meeting completely dominated from the platform; and proceedings culminated in the showing of an anti-Imperialist film of Zinoviev and Zorin visiting the Caucasus; after which the assembly dispersed emotionally singing the "Internationale."

At Moscow I visited Lenin in the Kremlin, and I had a glimpse of the administration of one or two government departments. I got an impression everywhere of casual and amateurish administration. The post office was completely out of gear—I saw youthful stamp collectors, entrusted with letter sorting, picking foreign stamps off the envelopes of letters at the frontier bureau—and the new régime had practically taken over the personnel and methods of the Tzarist police. There never had been much of a civil service in Russia, and to a large extent its function (in 1920) was being performed by members of the Communist party, who sat in slovenly requisitioned rooms, and made up in zeal for what they lacked in efficiency. Possibly this improvised civil service has learnt much in the last ten years, but Stalin, who has succeeded the scientific-spirited Lenin, seems to possess all the vindictive romanticism of a typical Georgian, and his methodical removal of one after another of Lenin's trusted lieutenants cannot fail to injure and cripple the working of the huge new politico-economic machine he is trying to create. One symptom of inefficiency is the constant trials and frequent executions of officials and experts that still go on. The methods of terror, says H. R. Knickerbocker, still rule in Russia. The Terror in Russia has lasted thirteen years. It is a cruel and wasteful substitute for civil service morale.

But we cannot, we repeat, expand the catalogue of constitutions and administrations here. Those who are bent upon human unity and the great peace of the world must needs spend some pensive moments over this imagined gallery of contemporary governments at work, before they go on with our argument. This assemblage of creaky, clumsy, primary governing machines with their underpaid, corrupted or underdeveloped civil services, their encumbering traditions of procedure and their obstinate inefficiency, this miscellany of machines, all different, without "interchangeable parts" or any arrangements for interlocking, constitute at present the only available legal apparatus for regulating and reconstructing the common affairs of mankind. Our hope of a satisfactory substitute lies manifestly in the unobtrusive evolution of a series of scientifically organized civil services with ideas of world administration in common.

A very important and necessary linking system between the official civil services and the general activities of the developing modern community, Finer points out, is foreshadowed by what he calls vocational associations, such organizations as trade unions, federations of this or that industry, chambers of commerce and the like. On the one hand, such bodies can influence and instruct elected legislators directly; on the other, they are called in by the Civil Service before laws are drafted. They can coöperate in the work of special committees. More and more of the real administration work of modern governments is carried on by accessory committees. Such advisory committees before the departments as the German Economic Council, the French Economic Council, the English Economic Advisory Council, are all organized (if rudimentary) arrangements to supplement the work of Parliament by more effective consultative methods.*

§ 5. *Assent*

Let us for a section revert to the elementary psychology of human association with which we have already dealt in Chapter the Eighth. It has been difficult to consider the existing governments of mankind from the point of view of an efficient discharge of function, without a note of derision creeping into the account. That note will pass into dismay and monstrous foreboding as this chapter proceeds to the consideration of international relations and the clumsy dealings of these inept governments one with another. But when we consider them, not from that point of view, but as aspects in the slow, progressive adjustment of a very ego-centred and recalcitrant animal to social life, the calm of biology returns to us, we see how inevitable these evils were, and the flavour of exasperation and indignation fades out of our description.

Before we take up the activities of war and the mutual injuries of states, let us seek an explanation of this outstanding ineptitude which still pervades political life and which contrasts

---

*Finer's book on *Representative Government* (1923) broke new ground in this matter. Since then Child's book on *Labour and Capital* in their relations with Parliament has analyzed the situation in the United States more closely and exhaustively. There is a compact and very suggestive discussion of these general administrative issues in Sir Arthur Salter's *A Scheme for an Economic Advisory Council in India.* 1931.

so vividly with man's present scientific and industrial achievement. Why are our ostensible governments so manifestly inferior in their working and adjustments to railway engines or telephone exchanges?

The answer is latent in the account we have given of social origins. Man, we have to reiterate, is social in spite of himself. He is by nature self-centred, fierce and resentful, and to make up society it has been necessary that he should be educated, cajoled and subdued. Fear, superstitions and the gods, religions, histories, initiations and educations, example and precept have all played a part in the complex, always imperfect, process of breaking him in to collective life. Beating, promises, flattery and training have each contributed to win his assent to his rôle in the scheme of things, his willing participation in the give-and-take of the community.

In the smaller, simpler, stabler cities and states of the past, it was possible to browbeat and accustom ordinary people to the obediences and coöperations of collective life. The community carried on. If any chose to be recalcitrant, disapproval and compulsion of a practicable sort were close at hand. If in return the ruler proved too oppressive, a straightforward revolt and a change of ruler could occur and clean up the situation.

But with the growth and increasing complexity of modern communities, assent became a less simple matter. Government became distant, it became distant in space, and it receded from popular view behind a growing thicket of intermediaries. It ceased to feel the fluctuations of individual assent. Britain lost her American colonies because, weeks and weeks away across the Atlantic, men could get together and say freely what they thought of taxation by Westminster, while Westminster unaware could do nothing to suppress them or reconcile them. The French monarchy collapsed because France beyond Versailles would not assent to continually increasing taxation. Most of the social and political stresses of the past three centuries have been due to the dissentience of people out of touch with, and refusing assent to, governments. The nineteenth century, from first to last, was experimenting with representative democracy in the hope of sustaining the minimum of assent necessary for the working of a continually more extended, detailed (and more costly and taxing) governing machine.

On the one hand the traditional ruler was relinquishing more and more of the detailed application of power to the skilled or routine-guided official, while on the other he was still held responsible for all this increasing amount of government. So he found himself in continually greater need of the general assent of the community. The modern politician has arisen, in effect, to meet the needs of this situation. He is a dealer, a merchant or broker in assent. He lives by assent. He gathers it in, or makes believe to gather it in, from the vague and fluctuating masses of the great modern community, he consolidates it, or seems to consolidate it, always with a view to the approval of the assenting mass and a continuation of its favours, and so he transmits it to the officials, police, teachers, tax-gatherers, judiciary and so on. He interprets to the officials what the community approves and what they may do, and the officials inform him upon what issues the community needs to be instructed and directed. He has to pose as giving orders to the one and inspiration to the other. He is something quite different from a Roman Imperial statesman, an oriental vizier, or a statesman of the Middle Ages. One must go back to the city democracies of the Mediterranean to find anything like him. He is not indeed a statesman at all, or he is a statesman by the way. He is much more akin to the actor, the writer, and the popular journalist. He deals with audiences, as they do.

To realize the intervention of these assent-organizing activities and the conditions under which they must work is to begin to understand the otherwise inexplicable inefficiency of contemporary governing bodies. It was unfair to compare them to boards of directors or to any rationalized industrial organization. They neither embody definite plans nor pursue defined ends. Nobody is quite clear and precise about what they are for. They balance and sway in the balance. The will to rule which is supposed to exist in the electorate is not there. The will to rule has evaporated from the organization of the modern state. It is being concentrated afresh in the minds of political thinkers, business organizers, financial organizers and the modern civil service. But the politician has to pretend and sustain with all his power the pretense that the will to rule resides in the electorate. Directly it is proved that the ordinary man has no wish to rule at all, the reason for the politician's existence vanishes.

Our museum encyclopædia would detail all the multitudinous ways of looking at the state, still operative in the world. The religious royalist—in Britain, at least—would say that government is "for God and the King." It has to sustain the peace and order of the realm. Such Puritans as those who founded New England would have it that it is the embodiment of God's will on earth. Many minds with a Latin tradition would turn rather to the phrase of the Re-Public or the Common Weal. And then ask for an expert dictator—though dictators are never experts. But for the past century and a half theocracy and autocracy have been more or less thrust aside by the democratic idea, the idea that the state is the "embodied will" of the people, that all power comes from the people and all governmental service is ultimately the service of the people and of their common rights and liberties. In most other systems the people are supposed to assent passively; an element of natural or divine right in the ruler or rulers is assumed, and the people are understood to recognize that; in modern democratic systems popular assent is figured as active and continuous. The people are themselves supposed to watch and understand government and to signify their assent by their votes.

The next stage to representative democracy is Anarchism, in which theory no government whatever is required, since the people are supposed to be directly and immediately capable of solving whatever collective problems may arise.

Manifestly our contemporary populations neither watch nor understand government. That they do so is a legal fiction. But we have to get along with that fiction for the present, because no one has yet invented and worked out any better way of getting a general assent to administration and legislation. A much better way cannot be beyond human contriving, but it has not yet been contrived. Meanwhile the collective affairs of mankind have to be carried on through the mediation of a patchwork of seventy-odd governments, mostly of the elective democratic type. There is nothing else to be done but to work them as well as we can until a better way appears.

Again the reader must turn his imagination to vast shadowy galleries in our Museum of Human Activities. There would be exhibits to display the past and present of electioneering and the organization of democracies for political ends. All the machinery would be displayed from public meeting to polling station and vote counting; there should be a complete collection of election posters, cinema records of American processions and demonstrations, and a series of photographs of politicians in full harangue, with their faces distended and their uplifted and gesticulating hands and arms. In the special library there would be a collection to illustrate the relations of the press to political crises and studies of bribery under past and current conditions, intimidation, personation, the falsification of returns and the strategy of seat redistribution, freak candidatures and the like.

It is impossible, under modern conditions, for politicians to mould or direct opinion. They have to pick up and marshal such feelings and opinions as exist already in the community, to "crystallize" them in catchwords, to use all the skill and science of the professional advertiser to impress their "personalities" and their panaceas on the popular imagination. Even when they are standing for a real end, its statement must be simplified down to the level of the average voter. Necessarily they must seek and use the cheapest, widest appeals to prejudice that the public intelligence will tolerate.

Cheapest and most effective of all such appeals is the appeal to patriotism. If patriotism had never existed before, modern politicians would have invented it. And almost equally powerful are class jealousy and class greed. Let the burthen of taxation fall on other people: that has always been quite naturally a very popular cry. Fear of the unknown is another great force for the politicians' purposes. All proposals for reorganization must have their complexities, which may need half an hour or so of explanation—and half an hour of explanation is nine-and-twenty minutes too much for the average man. All, too, involve some experimental reservations. A twist of misrepresentation, a misleading nickname, a bold assertion of the certainty of disastrous consequences, and the carefully elaborated scheme is doomed. The common voter, unless he is in a panic or entirely desperate, will go down with the ship, will stick to the ship, that is, so long as it is above water, rather than risk the frightful jump into the lifeboat. Much more will he hold back when there are politicians to tell him that the lifeboat is a life trap, and as the ship always *has* floated he may trust it to float forever.

As corrective to this law, so to speak, of the maximum cheapness of appeal in political life, there is nothing but a public understanding based on a sound general education—education not of the formal school type, but real education as we shall define it in Chapter XV. As the level of sound education rises in a community, the quality of the politician's appeal must rise. There will come a point at which the baser grades of claptrap will discredit, and the politician will have to qualify this claptrap he uses with a certain consistency and sanity. An alert, intelligent and honest press is a powerful restraint upon the worst impulses of the politician. It can keep things in mind for and against him; it can be a constant refresher to the public mind. Unhappily, economic developments have for a time cheapened the press mentality throughout the world. But this we shall discuss later.

Posturing, intrigue and unscrupulous appeals to fear, class-jealousy, and patriotism; favours, buttons, crystal and claptrap: these are the forces that bring the politicians of the great powers of the world to office. They come to government pledged to measures that must confuse economic life, cripple trade and promote those international stresses that lead to war. As far as possible, the permanent official, the sane man in a position of responsibility, does his best to prevent or delay the realization of those pledges. And the necessary legislative and administrative incompetence of the democratic politician is also very helpful in assisting him to break his word. Moreover, as soon as his election to office is over, he has no longer any strong inducements to keep his word; it is much easier and pleasanter to let his pledges—he never, if he can help it, pledges anything tangible—slide. He promised to save the country, and is not his presence at the head of things a sufficient guarantee that the country has been saved?

In this manner it becomes clear how it is that the multitudinous governing machines that now divide human affairs so strangely between them are so inferior in efficiency to the aëroplane, the telephone exchange or the power station. When we scrutinize the psychology of human association the wonder is, not that it works badly, but that it works at all. We have seen how in a comparatively brief period of time human communities have passed from their ancient forced assent to the arbitrary will of Gods and masters, into this present state of alleged free assent—which is, to put it plainly, *humbugged* assent. Uncertainly and desperately the educationally minded toil to overtake the blundering developments of this new situation. The problem of government remains still the obscurest of all the vital problems that now challenge mankind.

We may, perhaps, glance for a moment at various proposals that have been advanced for the improvement of the modern democratic governing machine. They are all rather hopeless proposals because they are more or less plainly and openly projects for the abolition of the contemporary type of politician, and it is only with the consent of the contemporary type of politician that they can legally be brought into operation. The proposals fall into three groups: those which concern the method of election; those which concern the size and procedure of the legislative body, and those which turn upon the necessity of the checks and delays established by our forebears.

It is maintained by a very considerable number of intelligent people that the prevalent method of election by the division of the electorate into one-seat (or in a minority of cases two or more seat) constituencies, necessarily subordinates wide to local considerations, gives no representation whatever to the minority, though it may be only a few votes short of the majority, and leads inevitably to a two-party system which mocks at essential change. At times a party which really represents only a minority of the population, by winning a number of seats by narrow majority and losing a few by enormous minorities, may have an actual majority in the legislative chamber.

One remedy suggested by Thomas Hare (*The Election of Representatives*) in 1859 and supported by John Stuart Mill is Proportional Representation. In its original and most logical form it was a scheme for treating the whole country as one constituency and allowing a candidate to collect votes until he could obtain a quota qualifying him for election. "Practical" men have modified this project in 300 (!) different ways, but the most genuine form would have large constituencies returning up to 15 members (so Lord Courtney before the British Royal Commission in 1909) and long lists of candidates would be submitted to the electors who would mark their preferences 1, 2, 3, and so on. A candidate who secured more than sufficient 1's to achieve the quota, would have his surplus of 2's divided among candidates who had not yet received a quota, and so on, until a sufficient number of quotas would be accumulated and only a surplus of less than a quota would be left unrepresented. But this would tend to the election of outstanding representative men who are not simply party politicians. On that account it is that we have those three hundred variations of the method, all designed to keep government in the hands of party politicians by insisting upon the voters' second, third and later selection being not free but confined to tortuously fabricated party lists. These sophisticated forms of proportional representation, contrived as they are to restrict government to the professional politician, lead to a representative assembly with an inconvenient mosaic of small parties and make government a matter of tiresome bargaining and intrigue.

But the plain fact of the case is that proportional representation aims to get rid of the party politician altogether and to substitute for his interventions a real council of the nation. The world wants—just as far as it can—to get rid of the politician in managing its affairs, just as it wants to get rid of the middle-man in trade. Both are interveners, making trouble rather than saving it. No true politician will ever concede silent working efficiency in administration if he can prevent it. He lives and dies by party. What has been overlooked in such experiments in so-called proportional representation as have been made thus far, is that the elected chamber must be much smaller than, for in-stance, the British House of Commons or the American House of Representatives, and that it should have no party structure. It must be a not too big committee of the nation rather than an unwieldy bilateral debating society. Its ministers must not be a block, going in and out of office together; they must be in-dividually responsible to the entirely more intelligent and more representative assembly the proportional representative method would produce.

We cannot enter here into the detailed discussion of the pro-portional representative project. The best case against it is made by asserting that an election in a modern democracy has a double purpose. Its first end is the appointment of a legislator. But equally important, say these critics, is the education of the common citizen in public issues by the speeches and canvassing of the candidates. This is only possible in small, accessible con-stituencies. No candidate could cover the ground of a fifteen-member constituency; and so his instructive and exalting per-sonality could not get into touch with the uninformed common man. Proportional representation would therefore throw more political power into the newspapers and (party) publicity machinery. But think of the average party candidate—as edu-cating anybody! The fact is that to-day the guiding influences in modern elections are the newspaper, the party propaganda organization, priests (in many countries), and "movements" which canvass. A change over to proportional representation would not really alter this at all. Further it is argued that great numbers of voters would not vote at all. That might not prove a misfortune. To abstain is practically to assent.

But most criticism of genuine proportional representation is based on an uncritical and unimaginative belief in the necessity for party government because of its supposed stability. It is held to be an excellent preventive of any essential revolution, because the party out of office (though it consists of politicians differing in no essential respect from those in office) can pretend to take up and act for those who find the contemporary government intolerable. A change of personnel is thus foisted upon people who want a change of régime.

The whole apologetic for modern democratic government on the old party lines rests in fact upon this action in diverting and minimizing the forces of change in the interests of stability. It is not realized that there may be too much stability and not enough change. But the form of government suggested by the more thoroughgoing proportional representationists—a single small chamber of the size of a big committee of from 200 to 300 members, a circular chamber, that is, and not a bilateral one, a chamber elected by immense constituencies returning from 10 to 18 members each, would certainly give better scope for the broaching of dissentient views and for compromises with them, than the present system. It would accept or reject the ministers appointed by the premier individually, and it could go to the country triennially or quadrennially for new blood and the elimination of persons who had become unpopular. It would have far greater continuity of will and personnel than any existing government.

The professional politician has always clung as long as possible to the two-party system. When a community (as, for example, the British) has become so manifestly bored and thwarted with the Box and Cox alternation of governments, which, the more they changed, the more they remained the same thing, and has, in spite of every mechanical difficulty in its way, evoked a third or even a fourth party, then the politicians resort to the trick of the Second Ballot or Alternative Vote. These contrivances are designed to come into operation when there are three or more candidates, and none of them gets an absolute majority. The hindmost is eliminated, and the remaining two share his votes either in a second polling or by counting the second choice already marked on each voter's paper.

These devices have recommended themselves to legislators because they admit a third professional politician to the chances of the election and nevertheless are entirely effective in excluding any publicist, however popular, who is not attached to a fully organized party machine. The trade in assent, with all its honours and profits, remains in professional hands and that, from the politician's point of view, is the most important consideration. It is hardly surprising that representative party government on such lines has been unable to prevent an anti-parliamentary revolution in Italy, Poland and various other countries, when a bored and apathetic community has submitted to, and even found a certain relief in, a frank dictatorship. And already we have studied the desolating ineffectiveness and want of initiative of the Mother of Parliaments in the face of the dark urgencies of our time.

The fact that the prestige of the two-party system arose accidentally, because of a peculiar dynastic and religious stress in seventeenth-century England, is generally disregarded in the discussion of electoral methods. But it is a vitally important consideration. The fluctuations in English affairs which led to the successive replacement of the first Stuarts, the Commonweal, the late Stuarts, the House of Orange, the Tory reaction under Anne, the House of Hanover and the raids of the Old and Young Pretenders, within the brief space of a hundred years, established an exceptional duality in English political affairs. On the one hand was the Tory, Royalist, Anglo-Catholic or Roman Catholic, and presently agriculturalist and landlord; on the other the Whig, Middle-Class Republican, Aristocratic-Republican with a tame king as figurehead, Constitutionalist, Puritan, Dissenter or Low Church, often urban and interested in industrial development. When the British colonies in America developed beyond the scale of an exploited group of satellites, Tory and Whig fought for subjugation or independence—the City of London was for the colonists—and the two-party system was transferred without any question of its naturalness to American political life and fixed there permanently by the adoption of a method of voting that practically necessitates the restriction of an election to one of two candidates. Tory disappeared in America, and Whig split into Republican and Democrat—we omit the intermediate phases—but the dualism remained. The economic and political prosperity, first of Great Britain and then of the United States, gave everything Anglo-Saxon a flavour of success throughout the nineteenth century, and as other countries began to modernize their governments, this purely accidental bilateral arrangement of affairs, with its alleged efficacy in burking attempts at fundamental change by diverting them into the harmless channel of "opposition" politics, became a world-wide institution.

But there is no natural necessity for it; none whatever. It is a contemporary superstition.

Equally superstitious is the almost world-wide insistence upon two legislative chambers, devised to check and thwart each other. No one can give any satisfactory reasons, except what we may call "artful" reasons, for this double digestion of the community will. No sane business organizer would dream of an upper and lower board of directors with an "opposition" on each board and a cabinet of managers, who every one of them would have to throw up their jobs, if any single one of them failed to satisfy the boards. But that is the form of the British directorate, and that is more or less the spirit in which most of the seventy-odd, distinct and separate governments in the world have organized the conduct of their affairs.

Long ago Bentham remarked, "If a second chamber agrees with the first, it is superfluous; if it disagrees, it is obnoxious."

We have now to consider some of the broader consequences of this seventy-fold division of human control, among governments organized for conflict and specialized for the most tenacious and inveterate resistance to improvement or replacement.

§ 6. *Frontiers and the Official Intercommunication of Governments*

The division of human government into seventy-odd sovereign states does not merely impede the effective treatment of fundamentally important economic matters—that alone would be bad enough, but it goes much further towards evil and human frustration than that, because it keeps up the tradition of the militant state and turns men's faces towards war and war preparation, and towards destructive economic warfare in preparation for the military conflict. Enormous quantities of human energy are dissipated by this fragmentation of government, economic evolution is delayed by it, and the whole future of our species threatened.

We have to deal with these things here mainly as economic disturbances and diversions of creative power. We shall say very little of the cruelties and abominations of war. They are horrible indeed, but they are secondary. What concerns us with war in this general economic survey is not its soul-destroying cruelty, but its futility and the barrier it may set to man's attainment of any life ampler than the one he leads to-day.

Throughout this work stress has been laid on the profound change in human conditions brought about by increased facilities of transport and communication generally. That also is the main theme of the *Outline of History*. But since there exists as yet no real science of social structure, the connection of the vast change of scale in human operations, this enormous lengthening of the human reach, with the intensified economic and political tensions of our time, has not been understood. It was not realized that a drastic revision of our political institutions and economic conceptions to adapt them to this change of scale had become a logical and urgent necessity. It is only now that any considerable number of people are observing that the frontiers of the old political systems and the old areas of sympathetic association which fitted economic needs fairly well in the eighteenth century are becoming intolerably narrow, tight and dangerous. The *Outline of History* explains how in certain instances, in the preservation of the unity of the United States, for example, in the development of certain modern "empires," in the unification of Italy and Germany, the new forces operated, unthanked and almost unsuspected, and now the science of work and wealth must develop this conception of areas outgrown and set itself to

a study of the "frontier" as a complication and an obstacle to
the establishment of that world economic state which is so manifestly struggling to come into existence.

I had thought at first that we should begin here with the
custom house as an ever present manifestation of this entanglement. But it opens up our discussion better to examine the
nature of the obsolete traditional machinery which is fighting
so obstinately to maintain the old patchwork of communities
against the synthetic forces of the world, and then to treat the
existence of tariff walls as one necessary concomitant of that
machinery. The organization and work of foreign offices and
of the diplomatic and consular services must first be brought
into the picture. Here is the cue for the Foreign Minister in
his becoming livery, the Foreign Office clerk, and even the
King's messenger, with his impressively sealed bag, to pass across
the stage.

All this is now established traditional stuff. But though its
spirit is very ancient indeed, its present form was assumed in
comparatively recent times. In its present form it is only about
three centuries old—nine or ten generations of men. We must
go back to the Peace of Westphalia (1648) for the inaugura-
tion of the system of international dealing we know to-day. Then
it was, writes a friend from Geneva, that "the equal right of
all states, whether great or small, Catholic or Protestant, to
existence and independence was recognized, and also the virtual
sovereignty of the princes and cities in the Holy Roman Empire.
The practice of establishing permanent legations in each other's
capitals was inaugurated at the Conference." And the board
was set for that game between the powers, the Game of the
Militant Powers, which has become now so monstrous a weight
on social and industrial life and so stupendous a threat to the
future of mankind.

Were we working on a truly encyclopædic scale, here would
be the place for a study of the training and occupation of diplomatists, the relation of the diplomatic to the consular service,
and the successful resistance offered by the diplomatic profession of the world, so far, to the natural consequences of the fact

that it is now becoming materially possible for any Foreign Minister to talk to and see the face of any other Foreign Minister in any part of the world.

The diplomat of the eighteenth century, says Professor Alison Philips in his excellent article in the Encyclopædia Britannica, was frankly a national advocate, an "agent" for the proprietary rights of his sovereign. "Diplomacy thus resolved itself into a process of exalted haggling, conducted with an amazing disregard for the ordinary standards of morality, but with the most exquisite politeness, and in accordance with ever more and more elaborate rules." He cites Frederick de Marselaer (1626), however, as declaring that "it was the function of an ambassador not only to study the interests of his sovereign, but 'to work for the common peace and to study the convenience of foreign princes,' " and he also mentions François de Callières (1716) and Vattel (1756) as speaking "of Europe as a kind of republic which it was the function of diplomacy to preserve." In the nineteenth century Professor Philips traces a considerable relaxation of the original narrowness of the diplomatic idea and a certain diminution of the importance and responsibility of ambassadors with the advent of telegraph and railway. But at the same time there was a specialization and intensification of the mentality of the diplomatic services. Originally any intelligent competent person might be a diplomat (Louis XI sent his barber on diplomatic errands). But after the Treaty of Westphalia, the division of Europe among "sovereigns" and the centralization of power and authority about their courts, diplomacy became an "art" of the genteelest pretensions, reserved almost entirely for men of good family, skilled in etiquette and intrigue. They had to mingle with the "highest personages," to know the moods and feuds of influential people; to propitiate and hoodwink, to report and suggest. After Waterloo, Britain adopted the system of sending out to her various ambassadors one or two "attachés to be domesticated in his family."

"The attachés of the various embassies and legations in the European capitals," writes one bitter critic with an intimate knowledge of legation life, have been "a godsend to middle-

aged women of position everywhere. They are State gigolos."
This is perhaps a little harsh, but the advancement of these
young men and their matrimonial successes are closely interwoven. An attaché who marries "beneath him" falls out of the
service. Two "Labour" governments in Great Britain, approaching diplomacy in a state of conscious gentility, have done nothing to alter this state of affairs.

So the tradition of an elegant, manœuvering, "confidential,"
undemocratic service was built up, and it rules still, a little un-
steadily, in the swaying and dangerous world of to-day. The
British Foreign Office clerk has been mingled a little with the
diplomatists proper, where knowledge and mental vigour were
plainly more important than what is called breeding. And occasionally men of exceptional originality, such men as, for example,
Lord d'Abernon in Berlin have achieved real creative states-
manship in spite of all tradition. There are also now always
the military and naval attachés, who are there to observe and
spy upon the military activities of the host country. And nowadays
a commercial attaché creeps in. But of course there are no
attachés whatever to study the scientific work, the philosophy,
the art, and the social progress of the land. That sort of thing
does not enter into Foreign Office mentality.

An ambassador has certain privileges; his embassy is treated
as being part of his own country (extra-territoriality) in which
he may maintain his native laws, and he is exempt from distraint
for debt and may commit many of the lighter offenses, such as
disregarding traffic regulations, indulging in prohibited drinks
and the like, without prosecution. His more public duties are
now largely formal; every contemporary ambassador is on the
end of a telegraph wire from home; but there are obscurer
activities for him to foster. The association of embassies with
espionage, and during war time in neutral countries with the
organization of incendiarism, the sinking of ships, raids and
suchlike plotting, was natural and inevitable, and so, on the
other side of the account, was the stealing of their code books
and the furtive interception and examination of their correspondence.

For many reasons the diplomatic representatives of the United States of America have varied considerably from the normal European type, but there has been an increasing social assimilation in the present century. If the ordinary American ambassador is not now a nobleman, he is as much a nobleman as circumstances permit. Owing to many instabilities in their status and their greater novelty, the social assimilation of the representatives of Soviet Russia has hardly begun. They remain more than a little alien to the rest of the diplomatic world and are subjected to slights and insults no other diplomatists would endure.

§ 7. *The Custom House*

The obstinate resolve to treat the subjects of each of the sovereign states of the world as a community distinct from and in competition with the rest of humanity, which still dominates the political and educational organization of mankind is everywhere in the harshest conflict with the development of a world economic system. Of that we have a disagreeable reminder whenever we cross a frontier.

Nationalism is a vested interest and defends itself with all the disingenuousness of self-protection. The admission that a political world system is the natural expression of the continually more common material interests of mankind, means virtual social suicide for a vast complex of traditionally important people. It means the disappearance of diplomacy, of courts and royalties, and of every type professionally dependent upon assertive and aggressive patriotism. It means the obliteration of the nationalist politician and "statesman," who knows that in a world system he will sink to provincial or parochial importance. Or to no importance at all. There is consequently a world-wide and desperate resistance to the economic forces of our time at all the present headquarters of human organization. The parties of the right are patriotic and brutally for warfare; the patriotic parties of the left talk peace and will not ensue it, take care not to ensue it. The politician who really sought the peace of the world would need the courage and creative ability to make himself a world politician. He would do it at great personal risk. Whenever he displayed an interest in world problems or tried to acquire a wider point of view he would have to turn a defenceless back to his rivals at home. They would explain that he was growing too big for his boots, losing touch with his own people, neglecting the interests of his fatherland or motherland in his desire to strut upon a larger stage, and so on. World politicians will appear in time, no doubt; men working through such things as news agencies, books, and powerful international associations rather than through legislative assemblies, and so organizing a cosmopolitan assent to world-wide reconstruction; but such methods have still to be elaborated and made effective.

Meanwhile the sacred frontiers of the pre-railway era, and the ideals of the Foreign Offices of the eighteenth century, these strange geographical divisions for which we live and our sons may die, have under the stresses of easier and easier transport to be fortified not simply against armed hosts but against marketable matter in motion; they have to be emphasized by a monstrous system of interferences with trade, to defend their obsolete romantic autonomy against the plain necessities of our time. The less the frontier is necessary the more it has to be exacerbated.

The story of the modern tariff system and its increase in importance after the eighteenth century is a complex and a curious one. Tariffs seem to have been first used extensively for quasi-belligerent purposes during the Napoleonic Wars. Originally a mere method of taxation for revenue—they have become a mitigated form of warfare, aiming at the relative advantage of the population interned behind the frontier and the relative damage and ruin of foreign industries. The nature of their interference, the way tariffs are imposed, their methods of administration, make a science in itself. A popular account of that science would have to be enlivened by pictures of custom-house officials at work; the searching of luggage upon a New York pier, for example, and the activities and methods of smugglers and revenue patrols. The profits and prospects of the professional smuggler, the salaries and opportunities for corruption of the revenue services would furnish interesting material.

How the normal hostilities of tariffs may be raised to the level of a blockade is shown by a study of the trade relations between Britain and Russia. Tariff obstruction at this higher level is, for all practical ends, *war at the frontier,* White War, the chronic as distinguished from that acute form in which invasion, bomb, bayonet and poison gas play leading parts, which more emphatic sort of warfare we may call Red War. It is not really a different thing; it is only a difference of tempo, instrument and colour.

Closely associated with the clogging and congestion of world trade by the custom house is the interference with the free movement of workers, business people, and the like, by the passport and permit system. The passport has other uses of a more strictly political sort, at which we shall glance later, but here it is, while we are still upon the subject of frontiers, that its origin and development can best be described. The passport grew out of a majestically feeble letter of recommendation addressed by one's foreign minister to all whom it might concern. That letter has shrunken to comparative insignificance in the contemporary booklet passport, which gathers impressions from the rubber stamps of all nations. Endless forms of trouble arise in various countries out of the passport mislaid, and there is a flourishing trade in stolen, transferred and forged passports wherever men and women go about their unlawful occasions.

§ 8. *War Preparation as an Industry*

From the passive and obstructive malignity of White War we must turn to the activities preparatory for the Red War phase in international dealings. In no other department of human affairs has tradition held its own so successfully against the creative forces of the new age and every reasonable disposition in mankind.

Our kings and presidents, in their military uniforms, our flags and sovereignties and the primary forms and conceptions

of our states, all come down to us from the time of the localized
community which was either predatory in a small local way upon
its immediate neighbours or defensive against them. They remain with us, as dangerous as cancer starting points, because the
development of the modern economic world system has so far
been a planless process due to forces that are only now beginning
to be apprehended as one whole.

At no time has the necessity of getting free from the outgrown rules and boundaries of the old régime been faced, and so
the world's war equipment has followed blindly upon industrial
advance until it has become a monstrous and immediate danger
to the community. An encyclopædic review of modern war equipment might very well begin with an account of eighteenth-century
war plant, its horse, its foot and its artillery of little field guns,
and trace the accumulating consequences of big steel production
and of inventions in gas and explosives, in transport, communication and the like. Finally that richly illustrated encyclopædia
would become vivid with pictures of tanks, bombing planes,
aëroplane carriers, battleships throwing out smoke-screens, and
of munition works and casualty stations in full activity during
the last great war. All that spectacle is part of the work of the
world and a great spending of wealth. It is essential to our
review that it should come well into the picture.

The still unassembled galleries of this museum of the science
of work and wealth we have dreamt of would display, therefore,
the scale of the industry and the multitudes of men in training
for it at the present time. And since the associated encyclopædia
would be a full résumé of human occupations, it would have to
give the abundant particulars of that training in its endless
varieties. It would summarize the good and evil of barrack life.

At least military service uproots the peasant. That is a good
thing. But this drilling of millions of young men, this incessant
training of young Frenchmen mentally as well as physically to
kill Italians and Germans, of Poles to kill Germans or Russians,
of Russians and British and Americans to kill anybody who
happens, is not a good thing. This morning ten thousand bugles
and drums were noisy about the world, calling the boys out to

the exercise yard, and hardly a moment passes without a machine gun rattling out its blank cartridges or a futile gun booming at a target for want of immediate flesh and blood to shatter.

There is a real breaking down of initiative in the well trained common soldier. The late Dr. Rivers in his brilliant report on "War Neurosis and Military Training," now reprinted in his *Instinct and the Unconscious*, tells how the army discipline exaggerates mental suggestibility until it may even induce that type of hysteria which is accompanied by partial paralysis and kindred crippling functional disorders. Numbers of men never recover from the drill-sergeant throughout their lives. They go out from the army and become citizens, to play a part in politics, to vote. But at the word of command they jump to attention.

Our encyclopædia would correlate these service disciplines with peace production on the one hand and the labour market on the other. On the one page it might give figures of so perfect a piece of mechanism as a modern submarine, and over against it photographs of the equipment of a one-roomed slum "home" in which heirs to our civilization have been born and are being reared. That home is what it is because neither labour nor material can be obtained to make it better. The home is subject to all the restrictions of private production for private property; the submarine is evoked by the collective buying of the community. Our schools wait; this ugly tribute starves our schools. The modern state "economizes" on schools; on submarines it dare not economize. We should have pictures of dockyard gates with the workers pouring in or out; the great workshops on which they toil and the streets in which they live. And there must also be an account of specialized technical training for warfare—specialized training as distinguished from the mere drilling of the rank and file. Every year in times of peace something between one and two thousand carefully chosen young men of exceptional physical quality are smashed, burnt alive, or otherwise destroyed in the training of the air forces of the world alone. There is also a steady destruction of choice young men in submarines.

Against this we must balance the braver shows of outright war. Our lavish encyclopædia would display kings, princes, and

presidents and other militant heads of states arrayed in the brilliant uniforms that emphasize their fundamentally belligerent
function, decorated with feathers, skins, manes of beasts, and
so forth, reviewing and inspecting troops, presiding over military tattoos, parades, the trooping of the colours. It would
give also a brief history of military and quasi-military costume in
connection with belligerent psychology. A few score coloured
plates might be devoted to the uniforms worn by the British royal
family. Are soldiers particularly addicted to corsets and cosmetics? Some students allege they are. Little is known popularly
of the motives and methods of those who design and vary the
adornments of the military. It may be possible to discover some
interesting symbolism from many objects that on the surface
appear to be very aimless encumbrances and incrustations. Why,
for instance, do the Grenadier Guards wear vast bearskins?
Where are they made, and what do they cost? How many hands
and eyes have been busied in decorating those unfortunate, bored
and fatigued young men who stand for long hours heavily ac-
coutred at the gates of Buckingham Palace? How long will it
be before the last sentinel is relieved there and the whisper of
the final password dies away into the eternal silences? These
poor sentinels do nothing. The real guardians of the peace, the
police, are there also, to save them from annoyance and preserve
the dignity of the household within.

From these adornments an encyclopædic study of warfare
would pass on to trace the progress in military methods, material, and machinery. The Science of Warfare is now a very active
occupation. It is a sort of ugly and dwarfish little twin sister
running at the side of scientific research. Her difference is that
she tries to be secretive, and her ends are murderous. She is
perpetually seeking to seize upon and pervert scientific advances.

But one must admit the fascinating vigour of many of her
newer adaptations. There is something that stirs our unregenerate natures in the foaming advance of a great battleship and
in the emphatic thud of gunfire, the flash, the swift ejection of a
ball of dense smoke which slowly unfolds. Most of us could watch
aërial warfare with undiluted pleasure if the promiscuous use of

bombs were barred. We should follow with sympathetic delight the nimble dance of the conquering ace flying for position, tapping out the bullets from his exquisite gun with finished skill, sending, amidst our applause, his dead and wounded antagonists spinning down, poor rabbits, to their ultimate dramatic smash.

It would need another work as long as this one now, to tell fully of the post-war development of the tank and the mechanization of land warfare. Hitherto men have been stabbed, blown to pieces, buried alive, suffocated, scalded, burnt and smashed and eviscerated by projectiles in every conceivable way, but in the next war they will also have the prospect of being pulped into a sort of jam by glorified tanks. It will be a new experience. A really exhaustive treatise on war technique would include also the development of mine fields in the future and the next phase of warfare under the sea. A ship may hardly know it is hit before it goes under.

An inexpugnable nastiness and repulsiveness, however, invades the brightness of military science at the thought of "gas." The professional soldiers dislike it extremely. Nobody likes it. Yet no one in his senses believes that "gas" can be excluded from the next war. And no sane airman with a gas bomb will withhold it from the enemy's G. H. Q. if he gets a chance of delivering it there. But it is poor consolation for a civilization shattered, to know that a large proportion of military leaders will probably be choked to death in an extremely painful fashion if they get the war of their dreams. We also shall get the war of their dreams.

A comprehensive and impartial survey of what men do and how they gain their livings, if it were worked out in detail, would give ample attention to the Gas Warfare Department, describe the physical and moral effects of the latest and best gases, and weigh the prospects of an honest and capable young man or woman who selects that as a field for his or her life work. It would go into much detail about gas that we willingly spare our readers, telling of Lewisite, the gentle and insidious, so that you hardly know you are dead; of phosgene, which seems a small matter at the time and kills distressingly the next day; of the suffering caused by mustard gas, and of the fine gases that can get through any gas mask to the wearer within. These last do not kill, generally speaking; their purpose is to produce an intolerable discomfort so that the mask is torn off, and the heavier, deadlier gas given access to its victim. Gas treatment can now be extended to whole countrysides. It can constitute lines of defense that are for a time impenetrable. In the United States of America at least considerable advances have been made in the methods of disseminating disease germs from the air. It was found at first that the deadlier bacteria were in some cases too delicate and died during the process. Patient study has now made it possible to breed tougher strains of these organisms, and there is every prospect that in the next war all the more dreadful airborne infections will be released abundantly in the great cities of an enemy's country. Work has also been done upon the distribution of cattle and crop diseases over the countryside.

That better informed encyclopædia which hovers phantasmally at the back of our minds would also give certain figures I have not been able to ascertain, the number of grave, competent human beings who are now at work studying and experimenting upon these astounding refinements of human intercourse.

§ 9. *The Rôle of the Armament Industry in Fostering Belligerence*

Here is the place for an exhibit, an individual instance of the interplay of nationalist traditions and modern industrial progress, the life of Sir Basil Zaharoff. It is the story of an entirely honourable and honoured human being, exceptionally energetic and capable, reacting in a perfectly natural and legitimate way to the laws, traditions and institutions of our time. If this figure should seem to some imaginations to cast a very dark shadow upon the human spectacle, the fault lies rather with the pinnacle he stands upon and not with himself. His story is told by Richard Lewinsohn* with the endorsement of M. Skouloudis, the

---

Zaharoff l'Européen Mystérieux.

founder of Sir Basil's fortunes and a former Greek Foreign Minister.

SIR BASIL ZAHAROFF

Sir Basil, it seems, was born in an obscure village of Anatolia in 1849 of Greek parents who presently took him to Constantinople. There a kindly compatriot paid for his education at the English school, and in his teens he was able to earn his living as a guide and commissionaire attached to various hotels. Then he became the assistant of his uncle, Sevastopoulo, a draper, an infirm man whose affairs profited greatly by the energy and capacity Sir Basil brought to them. The nephew was promised a share in the proceeds of this business, but the uncle, either through meanness or the fear of losing the services of his useful relative if he became too independent, would not assent to the payment of the amount due to him. Accordingly young Zaharoff, having access to the money of the firm, paid himself off and, in the hope of avoiding any unpleasantness with his uncle, went to London to begin life anew. But the uncle, in a resentful mood, had him arrested there, accusing him of robbery. Things looked very bad indeed against the young man; he knew no one to bail him out, he was detained in prison until his uncle came to England to prosecute him. He was only saved from conviction and imprisonment by the dramatic discovery in the pocket of an old overcoat at the last moment before going into court, of a crumpled letter giving him full powers as a partner to buy, sell and pay out money as he thought fit. He had been hunting everywhere for that mislaid letter. The day when he had to go into court was cold, and he bethought himself of his overcoat, and in the pocket was something. . . . Sevastopoulo, confronted with it in court, could not deny his own handwriting. So by a fortunate accident young Basil Zaharoff was saved from prison to become, it is said, the richest man in the world.

How did this penniless adventurer clamber to that position, and what did he give the world in return for the enormous purchasing power he won from it?

Lewinsohn tells of a return to Athens, of struggles and difficulties, and then of the coming of opportunity. Zaharoff had gained the good-will and esteem of Skouloudis, and one day (in 1877) Skouloudis received a letter from the firm of Nordenfelt, makers of the earliest form of machine gun, asking him to recommend them an agent. Zaharoff was appointed to the vacant job with the warmest recommendation of Skouloudis at a salary of five pounds a week. Therewith, paying off various outstanding hotel bills, he commenced his march towards the inestimable millions of to-day.

He was to achieve wealth with honour, he was to become a British baronet and wear the magnificent plumes and robe of a G. C. B. in which he appears in his best known portrait. He is also, I learn from Who's Who, a G. B. E. Oxford University has made him a D. C. L., and France has conferred upon him the Grand Cross of the Legion of Honour. And he has won not only honour but power. He exerted, says the Encyclopædia Britannica in an extremely insufficient and concise but extremely respectful biographical article, "a strong if indirect influence during the World War and at the Paris Conference, being a close friend and political admirer of Lloyd George, Venizelos, Clemenceau and Briand." To that we will return.

His first considerable step towards this influence and recognition was to sell a submarine to the Greek government. After years of trial, Nordenfelts had produced a submarine that not only went down under water but, generally speaking, came up again. It had been exhibited in the Sound between Sweden and Denmark, but the great naval powers had refused to take up this new engine of destruction. There seemed to be a conspiracy against it. The experts found it unnecessary and unpleasant. Zaharoff had the bright and patriotic idea of selling one on easy terms to Greece. He had friends in Greece. Then he went to Constantinople to tell them about it and ask what they thought of it. Turkey was indisposed to let Greece get ahead with a weapon that might prove effective in the Dardanelles. So Turkey ordered submarines also. The ball was set rolling. Russia could not let Turkey get ahead in this fashion. Soon the submarine was established as an item in armament competition.

But now the Nordenfelt gun was threatened by the invention of a certain Hiram Maxim. He had a machine gun one man could work; the Nordenfelt needed a crew of four. He exhibited it at Vienna. While he fired his gun at a target and demonstrated its powers, Zaharoff was busy explaining to expert observers that the whole thing was an exhibition of skill; that only Maxim could fire that gun, it would take years to train men to use it, that these new machines were delicate and difficult to make and could not be produced in quantities, and so forth. Maxim, after tracing the initials of the Emperor upon a target, prepared to receive orders. They were not forthcoming. He learnt that the Nordenfelt was simple and strong. This gun of his was a "scientific instrument" unfit for soldierly hands. His demonstration went for nothing. What had happened? He realized he was vis-à-vis with a salesman, a very formidable salesman. In the end he amalgamated with the salesman. Thereupon difficulties vanished, the Maxim gun ceased to be a scientific instrument and became a standard weapon. Nordenfelt and Maxim consolidated, and the fusion was financed with the eager support of the investing public. So Lewinsohn tells the story.

This was in 1888, and the instincts of the investing public marched with the spirit of the times. The age of armaments in which we still live had begun. The device of selling first to Greece was capable of infinite variation and repetition. Naval theory was developing and becoming more and more infected by mechanism—even though the military mind still resisted what Lord Kitchener called "mechanical toys." The armament industry knew no boundaries. It was entirely modern in its cosmopolitanism, and whenever it produced a model that met the taste of Great Power A, Great Power B was invited to inspect the novelty that might presently be used against it. Some powers increased their state munition works, but the private armament industry, conceived on a world-wide scale, was already growing larger and more inventive than was possible for any single state. Presently (1897) Nordenfelt-Maxim found themselves bought by the great British firm of Vickers for one and a third million pounds, and Zaharoff carried his financial gifts and his salesmanship on to a wider stage.

The Vickers firm was not merely an armament firm; it did a huge business in iron and steel; it could carry through every stage in the process from ore to battleship, a feat beyond the power of any state arsenal. Vickers armed both sides in the Boer War, and the British who were killed in that struggle had at least the satisfaction of being killed by bullets "made in England." The profits of the Boer War enabled Vickers to buy up the Wolseley Tool and Motor Co., and the Electric and Ordnance Accessories Co., and so the process of amalgamation went on. The prospect of any state undertakings rivalling the products of the vast combination either in price, quantity, or quality became remoter and remoter.

It was less, perhaps, through ambition than through business necessity that Zaharoff, the supreme salesman of this great system, entered upon obscure but effective political and propagandist activities. He had never paused in his brilliant career to indulge in philosophical speculations or humanitarian dreams, and it was a natural and legitimate development of his selling methods to avail himself of press support and, for example, to secure an interest in such an enterprise as *Quotidiens illustrés,* which published the well known journal *Excelsior* and to endow a chair of aërodynamics in the University of Paris to hasten the day when aëroplanes (by Vickers) would be a necessary part of armaments all the world over.

The Great War was harvest time for the trade in war munitions. It would be unjust to historians, diplomatists, courts and patriots generally, to say that the armament industry had sown the harvest, but certainly for half a century it had done everything possible to stimulate the sowing. In Britain the industry was put under public control and a formal limit was set to its profits, but its heads became very naturally the advisers and helpers of the belligerent governments. Greece was hesitating about her rôle in the struggle, and Sir Basil found the money needed for a propaganda that would bring her into the war on the part of the Allies. Newspapers were bought and Greece came in, as Lewinsohn relates in detail.

The end of the war found the world extraordinarily weary of warfare, and there was a considerable possibility that the hugely distended world-armament industry would find itself facing a dispirited and declining market for its goods. Under these circumstances it was natural for those who were interested in its health and vigour to exert themselves to revive the romantic spirit of national assertion. And also Sir Basil loved Greece. He belonged to the Gladstonian age of national patriotism. A sentimental patriotism is probably the broadest, least ego-centred idea that ever entered his head; and we must not suppose too hastily that his motives in securing Western support for Greek aggressions upon Turkey, if complex, were necessarily disingenuous. But for Greece, in the harder, disillusioned, post-war world, the manœuvres that carried Greek armies to Angora and overwhelming defeat, that led to their disorderly retreat to the coast and the expulsion of the Greek population from Asia Minor, were altogether disastrous. The history of Greece and Turkey in the years following the war is too intricate, contentious and generally "shady" to deal with here; for us now its only importance is that it marks the culminating and conclusive effort of Sir Basil to exercise political power. Thereafter his activities have gone into channels that have little or nothing to do with this section of our work; operations with the deflated armament firms, metallurgical industries and petroleum, the exploitation of the Casino at Monte Carlo, and so forth. Our concern here is with the psychology of the armament maker as exemplified in his case.

Indisputably this man has spent a large part of his life in the equipment and promotion of human slaughter. And it is unjust and absurd to blame him for doing so. It is so cheap and easy for the sentimental pacifists to be indignant about him, but all of us are involved in the complex of processes that carried him to wealth and all of us have a share in his responsibility. Circumstances beyond his control built up his ideology. He has simply been modest enough not to question the standards of the world about him but to observe them faithfully and intelligently. It is plain that he has always accepted the making of money as a justification for his operations. Monetary success ought to be the indication of social service. If it is not, the fault is primarily with the political and business system and only secondarily with the individuals who make money. The organization of killing is inherent in our accepted ideology. The picture of an Anatolian Greek, overwhelmed by his riches, adorned with the highest honours France, Britain and Oxford can bestow, and amusing himself by running a gambling palace in his declining years, displayed against a background of innumerable millions of men maimed, tortured, scalded, mutilated and killed, may be an effective indictment of our political traditions, but in no sense is it a personal condemnation. Millions of his contemporaries would have played the same game had they thought of it and known how. There was nothing in their personas to prevent it. If anything is wrong it is in the educational influences and in the political, economic and financial opportunities that evoked those personas.

ALFRED KRUPP

We have taken the case of Sir Basil Zaharoff as the most picturesque illustration of the exploitation of our outgrown political suspicions and animosities by a particularly gifted salesman. An encyclopædia of the science of human industry would supplement his story with a constellation of biographies of kindred and associated spirits, all men no doubt amiable and pleasing in their private lives, and show how, acting strictly according to the business standards of the nineteenth century and on the lines of the education then provided, they were instrumental in imposing upon the civilized world first a colossal misapplication of its industrial machinery, then a vast load of taxation, and ultimately such an orgy of death, torment and destruction as the world has never seen before.

Victor Lefebure in his excellent book *Scientific Disarmament* tells how Lord Armstrong, the British armament vendor, when his new breech-loading rifled built-up gun was refused by the

British government in 1863, went to Austria, Denmark, Spain and other countries and so put the British muzzle-loader out of fashion. It was the same forcing method that Zaharoff employed when he took the submarine to Greece. Lefebure gives also a brief résumé of the life of Alfred Krupp, another of these honest dealers in the destruction of mankind. Alfred Krupp was one of the earliest pioneers in the trade, and a pioneer also in that development of the steels which we have already described from the point of view of Substances, in Chapter II. Krupp's steel guns were little appreciated in Germany until, in 1856, the Khedive of Egypt quickened the business with an order for thirty-six of them. Prussia followed, and from that time onward for half a century the progress of the gun dominated European life. Krupp became the close friend of the first German Emperor William I and developed an unrivalled testing ground at Meppen with a range of fifteen miles, the world's showroom, as Lefebure calls it, for big artillery. Krupp reigned, the world's "Cannon King." No one could equal his guns; no one could equal his armour plate. For fifty years he toiled to achieve that immense superiority in heavy ordnance that Germany displayed at the outset of the war in 1914. The other countries laboured in a vain endeavour to keep pace with Krupp.

"How far," Lefebure asks, "would it help to remove war from reality if we could limit these unleashed forces of armament development under a definite policy of agreed control?"

Alfred Krupp, the Cannon King, died in 1887 at the age of sixty-five, and was succeeded by his son, Frederick Krupp, who died in 1902. His health was indifferent, and he died before he was fifty. This second Krupp had financial and organizing genius rather than the technical preoccupation of his father, and built up the vast industrial organization at Essen that flourishes to this day. He controlled an important section of the German press and did much to consolidate the aggressive patriotism of the German people. The third generation of the Krupp family was already passing the meridian when at last the final harvest, the second reaping after Alfred Krupp, arrived. Its members were already lapsing from the strenuous tradition of Alfred. One made an elegant withdrawal from the common life of mankind to the island of Capri, where his reputation mingles now with that of the Emperor Tiberius. In the excitement and resentment of the invasion of Belgium in 1914, many English writers, the present writer included, denounced the "Krupp-Kaiser combination" as the sole cause of the collapse of European peace. They forgot the Vickers-Armstrong side of the story and the aggressive British Imperialism of the Kipling period. The twin begetters of that war were the armament industry and aggressive patriotism wherever they appeared. Nevertheless, it was mainly the genius of Alfred Krupp, stimulating and being stimulated by the ambitions of the Hohenzollern dynasty, to which we must ascribe the full development of this strange, monstrous, morbid development of human industry, science, loyalty, greed, vanity and tradition, the armament trade. It has slaughtered twenty million people and still it towers menacingly over all human life.

§ 10. *Spying and Spy Hunting*

Our account of the war industry will not be complete without some description of espionage, counter espionage, newspaper corruption and secret service work generally. The prospective belligerent hides his plans, his inventions, his purpose, and he seeks incessantly to know what his neighbour is hiding. He wants to verify suspicions and sow the seeds of indecision and division in a camp that may at any time become hostile.

There are human types, and often they are by no means stupid types, which lend themselves very readily to the organization and performance of these obscure but logical developments of the patriotic spirit. There is an attractive element of mystery in the work, the possibility of intensely dramatic situations, revelations, the invocation of unsuspected power. There are also great opportunities of pay for nothing—except the taking of chances. A sound knowledge of languages is very helpful in the profession, a good memory, quiet observation, subtlety and histrionic ability.

Correlated with these activities of the spying sort and linking up by hidden strands with the overt diplomatic organization, every country maintains special bureaus, with classified dossiers, based largely on secret, unverified and often totally inaccurate informations made against a multitude of arbitrarily selected unfortunates, the "suspects." Being a "suspect" is an involuntary form of human activity of a particularly disagreeable sort. Nobody in the world knows what the secret service industry may not have filed against him in some police dossier of this or that country, or what threats, delays, inconveniences, arrests or physical injury may not descend upon him. He may merely have a name identical with or similar to that of someone else. The secret patriot is above reason or the law. Whether he is ever far above blackmailing is another question. And the curious reader who wants to know how much this branch of war work goes on in war-time, may read for himself in Somerset Maugham's grim *Ashenden* or in Compton Mackenzie's derisive *Extremes Meet* and *The Three Couriers*. Both these writers base their books on close personal experiences.

Our encyclopædia, when it comes to be compiled, may quote these writers, but it is to be hoped that much more exact details than they give will be available of the cost and range of this branch of work and reward, the nature of the duties to be performed and the emoluments of the practitioners. Few of us outside the profession realize the multitude of people now employed in watching the unwary, in sneaking about for information or pseudo-information, in steaming and stealing letters, playing tricks with the telegraph and telephone, provoking simpletons to indictable acts, filching documents, taking forbidden photographs, circulating rumours and so forth. It is a world screened and hidden. The census does not reckon with it, for all its practitioners mask themselves by professing some more reputable occupation. From secret service to the white slave trade, the drug trade and kindred criminality, seems but a step. All underhand callings tend to drift together, and the mentality of these activities is nearly identical, even if the relationship with the police is different. The arresting hand of the policeman is suddenly seized and lifted. "That man or woman is useful and not to be taken." The difficulty of suppressing this ugly development of the industrialization of vice is greatly enhanced and confused by the existence of this inevitable furtive fringe to modern war organization.

§ 11. *The Service Mentality*

But a complete survey of human motives and human interaction will have to go much more deeply into the belligerent process than the preceding sections have suggested. We have insisted and reiterated that this survey is essentially psychological. It seeks the roots of social motive. Its fundamental matter of study is "will systems." Shops, factories, railways, ports and shipping as we have passed them under review, are all realized will systems. They are to be explained completely as the product of desire and demand, experiment, suggestion, imitation and effort. Few people will believe that the continuing existence of organized White and Red War is completely explained by an association of traditional stupidity with self-protective blindness to manifest facts and mere shortsighted greediness. There is something better about army and navy than that. Let us now look on this better side of the military persona, the service will system.

Too much pacifist literature is devoted to the more manifest evils and absurdities of belligerence; too little to the hiatus that would be left in human life if, by a miracle, flags, frontiers, arms and disciplines were suddenly and completely abolished. The machine would not go on if they were merely abolished and nothing more. Something would have to replace them. It is comparatively rare to find any realization that when every allowance has been made for the inertia of tradition, for the blind vigour of threatened interests, and for the innate streak of fear-linked emotional cruelty in all men, there must still be other elements in the human make-up to keep this vast system of activities going. You cannot make a resistant system out of elements that are entirely rotten. Few people are prepared to declare that the professional soldier is simply a compound of idiocy, fierce cruelty, and dishonesty; and yet very little has been said here so far to admit any other interpretation of him. Yet most advocates of world peace and world unity have in their hearts a definite respect for the good soldier as a soldier, and for the spirit of military tradition.

It is when we turn upon the pacifist and confront him with that possibility of the concession of all his demands in the sudden obliteration of all the military systems in the world and ask him, "What then?" that we begin to realize the more fundamental and justifiable elements in the military and naval mentality.

And in the first place, it is well to be reminded, it is not our soldiers who are responsible for the horrors of modern warfare. To the best of their ability they have resisted the novelties forced upon them by civilian ingenuity. The British generals in the Great War refused to use and then failed to use the tank with a quite heroic obstinacy, and so they prolonged the indecisions of the war for two years. They completely defeated an attempt to mitigate the horrors and exhaustion of the journey to the front line by a system of telpherage. We have told of the British artillery authorities refusing Armstrong's guns and the Prussian War Office driving Krupp to sell a battery to Egypt before it could be brought to accept his improvements. Wellington opposed the adoption of the breech-loading rifle. Poison gas, mechanization, ironclads, torpedoes, submarines, aëroplanes, have all been forced upon unwilling service men by salesmen and financiers with the pitiless logic of material progress behind them. Such contrivances did not arise out of the intensely conservative service tradition. The civilian has been more reckless in his inventions and fiercer in their use.

In the next place it has to be remarked that the duty of preparing to kill and ultimately killing foreigners has never been recognized as more than half the work of the combatant services. Quite as important to the soldier was his rôle of guarding something central and precious, his rôle of protector. Only secondarily has he been a destroyer. Historically every specialized army system in the world had developed sooner or later a standing nucleus, a "Guard"—Pretorians, Mamelukes, Royal Guards or what not. Before that specialization, wars were wars of comparatively undisciplined levies, they were the wars of the natural man, and they were more cruel, predatory, indecisive, discursive, and destructive. The irruptions of Hun, Mongol, Northman and Moslim were far more frightful experiences than the conquests of Cæsar's legions.

We have already given the broad lines of a classification of the personas to which modern people shape their lives, and we have pointed out that the persona of the professional soldier is a blend of the nomadic with an increasing element of the educated persona; that he is not only a self-respecting fighting man but now also he is a specially disciplined and devoted, educated and educating man. To that idea we return. Let us compare the soldier with the scientific investigator, equally devoted and educated. Upon each there is impressed the same obligation to disregard mercenary considerations and all personal ends. Each has an acute and elaborate code of "honour," and each, it is assumed, would rather lose his life than save it at the price of betraying his essential purpose. But while there is this much resemblance, there is a wide divergence in the direction of the devotion. The man of science has to be devoted absolutely to the sense of truth within himself. He must doubt interminably rather than scamp his decisions to get to an end; he must not formulate half truths as truths. Until he passes from pure to applied science, he is rarely under the obligation to act. But the soldier lives alert for the call to a maximum of effective action. His, then, "not to reason why;" his "but to do or die." If his "orders" are to spy or cheat, he will obey.

His is therefore the type of persona most prone to uncritical loyalty. All his ideals march with the idea of saluting his superior officer and obeying "orders" implicitly. The navy is entirely with him in this respect. The "service" first and foremost, dominates such lives. Every established system, however decayed, has or has had its loyal, unquestioning "services." The King bolts to Varennes, but his Swiss Guard dies at its post. That is typical. Before everything else the good soldier fears attacks upon his own discipline and upon the discipline of the rank and file. He dreads the unsettling idea that creeps into his thoughts, and the leaflet at the barrack gates, with an equal unreasoning horror. To him these things mean not change but dissolution. He dreads that dissolution as much as the man of science welcomes the continual destruction and rebirth of generalizations. The "services" cannot be self-critical of their loyalties.

These loyalty systems radiating from the militant "services" devoted to the uncritical protection of the political institutions of the past, to King, however petty and absurd, and to Country, however restricted, are the living core about which the sweating employer, the munition profiteer, the financial adventurer, the beneficiary from old traditional privileges, the reckless journalist, the clinging adherent to bankrupt religions and every enemy of criticism, rationalization and open change, everyone who lives for to-day and not for to-morrow, rally and find their power of resistance. It is only by the capture of the imaginations that underlie every system of loyalty, by a gradual change in the direction of these loyalties as the error of their existing orientations is displayed beyond question, by the educational development of a new system of loyalties altogether and by the fusion and reconstruction of national services as world services, that the triumph of the new order can be attained. The new world state needs its own militant services, its own banded men of integrity and calculable action, even more than did the old order. If they are no longer needed to protect the State from the enemy without, they have to stand ready against brigandage, piracy and every form of disruption within. They have to keep safe the ways by sea and land and air from end to end of the earth. If they drop something of the decoration of the past, if they assimilate more and more to the realities of a land, sea and air police, they will, nevertheless, drop little of the sentiment and feeling that make the good service man what he is to-day.

Here, perhaps, we may recall the unsuccessful attempt of M. Léon Bourgeois to set up a cosmopolitan armed force at the disposal of the League of Nations and so provide the nucleus for a "world service" loyalty. M. Bourgeois has yet to be given his just meed of praise. He was, I fear, many decades in advance of his time. The need for such a nuclear beginning was also advocated very ably by the late Sir Mark Sykes.* It would be of extraordinary value now in allaying the irritation of minorities in such regions of mixed interest and mixed population as the Danzig corridor, Trieste and Macedonia. These obviously could be made into special neutral territories under direct League government, policed and administered by a more responsible international board of control. A League consular service is also an imaginative possibility, working to protect all foreigners in places where it is either inconvenient or undesirable to maintain separate consulates for each sovereign power.

Would that we had space here to enter more fully into the policing of the wilder parts of the world. In the section devoted to housing and town planning we have already noted the regulative work of the police in big towns, and we have linked it to fire-fighting and other necessary services. But the world knows too little at present of the life and duties of the various types of armed service beyond its immediate ken. We have but the vaguest ideas of the life of the police who guard the sea and carry order into wild places, and scarcely more of the realities of our protection against every sort of malefactor. Roads, railways, grazing lands must be patrolled. False prophets and crazy insurrection may spring up like weeds after an unfavourable change in the economic weather or for no traceable reason at all.

The whales, the seals, the wild things of the waters, the deserts and wastes and forests call now for vigilant services on sea and land and air to save them from destruction. Seals, penguins, many sorts of fish have to be protected from cruel and wholesale massacre by semi-practical fishermen who will fight if need be. Kidnapping, forced labour and forced prostitution have to be prevented. Wherever there are crowds, again, there is danger of the collective lunatic breaking loose. Race conflicts and religious conflicts are not likely to die out for many generations. Even in the United States the vendetta and Judge Lynch

---

*A book well worth reading in this connection is *The Problem of the Twentieth Century*, by David Davies (1930).

still hold out against the powers of law and order. No civilization can save the world from earthquake, eruption, storm and physical disaster, and properly trained and disciplined services must be at hand to aid and shepherd the victims and clean up the débris. No longer loyal to local king and partisan flag, the services must be loyal to mankind and themselves.

Et quis custodiet ipsos custodes? Our imaginary encyclopædia, in its exhaustive study of these matters, must find place for a discussion of the most subtle of administrative problems, how to admit complaints, reverse decisions and sustain an adequate criticism of protective services without weakening them or hampering their just activities.

In a little book *The Moral Equivalent of War,* William James the psychologist made an interesting suggestion that is well worth noting here. He believed that there was a considerable moral benefit in a year or so of compulsory military service for all the young men of the community. He thought something of the kind might with advantage be extended to young women.

He was writing before the war in America, where nothing of the sort existed, and he had in mind a comparison of the younger generation of that country with their French and German coevals. It seemed to him that the young Americans were growing up with an irresponsible quality, that they took the order and security of life too much for granted, and that they needed to be reminded by some such universal imperative, of their obligations to the community which had produced them and protected them. This was in the restless but abundant times before the disillusionment of the Great War, and it seemed to him that definite military training was likely to become less and less necessary in the world. He thought therefore that, although the year or so of service ought still to be exacted because of its moral value, it ought now to be directed to non-belligerent ends, and particularly to such onerous tasks as can never be properly performed by people working merely in order to get wages. For example, for young women there are nursing and many kindred forms of social work, in prisons and asylums, there is the care and cheering of friendless, old and infirm people, and of young children who have no one to look after them, and for the young men all that multitude of police duties, from fire-fighting to fighting pestilence, and from traffic control to gang control, where the individual is necessarily on his honour to give his utmost, his life even, with entire self-forgetfulness. And there are many forms of arduous or dangerous toil, at which it does not become a civilization to keep a man or woman for a lifetime, which could also very well be made into special services.

A constant flow of young conscripts through all these and a multitude of other parallel activities would, it seemed to William James, gave such organizations just that "ventilated" quality which would prevent them crystallizing into self-protective systems with a defensive attitude towards the general public—as they do tend to become if the whole personnel is making a life job of the employment. An ennobling quality would be given these services, and the associations of the conscript years would form the basis of later friendships and brotherhoods. Moreover, a large section of the general population would be brought, in this way, into touch with and watchful understanding of the official administrator.

Quite independently of William James, a parallel series of suggestions was made by his Austrian contemporary Joseph Popper (who died at Vienna in 1921 at the age of eighty-three), who is perhaps better known by his pen name of Lynkeus. His suggestion is of an economic conscription to produce all the necessities of mankind. He finds that from five to eight years of service will suffice. His chief work is *Die Allgemeine Nahrpflicht Als Losung Der Sozialen Frage* (Universal Civil Service as the Solution of the Social Problem). His book has not the psychological quality of James's; he sees the problem as a material one. It is not available in an English translation, but an account of his proposals by Fritz Wittels has been translated into English by Eden and Cedar Paul under the title of *An End to Poverty*.

We shall recall these suggestions later when we are dealing with the educational state.

§ 12. *Passive Pacificism**

Our panegyric upon the police and the service type of persona has taken us away from the main issue of the danger of war to modern life, and to that we must now return. We had made a brief review of the existing machinery of government in the world—except only the League of Nations, to which we are soon coming—and we had shown the broad elements in the nature of these seventy-odd organizations, which make towards further war catastrophe. We will now consider the efforts that are being made to avert fresh warfare in the world. *Homo sapiens* is no longer carried mutely from disaster to disaster. He is protesting and using his wits with considerable vigour in the matter. How far has he got towards prevention?

We have insisted in § 3, and we here repeat, that economic war, the White War of peace time, and Red War, when all pretense even of peace is frankly set aside are merely the chronic and acute phases of the same disease—militant nationalism. They constitute one problem. The clue for the effective solution of this supreme riddle lies, we have argued, in the reorientation of loyalties through a realization of the essential unity of our species. In a phrase, loyalties have to be diverted from world subdivision to world union. That will give us a useful criterion by which to judge a great variety of anti-war activities in the world about us.

It would be a complex task to frame a list and classification of the anti-war movements of the present time. They fall into two main divisions. The first of them that will have to be considered may be termed roughly the non-participatory type of movement. The movements of this class base themselves on a resolve to have nothing whatever to do with war, to refuse military service, payment of taxes in wartime and so forth and so on. The more fundamental idea behind such a resolve is the complete renunciation of force in the dealings of man with man. But the renunciation of force means the renunciation of posi-

---

*The fullest and most recent statement of the case for Passive Pacificism is Devere Allen's *The Fight for Peace.*

tive government. Fundamentally, therefore, in their absolute form, these passive pacificist movements are anarchist movements, and they merely apply the general non-resistance to evil professed by all Christians in their more exalted moments to the special case of war.

The second class of movement is more complex in its methods and less easy to examine and discuss. It looks to political arrangements, international courts, agreements between states, disarmament conventions, tariff unions and federations, to retard, mitigate, and ultimately abolish war. There are many intermediate shades of opinion and resolve between the definitive types of these main classes. Both are compatible with a vigorous agitation for that reform of history teaching, that change in the political basis of the normal persona, upon which so much stress is laid in this work. The new education, it goes without saying, is inherent in either type of proposal.

But before we can take up the positive proposals of our second class which aim at positive measures and laws to emasculate and end war, it will be necessary to make a very careful study of the mentality of the non-participating resister and to understand exactly why he or she takes up this curiously irresponsible attitude. They are very illuminating socially. There are wide differences in the conception of non-participation. There is first, in close approximation to the second group, what we may call conditional non-participation. Associations of various kinds exist whose members pledge themselves not to support their own government in war unless it has made the last possible effort to arbitrate the issue. Other associations go further. They will refuse service in any circumstances because they believe that it takes two governments to make a war, and that it is the business of all governments to avert a catastrophe at any cost. And quite logically they will refuse to receive or impart military training, because they declare war is now impossible without gross blundering on the part of their own government—whatever the enemy government may have done. Moreover, they hold, and perhaps soundly, that a government duly warned of the probable passive defection of considerable sections of its population will pursue a far less aggressive and confident policy than one assured of a unanimous people, ready to leap to arms at the roll of the drum, on no matter what occasion. And as a further step comes the public announcement, so to speak, of one's neutrality in *every* possible war. All these movements must weigh very usefully with governments in making them chary of belligerent gestures, but alone they may not only fail to prevent war, but, it is alleged with some show of reason, they may even provoke attack from without by weakening the potential resistance to some more predatory state with a smaller proportion of peace idealists in its community, or with ruder methods of restraining their propaganda.

After all, unless the whole story of human development told in this work is wrong, it is by forcible assertion that the will for creative order has thus far established its rule in the world. Let us not forget that Education as we shall show later is to a large extent repression—discipline. There is as much ape as angel in *Homo*. The policeman, not the saint, is the guardian of freedom in the highways and byways. The protective function of the militant "services" is not a sham. If it were not for the potential force of orderly governments the whole world would be given up to brigandage. Non-resistance has never been of the slightest use in abolishing brigands. And a modern belligerent state, waving its aggressive patriotism at its neighbours, boasting of its armaments and clamouring for expansion, differs only in the scale of its offensiveness from some brigand chief in possession of a Chinese province, and he again from the gangster in a Chicago district. If the resistance of the reasonable civilized elements in such a brigand state is inadequate to control its government, it is not simply the right but the duty of more civilized governments about it to restrain its aggressions. And surely it is the duty of everyone within that state or without it, to do whatever is possible to weaken its internal discipline, diminish its credit and hamper its armament. It is childish to pretend, as so many non-participatory pacificists do, that all governments are equally belligerent and equally pacificists. It is mere mental laziness to assert as much. Values cannot be so easily ignored in international politics. The power most closely associated with the armament industry was the power most responsible for the war of 1914–18, and ten thousand able writers can alter that. Preparation is aggression, and aggression is brigandage. Brigandage will cease only when the last brigand is dead or in the hands of the police. War will be at an end when the last bellicose sovereign power lays down its arms before the united forces of civilization. And not before.

These things the passive pacificists ignore with considerable pertinacity. And since they are often people of considerable culture and ability, it is necessary to enquire into the ideology that enables them to do this.

Their vision of the world seems to be defective in certain particulars. Many of them seem to be the children of comfortable, secure homes and prosperous parents. There is a failure to realize that human affairs have to be kept going by the positive effort of a number of people. Before the Great War there was a curious feeling in the minds of many, that in spite of the visible armament competition in progress and the extraordinary swayings of European diplomacy, a big European war was unthinkable. There was an irrational persuasion that somewhere, somehow, it was being held off. I shared that baseless feeling. I was one of those pampered children of security. August 4, 1914, was an immense surprise to me, and I believe that a great number of comfortable, prosperous Europeans felt the same astonishment. The guns, of which we had watched the loading, were really going off! Although the forms of danger had been all about us, we had lived in such habitual security all our lives that our thoughts were bedded softly on that reasonless assurance.

It had certainly never occurred to us that we had to do anything in the matter—until the war was upon us. In America the war seemed still more archaic and incredible. Very few people really wanted war, and that had seemed to dispose of the matter. So America came into the war with more internal violence, more social persecution than any other belligerent. The war spirit had to be forced and fostered, or it would not have been adequate.

It is in the nature of all animals, and man is so far an animal, to live tranquilly until the ambushed eater rustles forward to his leap or the pursuer is visibly in sight. The anticipation and prevention of public catastrophe is a recent enterprise of the mind. Formerly the final direction of things public and general was left to Fate or the gods. The natural disposition of man is to keep happy as long as possible by denying the active evil in powerful, but not immediately hostile, things, to leave them alone unchallenged as long as they leave him alone and get what is to be got out of life meanwhile.

A great factor in this inactive pacificism is the disposition of fine and cultivated people to save their minds and lives from the complex distresses the positive prevention and forcible suppression of war adventurers would certainly cause them. There are so many fine, subtle, delicate, interesting and delightful things in life that it is intolerable that one should be forced to occupy good gray matter with these loutish, cruel, stupid, and abominable violences. But war is no more to be ended by saying, "No more war" and "I stand out," and declaring that every government that went into the Great War was just as bad as any other and indeed on the whole worse, than is burglary to be ended by speaking in tones of remonstrance to a policeman who uses his truncheon.

War is a necessary consequence of the political fragmentation of humanity. Until humanity constitutes a political unity, the mass of reasonable people will insist upon preparations for defensive war, and preparations for defensive war are indistinguishable in their nature and moral reactions from preparations for offensive war. There must be the same study and development of new and more dreadful war expedients. The only alternative to belligerent forces in the world is a common repressive and defensive force. Such a force has still with infinite toil and perplexity to be organized. But these passive pacificists seem to believe that in some remote and mystical form such a force exists already and can be invoked.

Their refusal of service is not therefore so much an action against their own state as an incantation to that unknown, unimplemented God of Peace. In that god they put their faith—and so, gesticulating sceptical disapproval and moral superiority towards all who seek to grapple with Mars in his panoply, towards all who seek to subjugate chaotic by ordered force, they liberate their minds to ease and agreeable occupations. Other people will do the dusty and laborious job, and then, if these others succeed, will they not be justified in their faith in that unknown power?

§ 13. *The League of Nations and Other Experiments in Internationalism*

We can now take the League of Nations into our account. Some readers will have wanted to consider it before. But for several reasons it has been preferable to glance down the diplomatic gallery, finish with our politicians and the Civil Service and see something of Scientific War before we came to this part of our Museum of Human Activities. We may figure the Peace Section now as a vast unfinished new wing to the collection. Much of that wing has still to be built; it is in the phase of mason's work and scaffolding in the open air, and even the galleries that are glazed and finished with cases and tables and open are far from full. It is through the League of Nations' display that we must pass to the greater possibilities beyond.

It is not really a very impressive display. One may figure it as a little clutter of beginnings amidst great spaces that are still eloquently vacant. It is only natural that it should be like that. The idea of a world League of Nations was unknown before the end of the first decade of this century. The League itself was born in a sudden convulsion of human hope at the end of the Great War.

In the stirring up of men's ideas that resulted from the war catastrophe of 1914–18, there was a real disposition to break away from the competitive military and diplomatic methods that had contributed so greatly to bring about that disaster. There was much talk of "Open Diplomacy" and a phase when certain great political figures, and particularly President Wilson, had manifestly a world-wide appeal. The time seemed ripe for a bold break with the system of competitive independent sovereign states altogether and the establishment of a centralizing Pax Mundi, with the support and approval of the great majority of mankind. The thing seemed possible then. Whether it was really possible no man can say.

In the *Outline of History* we have told of the foundation of the League of Nations and shown how the nineteenth-century sentiment in favour of "little nations" which dominated the imagination of President Wilson, at a time when all the world was crying aloud for Federation, blocked the way to a reversal of the Westphalian tradition. The very name of League implies a binding association. But President Wilson did not pursue that implication. He was perhaps too much of an historian and not enough of a creator. He had surely a vision of what might be, but he was too punctiliously disposed to fit it into ancient and traditional formulæ. He thought not of mankind in chains to nationalism but of little nationalities struggling to be "free." The League of Nations from its birth onward, therefore, was dedicated to national sovereignty, and it was staffed largely by the diplomatic profession. It was to have made the world safe for democracy; it made it safe for more diplomacy. It has never yet recovered from this initial inoculation with the virus of nationalism. Perhaps it never will. It has displayed small power of growth or initiative in the past decade, and it has lost most or all of whatever hold it had taken upon the imaginations of common men. The world looks to it no longer as a beacon of hope.

Yet it was a very important initiative, and it would be premature to consider its possibilities as exhausted. Everyone interested in the present state of human affairs is bound to scrutinize its working and learn whatever it can teach or suggest to us, to be sceptical of its present pretensions and hopeful for its future usefulness.

A very good book on the organization and work of the League of Nations is Howard Ellis's *The Origin, Structure and Working of the League of Nations* (1928); another, *League of Nations; Ten Years of World Coöperation,* written and pub-

lished by the Secretariat (1930). A compacter work is Wilson
Harris's *What the League of Nations Is*. To these works chiefly
we are indebted for the facts we retail here. All these books set
out the organization of Geneva in as hopeful a light as possible,
and all make the reasons for looking on beyond it now to other
unifying processes very clear. The claims and the apologetics of
these writers are alike illuminating. A more critical study is
H. R. G. Greaves' *The League Committees and World Order*
(1931) and a useful treatment from the legal side is Norman
L. Hill's *International Administration* (1931).

President Wilson seems to have had no very modern political
philosophy. He had a legal rather than a psychological mind;
his intelligence was of the nineteenth rather than the twentieth
century; and the great opportunities of the time rushed upon him
unheralded. And perhaps he was over self-reliant. His mind did
not go out readily to others and he was apt to make or attempt
to make men of his own calibre, his subordinates or his antagonists, rather than his helpers. The League, as he seems to
have conceived it, was a sort of super-federal government, and
he planned its constitution on lines that might have been drawn
by one of the framers of the American Constitution. As he
brought it into existence it was a quasi-parliamentary government
of a type such as we have already criticized. It has an Upper and
a Lower Chamber. The Assembly is a house of representative
delegations from all the constituent countries of the League,
each delegation casting one vote. The Council is a gathering with
permanent representatives of the greater powers and a limited
number of representatives of other states, who come in and go
out of the Council at regular intervals.

We will not repeat here the story of Versailles and the subsequent refusal of the American Senate to allow the United States
to enter the League. That is given with all the essential particulars in the *Outline of History*.

Once a year, usually in September, this Assembly, this partial
parliament of mankind, meets, and the hotels of Geneva are
packed with a polyglot multitude. There are not only the delegations from the constituent countries, but a great multitude of

camp followers, journalists, publicists and interested people. Geneva becomes the most animated of towns; its quays are crowded, and everybody of consequence in international affairs seems to be hurrying in one direction or the other across the Pont du Mont Blanc. A delegation may consist of as many people as its country chooses to send, but it has only one vote. The Assembly meets first in full session in an assembly room near the Grand Quai, the Salle de la Réformation, with a sternly Calvinistic gallery for strangers; it debates upon current international issues, resolves itself into a chamber of special committees which report to the concluding plenary session, and after that has been held and the reports have been considered, the tension upon the hotels relaxes again, and the delegations disperse north, east, west and south.

There can be no doubt that so far the Assembly has served a useful purpose for the public discussion of various issues of world importance. It is also commended as a meeting place for the politicians of remote countries, and as a medium for what Howard Ellis calls "hotel diplomacy," that is to say quiet friendly tentatives and undocumented understandings. It has been a convenient instrument for the formal discussion and settlement of various minor clashes in which the issues were not too strongly felt, the cases of frontier violence between Italy and Greece (1923) and Bolivia and Paraguay (1928), for example, and the Mosul frontier delimitation; but as regards War, either what we have described as the incessant White War of tariffs, or the Red War of military preparation and menace, it has proved a very ineffective body indeed. In September, 1931, while the Assembly was actually in session, warfare began between Japan and China. Mukden was bombarded and occupied by the Japanese army—without, it is alleged, any orders from home. The army acted automatically in response to local irritations and proceeded to occupy South Manchuria. This conflict manifestly puts the League of Nations to the test, for both China and Japan are members of the League and Japan is one of the Big Five.

The Council now sits four times a year, though a proposal

was made by Sir Austen Chamberlain to restrict its annual total of meetings to three on the ground that foreign ministers had more important work to do at home. It has five permanent members (Britain, France, Germany, Italy, and Japan), and nine others are elected, three a year for three years, by the Assembly. China may give place to Latvia, for example, or Abyssinia to Peru, or Spain to Liberia or the Irish Free State: turn and turn about. It exercises a number of directive functions, but the world's interest in its proceedings has become more and more flaccid with the spreading sense of its essential ineffectiveness. It meets and disperses without any conspicuous excitement in the European or American press. It meets without a splash and sends no thrill throughout the earth. Most people in the world are unaware of its gathering or dispersal.

But behind these parliamentary organs there is the Secretariat, the Civil Service of the League. After our examination of the modern needs and methods of government it is natural that we should turn to this with a very lively curiosity. It is appointed by a Secretary General (Sir Eric Drummond) and the whole staff numbers 670 persons (1930) drawn from fifty-one different countries. There are a number of sections, Political, Economic and Financial, Transit, Mandated Territories, Disarmament, Health, Social Welfare, Intellectual Coöperation, Information and so on. There is a registry of treaties and various technical and advisory committees, some permanent and some gathered for special tasks, operate in correlation with the permanent sections. No part of this organization has any executive authority. It "studies," it "advises," it prepares material.

Except for leaves and vacations, the Secretariat is always to be found at Geneva. It has been housed in a number of converted hotels; the Hôtel National, which became the first Palais des Nations, being the chief; now special buildings are coming into existence to supplement these first emergency shelters. The personnel of the secretariat is drawn from among the available experts in political science and administration, and the original recommendation of the organizing committee in 1919 was that they should be men and women best qualified to perform the duties assigned to them without taking account of any supposed necessity for selecting persons from different nationalities. Qualifying this was a repudiation of any nation or group of nations monopolizing the staff appointments. Yet, clearly, if some one nation produces all the best experts, there is no sound reason why it should not "monopolize" all the service. "The members of the Secretariat, once appointed, are no longer in the service of their own country but become for the time being exclusively officials of the League. Their duties are not national but international."

It was hoped to develop in the Secretariat an "international" (i. e., a cosmopolitan) mind. But the spirit of national jealousy has never been exorcized from Geneva, and the personnel of the Secretariat is continually disturbed because this or that influential power objects that it is not getting a "fair share" in the official machine.

Now let us take one section of the League's activities and examine the spirit and vigour with which it does its work. Let us take as our sample that "Committee of Intellectual Coöperation" which was originally projected by M. Hymans at the Peace Conference of 1919 and organized in 1922. Unlike various other departments of the League's activities, it is a genuine postwar product; the League's very own.

Here we have a title, at least, which is full of promise. We think at once of a systematic enquiry into all the endless mental activities of mankind that are now calling for and feeling their way towards coöperative unification. The dream of a mightier Encyclopædism rises majestically before us. We think of men of science and influence coördinated to restrain the production of war inventions and to guide the spirit of our race towards unity.

Victor Lefebure, in his *Scientific Disarmament,* reproaches scientific men for the readiness with which they give their knowledge and inventive powers to the ends of national armament. He is particularly concerned by the possibilities of gas warfare. He wants a real pacificist organization of these at present irresponsible and mischievous experts. He wants a new scientific morale in regard to war, a cosmopolitan morale. This would be an obvious objective for a committee of intellectual coöperation throughout the world, but I find no evidence of any such attempt on the part of the existing organization.

The Introduction to this present work, and indeed all our present enterprise, is devoted to one of the main questions that such a committee should undertake, the question of a new education for a new age. The need to make over the schools of the world from the teaching of national to cosmopolitan history has been fairly evident since 1919. One man at least was alive to these great needs, that very original and creative thinker, that typical survivor of the old clear-headed French tradition, M. Léon Bourgeois. As he put it, it was to be a committee "to deal with questions of intellectual coöperation and *education.*" But the Second Assembly, which sanctioned the creation of this new organ, dropped the last two words and left the League with the Committee emasculated. Emasculated for such achievements as this—I quote a passage in the best prospectus style from the Secretariat's own *Ten Years of World Coöperation.*

"The Committee on Intellectual Coöperation consists entirely of persons chosen for their individual eminence in the world of thought. The object of the League in establishing it was to summon to its councils a carefully selected group of the best thinkers of the age drawn from the chief intellectual disciplines. Thus philosophy has been represented by the first chairman, M. Bergson, physics by Dr. Einstein, Mme Curie, Dr. Lorentz, M. Tanakadate, Dr. Hale and his successor Dr. Millikan, and, more recently, by M. Painlevé, Greek studies by Professor Gilbert Murray, literature by M. de Reynold, medicine by M. de Castro, biology by Mlle. Bonnevie and later by Sir Jagadis Bose, the arts by M. Destrée, history by M. Susta and law by Professor Ruffini (succeeded later by M. Rocco) and by M. Mariano H. Cornejo.

"To gather together such an array of talent, representing such a variety of specialisms, countries and intellectual traditions, was in itself no mean achievement, particularly at a moment when the contacts between scholars, which had been interrupted during the war, had not yet been renewed. The mere existence of the Committee has certainly been a considerable moral influence in favour of international understanding."

But did this astounding committee ever really exist—that is to say, as a conference with a purpose? What did it *do?* Nothing apparently for two years. In 1924 it suddenly remembered itself and its promise, and it found a material form as an institute lodged in the Palais Royal in Paris with an income provided by the French government and a staff and a secretary. But it chose to be limited by its terms of reference and displayed no power whatever, of conviction and will to break away from them. It has done nothing commensurate with our original hopes for the League. It has engaged in a few minor activities; the organization of a certain amount of relief for intellectual workers in countries impoverished by currency fluctuations, the exchange of publications between scientific societies, the formation of an "International Committee of Popular Arts"—whatever popular arts may be—and so on. These are very meritorious things to do in their way, but they have no more effect upon the broad intellectual processes of the world than the Council and Assembly have had upon the economic hostilities that impoverish mankind, or upon the gigantic preparations for another great war that are going on so vigorously everywhere. Perhaps the crowning achievement of this committee so far is the Resolution which, greatly daring, it passed in plenary session on July 25, 1931, on the initiative of Professor Murray and M. Painlevé.

"The International Committee on Intellectual Coöperation,
"Considering that the military burdens borne by the different nations render increasingly difficult the studies, the training and even the continued existence of an intellectual class, and thus hamper the intellectual progress of mankind;
"Considering further that the Committee has undertaken and is carrying out the duty of instructing youth in the principles of the League of Nations, of peace and of international coöperation;
"And that the whole development of the League of Nations is closely bound up with the progress of disarmament and of the international conventions ensuring Peace:
"Expresses the ardent hope that the General Conference which is to meet next February will achieve a substantial reduction in the land, sea and air armaments of the world under

such conditions as will provide international guarantees for the security of each nation."

After which the banded Intellectuals appear to have slammed down the window very hard and dispersed in a threatening and portentous manner. No armament manufacturer could fail to realize the gravity of their disapproval.

It may be objected that it is not fair to judge the League by one of its feebler departments,* but that department has been taken because it was the League's own child. The International Labour Bureau, which has certainly done good work—and which carries a United States representative—is really only a continuation of the International Association for Labour Legislation founded in 1900, which held annual conferences and brought off such achievements as the Phosphorus Convention of 1906, in pre-war days. The League simply annexed and reshaped it. It might have grown more vigorously outside the League. The International Court again is claimed as something new. It is, we are told, a "court of justice," and not merely a "tribunal for arbitration," like the Hague Court. That is what is new about it. But how a process in a court which has no power of enforcement whatever can differ from an arbitration is for the lawyers to decide. The pre-war court and the post-war League Court are linked closely together and share the same "Carnegie" Peace Palace at The Hague. The League's share in the business is chiefly an affiliation claim. Various other originally independent international organizations, such as the International Hydrographic Bureau of Monaco, have been brought under the auspices of the League without visible harm or benefit.

But it is not our purpose to indict the League of Nations for its very manifest superficiality and inadequacy. It puts up such claims as it can; the prospectus style of its account of itself was almost unavoidable. It does very little, and it puts a brave face on the matter. There is no touch of deep living pride, of high ambitions or creative imagination in its evasive and diplomatic

---

*For a criticism of the economic side of the League see H. R. G. Greaves, *The League Committees and World Order.*

direction, but in that way it escapes getting into difficulties with resentful governments. It might have been the rebellious heir of the old order, and it has become its clerk-valet. It does not lead the way to unity, but at times it makes a deferential and perhaps directive movement towards unifying courses. It has immobilized and killed that wide and dangerous desire, as it must have seemed to all diplomatists and most politicians, for a world super-government, that flamed out in men's minds in 1918. That desire may flame again as our troubles thicken, but one may doubt whether it will flame upon the Geneva altar.

Let us rather accept the League for what it is and for what it may be. It is a small achievement if we measure it by the scale upon which any real intellectual, economic and political consolidation of human affairs must be attempted, but it is an achievement. It is a ripple in the advancing tide of unifying realization. It is a useful, if modest, permanent addition to the governmental resources of mankind. If it is not the home of unity, it is for awhile a convenient postal address. It has been and is, and it may well continue to be, a point for assignations, for enquiries and meetings, and the preparation of more effective coöperations. It may play the rôle of a matrix for the casting of organizations wider in scope and more powerful than it can ever be. It will be serviceable in just the measure that it transmits, and it will be objectionable just so far as it attempts to arrest, control, annex and claim credit for, the unifying forces of the world.

THE RED CROSS

But now let us look at certain other experiments in internationalism, less pretentious than the League but possibly more illuminating in the way in which they have contrived to transcend nationalist limitations. Senior among these is the Red Cross. The Red Cross was founded by Henri Dunant in 1862, for the assistance of the wounded in war; it was begotten by his book, *Souvenirs de Solférino,* describing the horrible condition of things upon that battlefield. It has had Geneva for its headquarters since its inception and its International Committee treats with governments and with the League almost as if it were an independent sovereign power. It has sustained objections to various war cruelties. Its arrangements for the repatriation of prisoners after the Great War were ably executed, and it has recently developed a special "International Relief Union" for the prompter assistance of populations stricken by famine, earthquake or the like sudden disasters. Its work in sustaining a world standard of nursing and of medical material has been of inestimable value. It is a federation of national societies which among them all count somewhere about 17,000,000 members.

THE INTERNATIONAL INSTITUTE OF AGRICULTURE

Another very remarkable and important international experiment, which has the status of a sovereign power making actual treaties with governments, is the International Institute of Agriculture in Rome. This was the creation of an American, a man, as the world must some day admit, of a very wide economic and political vision, David Lubin. His object was to establish a continual survey of world production, a perennial census organization, first of food products and then of other staples, in relation to world consumption. Conventions were made in 1905 between Lubin and forty countries representing 90 per cent of the world's population, by which they agreed to furnish reports and subsidies to his institute. A special treaty was signed with the Italian government of Victor Emmanuel for the establishment of the Institute in a palace built for it by that monarch in the Villa Borghese. There it set to work. Its operations were shattered for a time by the Great War and Lubin never saw it restored to effective world influence. On the day that the main avenues of Rome were beflagged, crowded and lined with troops to receive President Wilson, fresh from the triumphs of Versailles, Lubin's obscure funeral was making its way by back streets to the cemetery.

It is only now that this potential economic world organ of his is struggling back to a functional existence. But the world agricultural census of 1930–31, which it has in hand at the time of writing, is evidence of its returning vitality. It has initiated congresses on meteorology, plant diseases and locust control, and collaborated on occasion both with the League of Nations and the International Labour Office. In the long run we may find that this institute, the International Red Cross and the modest bureau of the Postal Union at Berne—also sustained by contributions from all the countries of the world—are types of world coöperation more flexible and practicable than that rather old-fashioned pseudo-parliament at Geneva, with its upper and lower houses, its dreadful polyglot debates and its pervading diplomatic atmosphere. It is highly undesirable that these older tested experiments in internationalism should suffer incorporation with the League, or that the League should obstruct by any officious intervention the development of the many other similar federal organizations, the growing need for world action in such matters as disarmament and monetary and financial unifications, may evoke.

THE BANK OF INTERNATIONAL SETTLEMENTS AT BASLE

We have already noted in Chapter IX, § 10, the growing realization of the need to put finance (and possibly monetary affairs) upon a cosmopolitan footing. Very important in the development of this realization is the Bank of International Settlements set up in 1930 at Basle. Its ostensible objective was the handling and distribution of the payment of German reparations for the Great War of 1914–18. But from the beginning it was impossible to ignore the wider possibilities of any such institution, and it is already growing very remarkably beyond its original functions. It is empowered to assist in credit operations necessary for the development of countries arrested in their economic development. In other words, it is free, if it can, to weave together the highly industrialized countries of northwestern Europe into one economic system with the still mainly rural countries of the southeast. It has necessarily become a meeting place for the bankers of various countries and a centre of expert discussion. Its possibilities are enormous. Already there are attempts to evolve side by side with it a huge investment trust to lubricate the working of national industries throughout the world. A third possible member of this profoundly interesting embryo of a world business control is an international mortgage bank to irrigate the agricultural production of financially weak states by long term cosmopolitan lending.

Professor Gustav Cassel, the distinguished Swedish economist whose warnings against deflation before 1923–24 have been so amply justified by events, finds these international organizations insufficient in themselves. He supports a scheme, recently drawn up by representatives of the Bank of England, for a much bolder and larger international institute directing floating capital towards permanent investment, and organizing the central banks so as to coöperate in a radical and general reduction of interest upon those short-term loans which have played so large a part in the financial convulsions of the immediate past. (Chapter IX, § § 11 and 12.)

That is as much as we can say as yet of this new cosmopolitan banking. When, in a few years' time, this book is revised for a new edition, these paragraphs here may have to undergo a very considerable expansion. We may have to tell then of a world nucleus at least as important as the League itself.

OTHER INTERNATIONAL BODIES

Another international organ whose bureau is now seated at Geneva which has done very useful educational and organizing work, is the Inter-Parliamentary Union founded in 1888 by William Randal Cremer and Frédéric Passy. It holds annual conferences of cosmopolitan-minded members of parliament in various cities. At the Berlin Conference in 1928, 475 members representing 38 different countries assembled. And there is an International Bureau of Education with a constitution and an international status like the International Institute of Agriculture; it has been recently organized and as yet only a few countries have taken a share in it. So far it is no more than a poor timid, conferring body, afraid, it would seem, even of contemporary ideas. The blight of sentimental nationalism that cripples the Institute of International Coöperation manifestly lies upon it. Furthermore, there exist a multitude of purely propaganda organizations of a more or less thoroughly cosmopolitan trend, of which the British League of Nations Union and the Carnegie Endowment for International Peace under the presidency of Mr. Nicholas Murray Butler may be taken as samples. The latter organization distributes large funds, its publicity is wide and thorough, and the name of Nicholas Murray Butler has become a household word throughout the earth. With the International of Coöperatives we have already dealt in Chapter VII.

GENEVA AS A RENDEZVOUS OF SCHEMES

As an informal consequence of the establishment of the League of Nations at Geneva a multitude of voluntary organizations of every grade of scope and quality have concentrated upon the Lake. These too help to measure the scale of the League of Nations effort. Every question that has a world significance receives attention in this "Geneva outside the League," from the propaganda of Esperanto and the advocacy of suchlike artificial languages, to conferences on the bearing of sexual custom and hygiene upon population and international stresses. There are numerous organizations outside the pale which conduct enquiries and watch and seek to stimulate the League administration. Some act as centres for propaganda on behalf of the authority of the League. They have conferences; they sit in rooms talking, they constitute and reconstitute their societies, and no doubt they play a helpful part in maintaining international if not cosmopolitan ideals in a discouraged world. Many of the most active spirits in this outer circle at Geneva are wealthy Americans; many are less opulent students and enquirers seeking opportunity.

It is natural that a certain number of picturesque eccentrics should also be attracted to the lakeside to complete the picture. They walk on the quays, they cross the bridge to and fro, they wear rather distinctive costumes and carry important-looking portfolios.

Geneva is an interesting convergence of hopes and projects and pretensions, but if it is to be regarded as the sole centre and culmination of the organizing as opposed to the disintegrating forces in world politics, it is not a cheering resort for those who have any sense of the magnitude and urgency of the dangers which threaten our precarious civilization.

Happily Geneva is not all. Geneva is merely a rendezvous for a certain number of people who have been brought there or attracted thither by the expression it gives to creative forces that are at work everywhere. If Geneva and all that centres upon Geneva and the League were destroyed to-morrow, it would be a grave, but not an irreparable loss to mankind. These forces would find another rendezvous. The drive towards unification is in the logic of human association; it is the primary fact of history and social life.

§ 14. *Projects for Cosmopolitan Synthesis: Necessity Drives Us towards World Controls*

A distrust of the League's utility in the larger functions for which it was contrived is manifestly felt by most experienced politicians and statesmen. Ever since 1923 they have betrayed their dissatisfaction with the League by a search for supplementary devices to avert or mitigate war—whether White or Red.

It would need a long chapter of modern history to survey these supplementary efforts, from the Washington Disarmament Conference and Locarno, to the Kellogg Amphictyony and the proposals of M. Briand for a United States of Europe. It is necessary to distinguish clearly between such mere sentimental gestures as the Kellogg Pacts, however magnificent, and practical efforts to coöperate on super-national lines, however modest.

Perhaps the most hopeful element in all these post-war projects, conferences and the like, is their persistent resumption. There is a widespread uneasiness in the human mind that no fatuous renunciation of war "as a method of policy" will allay. Indefinable, various and universally dispersed urgencies are worrying the attention of our species towards some effectual unification, in spite of all the heavy thrust of tradition towards further conflicts.

Along one line of experiment we may note the various tentatives that have been made towards economic federations (with, of course, the correlative of military alliances) on a supernational scale. That may be as good a way as any of getting past the patriotic pickets. It may be true that Human Unity is too remote for a single imaginative stride. Pan-Europa seems, at the first glance at any rate, more practicable than Cosmopolis. Let us accept any proposal to go halfway there, in the sure conviction that once we are upon the road, we shall find our projected super-national combination no more than a wayside inn for the final political home-coming of mankind. M. Briand's scheme for the "United States of Europe,"* British projects for "Empire Free Trade,"† the reality of Pan-America,‡ the dream of an Anglo-Saxon alliance, and the like, may all serve a greater purpose. They may all help to break down the spirit of national and local egotism and to turn men's minds not simply to the possibility but the need of larger systems of coöperation. While such suggestions are materializing as negotiations and haggling their way to realization, the secular process of material liaison will continue its apparently inexorable advance and reinforce these suggestions by a multitude of practical confirmations.

None of these projects is very original. They have been schemes for the pacific unification of Europe since the days of Henri of Navarre. The Holy Alliance was an attempt to bring into European affairs the conception of a regal family, and Sir Charles Waldstein was advocating a United States of Europe project right up to the outbreak of 1914. No doubt a group of intelligent monarchs might have contrived a European merger at any time in the last two hundred years, but unhappily very few European monarchs in the last two hundred years have been even moderately intelligent, several have been stupidly and

---

*Based on R. N. Coudenhove Kalergis's *Pan Europa* (1923).

†See Lord Beaverbrook: *Case for Empire Free Trade.*

‡See C. E. Hughes: *Pan-American Peace Plans* (1930).

aggressively militarist, and most have clung like limpets to the romantic patriotic traditions on which their importance rests.

These practical proposals for political unifications we have considered, these unions, federations, empire free-trade systems and Zollvereins, are all attempts to achieve a partial unification of human interests geographically. But partial unification of human interests can also be arranged by function rather than region. World controls, it may be, are to be built up bit by bit. The world Postal Union, the International Institute of Agriculture, the International Labour Office, the Red Cross, are all examples of real cosmopolitan organs, working very efficiently for certain specific ends. Since the war the League of Nations may have obstructed rather than helped the development of further specific organizations of this type by its claim to be *the* international factotum. But, after all, such special conventions first for this end and then for that, may be the easier and better way to get past the Nationalist sentinels. The League was imposed upon the world by men whose imaginations were obsessed by the image of a legislative assembly in which politicians like themselves would play the leading rôles; they did not realize that world affairs may be handled and perhaps must be handled, by methods quite different from those of any modern sovereign government. Yet we may have a unified world securely at peace without either a president or a parliament of mankind. And even with most or all the old kings and presidents still robed and enthroned amidst their local gilding. There are possibilities of mediatizing the sovereign governments of the world bit by bit, with an extremely small amount of visible infringements of sovereignty.*

Consider first the problem of disarmament. The statesmen and diplomatists manœuvre and distinguish themselves, trust—I believe vainly—to the mercy of history for a favourable posthumous press, and achieve nothing of material importance.

---

*A good pre-war book on this subject, still well worth a student's attention, is L. S. Woolf's *International Government* (1916). A modern book (1931) which also sets out very plainly the large amount of international organization prior to and outside of the League machinery is Keith Clark's *International Communications: The American Attitude*.

But manifestly no effectual disarmament is possible without, first, a world convention to take the armament industry out of the hands of profit-makers altogether, and secondly, a permanent body, a commission, a convention, call it what you will, to watch, coördinate and restrain the armament of all the states party to the convention. Disarmament will remain the most ineffective of "gestures" until that International Armament Commission is in permanent authority. Sooner or later, if civilization is to go on, it *must* exist. The League of Nations is itself quite unsuitable for the function. The utmost the League can do is to facilitate and not hinder the establishment of that overriding body. And as soon as such a commission comes into being it will begin to develop its own personnel, and the world will begin the business of getting accustomed to and having confidence in its operations.

Next let us consider the growing realization throughout the world that the economic distresses of our time are world stresses and that there is no hope of restoring and maintaining prosperity throughout the world except through cosmopolitan action. In this field, again, there may be a rapid acceleration of activities, as economic and social troubles increase. We have already noted in §13 the extreme significance of the Bank for International Settlements at Basle and the buds it already bears. Its development into a real cosmopolitan organ is probable. Here, in another system of interests almost independent of the disarmament issues, we may presently find people adopting different agencies and different methods and working their way towards some sort of International Currency and Credit board. One can see that coming into existence by itself without any exacerbation of Nationalist feeling. It would need a considerable staff of its own even from the beginning. And from the beginning it could be in communication with the Disarmament Board.

The League of Nations Commission of Enquiry for European Union (1931), with its subcommittee on organization, with its examination of the world economic crisis, its projects for the international transmission of electric power and international coöperation in production, is an interesting preliminary explora-

tion (within the limitations of the League) of the possibility of
getting past political boundaries in economic matters.

Any such world boards or commissions would necessarily bring
together into effective coöperation considerable contingents of
the civil services of the various states. They would acquire ultra-
national attitudes of mind. The foundations of a real world civil
service, independent of national politics, would be assembled and
laid. (Already, indeed, at Geneva, the League of Nations has a
little rudimentary "world civil service" of five or six hundred
employees.)

In §12 we have already raised the possibility of international
boards for the administration and control of *"macédoines"* of
mixed populations and for a Geneva consular service. What we
are suggesting here links very closely with the discussion in that
section.

The Red Cross again could expand its work by degrees to
become an effectual control of world health, no patriot objecting,
and it could extend modern conceptions of sanitary regulation
throughout the world. There are similar possibilities of development in the International Institute of Agriculture which
might easily be associated with the Bank for International
Settlements at Basle and the projected International Bank for
Business Credits and the International Mortgage Bank in one
great scheme of world statistics and world bookkeeping. Those
who are acquainted with the writings of David Lubin will know
that his ideas went far beyond the range of a mere bureau of
statistics. He wanted not only a census of needs and production,
but also a survey and control of methods of distribution. His
own experiences as a merchant in America had impressed him
with the primary significance of freights in trading, and one of
his still undeveloped ideas was a progressive upward extension of
the work of the world's post office, from letters and postcards to
parcels of increasing bulk, until all the shipping and all the inter-
state transport of the world were brought into one tariffed
scheme. Is a development of that foundation in Rome until it
becomes a census and control—"control" because knowledge is
power—not only of agricultural production but of all staple

production *and distribution* also, an unthinkable thing? It would be something much less showy but infinitely more real than a world parliament.

An International Conservation Board, as the *Science of Life* shows, is already urgently needed for the protection of natural resources now being wasted, and particularly for the protection of many species of animals and plants threatened with speedy extinction. In less than a hundred years, while the statesmen and diplomatists wrangle, most of the forests of the world may be destroyed. Many smart men of business may make large fortunes out of the process, and that no doubt will reconcile them at least to living on a balder planet.

All these varied strands of world organization could be woven independently of one another, provided that we release our minds from the suggestion that now it is only through the straight and narrow way of the League of Nations that such things are to be attained. And another great power could be evoked if that Institute of Intellectual Coöperation could be rescued from the petty aims and the ridiculous nationalist ideology that affect it like a disease, and made an independent organization, open and accessible to all who are concerned in the intellectual processes of mankind. The original educational objectives of M. Léon Bourgeois could then be restored, and the vitally important task of examining, protesting against, controlling and ultimately suppressing patriotic and belligerent teaching throughout the world could be undertaken with some hope of success.

Later on (in Chapter XV) we shall return to the possibility that this Committee of Intellectual Coöperation might assist or direct the production of World Year Books and a World Encyclopædia.

Towards all these various ends people are working now. Every one of these desiderata carries with it vast possibilities of international confluence between public services and of international confluence between educational organizations. All such projects for world-wide special boards and services march side by side not only with each other but also with political projects for confederations and economic alliances, towards unity. The two types of coalescence, the geographical and the functional, are not in conflict. Together these two sorts of movement already constitute a very impressive array of devices, possibilities and hopes.

The greatest danger to such hopes seems to lie in the years immediately ahead. All this experimenting and muddling towards world organization takes time. Meanwhile the old traditions remain very strongly established—in the legal forms of government, in social habit, in our schools. Particularly in our schools. The armament firms remain. They have not yet been brought to heel. The press, ignorant and short-sighted, is still very largely on the side of mischief.

This search for the methods of a world pax is essentially an intellectual matter, a psychological problem; it is an attempt to save mankind from the insane obsessions of patriotism; it is a race of education to avert another and greater catastrophe. The fundamental thing in human association is and always has been education; for what our education is, that also is our social organization and the quality of our lives.*

---

*The student who wishes to expand the matter of this and the preceding sections should read A. C. F. Beale's *History of Peace*.

CHAPTER THE THIRTEENTH

THE NUMBERS AND QUALITIES OF MANKIND

§ 1. *The Increase of the World's Population.*
§ 2. *Impact of Races and Cultures.*
§ 3. *Eugenics.*

CHAPTER THE THIRTEENTH

The Numbers and Qualities of Mankind

§ 1. *The Increase of the World's Population*

WE CAN now take up another important aspect of the lives of these nineteen hundred million inhabitants of the human ant-hill: their multiplication. That multiplication continues as I write. In the last minute the grand total has increased by twenty. It has been increasing for a long time, for several centuries. It is increasing now by about thirteen million yearly. It may never have been nearly so great in any previous time.

Is this human population too great? Is it already consuming more of the available resources than nature renews? Or is it rapidly approaching that state of affairs? In a hundred years' time (A. D. 2031), at its present rate of increase it will number 4,000 millions. In two hundred years, 8,000 millions, in three hundred years 16,000 millions. These are overwhelming figures, the forecast of a stupendous breeding storm.

The answers to the questions we have asked here are discussed at greater length in the *Science of Life* and we have also approached these issues in Chapter IV, § 4 of this work. The earth is not fecund without limit, and in some of the needed alimentary substances it is even parsimonious. It seems, for example, to be grudging in its supply of phosphorus. The present great multitude of our own species is not now feeding upon the spontaneous gifts of our planet as other creatures are. Earth's gifts to us are in part already forced gifts. We depend on fertilizers for the fodder of our meat supply and for our vegetable food. And there is a limit to the supply of fertilizers. Every year the pressure on that supply increases. If the expansion of population continues, a time will come, whatever our efforts, when our species will return to the normal condition of most other species; that is to say, it will return to universal want and to a competition for bare subsistence.

In some parts of the world, in parts of Bengal, for example, humanity is now already at that level of bare subsistence. The peasants are so cheap that it does not pay to give them adequate protection against wild beasts. It does not pay. Every year thousands of them are eaten by leopards, tigers and other carnivora. Man-eating beasts will come into their villages and carry off people in the night from their houses. Locks, bolts and bars cost money, and Hindus cost nothing. They possess barely any clothing or furnishings, and though they breed abundantly, their rate of increase is kept down by their weakness and high mortality.

In a little while men of science may be in a position to estimate exactly what human population this earth can carry and go on carrying, at a tolerable level of existence, at a level of freedom, happiness, variety, direct relations to wild nature and full and complete living. At present such estimates are based upon insufficient assumptions; they are of no practical value. That estimated "optimum" of population, when we get it, may turn out to be above or below our present numbers, and it will certainly vary widely with what is taken as the standard of life. American authorities have put it as low as 350 million.* No doubt the earth could carry at a level of bare subsistence, for a few dismal decades, an enormously greater population of degraded human beings than 1,900 million. Some authorities go as high as 7,000 million. But who wants that? However high or low our standard may be, it will still leave us face to face with the facts that there is a limit to human increase and that it can be regulated and restrained or within certain limits encouraged and stimulated.

Since the time of Malthus it has generally been assumed that the human animal, like most other animals, has a reproductive

*See *Nature*, February 7, 1931, p. 217. Account of discussion of American Society of Naturalists, New Year's Day, 1930; Professors W. F. Ogburn and E. M. East.

urge sufficiently strong to keep its numbers pressing steadily upon the means of subsistence. But the readiness with which almost any human community to which the necessary knowledge was made available, has accepted and acted upon the suggestion of Birth Control, throws an increasing doubt upon that assumption. In various European countries, without any compulsion or any great pressure, merely through rising standards of life and the disinclination to bring children into the world at a disadvantage, the "natural" increase of the population has been checked and even converted into a decrease.

There are many interesting subtleties about the statistics of population into which we cannot enter very fully here, but, roughly stated, between 1876 and 1926 the birth rates of various European countries have fallen as follows: England and Wales 36.3 to 17.8 (16.3 in 1930); Germany 40.9 to 20.7; Italy 39.2 to 27.8; Sweden 30.8 to 16.9 and New Zealand 41.0 to 21.1. These are birth rates per thousand living at the time, and it is obvious that New Zealand, which was subjected to a steady immigration of people round about the age of marriage, was in a very different position from Great Britain, from which such young people were emigrating in considerable numbers during the last quarter of the nineteenth century. The New Zealand fall is really more striking than these figures at the first glance suggest. The British is less so. Yet, though such considerations mitigate or intensify the crude facts, they do not do so enough to alter their essential significance.

This fall in the birth rate has been accompanied by a fall in the death rate which has minimized its effect upon population totals. The figures for the countries just named are England and Wales 20.9 to 11.6 (11.5 in 1930); Germany 26.3 to about 11.9; Italy 28.8 to about 16.8; Sweden 19.9 to 11.8 and New Zealand 11.8 to 8.7. This gives an apparent fall in the rate of increase of population of all these countries of about 9 per thousand in the case of England and Wales, 7 in the case of New Zealand and similarly for the others. Had the death rate not fallen also, the "natural increase" would have been wiped out altogether and replaced by an actual fall. During the period we are considering, the progress of hygiene saved so many infants that would otherwise have perished, and prolonged the life of so many people beyond middle age who would have died under earlier conditions, that the falling off at the source did not produce anything like its full effect upon the aggregate numbers. (The infant mortality for England and Wales sank to the record figure of 60 per 1,000 births in 1930.) It is only the saving of infant lives that has a real continuing effect on population. They will live and reproduce, but the increased proportion of people over the age of forty-five (from 18 to 25 per cent in twenty years in Great Britain) will add little or nothing to subsequent generations. The actual state of affairs is better displayed in another form. The number of children under fifteen in Great Britain in 1921 was no greater than in 1891; the number of scholars in Public Elementary schools in England and Wales reached its maximum in 1915 and has declined steadily ever since. In 1881, 883,600 children were born in England and Wales; in 1924 only 729,900.

So far as gross numbers are concerned, the problem of over-population is evidently not an insurmountable one. As modern civilization spreads a rising standard of life about the world, the fall of the birth rate goes with it. The full effects of a fall in the birth rate take some time to make themselves felt. If the birth rate in Great Britain remains at its present level, the population will cease to increase in about ten years' time and will then begin to diminish. No further cut in the birth rate is therefore needed in order to bring about a reduction of the population in the near future. The same holds good of all the countries of Northern and Western Europe.

Partly this falling off of births is due to a retardation of marriage, but nearly all authorities are agreed that it is due mainly to what is now known throughout the world by Margaret Sanger's term of Birth Control. This is the deliberate avoidance of offspring (by methods discussed more fully in the *Science of Life*), particularly during the earlier and formerly the most fertile years of married life (i. e., between twenty-five and thirty-five). It has become a general practice throughout the modernized Atlantic communities. Its onset follows a practically uniform course as industrialism progresses, and as production and the standard of life rise. To begin with, in the ugly and "sweating" stage of industrial employment there is a phase of expansion, and only after that does the brake come into action.

The first result of modern industrialism in its cruder and crueller phases has always been to produce relative plenty at the price of onerous labour conditions. Anyone could "get a living" under the new régime, though it is a bare living of the most miserable sort. Previously there had been plain starvation. The new factory workers, ignorant, at a low level of subsistence, mostly young and thrown together with few restraining influences, were practically unable to avoid reproducing their kind. The first result of industrialization therefore was to foster a multiplication of the low grades of population. A rapid increase went on in Great Britain from the first appearance of factory manufacture in the eighteenth century up to the seventies of the nineteenth. Only then did a checking influence appear. Great Britain is the type instance in these matters. The story of the other industrialized countries upon the Atlantic, though it is not strictly parallel, is essentially similar, and the rest of the world's populations seem likely to follow these precedents one after another as industrialization reaches them; first will come proliferation through improved sanitation and increased production, then retardation.

The opening phase of proliferation has occurred in Japan and in the modernized industrial centres of India and China. In Japan, population which had been practically stationary for a century (between 1723 and 1846) at about 29 million, leapt up with the extensive adoption of European methods of production to its present congestion of 60 million. Japan is now, as Carr-Saunders has pointed out, in practically the same phase as Great Britain in 1875, and there is no reason to suppose she will not presently follow the other modernized countries towards a reproductive arrest. This is the more probable since her people do not emigrate readily to uncongenial climates, and most attractive emigration areas are closed to them. They will feel the pressure the sooner for that and resort to restriction sooner.*

We are still very ignorant of the state of affairs in China as a whole. India, from the point of view of population, is a quite abnormal mass of human beings. The heavy, protective paternalism of the British has maintained a state of peace, prevented disease and famine, the natural checks upon numbers in a barbaric community, and yet has done hardly anything to educate or raise the standard of living of this multitude. The Indian population in 1921 was 318,942,480. It had increased in spite of a high infantile and general mortality by 3,780,000 since 1911, and it continues to press upon the means of subsistence. This is a rate of increase, however, of about .12 per cent per annum, which is much lower than 1.1 per cent, that of the more advanced European countries to-day.† It is well to keep that ratio plainly in view. As we have just shown, the natural increase even of England and Wales is still about .62 per cent per annum; Italy stands at 1.1 and New Zealand at 1.24 per cent. The population of Russia, which probably declined in the terrible early days of the Revolution, is now (Chapter X, § 8) sweeping forward at the rate of 3¾ millions per annum, ten times the Indian increase. The proportion of Indians, therefore, to the rest of the world's population is not increasing; it is falling, and this is probably still truer of the uneasy multitudes of China. India and China are no doubt going forward in the population race, but the European and American communities are still going forward much faster. The popular idea of India and China as great overflowing tanks of population ready to burst upon the rest of the world is quite a mistaken one. But it is constantly appearing in the discussion of these questions. In Chapter VII we have described a cruel and systematic depopulation of equatorial Africa during this current century. The "Rising Tide of Colour" is a scaremonger's fantasy.

It is not our affair here to speculate about the possible future of India and China. Both regions are manifestly in a phase of

---

*See *The Japanese Population Problem*, by W. R. Crocker.

†But note that the years after 1921 show a rising rate of increase for India.

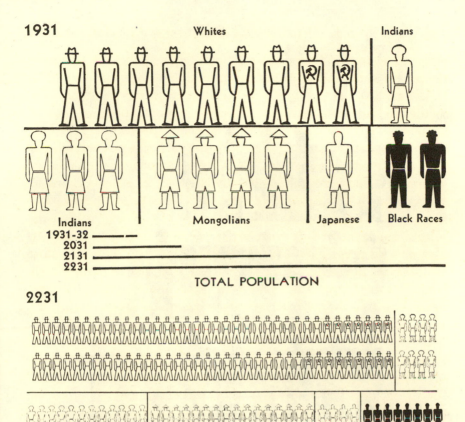

THE PROBLEM OF POPULATION

THE diagram at the top shows the present racial distribution of the people of the earth. The lower diagram, drawn within the same area, shows the crowding of populations three hundred years from now, provided that the present rate of increase is not checked. In both cases the figure of each man represents one hundred million people. The lower diagram indicates the tremendous overcrowding which increasing population will bring.

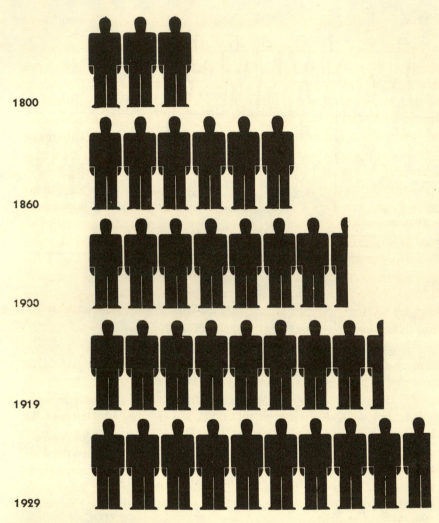

1800

1860

1900

1919

1929

THE GROWTH OF POPULATION

How the world's population has grown through the last century. Each figure of a man represents 200,000,000 persons.

great change and reconstruction. But it is as reasonable as not to assume that the same economic and social forces that have brought, or are bringing, the advanced communities of the world nearer and nearer to a stabilization of population, will ultimately become operative throughout the whole planet. As the obsession of jealously competitive nationalism lifts from the still crazy mind of our race, there may even be a concerted return to an ascertained optimum lower than 1,900 millions. The lean Indian in a loincloth, living in a hut with a cow-dung floor, who tethers his worn-out cow on the jungle edge for the tiger to kill, because he must not kill her himself, is no more a permanent actor in the world spectacle than were the British savages in woad, or the Arab pirates and slave traders who raided the coasts of Provence in the Middle Ages. The Indian ryot is not there forever. The stuff that will be stirring in the brains of his grandchildren may be so different from that in his own, that his way of living may have become an almost incredible horror to them.

We are too chary with our imaginations about modern possibilities. The forces of modernization have still to play upon those Indian peasant swarms. The elementary school, the newspaper, the cinema, have not yet brought home to them that there are other ways of living than the routines they still accept as the inevitable formula for life. There has been a certain drift of a few millions altogether from the countryside to the dreadful factories of Calcutta, Bombay and Cawnpore, where conditions recalling Lancashire at its worst phase have been produced, but the greater part of that immense village population, so poor, so weak, so monotonous in its toil and debt and hunger, remains intact. A few decades of native administration may restore the vital balance to the stability of pre-British days.

So we put the vast sad sunlit plains of Bengal and its hundreds of millions toiling only to eat sparsely, into the background of our general survey of human activities. They are playing only a passive part in the drama. They are living, as it were, in a dream, and it is impossible to anticipate in what fashion the call of creative energy will presently awaken them to take up a positive rôle in our renascent world.

So far as present conditions go there does not seem any probability worth considering of very great change in the proportions of the human population in the years immediately before us. The total in hundreds of millions is rising towards 20; of these about 7 will be the children of the Europeans and Americans at present living under the modern capitalist system, of which 7.2 will be English speaking; there will be 2 deriving from the present Soviet republics; 4 from the Indian mass and 5 Mongolian, of which something approaching 1 may be Japanese. There are thus 9 out of the 20, of what we may call the already Europeanized peoples, or 10 if we count in the Japanese. Two hundred million (or fewer) black people, chiefly in Africa, will complete the total. These are the great blocks which have to be built together into the coming world state. As their economic lives assimilate, their vital statistics are likely to move in unison, and the rate of increase or diminution become the same throughout the planet. There may be fluctuations in these proportions, but there does not seem to be the slightest probability that any section will be "swamped" by any other.

It is interesting to note how few are the people who may be considered answerable for the very great changes in the pressure of the more civilized populations we have just been considering. Until the last quarter of the nineteenth century birth control was a secret and shameful practice, known to occur but never discussed except to be disavowed or denounced. A few obscure societies, whose publications were in constant danger of prosecution, maintained what was then called the doctrines of Neo-Malthusianism in a world that feigned to ignore them. They had been active for three quarters of a century. Birth-control handbills were circulated in Manchester in 1823, it is believed at the instance of Francis Place, and books advocating birth control were published in America, the *Moral Physiology* of Dale Owen in 1830 and Dr. Knowlton's *Fruits of Philosophy* in 1833. *The Elements of Social Science* was published in London by Dr. George Drysdale in 1854.

The new views spread widely but quietly. They found their maximum application at first in France. They were talked over and applied more and more extensively, but it was left for quite a small number of resolute people to break the obscurantist convention and bring this fundamentally important issue in human affairs into the full light of open discussion. They did so under the provocation and threat of new prohibitive legislation, particularly of the laws passed by Congress and various state legislatures in America at the instance of Anthony Comstock's "Society for the Suppression of Vice." Anthony Comstock was not exactly the parent, but he was the stimulant of modern popular birth control. The pioneers for outspokenness in the English-speaking world were Charles Bradlaugh and Mrs. Besant, whose defiant republication of Dr. Knowlton's *Fruits of Philosophy* in 1877, and their subsequent prosecution, make indeed an epoch in human biology. A marked fall in the English birth rate followed this trial. The battle for the frank popularization of this kind of knowledge was fought and won in America by Mrs. Margaret Sanger, and in England by Dr. Marie Stopes. Margaret Sanger was a hospital nurse who had specialized in obstetric nursing. "During fourteen years of nursing in the homes of the New York poor," she writes, "I was brought face to face with such unbelievable misery that I reached the point where I could no longer face my own conscience without devoting myself to the relief of that misery at its source." Although she was happily married and the mother of three children, she embarked boldly and methodically upon a campaign first for the publicity of the issue, and then for its scientific development. Both she and her husband were imprisoned under the repressive Comstock Law—she twice—and she fought a stormy battle before she could win over public opinion to a rational attitude in the matter. Dr. Marie Stopes was a young doctor of science and a botanist of some distinction, who plunged into a parallel conflict in England, moved by the same pity for feminine wretchedness. England has had no Comstock, and it was not necessary for her to go to prison. Now in the English-speaking world at least, thanks mainly to these two valiant women, we may all talk, think and write without embarrassment of this quintessential of human biology.

But this freedom is not universal. In France and Italy, for example, the public discussion of birth control has been prohibited under penalties. In South Ireland also. Married women, in these countries, are in effect to be forced to bear children whether they want to do so or not. This does not prevent a fall in the birth rate in all three countries, but that fall is the result of forbidden knowledge, and it is associated with the utmost furtiveness, dirtiness, and shame. Indoor domestics, even when they are young married people, contrive to be as sterile in these lands of mystery as elsewhere, and the wife of the labourer and small shopkeeper no longer bears children until she dies exhausted in the good old fashion—whatever the authorities may forbid. But no one dare tell openly what is done. In France this obscurantism is by no means absolute. Those greater and better concepts of intellectual and personal freedom which are so inextricably interwoven in the French tradition, war against any such limitations of knowledge, and by way of medical and scientific conferences, more and more freely reported, and such courageous books as Victor Margeuritte's *Ton Corps est à Toi*, the possibilities of birth control are kept before the general mind.

The attempted suppression of birth control information in the Latin communities seems to be due mainly to a grotesque alliance between military feeling and the Roman Catholic organization. In Ireland, however, it is purely religious. The teaching of the Church as interpreted by the Papal Encyclical of January 8, 1931, denounces as sinful and unnatural any use of matrimony by which the production of offspring is evaded. (It is, indeed, as unnatural as stopping a tooth or wearing clothes.) No considerations of health or economics, says the Encyclical, are to justify this abstention. The good Roman Catholic must marry and breed or abstain, or he must not marry. Happily many Roman Catholics are not good Roman Catholics. Sterilization of the defective His Holiness declares is equally against the law of God. Sterilization, it is conceded, may be used by the civil power for the punishment of criminals but not as a social preventive measure. You may sterilize people to hurt and humiliate them, but not to do them and the world a benefit. The prospect of a world population of 16,000 million with an increasing population of imbeciles, in which no vow of poverty will be necessary, does not dismay the Church in the least.

This is "Providentialism" to the superlative degree; man is absolved from all practical responsibility in the matter, he is to observe the dogma and trust to the Church and Heaven. An age of famine and distress will afford great opportunities for holy living. The more sufferers, the more souls to be saved. There is a dreadful logic in this teaching.

This emphatic repudiation of any birth control whatever by the Roman Church is in marked opposition to the temporizing attitude of the Anglican Bishops expressed in the Lambeth Conference of 1930, and to the general disposition of enlightened people of all creeds; and from our present point of view at least it is regrettable that the mighty and venerable Roman Catholic organization should now have been put definitely and finally in a pose of antagonism to ordinary human welfare and happiness.

The opposition of the aggressive patriot springs from other than theological sources. It seems to be grafted upon a crude, brutish, and ignorant interpretation of what is called the "struggle for existence." President Roosevelt, for example, in his most "Bull Moose" style, reviled birth control as "race suicide." Why an attempt to husband the resources of mankind should be called race suicide, is difficult to imagine. A family that has restricted itself to three or four children has no more committed suicide than did Roosevelt when he took violent exercise in the presence of the reporters to keep his weight down. But the fear of being "outbred" by some imaginary, nasty but prolific "inferior race," though it has no support whatever in the figures we have just given, can be worked up into a very savage feeling indeed. To this terror of a pullulating flood of little brown, black and yellow babies which makes strenuous white men wake and cry out despairingly in the night, we will return when we discuss eugenics.

The Roman Catholic Church forbids birth control, but it makes no direct attempt to persecute hygienic propaganda. That it leaves to the secular arm. In France and Italy alike it is plainly not piety but the patriotic obsession, the insane entanglement of the mind with military delusions, which stands in the way of a frank and self-respecting practise of birth control. One must bear children for *la patrie*. "La France" wants soldiers, Italy's "destiny" is to recover the empire of the Cæsars. The Prince of Peace plays quite a secondary rôle in the active suppression of the Birth Control movement. He is merely an auxiliary argument. He stands for the crucifixion of the flesh rather than the glories of warfare. It is not souls to be saved but sons to be shot that the patriot is after—and particularly is he after other people's sons. It is to pacify the patriot rather than the priest that the poor tuberculous woman in the Parisian or Neapolitan slum is allowed, unwarned and unpitied, to bear her ninth or tenth diseased and hopeless child.

The general scheme of this work is to display human activities in one ensemble. But here we seem to be dealing for the most part with activities avoided rather than actual activities. We can add to our scene only a few figures here: a committee room with the mixed ingredients of every committee where "movements" are concerned, public halls and meeting rooms where an earnest speaker, often a woman, addresses a mixed crowd, or more intimately a special gathering of wives and mothers, or conferences of medical men. And we would evoke, too, a little room in a back street, which proclaims itself not too obtrusively a "Birth Control Clinic." Anxious furtive women with drawn faces and a persecuted expression come creeping in to tell a story in undertones.

If the reader wants to know the sort of stories they have to tell, he should read Margaret Sanger's *Motherhood* or Marie Stopes's *Mother England*.

Some of those who advocate a popular propaganda of birth control, like Professor MacBride, advocate it for others rather than for their own type and class, and they would supplement it with compulsory sterilization. Their minds are troubled by something called the "Rapid Multiplication of the Unfit," and by a gnawing vision of their own relative worthiness drowning in a sea of inferiors. This sort of birth control advocate is not really thinking of the population question at all, or, at any rate, he is making it a quite secondary consideration. What he has in mind is Eugenics, that is to say not Limited but Selective Breeding.

It is necessary to distinguish much more clearly than is usually done between these two different and separate ideas about reproduction, the idea of Birth Control and the idea of Eugenics. The former idea is an economic one based on the plain prospect of severe pressure upon the means and subsistence ahead of us, and it insists upon our attention here. The gross increase of population creates a problem immediately confronting mankind. This was the problem Malthus had in view in his celebrated *Essay on Population*. But there is also this other possibility, the possibility of improving the race by selective breeding, as races of dogs and horses have been improved, and as new and better Indian corn and wheat have been produced in recent years. This is a question for the biologist rather than the economist. In the *Science of Life* we tell of recent work in economic biology and we discuss and point out some of the difficulties in the way of human eugenics. We will recall these conclusions in a brief section following this one, to make it clear why Eugenics is not yet to be regarded as a practical proposition.

The question of Birth Control is a fairly straightforward one so soon as it is stripped of its eugenic entanglement. It has nothing to do with a "human stud farm," as some antagonists say it has. It is independent of quality. It is essentially a question of numbers and of quite practicable checks on their inordinate increase. The experience of the past few decades proves abundantly that where the standards of life are high, human beings, directly the conditions of parenthood become at all difficult and the necessary knowledge is available, are extremely ready and willing to lighten the burthen and anxieties of parentage. The possibility of overpopulation is formidable only in a darkened and ignorant community invaded in spite of itself by life-saving and food-increasing inventions from within or without, and even then it can be but a passing phase of distress.

§ 2. *Impact of Races and Cultures*

Our review of human lives as they are being lived at the
present time takes us from high lights of spacious hopefulness
to teeming wretchedness in the blackest of shadows. Our
blackest, our most horrible section has been §7 of Chapter VII,
and frightful and disgusting as that section is, it has nevertheless
been mitigated and toned down to make it endurable by the
ordinary reader. It is really cannibalism that is occurring; not
indeed the devouring of one man by another but the devouring
of one human society by another. Whole populations have been
and their remnants are still—now while the reader sits over this
book—being tormented and crushed to produce saleable products,
very much in the same fashion as the penguins of the Southern
ocean are massacred and crushed for marketable oil. There is no
Humanity, no *Homo sapiens*, embodied in a world government
to protect them; there are only competing sovereign states,
not concerned by their extirpation. How the "policies" of these
competing states have barred enquiry in one case, we shall note
later. It would be inhuman to leave this account we are giving of
human populations at this; to give merely the account of these
miseries without some discussion of what is being done and what
is being promised and attempted to alleviate this frightful pressure of raw and undisciplined modernism upon backward and
defenseless populations.

In the preceding section we have shown that in all probability
the main pools of human population are likely to remain, for at
least a very long period, with their general proportions to one
another and their innate characters and qualities unchanged. But
they are all under the influence of parallel cultural changes, and
they are all being brought now into the same economic net. At
a great number of points the chief "races" are either blending or
becoming joint occupants of common territories without blending, or with various political and cultural complications they are
in active conflict for the possession or control of disputed areas.
The inequalities of social and economic progress during the past
two centuries have given the "white" races and governments an

inordinate destructive material advantage over the black, brown and yellow peoples, and the absence of any world government, and indeed of any operative world ideology for the common good, makes the regions of racial and cultural overlapping regions of disastrous dominance, brigandage, subjugation and revolt, while the world-wide exploitation of natural resources by white finance and economic enterprise is the cause everywhere of a hundred distresses for the disadvantaged millions of colour.

The broad reply to the question, "How is this present enslavement, torture and conflict of races and peoples to be ended?" is plainly to press on as fast as possible from our present division of the world's control among seventy-odd sovereign governments towards a world control and the scientific and comprehensive treatment of the matter as one whole. World controls and scientific planning are the broad remedies for most human ills. But that answer is so broad, so very broad, that it leaves us still without any clear ideas of what to advocate and what to do for the miseries of to-day and to-morrow, the immense miseries that actually oppress and threaten millions of our species who will never see and much less benefit by that world rule and world plan towards which things are moving. Nor does that broad reply give us any criterion for judgment upon the actual methods of dealing with these things at the present time.

Two preliminary questions, however, have to be asked before we can pass any judgments at all in this field. The first is the question whether, of the main races of mankind, some are "superior" and some "inferior," or whether there is a practical human equality throughout the earth. The second is whether there is anything formidable and undesirable about free mixture between the peoples of these broad divisions. Upon both questions there is a voluminous and unsatisfactory literature, only to be compared in quality and temper to the unlimited frothings of prejudice and rubbish, of which we have already complained in Chapter XI, evoked by the discussion of sexual relationships. As between white, yellow, brown and black, considered as wholes, it seems impossible to fix a scale of gradations that justifies any social subjection or servitude. The question is complicated by the existence of really primitive and undeveloped peoples in small numbers, like the white hairy Ainu or the pigmies or the Australian black-fellows, and by the fact that in populations of every colour inferior strains are perceptible. But these ethnological pockets and these bad streaks do nothing to justify broad colour generalizations. Professor J. W. Gregory* quotes ample authorities to sustain a virtual innate equality in the case most in dispute, the case of the American Negro. The Negro is different from the white or yellow man; that gives him advantages as well as disadvantages; he is better at this and worse at that; but it is only by marking all the points of difference in the white man's favour that the thesis of the white man's intrinsic superiority can be sustained. The "poor white" strain in Georgia compares badly with its coloured neighbours. In South Africa the black is so far from being inferior to the white that the Kaffir is debarred from education, skilled trades and various professions, to *protect* the white from his competition.

But while Professor Gregory admits the virtual equality of all men and would have no race subject to another, he displays a strong conviction against inter-marriage. He has collected various casual opinions about the inferiority of half-breeds to individuals who are what is called racially "pure," and he brings in his own widely travelled impression of the inferiority of the "mulatto." I note his impressions with respect but not his conclusions, and against them I put the much wider and more intimate experiences of such observers as Lord Olivier and Sir Harry Johnson.† Lord Olivier knows Jamaica as few other observers do. He was once Acting Governor, 1900–04, and once Governor, 1907–13, and he has revisited the island in 1930 and 1931. The population of Jamaica is about a million, of which 1,500 claim to be "pure white" and 150,000 mixed. The rest are definitely "black," but black drawn from very various African sources. "The administrative, professional, commercial and

---

The Menace of Colour (1925), *Human Migrations and the Future* (1928), *Race as a Political Factor* (1931).

†Particularly his *Negro in the New World*.

clerical classes are predominantly white or coloured, but include
some who are pure black. The owners of the large estates are
probably in most cases white, inheritors of the former white
'plantocracy,' but many are coloured, and there are great numbers of coloured and black proprietors of smaller farms and
about 11,000 black and coloured landowners having from one to
fifty acres. In this community there is no policy whatever in relation to contact between races. There is no colour bar and no
discrimination of civil rights. There is a constant tendency to
economic and social advance of the coloured and black people.
The capable white people hold their own, and there is practically
no poor white class in indigent circumstances. There is an aver-
sion on the part of 'pure white' people to intermarriage with
the coloured; but such marriages with near whites or reputed
whites are not uncommon. The people of mixed race do not tend
to disappear, nor do they constitute a separate class. Their proportion increases. Physically and intellectually they are vigorous.
There is a very fine physical type of dark coloured men and
women commonly called 'Sambos' which seems well established.
They are energetic and independent in character."

Since he first knew the island Lord Olivier declares that the
progress of coloured people has been conspicuously recognizable. There is still a certain amount of colour prejudice as between adjacent groups. But it is much less than it was forty
years ago.

"Since I have been acquainted with Jamaica," writes Lord
Olivier, "there has been a great increase in the facilities for
the secondary education of coloured young persons of both sexes,
and this has involved improvement in hygiene and athletic nur-
ture. Coloured and black youths now hold their own in sports
with those of any other race in the world. Note, for example,
the recent performance of the West Indian Cricket team in
Australia. . . ."

In "Jamaica, a Racial Mosaic" (in *Opportunity*, May, 1931)
R. L. Buell insists that differences are more cultural than racial.
"Black Jamaicans who are educated and well mannered are
received upon a basis of complete equality."

The evidence of Lord Olivier is first-hand evidence of a very competent witness indeed, and it contradicts Professor Gregory flatly. It is Lord Olivier's opinion that the half-breed is so often a moral and social failure because he is a misfit; he falls between two stools; there is no established culture for him, and there is prejudice against him; given proper opportunity he might just as probably as not prove an interesting and successful blend of qualities; and there is nothing in the uncontrolled verdicts Professor Gregory assembles to affect this explanation. Basing myself upon this evidence I do not share that fear of a free social and economic intercourse, even to the point of intermarriage between *all* racial types.

Another apparently successful mélange of races is to be found in Hawaii. There, says Professor Romanzo Adams, the Professor of Sociology in the University at Honolulu, practically all the main races of mankind mingle socially and genially.

Captain Leo L. Partlow, in an interestingly illustrated article in *Asia* for June, 1931, says:

"Former Governor Farrington once called the Territory of Hawaii 'the world's greatest adventure in friendship.' It may seem sentimental rather than scientific to suggest that there is such a thing as the 'Hawaiian atmosphere,' in which goodfellowship between races seems perfectly natural. Yet the various races in Hawaii do seem to accept one another as a part of the environment, without prejudice or favour. I should not quite say that they freely intermingle socially nor yet that they remain good-naturedly apart. They attend to their own affairs, and, if those affairs bring them together, they come together without antagonism or self-consciousness. If any but the whites have a feeling of racial superiority, I do not detect it. . . . Racial intermarriage is practised to some extent between all the various groups, but there is no indication that it is, or tends to become, general. Indeed, the Japanese never have intermarried to any great extent with any other race, and the inter-racial marriages of the Chinese—principally with the Hawaiians and Filipinos—are decreasing rather than increasing. Whatever may be the eventual outcome, nothing now indicates a homogenous physical blend."

To leave intermarriage free, one must remember, is not to make it universal or obligatory. It is a matter for individual preferences to settle. Mostly, I believe, like will marry like. I see nothing alarming, but much promise of varied interest, in a marginal mixed society—which is always likely to remain a marginal and intermediate society. The main pools of population will, I think, continue to absorb and assimilate what falls into them by virtue of the better adaptation of the regional type to regional conditions, and of its acquired resistances to local disease, and I see no necessity for emphasizing by bars and prohibitions racial conflicts and struggles in the areas overlapping. The setting up of racial barriers and segregations I regard as reactionary and mischievous and doomed to painful failure. These are, of course, merely personal opinions in a region of thought in which nothing better than opinion is yet possible.

So far as restrictions and prohibitions go, Lord Olivier is very insistent upon their bad imaginative results. "They will," he remarks, "produce very silly and very bloody romances." . . . They may produce such tragedies in great numbers. Plainly down that vista one can see race outrage and the moonlight pursuit, Judge Lynch and the Ku Klux Klan. And no end to that vista.

Obviously, with these primary issues still so much in dispute, our judgments upon actual methods of racial adjustment to modern stresses must remain to a large extent individual and provisional. Two systems of will and intention play against each other in this business. This has been very clearly expressed by Lord Lugard in his *Dual Mandate*. On the one hand there are the urgencies arising out of the idea of a modern world economy, using all the natural products of the earth, freely and thoroughly, for power and plenty. To that economy the distinctive products of every region of the earth must contribute, and it is necessary that, in unsettled or socially and politically backward lands where the local population is living under an ancient traditional savage or barbaric régime, some methods of exploitation should be adopted to bring these natural products into the new world system. Some invasion of the indigenous culture is inevitable, if the new system cannot work and cannot balance itself without these products in abundance.

How is that invasion to be made? The gravitation of these natural products to the modern centres of manufacture is so great that if the business is allowed to occur without control, tragedies of brigandage and cruelty, legal or quasi-legal, on the Congo and Putumayo pattern are inevitable. Free invasion and uncontrolled conflict is the way of nature, and the way of nature is not only cruel but disastrously wasteful. Like all exploitation for immediate private profit, like the present exploitation of forests everywhere, like the whale and sea fisheries and the penguin massacre, the modern private-profit system in these regions of coloured labour is getting natural resources too abundantly and too cheaply now while creating a shortage in the future. And in the cases we are now considering it is enslaving and destroying human beings to do so.

As this is apprehended there comes into action the second series of motives, the other command of the *Dual Mandate:* care not only for economic output but for the present and future welfare of the native. The economic invasion of these productive backward regions, we admit, must occur, but their human and other natural resources must be protected and conserved. This means a protective interference with the social life of the native in the place of a massacre. There is no other alternative. But that interference, it is held, can be and must be for the native's ultimate well-being. The economic annexation must needs be rapid, but the assimilation of the native into the world commonweal may need a lengthy education. The haste, therefore, must be canalized and restrained. The obvious dangers of hypocrisy and of a sham and enslaving "protection" are plain enough. Just how much interference there may be and what should be the quality of the interference is the question.

Now, there are four chief methods of interference possible. The first is to push the native aside from the coveted region of mines, forests, or cultivatable soil, into *reserves,* and to plant workers from some other region upon the district of exploitation. Usually under this method the native in the reserve dwindles away. The reserve is all too often a shrinking area of undesirable land. Imported white labour and imported Asiatic labour have proved failures in South and East Africa, but the Negro was established in this fashion in the days of frank slavery in the West Indies and America.

Or, secondly, the native can be pushed aside into a reserve, but from that reserve he is tempted to emerge as a wage-earner in the region of exploitation. The reserve is thus made a labour tank of supply. The trouble is that usually he will not be tempted in sufficient numbers to satisfy the impatient white planter or mine owner.

So we come to the third system of treatment, dear to the whites of British East Africa, for example, "pressure" on the reserves. The natives are, for example, taxed, a head tax or a hut tax, and the tax is payable solely in money, which can be got only by plantation work. Or in other ways up to actual conscription by the chiefs, the native is to be compelled to come in. And to keep him in the desired path he is to be restrained from occupations by which he may earn on his own account. Education which might "put him above" mine or plantation work, is to be denied him. So native labour, it is supposed, can be kept cheap, poor, inferior and submissive, and the white settler can have a reasonable prospect of an indolent competence while directing the exploitation of the invaded mines or lands. This is the Afrikander policy. In South Africa things are making clearly towards a dangerous two-caste society, in which a minority of whites will rule over an artificially restrained, uneducated, disenfranchised coloured labour majority. Olivier's *Anatomy of African Misery* (Chapter XI) deals faithfully with the frank economic purpose of Hertzog's Native Land and Labour Bills,* and he has been largely instrumental in the appointment of the Joint Select Committee which has arrested the development of a similar state of things in Kenya.

In his book, *Kenya*, Dr. Norman Leys indicts the white settlers of that colony very forcibly and effectively. General Smuts, in his *Africa and Some World Problems*, propounds a scheme

---

*See also Olivier's *White Capital and Coloured Labour*, chapters XIII and XIV.

for an Africa dominated throughout by a backbone of white settlers in the highlands, a scheme subjected to very destructive criticism by J. H. Oldham's *White and Black in Africa*. A network of restrictive legislation seems to be closing about the black peoples of the Dominion of South Africa. They are being deprived of educational opportunity and political expression. They are being driven towards the alternatives of mass insurrection or complete degradation.

A fourth line of treatment—which has a weaker appeal to the white settler in a hurry—is to treat the native fairly, to police his country, to teach and show him how to cultivate the desired product, to make it worth his while to produce it and gradually bring him into the position of a tenant farmer, with technical guidance and help and a sure market for his produce. This has been the British policy in the new cotton-growing areas of Nubia.* It marches with what we have developed in Chapter IV on the trend of agricultural reorganization throughout the world. In this way an intelligent native population might be brought step by step and freely and happily into line with modern conditions.

In Jamaica practically the same method has been followed, and a prosperous and contented black and coloured peasantry has been raised from its original status of imported plantation labour to a level which compares favourably with many southeastern European cultivators. It is certainly as well prepared as they are to pass on towards that scientifically organized individual farming by state tenants under central control which we have given reasons (in Chapter IV) for regarding as the probable normal method of production in a completely modernized world.

The Gold Coast and the not very distant Portuguese islands of San Thomé and Principé are interesting exhibits for us here, since they offer a vivid contrast between the system of justly treated native production and what is practically slave labour. The cocoa-growing of the Gold Coast is due to native enterprise. The cacao tree is of South American origin; it has long

*See Odette Keun's *A Foreigner Looks at the British Sudan* (1930).

been grown on the island of Fernando Po, and in 1879 a native blacksmith named Tette Kwesi had the energy and intelligence to bring a few pods to the Gold Coast. Other natives took up the cultivation, and in 1891 the colony exported eighty pounds of cocoa. The Gold Coast government follows the policy of encouragement to native farmers and prohibits the acquisition of land and the formation of plantations by white adventurers. Buying firms insist upon standards of quality and the Gold Coast Agricultural Department provides instruction in planting, cultivating and preparing the cocoa. And behold the result! By 1929 that initial export of eighty pounds had grown to 233,000 tons, about 43 per cent of the whole world output, all grown by free native farmers, sanely governed and guided. In Ashanti and Nigeria the same methods have been adopted with a parallel success.

In San Thomé and Principé, a few hundred miles away, the plantation system rules in all its ugliness and misery. The attention of Cadbury's, the British chocolate makers, was called to this fact in 1901 by the offer for sale of a San Thomé plantation in which among other assets was an item of so many labourers at so much a head and an inferior grade of labourer at a lower price. The offer was declined, but that listing of labourers as chattels rankled in the mind of Mr. William Cadbury and led him to investigate further. He secured the coöperation of two other British firms, Fry and Rowntree, and the German firm of Stollwerck, and an investigator named Burtt was sent to prepare a report. It appeared in 1907 and was a thoroughly black one. It was a plain case of slave labour masquerading as contract labour. Most of the workers were caught in Angola, brought chained and under conditions of great hardship and cruelty to the coast, and shipped to the islands. There, with a view to outside criticism, they were made to go through the farce of signing a contract. But none was ever repatriated. When the contract expired they were forced to sign another.

We will not go on to tell the story of the efforts to end this state of affairs. They involved a libel action and other complications from which the cocoa firms concerned emerged very honourably. Foreign policy required that Great Britain should show great consideration for Portuguese feeling. But the cocoa firms named were able to secure the coöperation of their leading American competitors in a boycott of the tainted product, and by 1918 considerable reforms had been effected. How far these reforms were permanent is unhappily in doubt. San Thomé and Principé retain the plantation system, and in 1930 when the British Delegate at Geneva pressed for enquiry into the general question of slavery, the French, Italian, Portuguese and Abyssinian delegations opposed it successfully. France and Belgium have also refused a Forced Labour Convention with Britain. The better chocolate firms, the best known makes and names, still boycott plantation cocoa, but it finds a ready sale among their less scrupulous competitors. Thus, within an hour's flight of each other by aëroplane, you have the two contrasted systems of production in active competition. You have one black population being civilized and another being degraded and destroyed. And you have some intimation of the tangle of international politics which protects the evil method.

Let us return now to that other aspect of this problem of racial impact, which is raised by an exaggerated fear of miscegenation and by the prejudices of hates arising out of that fear. Here the writer's bias in favour of one human community is so strong that he finds it impossible to state the case against his own persuasion. He is convinced that in a properly educated world people can live in a state of racial mingling without any tragedy at all, civilly and kindly. He disbelieves altogether in bars and permanent reserves. He accepts Jamaica and Hawaii as his justifying experiments. He believes that race hatreds and conflicts are due mainly to economic tension, bad traditions and diverse conceptions of pride and behaviour. They are stupidities, they are vulgarities that the schoolmaster should anticipate and destroy. There is indeed hardly any race conflict in the world that is not deeply rooted in economic motives. But since that is an abnormal point of view, let the writer stand aside here for Dr. Malinowski, Professor of Social Anthropology in London University, who has written as follows (*op. cit.*) :

"What is the conclusion, then, to which we are forcibly driven by facts? Obviously, that the co-existence of two racial stocks side by side is inevitably a source of serious dangers and a starting-point of a long series of troubles. Once the process of mixture and conflict begins, the best we can hope is that one race should oust the other, or that a new preserve should be founded for the new mixed race. Why, then, not avoid the tragic process with all its evil implications and consequences? Why not frankly state that the only sound policy is that of racial and cultural preserves: the policy, that is, of indirect rule, of limited settlement for administrative purposes only, and the development of indigenous colonies on indigenous lines and, as far as possible, through indigenous enterprise? It would be untenable to object that this is not a practical policy. It is *de facto* the main principle of the policy of indirect rule which is, more or less, consistently carried out in the West African colonies. It has led to good results in Nigeria and in Uganda, in the Gold Coast and in the native protectorates of southern Africa.

"Moreover, the policy of racial exclusion is being carried out on a vast scale, consistently and efficiently. White Australia has resolutely closed its doors to superior Asiatic immigration, and it has deported in bulk inferior Kanaka labour. Similar racial preserves have been proclaimed in the Union of South Africa and in Canada, in Kenya and in many other white colonies. The United States of America have closed their frontiers completely on the West and very tightly on the East. Within Europe, Great Britain has excluded foreign immigrants.

"In all this we recognise a right policy, and we do not speak about violating the 'Dual Mandate,' though the 'world at large' would benefit appreciably if a score of million Asiatics were distributed over Queensland and the Pacific States, over the Northern Territory of Australia and the plains of Canada. Here is an immense wealth of fertile, unexploited regions wasted for the world, because the uplifting influence of effective Asiatic labour, of Chinese industry and Japanese organisation, is not being applied to it. This is the same moral argument as is used now to justify white settlement in East Africa. But both moral attitudes are wrong. Australia is not the yellow man's country, because, unless he could exterminate the few million whites there resident, he would create trouble for them and for himself. East Africa is not the white man's country because, again, he cannot exterminate the Negro; because he does not want to be blended racially, and because the only solution, a stratified community, is wrong all round."

Let there be a brief interpolation here. Dr. Malinowski was educated as a Pole, as a conscious aristocratic patriot (see Who's Who) in conflict with the central European synthesis. Most of us were brought up also on sound patriotic lines, and we cannot cast a stone at him on that account. But in what follows is it the Polish patriot or the emancipated London professor who is thinking?

"One more point must be made. The steam-roller of universal Western culture is undoubtedly levelling the cultures and societies of the world. . . . But, against this universal levelling, there is developing a strong reaction. The powerful assertion of political independence by the small nations in Europe was, perhaps, its initial symptom. National languages are revived, national religions set up, forms of national art and national literature cultivated, in opposition to the prevalent internationalism. Outside Europe, Egypt has claimed and received a considerable measure of independence; Turkey, while superficially adopting European ways and manners, has reasserted her national autonomy; Afghanistan has dealt even more drastically with spurious Westernisation; India is on the way to dominion status. In America, there is a strong resistance by the Latin-Indian nations against the cultural conquest of the North. Japan led the way in the fight for Eastern self-determination, and China may, in the future, completely reassert its cultural autonomy and achieve its national unity."

I repeat that I quote these views to disagree with them. This renewed fragmentation of mankind which Dr. Malinowski seems to welcome, this flickering back of his mind to nationalisms and autonomies, is a relapse from cosmopolitanism to Polish patriotism unworthy of the London School of Economics. The trend of material forces in the world is all towards unification of control however traditional sentiment and prejudice may resist that trend. Those more elemental directive influences will not tolerate these particularisms, these reversions to nationalism, these failures to tolerate or combine. Those post-war setbacks he cites, to the movement towards one great confluent human community having darker and fairer regions indeed but with no boundaries, castes or other fixed divisions, have occurred because that movement was, to begin with, so clumsy, planless and unforeseen. What Dr. Malinowski calls "the steam-roller of universal Western culture" was in fact not a culture at all. It was a steam-roller of blind forces, that has yet to produce a conscious world culture. It was an economic rolling preparing the soil for a world culture. A halt and even a phase of reaction may be inevitable, but at best that is no more than an interlude, a resting pause, a phase for thinking things out better, before the conscious, measured and designed establishment of a world order and a world law in which all men will live at peace together is resumed.

§ 3. *Eugenics*

To make our review of human affairs comprehensive we have had to plan a considerable number of sections, bringing in this activity or that possibility. Here, for once, is a section about something that hardly comes in at all, Eugenics. We have to make clear as briefly as possible, why at present the practice of Eugenics does not come into a survey of contemporary mankind, and then we can dismiss the subject and proceed to other aspects of the human spectacle.

Eugenics dates from 1885. We owe the word to Sir Francis Galton, the founder of the science. He died in 1911, leaving money to found a Chair of Eugenics at University College, London. He worked in the days before the development of the science of genetics and before the dawn of any adequate classification of human quality. He was eager for immediate applications; he wanted to set about improving the race without any close critical examination of the assumptions on which his plans were to be based. He thought there were large, indisputably superior people in the world, moving about amidst the small inferior multitudes, and that it would be possible to pick out, mate, and breed these superiors. This he termed "positive eugenics." He thought also that there were people definably inferior whose breeding ought at all costs to be prevented. That was to be "negative eugenics."

But human relationships are complex and subtle, and the

various attempts that have been made to measure "intelligence quotients" and the like, so as to show that there are social elements which have in their heredity a class superiority or a class inferiority to the average, are all open to very destructive critical objections. The only case that has been made out with any degree of conviction is the case for the segregation and sterilization of mental defectives.

There does seem to be a reasonable assumption that congenital defects of certain types are, so far as very many of them are concerned, heritable, and at any rate, since restriction upon population is a world necessity, there is no reason why the slight unobtrusive and practically painless operation of sterilization should not be performed upon them. Nor is there any sound objection to the sterilization of criminals convicted of brutish violence. The balance of evidence tilts towards the conclusion that such qualities are transmissible and, even if that conclusion is unsound, nevertheless the suppression of offspring in these categories will eliminate the certainty of a number of children being born in unfavourable surroundings at a great social disadvantage. Again there is every reason for the temporary or permanent sterilization of those who have contracted hereditable diseases. For a fuller discussion of these points than is possible here the reader should consult Carr-Sanders' book on *Eugenics*. The sterilization of certain types of defectives is now (1930) the law in California, Connecticut, Delaware, Idaho, Iowa, Kansas, Maine, Michigan, Minnesota, Mississippi, Montana, Nebraska, New Hampshire, North and South Dakota, Oregon, Utah, Virginia, Washington and Wisconsin.

When we pass from such extreme and obvious application of negative eugenics towards positive eugenics, we find ourselves passing from a field of reasonable probabilities into a tangle of riddles.

In the early days of Galton it seemed reasonable to assume that a child was essentially a blend of all the qualities of its parents. Only a few acute observers, then, doubted that assumption. But the science of genetics has made it clear to us that the characteristics of an individual are not the expression of all his hereditable possibilities. In the *Science of Life,* with the help of diagram and full explanation, we have made clear how it is that this should be so, we have described the splitting of chromosomes, and we have shown how "recessive" qualities can be transmitted by parents in whose personal make-up they do not appear. Only the half of a human being's full equipment of hereditable qualities is handed on to any particular offspring, the other half comes from the other parent, and the combination of these two half sets may be quite a different selection from what appears in either the mother or the father. To take a simple instance, having blue eyes is, it seems, a "recessive" quality in heredity. Two brown-eyed people may each be carrying this recessive latent in their reproductive cells, and chance may pick this out from both of them to blend in making a blue-eyed child.

Manifestly, then, we are not going to produce miraculous beings with any certainty by mating people of outstanding beauty and intelligence. The delightful combination of these qualities in either case was an accident not easily repeated. All sorts of recessives may pop out to grimace at us from such a coupling. Who among us cannot recall the half handsome children of the beautiful, the not very brilliant offspring of the genius? Now and then, of course, there may be a run of luck, but our best chance of getting any quality repeated, say the biologists, is to inbreed closely, which at once brings us up against the restrictions of current morality. We should turn back towards the primary social sin, incest.

Even in negative eugenics there is no assurance that undesirable qualities will be eliminated altogether. Certain types of mental deficiency are supposed to be "recessive." It is quite possible, therefore, that two quite admirable people should have a defective child. Such tragedies occur. The sterilization of defectives will not end, it will only diminish, the supply of defectives. Recessives can hide from generation to generation waiting to meet a kindred gene. When, therefore, biological workers seek to evoke and fix a new variety of some plant or animal, they resort to expedients quite outside our present liberties with human material. The first thing is to discover the recessives by the freest promiscuous breeding and interbreeding. Every undesirable recessive thus brought to light is then thrown out of reproduction; every individual known to carry a recessive is also cast out. When at last a "pure" strain is achieved, all the rest are destroyed, sterilized, isolated, or otherwise put beyond the possibility of reëntering the reproductive stream.

And also, be it noted, in the case of plants and insects and so forth, the breeder works for one simple quality. He wants a bigger ear of wheat, he wants resisting power to some disease or to some degree of cold. Nothing else concerns him. Everything else he can sweep away. But we do not know with anything like that much narrowness what we want in human beings. We do not want human beings to become simply taller or swifter or web-footed or what not. We want a great variety of human beings. And the qualities we want are complexes, not simple hereditable elements. It sounds paradoxical, but it is probably true that a large proportion of distinguished men and women are distinguished quite as much by a defect as by an outstanding gift. A man who has a "gift" generally needs, in order to develop it, exceptional freedom from secondary motives. He will specialize and concentrate all the better if there is no other strong impulse in his composition to distract him from the call of his gift. So we hear that among distinguished people so and so is sexless; so and so, strangely heartless with women; so and so is incapable of managing his household or his business affairs; so and so, absent-minded and forgetful of engagements to the pitch of gross incivility. Yet one of these is, say, a great artist, another a great mathematician, a third a distinguished lawyer, the fourth a statesman. All of them might give the most disconcerting results with intelligence tests. A story is told by Einstein against himself that comes in amusingly here. He is a great mathematician, but he is not a ready reckoner, and during the crisis of the mark he thought that a tram conductor had given him back too much change—a hundred thousand marks or so —and had to be convinced of his error. "Everybody," said the kindly tram conductor, "hasn't the gift of calculation with these big figures. I mustn't take advantage of you. . . ." And Laplace, one of the greatest mathematicians the world has ever known, was dismissed from the Ministry of the Interior by Napoleon for the grossest incompetence. But our organizing world requires these exceptional individuals far more than it does an endless multitude of fairly-good-all-round people.

That is how things stand at present. Biology, like all sciences, may spring the unexpected upon us at any time, but unless some such surprise occurs, no deliberate improvement in human quality is likely to be attempted. We must tolerate much that is odd and weak lest we lose much that is glorious and divine. For man reproduction is so slow, and his conditions of survival so complex and individual at present, that no natural process of selection can now be in effective operation, whatever may have been the case with his shorter-lived ancestors. There is considerable finality about *Homo sapiens*. For many generations, and perhaps for long ages, we must reckon upon a population of human beings not very different from those we have to deal with to-day. We shall meet with the same mental and temperamental types and the same racial characteristics that we encounter in the cast of the human drama to-day. The deliberate improvement of man's inherent quality is at present unattainable. It is to a better education and to a better education alone, therefore, that we must look for any hope of ameliorating substantially the confusions and distresses of our present life.

CHAPTER THE FOURTEENTH

THE OVERFLOWING ENERGY OF MANKIND

CHAPTER THE FOURTEENTH

THE OVERFLOWING ENERGY OF MANKIND

§ 1. *A Short History of Leisure*

CHAPTERS XI and XII and XIII are the darkest chapters in our survey. They have dealt with waste and poverty, with the weaknesses of governments and the mischief of bad government, with war preparation and economic war, and with the black cloud of approaching over-population. They have also shown man apparently unable to save himself from grave disasters, caused by his own defective monetary arrangements. He is seen injuring and perhaps destroying himself—without waiting for external Nature to turn upon him. The note of confident progress that pervaded our recapitulation of human achievements grew weak and died out altogether in some of those sections.

But hope remained, waving a tattered flag above the panorama, if at times it was difficult not to wave it very much in the manner of a danger signal. We have now said about all there is to say in a work of this sort, about these vast instabilities. We shall glance at them once again in our chapter on Education, and weigh their gravity in our conclusion. But for the rest we will disregard them. If civilization crashes, the story ends, and this work is no more than the measure of a frustration which will matter in the end to no one. But civilization need not crash. If it does not crash, then it will go on, we may be sure, to the fullest realization of the hopes and liberties, scientific and mechanical progress has made possible.

One inevitable consequence of continuing human progress is a steady increase of human leisure and human resources. At present much of that leisure takes the form of unemployment and impoverishment, but that need not be so, and also, as needlessly, much of the wealth and vitality we have accumulated is guided by patriots and munition salesmen into the disagreeable and unprofitable expenditure of war preparation and the consequent war orgies. Nevertheless, for the present, at any rate, humanity enjoys much more surplus time and energy than the past ever knew. How that surplus time and energy is employed is a necessary part of the human spectacle. It is a developing aspect of that spectacle. It opens out a vista of very important and perhaps even very novel activities in the future.

No sociologist has yet attempted to measure the leisure of a community. No biologist indeed has yet devised a comparative scale for the surplus energy of a species. To the *Science of Life,* Julian Huxley contributed some very interesting and suggestive material on the play of animals. He wrote that living species for the most part stick closely to business; they do not play. Play appears only with the more intelligent vertebrates. It is of definite biological importance, and it is for the most part confined to the young. It is almost entirely an educational rehearsal of the serious activities ahead of the young. But among creatures at the level of dogs and cats, even the adults, in times of abundance, will lark about and exercise themselves. Generally, indeed, when they are grown up they sleep, digest and recuperate between exertions, but the play is there. When we come to the monkeys and apes, there is considerable restlessness and activity, even on the part of the mature, outside the food hunt and the sexual storm. They are not only sexually excessive but curious and experimental. Many birds also release exuberant energy in song beyond any biological need, and penguins, ravens and jackdaws will play in a very human manner.

Nomads and savages, in favourable seasons, have time on their hands and a surplus of energy to expend. They exercise and dance and play games, decorate themselves, make amusing objects. But the onset of the larger cultivating community, the onset of foresight, that is, and enforced toil, restricted the spontaneous activities of the multitude very greatly. Only a limited proportion of the people won to any notable share of free time and free activities. The mass was caught and remained entangled in the net of unavoidable work.

Throughout the ages of cultivation, the peasants, the great majority of mankind, have had little leisure or surplus energy. The life of the peasant is still a very continuous round of labour; in Christendom he goes to mass (itself the vestige of a fertility blood sacrifice) on Sunday morning, but often before and after that on Sunday he finds something to be done to his ground. His wife and womenfolk, and the wife and womenfolk of the smaller townspeople, seem unendingly busy. As the proverb goes, "A woman's work is never ended." Over all the countries affected by the Hebrew tradition there is indeed the Sabbath, but that is not a day of leisure and the release of surplus energy; it is a day not of enjoyment but of ceremonial inactivity, a day of restraint. Chess may be played by the orthodox but not games for money, and the gad-about is restricted to the limits of a "Sabbath day's journey." The relationship of the Judæo-Christian Sabbath to other days when work is taboo, for workless days are found all over the world, is discussed in Hutton Webster's *Rest Days*.

The festivals of the cultivating communities, apart from seed time and harvest sacrifices, are few; they have lost the frequent dances, so stirring and hygienic, of the more savage people. Man, as we have insisted throughout this book, is not by nature a toiler: toil is a phase in his development; he has had to be subdued to toil, and whenever an excuse appears cheerfulness breaks through. Nevertheless, through the ages in which the main human community has been developing, through the last seven or eight thousand years, that is, the great industrious working majority has been almost devoid of leisure and spontaneous activities.

It was only at the centres where wealth accumulated or where a strong element of nomadism remained in the social mixture that holy days lost their severity and became holidays. The pastoral peoples have never given up their races, that exciting trying out of horses, and among them we find also the bull fight and suchlike sports. These mingle with foot races and combative exercises. The nomad trader brought his more eventful habits to meet the peasant spirit in the market and fair. The gipsy stirs up peasant life. The fair with its shows is a very ancient thing in social life. A few score times in his existence the peasant goes to the fair, partly to trade, but also to feast, dance, get drunk, fight, and, for a few precious hours, relax from his lifelong servitude to the soil.

Great towns, in which a large element of the population, like the Roman voters, for example, was exempted in some exceptional way from the need for continuous labour, display the maximum of leisure in the ancient world. In the classical period the architectural evidences of real holiday-keeping appear in amphitheatres and hippodromes. We find those clubs of the ancient world, the baths, becoming important features ·of the urban life. There and in groves and temple precincts we find also gentlemen of leisure meeting to walk and gossip, and presently to engage in philosophical discussion.

Except for the leisure of these favoured centres, a leisure which vanished again for long centuries with the collapse of the Roman system, the ordinary human life in the cultivating communities throughout history has had neither leisure nor recreation. It is only with the coming of power machinery and large industry, that the work of the common human being begins to be limited to regular hours leaving a daily margin of daylight and activity, and that a grudged but increasing amount of holiday appears. Nowadays there is leisure for all. The modern worker, under good conditions, gets his daily, weekly and annual leisure as he gets his daily bread. Never did the mediæval worker waste daylight as he does. It is quite a delusion to think that the past was a leisurely time and that this is a driving time. The past was a time of almost universal drudgery and insufficiency, and the ages of leisure and plenty lie ahead.

Some interesting books about leisure (C. E. M. Joad's *Diogenes or the Future of Leisure*, for example) have been written recently, but there is as yet no comprehensive survey of the ways in which this expanding element of surplus time and vigour is being used. That limitless encyclopædia of which we

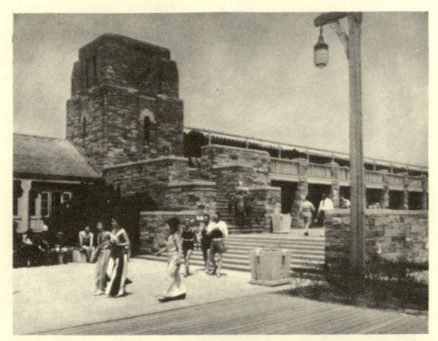

MANKIND AT PLAY

A VIEW at Jones Beach, a new resort development on Long Island, owned and operated by the State of New York. It is one of the finest beaches in the United States, and almost the only one which has been designed with forethought and good taste.

THE CROWD RELAXES

THE beach at Coney Island, the greatest of all beach resorts in the United States. There is more than a mile of public beach, all of which is densely covered on a hot summer's day.

are always dreaming would trace in its ample pages how leisure has spread down from class to class in the last century or so, and how new occupations have been found for it. Man does not like prescribed toil, but man is an energetic creature and leisure has never meant idleness for him. Probably our encyclopædia would classify man's leisure activities roughly after this fashion: as (1) exercise and sports, (2) hygienically unprofitable games, (3) sexual dissipation, gluttony and drunkenness, (4) gossip, parading in costumes and loafing about, (5) seeing shows, (6) wandering and travelling to see and learn, (7) making things for pleasure or, as the Victorians called it, "hobbies," passing insensibly into (8) art, (9) philosophy, scientific enquiry and experiment.

The student of the general history of leisure will go very largely for his material to the contemporary novels, plays and accounts of lives and "characters" of the past. These begin to bear their witness about the period of the Reformation after a phase of pestilence and social warfare had strained the mediæval economy severely. There was little fun upon the toiling, needy countryside then except for the seasonal holidays, "May games, Whitsun ales, Morris dances, leaping and vaulting." The village seniors played skittles and quoits and drank beer, and the visit of a garrulous peddler was an event. A book of ancient "sports and pastimes" would not rouse the envy of a slum child to-day. Except perhaps the bull and bear baiting. The town worker had to practise his archery in any time he had to give it, and, to make sure that he did so, lapses into football and other games were legislated against and severely punished. Bowling was prohibited altogether in England "for the meane sort of people." After darkness stopped the work, before they went to sleep, there was taverning, "eaves dropping" in the villages and mischief in the dark streets. Only the fairly well-to-do had light enough for reading. The leisure of the common people, if one reads between the lines of the increasing literature of the times, shrinks rather than expands throughout the seventeenth and eighteenth centuries. People do not seem to be working vigorously, but they are incessantly drudging. They knew no better; they did not complain.

Meanwhile, in the accumulating mass of more prosperous people, the beginnings of all the nine categories of activity just enumerated were appearing. People who once rode about their business and hunted by necessity, now rode and hunted for health and pleasure. The deadly pastime of card games was elaborated, and a touch of reality given to its futility by gambling. It is less trying to the eyes to play cards than to read by candlelight. One got drunk in the dining room and made love discreetly in the drawing room, and the gentry periodically left their estates to their stewards and foregathered at Bath and Tunbridge and in London, observing and getting excitements out of the novel people they encountered. The theatre reappeared; not the informative miracle play of the Church, but the comedy and tragedy of the classical world adapted to modern needs. Much attention began to be paid to witticisms and sentiments. The reader may find the sort of witticisms in Swift's *Polite Conversation*. The novel developed.

There was, however, a steady resistance to "frivolity" in the puritanical household that played so large a part in the development of the capitalist system of business (see Weber's *Protestant Ethic*). This retarded the spread of leisure to the employee and directed the mind of the employer towards serious literary and scientific interest. Reading increased. The novel, at first merely tolerated on week days, presently, under a false claim of edification, invaded the Sabbath. The state of affairs for the employee in the early nineteenth century is shown in Samuel Warren's *Ten Thousand a Year*. His poor poverty-struck shopman works intolerable hours and has no form of leisure occupation at all, except dressing up "above his station" and going for a walk on Sunday, pretending to be a gentleman. "Going for a walk" was an important phase in the life of everyone who could afford the time in the serious nineteenth century. It was healthy; it was not frivolous. A hundred years ago it was the chief relaxation of the university student and the university don. All the country round Oxford and Cambridge was dotted daily with intent, wide-striding men. Sport, as an integral factor in university life, had still to come.

The onset of the annual "holidays" in civilized life would be matter for an interesting special monograph. In the Middle Ages the migratory urge, which has never been altogether eliminated from the human make-up, found a relief in pilgrimages. We do not know what proportion of the population went on pilgrimages or how often they went. Nor do we know the quantitative proportion of pilgrims in the world of Islam to-day. The German student and the German artisan have a mediæval knapsack tradition, but the latter wandered not so much for fun as to find work as a journeyman and settle down ultimately for good. For the bulk of people there was nothing like "the holidays" of the modern community, until the dawn of the railway era. Restless souls answered the call of the seas, of overseas adventure and of emigration. Lively lads enlisted or ran away to sea. For the most part, these restless souls went for good and never returned. Ordinary folk stayed where they were from start to finish. Samuel Warren's draper got no holidays, and had he got holidays he would have been hard put to it to find where to go. But people in prosperous strata above were already observing a seasonal migration to "town" and the "spa" in the seventeenth century. Directly the railways arrived, this fashion spread down into the middle classes. The railways assisted, by the introduction of excursion trains, which truly "supplied a long felt need." Now the whole working world takes holiday and our encyclopædia would have long histories of the seaside resort, of the battle against mixed bathing and against modern relaxations of costume, of the development of winter sport, of mountaineering and tourism. It would be a continuous unfolding of freedoms and refreshment, of new methods of catering and attraction, and on the whole it would be a very cheerful and encouraging history.

And, moreover, this great extension of leisure and this very considerable development of leisure occupations bear very importantly upon the economic and social difficulties we have discussed in Chapter XI, § § 5, 6 and 7. The primary needs of mankind, we have shown, are being satisfied by a smaller and smaller proportion of workers. Therefore, unless the standard of life rises, there must be a steadily growing proportion of the population unable to earn money, without spending power, and therefore without the ability, unless some form of "dole" steps in, to get and consume even their primary needs. By shortening hours, introducing more and more holidays, cutting down the working life at both ends, this surplus of unemployed workers may be reduced. But if also the standard of life for the primary productive workers rises by the development of leisure occupations, amusements, holidays and entertainments, there will not only be an increase of the numbers—or at any rate a check upon the shrinkage of the numbers employed in primary production, but also a new world of secondary employment will open up that may at last become as great a spectacle of activities as the old. This, indeed, without a revised currency credit system and a secure world pax, will not solve all the present perplexities of mankind, but it is a factor of very great importance indeed. Want more, live more fully, is the command of the new civilization; enjoy that others may also serve and enjoy.

§ 2. *The Travel Bureau*

There must be a section here, even if it has to be a very slight and allusive section, about the readiness with which human beings will at the slightest chance escape from fixed locality and everyday routines and set out to see the world. Hitherto there was not much chance for the generality of people; now every railway station appeals to the migrating impulse with gaily coloured posters of foreign scenery. Before the present age "over the hills and far away" was for most people an unrealizable reverie. There must have been a certain amount of coming and going in Greece at the season of the Olympiad. Tourists went up and down the Nile in the great times of Egyptian security and scratched their names on monuments and buildings already ancient and wonderful. And pilgrimages creep into history very early. There were pilgrimages in Egypt and Babylonia. I do not know of any good history of early travel, travel for piety or curiosity, or for the latter disguised as the former. The command of the prophet that all faithful Moslims should visit Mecca at least once in a lifetime made that form of wandering a great feature over all the East, and Christians began to resort to Jerusalem from the third century onward. All through the Middle Ages the pilgrim bands journeyed about Europe to this shrine or that, and for the sheer gad-about element in these wanderings see Chaucer's *Canterbury Tales*. In pre-revolutionary Russia the roads were pleasantly infested by tramps, each with his bundle and his kettle, seeing the world and living casually en route to pilgrimage centres. But there has never been anything before like the vast volume of journeys made frankly for pleasure that goes on to-day. Catering for pleasure travel is now an important industry.

There is no need to expand here what the reader can expand very amusingly for himself by applying to any travel agency. As this page is being read there must be hundreds of thousands of people in great liners upon the high seas, on pleasure journeys halfway round the world. There are scores of thousands of hotels full of transient visitors, trains of excursionists and trains de luxe rattling from country to country, and hardly a mountain pass or lovely highroad without its omnibus motor car of passengers agog.

It is plain that, given prosperity and spare time, the great majority of human beings would go round the world two or three times and gratify an ample appetite for novel scenery and the different ways of men.

§ 3. *The World of Sport*

With the brief time at our disposal the writer and reader must now walk very quickly through another long, airy and attractive gallery in the vast museum of human activities this present work has evoked. This gallery is to represent all that efflorescence of athleticism and of looking-on at athleticism which goes on under the name of sport. It is an enormous and conspicuous aspect of modern life, and it may be capable of much further development.

Our gallery would pay its tribute to the athleticism of classical times. We have little record of sport in the older civilizations, except kingly hunting and the bullfights, gymnastics, and funeral games of the Cretan and other Mediterranean peoples. Those were palace affairs. The Aryan-speakers seem to have brought the chariot race with them when they flowed over and subjugated the ancient civilizations, and they seized upon and developed the sports of their predecessors. There were races on horseback so early as the third Olympiad, but the horse race never rivalled the chariot race in classical times.

We should trace the development of the Olympic games from a village festival to a great meeting which united all Hellas, and we should show how the gladiatorial fights of the Roman amphitheatre arose side by side with the Aryan chariot race in the hippodrome, out of a revival of the Etruscan sacrifices. Running, wrestling, boxing, weight throwing, were the main sports of the Greek meetings—and of all the ancient world. Roman gentlemen tossed balls to one another in the Baths, as Petronius tells us, but the widespread, regular playing of set ball games for exercise, from cricket and tennis to golf, seems to be a recent thing. There is scarcely a trace of it in the classical literature. Games more or less like tennis and polo appear obscurely and intermittently in Persian, Arab and Egyptian records, but never as widespread practices. They were associated with mediæval courts and chivalry. To play tennis, the hard original tennis, you needed a castle moat.

The modern expansion of sport followed upon the industrial revolution and is closely associated with the revival of the universities. In the eighteenth century these institutions had shrunk very greatly, through the imposition of religious tests and the diversion of intelligent minds from scholarship to more interesting occupations. But the development of new types of well-off people, aware of a cultural inferiority, the general increase in wealth and the relaxation of sectarian jealousies, led to an influx of prosperous young men in the schools and colleges, anxious to become young gentlemen, but indisposed for any severe intellectual toil. The aristocratic conception of education through physical exercise appealed to them strongly.

The "sportsman" was already appearing in the first half of the eighteen hundreds. But "sport" was then a business of illicit boxing matches, dogfights, race meetings and the like, rather than real athleticism. It was frowned upon by the authorities. Cricket was discovering itself in England, indeed, and one or two English public schools had crude games of football with distinctive local rules. One found local sports of a traditional type in Scotland, a few Swiss villages and scattered unimportantly over the world. The big expansion of sport belongs to the latter half of the nineteenth century.

Then things went ahead very rapidly. The first athletic meeting in modern times, says Captain Webster in his British Encyclopædia article, was promoted by the Royal Military Academy, Woolwich, in 1849. Exeter College, Oxford, was next in 1850. Cambridge sports came in 1857. Oxford followed suit in '60, the Oxford and Cambridge meetings began in 1864, and English championships date from 1866. The American inter-university meetings came soon after these British beginnings. International meetings appear in the record in the eighties. Thereafter there is a crescendo of sport. Our tale passes on to the revival of the Olympic games at Athens in 1896 and the appearance of great stadia for these gatherings, to remain as permanent additions to the athletic resources of the city of assembly. To such meetings Amsterdam owes its stadium; Paris, the Colombe stadium; London, the stadium at Shepherd's Bush (seating 50,000), Stockholm a stadium accommodating 15,000. These are far outdone in capacity by the Chicago (150,000), Yale University (80,000), Illinois University (60,000) and Ohio State University (75,000) stadia, and London has since added to its resources the Wembley stadium of ten acres holding about 98,000. The greatest capacity in the British Isles is now Hampden Park, the Glasgow Rangers' ground, which held 129,510 in 1930. In America, says the Encyclopædia Britannica (from which most of these figures are taken), there were only five stadia of importance in 1913, and now (1930) there are thirty. There is accommodation for two or three million spectators of athletic sport on any fine afternoon in the United States alone. The *English League* and *Scottish League* grounds (ignoring the hundreds of minor amateur and professional grounds) open every Saturday for football spectators are well over two and a half millions in capacity. There are four grounds holding over 60,000 in London alone (Wembley, Arsenal, Chelsea and the Crystal Palace Corinthians ground) and three others near 50,000 if not over (Tottenham, West Ham and Millwall). The original stadium at Athens which was reconstructed in marble upon its original ruins for the 1896 occasion held 60,000 people. The Roman amphitheatres were never quite as vast as this; the very greatest, the Colosseum held, it is now estimated, about 50,000 (Talbot F. Hamlin).

These figures help one to understand the dimensions of the sporting world to-day. These gathering places are not like the Greek Olympic centre, used only once every one or two or four years. They are in frequent and habitual use. They add to our spectacle of factories, mines, plantations, transport, a vision of swarming myriads of usually sunlit folk in their places and in the arena, the shining bodies of beautifully fit and active racers, players and combatants, and the well drilled ranks of athletic associations in display.

And these stadia are not all. To them we must add the race courses with their grand stands, their coaches and parked automobiles, and the vast crowds of spectators and crowd-followers that assemble for such festivals as the English Derby or the Ascot week, and also we have to indicate such grounds as Lords and Kennington Oval, where they play cricket, and Wimbledon, with its tennis courts established for fifty years, must also come into the picture. And then from these culminating centres our eye must go outward, and all over the countryside of the modern communities are the football fields and baseball fields and cricket fields and tennis courts, where the balls fly and the healthy bodies flash to and fro. And then, in the less sunny weather, there are the running associations in vests and shorts, the "harriers" and paper chases, and so forth, and the resolute walking men, and the men in training loping cheerfully through the mud, fists clenched and lungs and heart at their steady busiest.

Add now to all this the paddled canoes, the single outriggers, the fours and eights and all the more leisurely rowing boats, that swarm upon every river near a great town. Add also the diving and swimming that go on in rivers, lakes, swimming pools and public baths. Add also the swarming beaches, the bathing places, and the basking lightly clad multitudes wherever there are sands by the sea. Bring in also the immense activities and pleasures of the snow sports that were almost unknown until the last decades of the nineteenth century, the luging, the ski jumping and the ski excursions. And the ice sports, the skating and curling. Mountain climbing is an older delight, but except for a few pioneers—De Saussure climbed Mont Blanc in 1787—it does not go back more than a century. And these pleasures are no longer monopolized by a small rich leisure class. There has been a great cheapening and distribution of athletic material— I do not know how far the development of rubber described in Chapter III has not made the balls so necessary for many games accessible to medium purses. Modern industrial methods have given the world cheap standardized balls. Without such balls the contemporary development of games could never have occurred. Football, one of the cheapest of games, has spread from the English industrial districts all over the Westernized world since the war. Any afternoon now one may see in the London parks a string of boys from some East End elementary school, who would already have been factory workers half a century ago, going out with a schoolmaster in charge of them to play their weekly game of football. Even in Egypt and the Sudan now the small boys play football.

All this in itself means human happiness on a world-wide scale. And never was there anything of the kind on earth before. Just like the swelling human population and the overwhelming pro- duction of staple goods, it is a consequence of the invention and discovery of the past century. There is no reason why we should not hope to see free, ample and lovely exercise in the open air brought within reach of every human being. There can be no limit to the beneficial extension of athletics.

But when we consider not the extension but the specialized intensification of athletic exercises and the domination of public attention and leisure by these activities, it becomes necessary to qualify our benedictions. It is good for a man to be fit and well developed; it is quite another matter when he gives, and is incited and driven to give, his whole being to the extreme exploitation of his neuro-muscular system. It is good for a community to have plenty of exercise; it is very bad for it to subordinate all other interests to sports and games. Athleticism in the present generation goes, it is admitted, too far. Reasonable sport accumulates energy, but excessive sport wastes it. From Euripides to Rudyard Kipling, with his "flannelled fool at the wicket" and his "muddied oaf in the goal," public-spirited men have had harsh words for the specialized athlete and game player.

The ascendency of sport is particularly remarkable in the United States of America. And from the United States universities come the boldest apologies for this tremendous concentration upon athleticism. Before the end of the nineteenth century university sports were mainly in undergraduate hands in America, as elsewhere. These were in part insurrectionary against the prevalent mental education. But the insurgent spirit of the richer and bolder students put the sporting side of the collective life into such prominence that the faculties of instruction had to accommodate themselves to the realities of the situation. The great "educational" value of sport was officially and formally discovered. An Intercollegiate Conference found sports could be used to "supplement and broaden modern education" and made the peak of a "physical education pyramid."

The "physical education pyramid" one can concede, but how careering about in fields in a semi-nude state can be supposed to "supplement and broaden" anything that an honest man would call education staggers the imagination.

However, on these assumptions and by much unsubstantial assertion of the moral benefits—"clean and healthful living" of athletes, for example, and "development of loyalty to the institution and to fellow members of the college community" (the gang spirit, in fact) the way was paved for the partial conversion of the American universities into athletic training centres. The athletic coach has now become the equal or superior in pay and dignity of the merely intellectual teachers, and the exhibition of sports an important source of funds for these institutions. Sport has indeed assisted in the financial revival of several state universities, whose merely intellectual teachers had failed to attract students in paying quantity. Conceivably some of them indeed might do even better financially by scrapping their intellectual faculties altogether, competing by scholarships for youngsters of athletic promise, and concentrating upon the stadium. The coach, the new "broadening" type of American professor, is sometimes a man educated on the older lines, sometimes a professor of modern hygiene, but often a promoted trainer or rubber or masseur.

In a list of "secondary objectives" in the statement of the Intercollegiate Conference, the realities of the situation peep out. Objectives 4 and 5 confess that these sports "provide opportunity to 'animal spirits' for legitimate physical expression" and "further the educational viewpoint and needs by securing and maintaining active interest of *alumni* and general public in the educational institutions through the field of greatest common interest and appeal." This concentration of sport in the universities is not in fact a development of education, but a distortion of the educational machine through an exuberant economic growth of the community which has swamped the country with endowments and with a multitude of people anxious to give their sons and daughters the social prestige of university graduation.

This inflation of sport is a natural and necessary result of the atmosphere of boredom created by crowding healthy adolescents who do not want to learn, into classrooms with teachers not particularly anxious to teach and not very clear about what should be taught, and its value as advertisement and its financial possibilities have been duly exploited by the college authorities. The influence of this development upon the general education of the community, and the desirability of withdrawing a large proportion of the better-class youth from general social and economic development to specialize as stadium performers and develop a gang feeling in intra- and inter-collegiate rivalries, lest worse befall, we will consider in the next chapter; our concern here is only with the physical aspect of the business and its radiation of health and excitement throughout the modern community. That radiation in undeniable. The health is for the moderate majority rather than the experts. The Encyclopædia Britannica states on the authority of the Carnegie Foundation for the Advancement of Teaching that twelve out of every hundred university football players receive "serious injuries." The figure given for all games is 3 per cent. These are the strenuous ones who are crippled, the vicarious offerings made for the well-being of the rank and file.

The same influences are at work in the promotion of athletics in the educational institutions of Europe as of America, but the European developments have not attained the same enormous scale nor devastated the intellectual life of the colleges to the same extent, because in their case there has not been the same steady advance in prosperity and spending power during the past two decades. The nearest approach to American conditions in Europe is to be found in the older English public schools. There an undernourished, underdeveloped slip of modern education travels, like an unwanted passenger in an overcrowded omnibus, between the captain of the cadet corps and the mighty cricketers and athletes whose attainments in the playing fields have determined their selection for the teaching staff.

One interesting aspect of athletic recreations is the organization of "records." In the past half century authoritative organizations have made the most precise and careful observations of human bodily achievements. We know now that man at his best can run 100 yards in 9 3/5 seconds. This has been done four times, by D. J. Kelly (1906), H. P. Drew (1914), C. W. Paddock (1921), and C. Coaffee (1922). Possibly it is a limiting record. C. W. Paddock also holds the 100 metre record

($10^2/_5$ seconds). For longer distances the achievements of P. Nurmi, a Finn, remain unsurpassed. He ran a mile in 4 minutes $10^2/_5$ seconds (Stockholm, 1921), and he held all the records from 200 to 10,000 metres until Jules Ladonmègue did a mile $^1/_5$ of a second quicker in October, 1931 (Paris). The highest jump so far recorded is 6 feet 8½ inches, by H. M. Osborne at Chicago in 1924, and the longest is D. H. Hubbards', of 25 feet 10⅞ inches at the same meeting. J. Weissmuller swam 100 yards in 52 seconds and 100 metres in $57^2/_5$ seconds. But lists of records in a score of sports are to be found in every book of reference, and there is no need to give more of them here.

There seems to be no sensible objection to this exploration of human possibilities in every sort of bodily exertion. But in some directions a record hunt must necessarily take a murderous turn. For example, there is ski jumping. There is hardly any limit to the height a ski jumper, *with luck,* may not jump down and get away from. Up to a reasonable limit, men may compete and none be injured, unless for a broken ankle or so. Then as the dimensions increase, the adverse chances increase. So that while people are willing to risk almost certain death or crippling injuries, there need be no limit to the record ski jump.

The same principle applies to many forms of mechanical record making, speed boats, aëroplane and motor-car races and the like. In these cases one is not dealing with a wholesome definite physical limit, nor is one really testing out a machine. More and more one is chancing the perfect smoothness or the perfect banking of a track or the limit of strength of a wing. Sir Henry Segrave was killed in his motor boat, *Miss England II,* on Lake Windermere, in an attack on the speed-boat record. The boat hit a scrap of flotsam at a speed of over 98¾ miles per hour, turned over in a cloud of spray, and sank stern downward. Mr. Hallwell, an engineer, went down with her. This *Miss England II* was recovered from the bottom of the lake, reconditioned, and on Lake Neagh, after a preliminary reconnaissance by aëroplane to make sure that the water was clear of driftage, Mr. Kaye Don got to an unofficial velocity of 107 miles per hour. But his official record made at Buenos Ayres was under the hundred and he capsized but escaped uninjured in a later race. Previously Sir Henry Segrave had made the record for automobile velocity on the Daytona beach 231⅓ miles per hour, but his achievement was subsequently bettered by Captain Malcolm Campbell, who made an unofficial 260 miles per hour and an official record* of 246 miles per hour with the specially built car *Blue-Bird II*. A flight record of 357¾ miles per hour was made by squadron-leader Orlebar in September, 1929 and this was outdone by flight lieutenant G. H. Stainforth at Calshot on Sep. 29th, 1931, who reached a speed of 415.5 miles per hour and averaged 408.80 in four runs along the three kilometre course. Blériot, who was the first to fly across the Strait of Dover, is offering a prize for the first man who in any mechanical contrivance whatever achieves a horizontal speed at 1000 km.=621.37 miles, per hour. Quite possibly this is an attainable speed, but its attainment will exact a heavy toll of human lives.

It is possible that the development of record-breaking and display athleticism may be approaching its maximum now, or that in America it may even be passing its maximum. All the rational feats of bodily strength and skill may presently have been tried out to the limit. People will cease to beat records and only aspire to touch them. If the world's prosperity goes on increasing, the great majority of people may tire of the spectator's rôle in the stadium. They may find competing attractions. They may go to look on less frequently and less abundantly. There may be changes in the economic and industrial ordering of the world that will diminish the present supply of honourable amateurs for public games. Prosperous people may find some better method of launching their sons and daughters upon life than in offering them up to athletic uses. Public shows of games may become mainly professional displays of an exemplary sort. But this may not affect the wide diffusion of open-air recreation. That may be a permanent gain. If leisure increases,

---

Nature, February 14, 1931.

it seems likely to become more and more general, more and more a normal element in life.

THE SPORTING ELEMENT IN WAR, INSURRECTION AND MANY MURDERS

In a survey of human activities so essentially psychological as this that we are making, it is impossible to leave the question of sport and the sporting mentality without noting how closely allied are many of the impulses and motives that have been active in developing the world of modern sport, with those that are operative in maintaining war, and how closely allied complexes militate against order, tranquillity and security in everyday life. We have again to recall this fundamental fact in the human problems, that civilized man is a very imperfectly domesticated aggressive animal, that in each generation he has to be broken in again to social life, and that, whatever may be done to suppress, mitigate, or sublimate his fiercer, more combative impulses, there they are pressing against law, order and compromise. The American educationists find in athleticism a "legitimate" release for "animal spirits." Whether it is always adequate may be disputed, but there can be little dispute that the French Apache, the British Hooligan, the young American Tough on his way to become a gangster, are impelled very largely to their anti-social activities by impulses practically indistinguishable from the sporting spirit of their social betters.

So far we have said very little of hunting, shooting and other "blood" sports. We have still to note, for example, the almost pathetic spectacle of pink-clad huntsmen and hounds chasing rare and unpopular foxes, in spite of barbed wire, market gardeners, light railways, automobile-infested roads and chemical manure, across the suburban landscape of England, or rousing even the meek Egyptian fellahin to murderous protests. And here too we glance at the lined-up guns of a battue of pheasants, raised at great expense for the slaughter. These massacres are the last vestiges of the habitual amusement of monarch and noblemen throughout the whole course of history. The stir and effort, the triumph of slaughter, given by the hunt, have made it the dominant occupation of men of every race, who have found themselves free to follow it. And from the hunting of beasts to the man hunt was but a step. The two things mingle upon the painted walls of Egypt and the Assyrian sculptures. War and conquest was the sport of kings. And in all antiquity it is conquest and killing that is glorified. There is no trace in the record of any honest appreciation of an equal conflict fought out stoutly to an indecisive issue.

The American Indian was so great a sportsman that he subordinated all the rest of his life to the exaltation of the warpath. He inaugurated the season with mystical dances, and scalped and destroyed according to a precise and picturesque ritual. Throughout the ages, the historian can tell of communities, from the Huns to the Zulus, which have given over themselves (and their neighbours) altogether to the master sport of war. Clearly we have something in the human make-up here, very fundamental, fundamentally ineradicable, needing suppression and sublimation and likely to crop up again very obstinately whenever the suppression and sublimation relax. It is charged against the German Kaiser that he saw war as a sport and so precipitated the crash of 1914. It is at least equally true that Mr. Rudyard Kipling and his school, had presented imperial conquest as a sport to the minds of the British ruling classes. Only a few days before this was written some gallant British major-general—I made no note of his name—escaped from the control of his wife and wrote to the papers to say that war, the "man hunt," was the supreme sport of mankind.

How gladly would the unregenerate sportsman in ourselves chase that gallant gentleman into a gas cloud or drop him into a poisoned dugout and leave him there!

These "animal spirits," the American educationists recognize, crop up not only in the ragging and insubordination of students and the criminal violence of lower-class adolescents, but also, it is plain, in a certain proportion of adult crime. It is clear that certain uncontrolled human types, when they get the chance, will kill, as a cat or a tiger will kill, because it is in them to

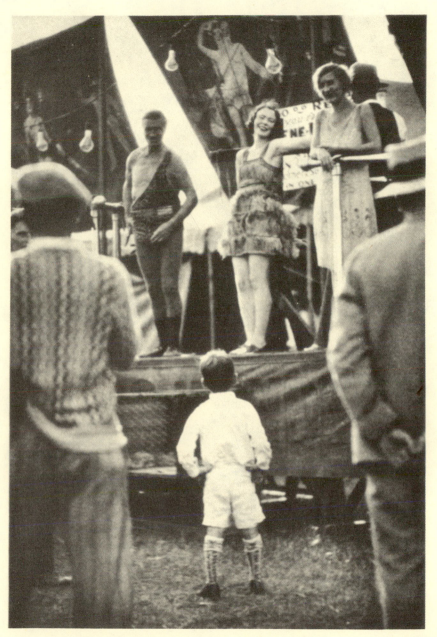

THE WORLD OF ENTERTAINMENT

THIS is a side of life that may have great developments if material progress continues.

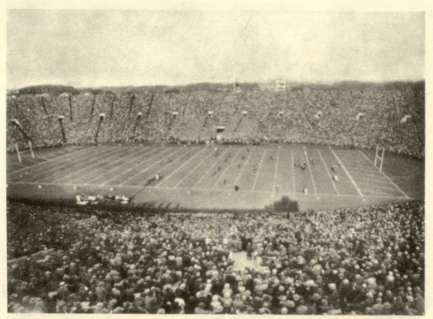

THE UNIVERSITY AND SPORT

ONE of the great football stadiums, that of Yale University at New Haven, Connecticut. The game in progress is one between Yale and Army, and more than eighty thousand spectators are present.

do so. We are not speaking here of lunatics; we are speaking only of a slight individual exaggeration of what is inherent and normal in man. Every man is a potential killer, warrior or murderer, and it is absurd to disregard that reality when we deal with the problems of economic organization and social and political control. Insurgent movements, insurrections, are a vast relief to the boredom of a countryside. Consider what a relief it must be to some poor devil, obsessed by a sense of social or racial inferiority, to make and throw a bomb, or waylay and murder a policeman, or riot and burn.

Many a revolution has been brought about by the want of sporting release, and as for war, the drums and trumpets, the martial music, the flags, the serried uniforms, the rhythmic jingle and tramping of marching men, and above all the sense of going off to a dramatic objective, call to all of us. It was necessary to spoil the sport of war by poison gas, air bombs, propaganda and the plain prospect of universal bankruptcy, before men would think seriously of giving it up. And when, if ever, we have "abolished war," we shall have to reckon much more thoroughly than we do now with the "blood" element in the sporting .motive. Some forcible men will train and drill themselves and develop the service mentality, but not all; some bold spirits will hunt with a camera instead of a gun and be content with a picture instead of a skin, but not everyone will do that. Yet, if we can detach the adventurous element from cruelty, society will be the better able to keep cruelty under. With that first great pax in the world, the Roman Empire, the arena, the blood show, spread all over the civilized world. The civilized countries of to-day which are furthest removed from war display the greatest ruthlessness in sport. There is need for public watchfulness against the release of cruelty in sport. The world of sport, elaborately developed and firmly controlled, seems to be *inter alia* the most hopeful organ for excreting the more violent and adventurous ingredients in the surplus energy of mankind. "*Inter alia*," we write, because sport leads also to greater fulness of life and beauty.

BETTING, GAMBLING, AND THE LOTTERY

Our survey of sport, to be complete, should include the betting world, gambling and playing for gain. One may raise the question whether these things are to be looked at under the heading of sport, or whether it would not have been advisable to treat them as an erratic branch of finance. And we may set aside either alternative with the suggestion that the reality beneath these things and beneath the lottery, which is prohibited in Great Britain, Belgium, Sweden, Switzerland and the United States, is something which is neither superfluous energy nor abnormal finance, but a craving to relieve a rather too dull everyday life by streaks of hope. To buy a lottery ticket is for most purchasers to buy something much more exciting than a novel or a cinema show. Until the drawing, the mind is pleasantly occupied by dreams of what will be done when the prize is paid. A bet (on reassuring information) at long odds, or a lottery ticket, is, at the worst, the key to many days of pleasant reverie. It is the imaginative stimulus for a dream that may come true.

That is from the point of view of the individual maker of bets. Energetic, fully and happily occupied people do not want these mitigations of an orderly life, and we may suppose that in a world growing more prosperous, various and interesting, betting will decline. The evil of betting comes in with the exploitation of this natural desire suddenly to get much for very little and so experience a bright, rare enhancement of life. The gambler soon comes to bet not with his odd superfluous coins but with his necessities. People will buy hope in such quantities that they deprive themselves of the necessities of life; too hopeful employees will borrow from the till on the strength of some tip or dream they have had; women will stake the housekeeping money, and men their wages. When the law intervenes with prohibitions, an illegal organization of betting arises in response to the attack. A full encyclopædia of human activities would include a small library upon anti-gaming and anti-gambling legislation and its evasions. It would be neither very entertaining nor very illuminating. Pictures of lottery drawing are very dull pictures. The only really agreeable thing about this complex dreary business is its multitude of gleams and states of hope. The actual prize winner, especially if the prize is big, is rather to be pitied than envied. Projected onto an unfamiliar plane of prosperity, socially transplanted, he or she in too many cases is destined to learn how little happiness can be bought in the world by an inexperienced buyer.

The habitual maker of bets and buyer of lottery tickets always loses in the long run. But specially attentive and industrious classes are able to make a living by ministering to the general gambler. Here we have no space for the ways and habits of tipsters, bookies and the like; for the journalistic side of gambling with its special sporting editions devoted to tips and starting prices, the organization of gambling clubs and houses, the corruption of games and the turf due to betting. From the prince's baccarat and Monte Carlo's roulette and *trente-et-quarante,* to the soldier's crown and anchor and the errand boy's pitch and toss, it is a history of stakes lost, relieved by incidents of irrational acquisition. It is a history of landslides in an account book. It is a pattern of slithering cards, dancing dice, spinning roulette wheels, coloured counters and scribbled computations on a background of green baize. It is a world parasitic on the general economic organization—fungoid and aimless, rather than cancerous and destructive, in its character. A stronger, happier organization would reabsorb it or slough it off altogether.

§4. *The World of Entertainment*

A field of human activities which seems certain to undergo great expansion and elaboration as human leisure and surplus energy increase, is the field of entertainment. Here the detail is enormously abundant and varied, and the alternative to a labyrinthine assembly of histories, panoramas and anecdotes of theatres and travelling companies, gipsy shows, bear-leaders, gymnasts and conjurors, street singers, menageries, circuses, clowns, fairs, hand, horse and steam roundabouts, minstrels and organ grinders, sing-songs, music halls, "variety" in all its forms, cabarets, revues, star actors and starry actresses, obscure actors and actresses, singers, musicians, music festivals, chamber music, concerts, Wagner, Reinhart, Crane, Barnum, Lord George Sanger, Mark Twain's immortal letter to Queen Victoria on the showman element in royalty, Maskelyne and Cooke, Mr. Charles Cochran, Mr. Ziegfeld, Mr. Frohman, the cinema, broadcasting, auditoria, admission, licensing, Sunday closing, censorship and prosecutions, books that profess to entertain, novels, novelists, playwrights, comic writers, comic papers, the newspapers as entertainment—is again to say "Museum" and evoke another ten miles or so of imaginary floor space, a cheerful deafening nightmare of glare, uproar, spangles and display. The record would go back into pre-history. The "funny man," the jester and the juggler, are probably as ancient as mankind. So are the singer, the story-teller, the acrobat, the dance and dressing up, the strange beast led about.

We may add, perhaps, a few general remarks about the entertainment world as a whole, about its atmosphere of thought and feeling, and then about what one may call its strangulation. For the strangling of entertainment is also a serious business activity.

The psychology of the entertainer is peculiar. His persona lies outside any one of the three main types of persona described in Chapter VIII. Entertainers may be drawn from any class of mentality, but their peculiar circumstances lead very rapidly to the exaggeration of reactions that play only a secondary part in the lives of most human beings. The peasant's guiding principles are safety and profit, the nomad's, glory and swaggering advantage, the educated types, service and sound achievement. But the breath of the entertainer's nostrils is attention and applause. Only the modern politician approaches him in his sensitiveness to attention and applause. By them he lives, and for want of them he perishes—as an entertainer.

To a large extent entertainers are entertainers by heredity. This is truest of circus folk and performing folk generally, and least true of writers. Musicians are drawn very largely from professional musical families and music shops, if only on account of the advantage of early access to instruments and early stimulation. Nowadays, however, schools of dramatic art and music schools, and in America courses in story-writing and play-writing, introduce an unprecedented volume of new blood into the succession of those who would amuse.

Dependence upon applause produces characteristic traits. Applause is what the entertainer seeks, but what the normal human being desires in an entertainment is before anything else elation and laughter. Elation and laughter are the characteristic gifts of the best and most entertaining novels, plays, music and operas. These qualities compel applause. But since the great majority of professional entertainers have no very exceptional power of delighting, cheering and producing those happy surprises that stir the human heart to laughter, and since they have to live, they put it upon the common man in the audience that there are serious qualities in their work to which he must bring care and attention, that it behoves him to discriminate, to submit himself to instruction and learn to applaud not spontaneously but *properly*. He must be advised and shepherded by critics and reviewers, guided by a claque, and brought up to the applauding point in spite of his fundamental lack of response. Such are the essentials of the comedy of the entertaining world and so it is that that world is full of argument, assertion, detraction, plots and vile conspiracies, and infested by a great multitude of professional appraisers and praisers and suchlike critical journalists, clique organizers and advance agents; and why at the end of this chain of intermediaries the modern citizen sits before a long list of plays, shows, and entertainments of all kinds, by no means entertained, wondering distressfully where, if anywhere, he can go to find those rare, precious golden threads of self-forgetful happiness, those glittering, exalted moments which are the sole justification for any kind of entertainment whatever. And who among us has not stood before a row of books in a shop window, full of the same perplexity, gathering resentment against the authors without inspiration, the critics and publishers without discrimination, who live and flourish by seeming and failing to satisfy our universal frustrated desire?

Next only to prostitutes, no social class has been so needlessly pursued and vexed by administrators and magistrates as entertainers, and none has been so ruthlessly forestalled, hampered and crippled by commercial cunning. The entertainers, the artistes, preoccupied by their essential need for applause, and intent upon producing their effects, have little time or intelligence left over for the material arrangements of the publication or show. Here step in the impresario and the makers, owners, and conductors of exhibitions, theatres and other show places. They mediate between the public and the more or less gifted persons who would entertain the public, and they make their profits, and seek to make the utmost profits, according to the traditions of the ordinary entrepreneur.

There is consequently a disposition to restrict the output of popular displays with a view to higher prices, there are conspiracies to syndicate and monopolize theatres, music halls, and cinemas, to ration the most attractive stuff and serve it out diluted with less amusing or exciting matter, to buy up and monopolize and restrain the performance of star performers, and to cut the market of outstandingly original star performers by advertising and pushing inferior rivals and mere imitators into prominence. These traders in entertainment corner joy; they ration joy; they adulterate joy. All these activities intervene between us and our moments of real happiness in entertainment. They thwart and irritate us.

No need for museum exhibits here, for nearly everyone can fill in these general statements from what we have all known and felt. Not only do we not get nearly all the good entertainers and delightful entertainment or anything like the amount of their work that we might have, but we have a quite excessive amount of weak, plausible, sham entertainment foisted upon us. It is well to have a rationalized oil or coal industry, because here we deal with a standard commodity, but entertainment can never be standardized, and these ingenious people who quasi-standardize it and flatten and deaden it are real destroyers of human initiatives and of human happiness and well-being. This is

one side, the commercial side, of this very real problem of contemporary life, the restriction and strangulation of entertainment.

It is a complex and difficult problem, and here we can offer no
suggestion of how free trade in entertainment can be established and maintained. The municipalization of theatres and
show places and their separate local management may alleviate
this unofficial commercial strangulation of the entertainer. A
municipal free-house working in competition with just as many
private entrepreneurs as appear would check monopoly, but
combined with a municipal regulation of privately owned show
places it may easily develop into the second form of strangulation—strangulation by authority. A public authority may very
well require that a show place for the public should be safe,
sound, healthy and with a reasonable standard of comfort and
elbow room. Further than that it is doubtful whether the public
authority should interfere. But it does interfere most persistently.
In all ages rulers, religious organizations and governments
have regarded uncontrolled entertainment and particularly uncontrolled mirth, with suspicion. Mirth is a powerful solvent:
the *aqua regia* of thought. All human authority is more or less
haunted by the fear of ridicule. No doubt the Old Man in the
primitive squatting place became restive at any unexplained
laughter. Few people, even the most potent and flattered, are
free from some element of self-distrust, and laughter is the
natural enemy of all authoritative conventions. Even the court
of Louis XIV must have had moments when it realized that
it was just a little preposterous, and the Church of his time,
that it was more than a little pretentious. The laws against
sceptical or disrespectful jesting in the eighteenth century were
severe. Actors and minstrels were vagabonds. No writer who
wrote against authority could call his ears his own or hope to
keep out of the pillory. And for the better protection of the
realm, all who would act must be licensed as the King's Servants.
Academies were founded in France to elevate the aims and
ambitions of writers and keep the intellectual life of the com-

munity in due subjection to the great apex of the pyramid, and every English poet who did not delight outrageously might hope to become Poet Laureate. There was a real sustained effort during the eighteenth century, in Catholic quite as much as in Puritanical countries, to stand between the industrious masses of the realm and levity. Reading "light books," such as novels or poetry, was discouraged in the respectable home. "Fun," said the ruler, "by all means," and begged the whole question by adding, "innocent fun."

Is there ever any fun without its streak of naughtiness?

There has been much emancipation since the phase of high control in the eighteenth century, but not by any means complete emancipation. A cat may look at a king in all his majesty, but it will certainly be indicted for the worst possible taste and probably turned out of doors if it laugh aloud at him. The utmost absurdities of theology are still taboo. Only very little, remote, pearl-eyed, shark-toothed Polynesian gods may be laughed at freely. People may now protest "seriously" against current sexual institutions and sentiment, but good honest laughter in these matters is decried. You may leer and snigger a little, but Peeping Tom's giggle is the very opposite to the healthy "ha-ha" of a mind released. The absurdest military or naval proceedings, again, command and get attitudes of respectful homage. A marshal, spurred and feathered like a Bantam cock and claiming credit for a victory that happened to him, overwhelms us with awe. Who dare mock him on the stage? At the loyal and patriotic anthem we stand up and look as stiff and meekly dangerous as possible. People dare not laugh at these preposterous things, cannot laugh at them, because they have never been shown how to laugh at them. Yet the world is full of vast, solemn, disastrous old conventions and institutions that only a gale of laughter or the despairing fury of revolution can ever sweep away.

And so we go out from our entertainments into the streets again smug and subdued, like a genteel congregation leaving church; elation and laughter well drained out of us.

§ 5. *Art as a Product of Leisure*

Between Entertainment and Art there is no boundary. All entertainers claim to be artistes, even if there is much Art that does not condescend to entertain. Art is the larger term, and we are bound to attempt some generalizations about the immense variety of forms in which it expresses itself, before this chapter can be considered complete.

What is Art? That question was asked and answered with endless variations in ten thousand nineteenth-century debating societies. But from the biological approach it is seen as a special form of play which takes a constructive form. There are no precise boundaries between other forms of play at which one can say: Here play ceases and Art begins. Play is the happy overflow of energy of a more or less secure and satisfied creature under no immediate practical urgency. With dogs and cats and young human beings it takes the form of wild caperings and mock battles. Such caperings become rhythmic, pass insensibly into dancing, just as shouts and noises pass into song.

Human life is full of overflow and by-products. Nature, we may say, supplies the urge and conditions of life; the creature she evokes must have impulses to drive it, senses, feelings, preferences, discriminations. Then it will survive and multiply itself, and that is as much as concerns her. It is no affair of hers if the impulses are in excess and if these senses, feelings, discriminations and preferences open up beyond the world of mere existing propagation and survival, realms of effect beyond utility, and delights and emotions that serve no manifest biological end. You may say that all this world of feelings and responses that art explores is a mere superfluity upon the material scheme, like the colours of a bubble or the delight and beauty of a flower. Or you may say that it is an escape from the material scheme, that Nature, the careless old sloven, has quite heedlessly put a key into our hands that opens the portals of a universe of super-reality, more important than material being, a sublimated universe of emancipated and intense effectiveness.

This last attitude is that generally adopted by the artist and the art critic. They have to choose the alternatives we have stated, and the latter is the one they are practically obliged to choose. The former alternative would be intolerable for an artist with a normal persona, an admission of triviality that would take all the spirit out of life for him. Hence the artistic persona is almost always a mystical and arbitrary one, and the attentive critic toils, vaguely expressive, in pursuit. The real artist, with his music, his paint, his chisel, his pencil or his pen, explores his kingdom beyond space and time, explores his magical overworld, and endeavours to convey his not always very certain impression of his discoveries to appreciative minds. He shows. You must take it or leave it—if you do not get it then it is not for you— and therein he differs from the man of science who explores as boldly as the artist, but within material limits and with repeated experiment and reasoned demonstration so that he can prove and compel your acquiescence.

For this part of our survey of the human ant-hill we need invoke no imaginary collections, for all over the world there exist art museums and galleries; it is impossible to guess how many hundred miles of Art have been segregated from the general life and come to rest in these places. And we can point, too, to countless myriads of books about art, and still there will be the poets and the romancers and the fine writers to consider. But let us turn from these accumulations of achievement to the activities of painters, composers, poets, designers, contemporary playwrights and novelists. It is in many ways a distressful life. No artist is an artist all the time; he has his moments of serene divinity when he is absolutely sure of himself and his vision; the great artist has long periods of such assurance; but for the rest, the artist is an unsure, straining creature, miserably in need of reassurance and failing in courage. He has glimpses of his kingdom, and then it is hidden from him. And since in our present state of affairs much prestige and some profit come to the successful artist, he is jostled by a great number of pretenders, without vision, who imitate and put out the results of a pretended and fabricated inspiration. Many of these pretenders do indeed have gleams of artistic insight mingling with their dross, no great artist has been altogether free from dull moments of forced and routine performance, and there is every gradation between the almost perfect genius and the absolute impostor. The world of art is made feverish and miserable by its evident need for continual criticism, appraisal and condemnation. Critics are mostly very human in the worst sense of the word, so that no artist gets his perfect praise. Not for him is the full-bodied applause that greets the successful entertainer, nor the sure and certain "record" of the athlete. He may have done his utmost and be driven frantic by some stupidity of interpretation.

It exacerbates the sensitiveness of the genuine artist that he has generally to make a living by his art. He must sell his picture or his novel, he must get his composition performed. He cannot keep his mind indifferent to those banalities of criticism and publicity, on which his reputation and his income depend. And in this world of shareholders he finds himself working amidst a half competitive swarm of people who have larger or smaller independent incomes, who are attracted by the charm and picturesqueness of a literary or artistic atmosphere, who feel they "want to do something."

But we have said enough to account for the expression of tormented defiance that looks out upon us from under the extravagantly slouched hat and disordered hair and over the wild large tie of the artist. He is a tragic hybrid. He is divine; he is pitifully human. We can hurt him even without malice, stupidly and enormously. He puts up his distinctive fight against us in his own fashion.

Here we will but name the rest of the world of art and artistic literature, the picture dealers, the exhibitions, the publishers, the musical recitals and concerts, the new multiplication of music by radio and gramophone, a world which passes without any boundary into the world of entertainment. We can but glance and pass on.

Steadily through art, life explores the realms of human possibility beyond the limits of material necessity, as athleticism explores to the utmost the physical possibilities of human life, and entertainment sustains its continual protest against a purely rational interpretation of existence. "Eat and drink," says the hard rationalist, "and be merry" adds the entertainer, and opens one door at least upon the wonderland of art. It seems inevitable that as man conquers the three major problems that at present confront him, as he escapes from the suicidal obsession of warfare, the plain danger of overpopulation and the perplexities of economic strangulation, his released energy, his ever increasing free energy, will find its satisfactions very largely in immense artistic undertakings. No doubt it will also flow into the service of science, but though science illuminates, its main product is power—and it is art alone which can find uses for power.

Therefore, if we are not on the verge of a phase of disaster, it seems plain that we must be on the verge of an age of mighty art, and particularly of mighty architecture and musical spectacle. Architecture and music may be regarded as the primary arts. Painting, sculpture, all furnishing and decoration, are the escaped subsidiaries of architecture, and may return very largely to their old dependence. Spectacle is architecture animated, and music also, through the dance and the sound drama, leads the way to spectacle. There may be a very great rehabitation of poetry and fine prose composition under the influence of radio. For two or three generations we have read our poetry in books; we may return again to hearing it.

But it is not for us to attempt a prophecy of the coming forms of art. It is absurd to suppose that all that we now call art, the masterpieces, the supreme attainments, is anything more than an intimation of what the surplus energy of mankind may presently achieve.

CHAPTER THE FIFTEENTH

How Mankind Is Taught and Disciplined

CHAPTER THE FIFTEENTH

How Mankind Is Taught and Disciplined

§ 1. *What Is Education?*

SO WE come to the culminating chapter of our review of human activities. We have shown the factories at work, the houses being built, the armies drilled, the trains running, the food distributed, the population clothed, and the human race maintained and reproduced and increased from day to day, by the interplay of need and desire, guided by idea systems, by conceptions of how and why one ought to behave, and what is due to self and to others in this vast coöperation. We have introduced Jung's convenient new term, the persona in that exposition, and it has proved very useful indeed in handling this discussion. We have attempted a rough, obvious classification of the various types of persona by which human conduct is guided, and we have indicated how the social economic life of our communities is shaped by the multitudinous interplay of these various kinds of persona. But so far we have been vague upon the way in which these guiding personas are built up in human brains. Yet obviously, unless the entire psychological analysis on which we have based ourselves is wrong, the building of these personas and their associated ideology in the one thousand nine hundred-odd million brains of mankind is the central reality of human association.

Every human being is to some extent an educable creature. If it were not so, the loosely knit world community which already exists would be impossible.

And here we use educable and education in the widest sense. We are using it in the biological sense of the modification and elaboration of instinct, of innate dispositions that is, to behave in this way or that, through experience. Experiences enhance or restrain the original mechanical responses; the creature learns. As the *Science of Life* explains very carefully, this educability is vastly greater in mammals than in any other creatures, greater in the primates than any other mammals and immensely greater in man. In all these "higher animals" there is a distinctive organ, the cerebral cortex, which is specially associated with this learning through experience. But in many animals, and particularly among the primates, there appear the rudiments of deliberate instruction. In man educability is carried to unprecedented levels by the use of symbols and particularly by the use of words. And now almost universally he draws and writes and so supplements his gestures and talking in their task of conveying and receiving suggestions. The education and instruction of even the highest anthropoid ape is quite immeasurably below the education of the most primitive savage.

The education of the savage, and also the education of a great proportion of simple and primitive people, is limited to the precept, examples and warnings of the small social group in which the individual is reared. He is shown and told what is needed for conduct in that restricted group in which he is to play his part. If he is a savage, he is shown the use of weapons, the simpler tactics of war and hunting, the use and manufacture of a few implements. It is suggested to him that certain things are things to be proud of and certain things are things to be ashamed of. And there are the imperatives of primitive law, the tabus, sexual limitations, respect for the property of others, minor specific restrictions, which must be observed under penalty. Everyone drums them into him. Everyone will see that he observes them. That suffices for his elemental needs. In the more restricted and specialized sense of the word, the normal sense of the word "educated," he is not educated at all. He is in ordinary language an uneducated person.

In that narrower sense he only begins to be educated when he is given definite and deliberate instruction in the exacter use of words, almost always with instruction in the elements of writing and counting, and when he is made to learn and remember histories which seem to explain the group and the world to him and assist him to play his part not only in the intimate domestic life, but in wider relationships. Even that much education is not yet administered to the whole of mankind. Up to a very recent date it was the privilege of comparatively limited classes even in the most advanced societies. Universal elementary education in a community is a thing of yesterday, and it is still imperfectly established. The extension of education to the whole of adult life in every class has hardly begun. Education is only dawning upon the world.

But education is being forced upon everyone by that rapid increase in the range, complexity and instability of social co-operation that is the fundamental characteristic of contemporary experience. Men have to read and write if only to understand messages, render accounts and adapt themselves to incessantly changing processes. You cannot train them and leave them. The traditional equipment of the peasant and the wandering herdsman and hunter has now to be enlarged and supplemented at a hundred points, if he is to maintain himself among the constantly multiplying exigencies of the present world. Everywhere, now, the teaching of reading and writing spreads: into the peasant life of Russia and Turkey, into the wilds of America and Siberia, into the dense peasant masses of India and China. That is to say, thin threads of understanding relationship are spreading into the minds of populations whose towns and villages were formerly as incoherent one with another, politically and economically, as grains of desert sand. The need for an extension of education created by the new economic life has been perceived, and perceived so plainly, in all the Western communities that, in spite of the jealous opposition of the baser sort of employer and of privileged people with limited ideas, it has already been carried through to the extent of creating an almost completely literate population. Nearly everybody in America and western Europe has learnt to read and write nowadays. Illiteracy recedes everywhere.

That an extension of the educational elements was bound to bring great changes in the ideology and the personas of the newly instructed was not at first evident. But reading and writing involved the penetration of general ideas into a majority of minds that had hitherto been untouched by them.

Instead of certain instructed and privileged classes the whole community is now accessible to wide general ideas and capable of incalculable interventions in the economic and political organization. The broadest ideology may appear now in action at any level in the social body. The educated persona which dominates the public services more and more, which has permeated even into the militant services, is now infecting and changing both the entrepreneur and the worker. The sense of service is spreading; it is becoming an ingredient in a growing proportion of personas. We are visibly moving towards an entirely literate and disciplined world, more and more clearly informed about its origins and its destinies.

The civilized world-state of the future will develop and can only develop in correlation with that spread of the educated persona. In the end that, with its variations, must become the universal human persona. The motive of service must replace the motives of profit and privilege altogether.

§ 2. *The Nature of Primitive Education*

When that encyclopædia of work and wealth we have projected is completed, or when our industrial museums have been extended to cover the whole field of human activities, there will be great sections devoted to education in its more specialized sense. They will show a continually broadening scope and a steady invasion of the everyday persona by large ideas.

The earliest formal education must have been instruction in the meaning of hieroglyphic signs and symbols, the teaching, that is, of reading and writing and the art of counting. There are learners' cuneiform writing tablets still in existence, four thousand years old and more, Sumerian pot-hooks and hangers. This was the substantial basis of all education for vast ages. To that was added a certain amount of explanatory lore. In our sufficiently spacious museum we should have models or paintings as well as specimens to illustrate types of primordial primary education; pictures of hedge-schools and dame schools, samples of horn books and alphabets, the abacus in use, slates and slate pencils, copy books and the like. That great educational museum of ours, which has yet to find its Oskar von Miller, will show scores of charming groups of the world's children at work upon their "elements." Rabindranath Tagore described to me how, in the schools he endowed upon his family estates, little Indians sat under trees in the open air learning after the fashion of the past to make their letters with styles upon big leaves. I remember learning my A B C from my mother with the help of a sheet of letters which she had stuck up in the kitchen, and the first word I wrote was "butter" on a scrap of paper put against the window to trace over the copy she had made. From such primitive methods our museum will ascend to that more systematic and scientific training, not only in letters and figures, but in shapes, colours and outline that has been developed from Froebel's initiatives in the kindergarten.

Many of my contemporaries got their "elements" in the same old-fashioned way as I. They learnt the numbers as shapes and their "tables" of multiplication, and so forth, long before they realized what it was all about. Such propositions as "five and two are seven" or "twice five are ten" were learnt as dogmas. A single unsoundness in the set of dogmas thus acquired was enough to send all their summing wrong and give them a life-long dread of the uncertainties of calculation and the perplexities of mathematics. Their "sums" came out wrong, and there was no way of checking and discovering the faulty tendency. A little boy who had slipped into the heresy that $5+7=11$ or that $7\times8=48$ might have his life embittered and suffer punishments and impositions for years through the operation of that one undetected defect.

Interesting modern developments will be displayed in these collections showing how the accidental misconceptions and physical idiosyncrasies of children can now be observed and detected and corrected. Hitherto astigmatism and other optical defects have made adding and suchlike processes in column, and the swift recognition of figures, difficult for multitudes in every generation, and have stamped this swarm of unfortunates with an unjustifiable sense of their lack of "gift" in these matters. Defects of hearing and obscure mental resistances have led to a similar imputation of stupidity in the use of words. The old elementary teaching was a wasteful process because it was unobservant. At every stage it left crippled and uncompleted minds by the wayside.

Superposed on the necessary first-grade instruction in the codes of intercommunication comes the teaching of social explanations, the teaching of the common ideas that hold the community together, its history and its usages. This lore and the way in which it is imparted vary enormously throughout the educational spectacle. Here again we contemplate a vast region of fact that still awaits the labours of an army of investigators. The persona of the adult is made in the mould of this elucidatory and initiatory teaching, and through the aggregate of the personas of the community flow all its activities. At this most important part of our enquiry into the motive forces of the human ant-hill we find ourselves again in uncharted and unsettled territory.

That anthropological part of our coming encyclopædia, that still uncrystallized Museum of Human Education, when it has been brought into being, will display, arranged in order, an intricate, strange variety of methods adopted by savage and barbaric peoples throughout the earth. Just as there was a stage in the development of agricultural processes when the sowing of seed and the beginning of a new year seem to have been inseparably associated with human sacrifices, so almost everywhere we find traces of cruel, dark and grotesque ceremonies at the dawn of sexual maturity. Fasts, vigils, torture, mutilations, the knocking out of teeth, the tattooing of the body were inflicted. And after various dire tests and strains, there generally appeared a pretense of imparting profound secrets. The incidence of these initiations varied widely. Some were the lot of everyone in the tribe, or they fell most heavily on the men, or they were restricted to particular ranks in the social body or made exceptionally onerous for those ranks. They were the crown of the popular education of all the folk concerned, or they were the culmination of the special education of the priests and medicine men.

The teaching of the young savage about himself and the conditions of his life, what he was, what the tribe was, what he might do, what he might not do, what powers he should respect and why, was manifestly threaded into this testing, straining, and breaking-in process. But at present our knowledge of the psychological forces concerned, what were the motives and ideas of the elders who imposed these ceremonies, and how they reacted upon the persona of the neophyte, is very obscure. Even our accounts of the actual rituals in many cases are extremely imperfect and unsatisfactory. More often than not the idea which led to the adoption of this or that ceremony is lost completely in the remote past. Each generation has gone on repeating what was done before, with occasional elaborations and mutations of the things done, reverence increasing and deepening as the last rays of rationality vanish. When the ceremony has become a mystery and a sacrament, then its establishment is secure.

There is a streak of original cruelty in the human make-up, a disposition to experiment upon our fellows, a taste for strange, impressive, and terrifying behaviour. All peoples seem to like grotesque masks, monstrous images and antics, throbbing and menacing music and ceremonious dances for their own sake; but the normal human disposition is all against admitting that these things are mere play and purposeless excess; they are justified therefore in inventing deep reasons and grave imperatives. In an earlier chapter of this work (Chapter I, § 5) we have shown how the human community grew against resistances and particularly against the dispersive influence of the jealousy of senior for junior. There may be an appeasing element mixed up in initiation; there may be a vindictive and dominating factor in the primitive educational process. The jealousy of the seniors works itself off. We do not merely teach the young, we "larn 'em."

The disposition to inflict suffering and impose submission is still plainly perceptible in our records of the education of the growing civilizations of ancient and modern times. The teacher approached his pupil in the mood of a snarling dog, hardly concealing the implements of discipline, the rod, the cane, the birch, the leather strap. It is all too plain that he did not mean to use them only in the last resort; he meant to use them at the first opportunity. Our Educational Museum will have cases and diagrams of these once necessary instruments, and all literature will be ransacked for our encyclopædia to find illuminating quotations about this flagellatory phase in the teaching of mankind.

Even the "elements" were taught harshly and clumsily in primitive education, and the comparison of savage initiations with one another and with classical and mediæval educational methods will, I think, reveal more and more that the second stage of education has aimed partly indeed to impart a history and an explanation, but mainly to cow, abase, break in, and so socialize the presumably recalcitrant and insubordinate newcomer. Even to this day it is charged against the English public schoolboy that he has been given a morbidly exaggerated sense of "good form," that he is a moral coward, afraid to think for himself or look hostile public opinion in the face. He is subjugated not only by the teaching staff, but by the conservative influence of the senior forms entrusted with the "traditions of the school"; he has all the individual "nonsense" knocked out of him. So the prize boy becomes the orthodox second-rate man. That particular indictment we will not discuss here. But it is plain in any realistic and circumstantial account of schools throughout the ages that the pedagogue has had a very aggressive way of leaping upon his human material and driving it before him. And much of the amelioration of upper-class schools in the last hundred years or so has been rather a relaxation of pedagogic energy, fierceness and clumsiness, under the protests of parents and public, than any very definite revolution in the teachers' conception of educational method.

The extensive disappearance of violence and dogmatic compulsion from education in recent times is apparently only one aspect of a general mitigation of the relations of human beings one to another. It has gone on parallel with the decline in the beating and ill-treatment of servants and workers, and the diminished arrogance of employers, and it is due to deeper causes than any specific educational reform. We have already indicated how far the greater prosperity of our species and the civilizing influence of the machine have contributed to this amelioration of life. "Democracy" is one of the terms we use to express this changed spirit in the world. We are not so sure who are inferiors and who are superiors as we used to be. Projects are explained to people instead of being imposed upon them, and the imperative mood gives place to persuasion.

The world has discovered that the common man is neither so stupid nor so obstinate as was once supposed; a large part of industrial progress has consisted in taking the worker into the confidence of the entrepreneur, and a quite parallel change in spirit has gone on throughout the educational organization. The declared object of education is no longer to make a suitable instrument for the carrying out of a subjugating and restraining tradition; it has become the stimulation and release of a willing collaborator in an adventurous enterprise.

This implies not only an extensive change in the spirit and method of teaching, but also a revolutionary change in the content of education. The persona evoked has not only to be of a different quality, but it has to look in a different direction.

To the development of that change of direction this entire work is devoted, and we now approach its concluding definition.

§ 3. *Religions and Education*

Here it is we must bring in the church spires, the towers, the minarets, the modest chapels, the cathedrals, cloisters and episcopal palaces, the church house, the monastery, the nunnery, the lamasery, the religious retreats, pilgrimage centres and wayside shrines, scattered about our world. Or rather we must bring in the activities of all the men, women and children which centre upon these, who perform ceremonies, celebrate occasions, chant, fast, pray, and watch in and protect these picturesque and often very beautiful aspects of the human landscape. What do they signify to us in our review of the human ensemble?

What in fact is the social significance of religion?

Let us recall the limitations we have set ourselves in this work. As we defined our scope in Chapter II, § 4, we are dealing with "man's gradual and at last methodical extension of mastery over the forces and substances about him—in space and time as he experiences them, in existence as he knows it." We have refused to follow the new-fashioned mathematician or the old-fashioned theologian beyond this everyday life, and we are concerned with religion therefore only in so far as it now influences the activities of people and affords occupations for them. It is not for us to discuss here whether this universe has in fact existed forever or (what is for all practical purposes the same thing) that it was flung into being in the year 4004 B. C. as a going concern so contrived that it implied an infinite past. It does not concern us whether (in some profoundly symbolic fashion, of course) the cosmos rests on a tortoise which rests on an elephant whose legs reach "all the way down," or that it is all a thought in the mind of a Jeans-like Deity whose symbol is the square root of minus one, who started his vast meditation with the simple proposition, "Let there be light" and gradually worked things out—a game of Patience played by a Being of Infinite Leisure—to produce a recognizable reflection of Himself in the mind of a popular savant. These and every other form of cosmic poetry, logomachy and "mystical" interpretation of Being are outside our scope altogether. We refuse all theological controversy. We do not interpret Being here. We accept Being. However Being may be interpreted, it remains for man mainly an affair of economic coöperation in which his to-day is filled with the cares of to-morrow. That employs him, and that is what concerns us here. We deal with Being here only as it presents itself in the everyday life, and with religion only as a social fact in a spectacle of facts.

In fact, religion appears at first in the human story as something as practical as a flint arrowhead. Its gods were once as actual and material as men. Its chief festivals turned on seed-time and harvest, and its sacrifices and the benefits it promised were, so far as we are able to tell, entirely mundane. Even when the idea of immortality came in, it was to begin with a quite materialist immortality, a resurrection of the actual body, or a life in happy hunting grounds as real as earth.

We are profoundly ignorant of the religion of palæolithic man. There are guesses that he had a sort of fetishism, and that he imagined minds and wills in everything. They are just guesses. It is doubtful if the present beliefs and customs of still savage people furnish very sound indications of the working of those archaic minds. A savage is as many generations away from primitive man as we are.

Still less do we understand the mental operations of the generations transitional to the early agricultural peoples. Advancing psychology may presently find acceptable explanations of the steps which led to the specialized priest and the altar. Through stage after stage we may build up again in our imaginations that mighty growth of fears and personifications, of symbols that were living realities to the worshipper, of vast overhanging imperatives and assurances. Now it is only in rare flashes of intuition that we glimpse the gods and spirits and powers that our ancestors knew for real. The early civilizations, as archæology reveals them, show a threefold society of peasant, of nomad conqueror and trader and of initiated priest, already established, believing in the gods and in the guidance of those gods. The religion as prehistory displays it is intensely practical, and the priest monopolizes the thought and knowledge of the community. He is astronomer, man of science, doctor, lawyer, banker, architect and art director. He is subjugated to his god and to his order, and he is saturated with the idea of service. The whole mental life of the community is in fact at that early stage religious.

So, still very largely unexplained, Neolithic society breaks upon our knowledge.

The collective mental life has long since lapsed from its homogeneity in the early communities, by the distinction and disentanglement of the learned and technical callings from the religious priesthood, pure and simple; by the escape through specialization of this great service and of that, from immediate association with the temple. The professions specialized away from the religious body, but the religious body to the best of its ability remained generalized and directive. It did not accept any specialization, though a sort of specialization was thrust upon it. By the later Middle Ages, the lawyer and the study of law, the medical profession, philosophy, science, finance, banking were all practically secularized, and the formal religious organization, though still the directive power of society, no longer permeated the whole net of intellectual activities.

Finance had indeed been secularized since classical times. When the great Semitic civilizations of Mesopotamia and the Mediterranean had collapsed before Aryan conquerors, the cruder religious organization of these latter never took over the banking, loaning and insurance of the ancient Temples. That remained in Semitic hands.

From the time of the Greek republics onward, whenever a class of independent gentlemen arose there was also an escape of philosophy and science from the priests. But though they escaped they were still subordinated. If men thought and experimented with a certain freedom they did so under God or under the gods. Plato, Socrates, Euripides pursued the most penetrating and subversive enquiries, but they saluted the gods with respect. They could think and say what they liked within limits and to their own special circle, but they had to respect the divine control of the general community. The earliest scientific society dedicated itself to the Muses.

Education has been the last field of intellectual activity to pass out of religious control, and it is still imperfectly and doubtfully released. General education was still almost entirely in consecrated hands in the sixteenth century, and most of the great statesmen were still clerics. There is a manifest reason why there should be this sustained association of school and altar. The lawyer could begin as a special sort of priest and presently cease to be a priest at all, because explaining the moral order of the universe and keeping contact with the gods had manifestly ceased to be any part of his business. But the teacher who began as a special sort of priest has remained priest because he has, even more than most priests, to explain the moral order of the universe and keep up the contact between the learner and the gods.

In our own times in England and France we have seen a great movement to "secularize" education and a powerful resistance to that movement. The conflict has played a large part in the political life of both these countries for half a century, and the disentanglement of school and Church is still very incomplete. It is, in fact, an impossible disentanglement. The moral order of the community must be expounded in some fashion; if the gods and creeds are to go, there must be another story told and a fresh creed explained.

Secularism cannot do without the religious function; it cannot banish a rationalized devotion. Quite as much as religion it has to present life in an ordered series of values in which self takes a subordinate place.

If the reader will recall the chief religious revolutions, revivals and new beginnings throughout the world, he will, I think, agree that in all cases they were animated by the desire to restore the original comprehensiveness of religious direction. They are educational resumptions or attempted resumptions, a bracing up of education. They all arose in times of change and mental confusion, and either they sought to recall the old gods or formulæ in an invigorated state, 'or they attempted to substitute new ones. Buddhism, Christianity, Islam, Communism arose, all of them, not as new and interesting discoveries (or denials) in the field of theology, but as complete new ways of life, to which law, hygienic régime and medicine, social custom, thought and enquiry had to be reoriented. In each the convert had to be "born again." He had to come out from the City of Destruction. He had to learn a new way of life. They were all "teachings"; they were all in essence educational, a new sort of training for a new sort of living.

Throughout the ages religion in its various forms has always been providing or attempting to provide *the common explanation of the community;* to state, so to speak, the community's "articles of association." It has held communities together even if it has never, in historical times and so far as we know, completely and entirely bound them into perfect organized unities.

If we consider the histories of the main religious beginnings and reform movements of the historical period we shall find a sort of parallel development among them all. They arise with a sort of glory in men's souls. The common things of life are transfigured. To begin with, the new faith is always intensely practical, always. It demands a change of the whole life. Things have got into a dreadful state, and they have to start afresh. Whatever the revelations, theories and mysteries on which the new teaching professes to be based, a new sort of behaviour is its substantial aspect. The normal everyday life, the "world," has to be renounced altogether. It is the new religious life or nothing. The rich young man has to sell all that he has and follow in the footsteps of the Teacher. All men are to be converted and brought under the yoke of the faith. Manifestly all education has to be renewed from the ground upward.

But soon the teaching is taken up by disciples who hand it on to other disciples. They go out from the inspiration of the Master to obdurate and inattentive people already set in established ways of living but who, they feel, ought to be attracted and persuaded. And presently the Master is no longer with his disciples to revive their flagging zeal and criticize their interpretations. Compromise creeps in. The new faith reduces its terms. Things are made easy for those who will come part of the way but not all the way. A distinction is made between those who lead a full religious life and the lay adherent. Times and seasons are prescribed for religious duties, and the rest of the daily life is tacitly released from the grip of the advancing religion.

A process of "spiritualization" begins. The Master taught, perhaps, that the spirit was more important than the letter, but now this is interpreted to justify a mitigation of practical applications. A distinction is drawn between *deadly sins*, like denial, blasphemy, failure to respect the prescribed sacraments and the like, which break up the organization and so remain of vital importance, and *venial sins* which merely disregard the rules of personal conduct. Sins of the flesh, usury, dishonesties, these the religious specialist will forgive on reasonable terms so long as you will not attack the fundamentals of his organization and creed. Make the sign of the cross, or repeat the formula that Allah alone is God, admit that your sins are sins, and you may sin in comparative peace.

And not only is the practical influence of the spreading faith thus attenuated and detached, but also it becomes "tolerant." It is tacitly admitted that it is, after all, not supremely important. Islam, which began with the alternative of conversion or the sword, presently arrived at the more practicable alternative of conversion or tax-paying. The believer and the damned meet with increasing amiability as this attenuation of religion proceeds.

It becomes less and less possible to distinguish the converted by any external tests. Even their spiritualized religious exercises begin to be neglected. The formulæ remain devitalized and dying. Yet the organizations fight for existence, and the sincere believers fight against this broadening decadence. Many are diverted into partisanship and into a preservative persecution of the scoffer and the open unbeliever. There is a struggle against mixed marriages, against unsympathetic talk and books, against novel practices. Instead of the "glad tidings" of the opening phase appears orthodoxy indignant in an inattentive world. What was once an inspiration has become an obstruction; from conquest the creed has passed into opposition. Religions begin as the dawn of God and end with their backs to the wall.

Such is the common history of religions as the world has known them since history began. It is as true of sectarian departures, of Quakerism and Calvinism for example, as of Christianity as a whole. Religious impulses are always "fading out" and always being renewed. They do not disappear, but they lose emphasis. They lose fire and quality. They are great impulses in life, and they spread and spend themselves in conquest. The flash ends in ashes.

Yet the need of religion for a comprehensive statement of life and right conduct is perennial. Religion after religion is evoked by that need; each tries to recapture that completeness of control over life which was originally exercised by belief and fear in the early communities, and each in its turn fails.

At present great multitudes of us are living in a state of faded religiosity. The formal religious organizations of the Atlantic world are little more than the spiritualized husks and trappings of long abandoned efforts to begin a new way of living for mankind. About each there has clustered an accumulation of buildings, endowments and methods of feeling and behaviour. These things go on by a certain inertia and by the imponderable elements in the human make-up. The new way of living, the new rule of life has largely or entirely disappeared or become the "rule" of some professing order, but the "spiritualized" functions and ceremonies still exert an emotional and habitual appeal. So far from revolutionizing life and taking people out of worldly routines, religions in their last phase serve rather to allay restlessness, silence uneasy questionings and reassure by their atmosphere of conviction and ultimate knowledge.

Least faded of all the variations of Christianity is the Roman Catholic Church. This does maintain not merely a struggle for its own existence and an obstinate grip upon its schools, but a stout and definite attempt to control the lives of its adherents. Not in economic life. In economic life the control of the church is and always has been very weak, it repudiates Socialism without any clear definition of the sin involved, but in things biological and intimate its determination to direct is real and living. We have noted this already in Chapter XIII, § 1. Upon the fundamental issue of birth control there was a phase of hesitation on the part of the Church. Bishop Bovier of Le Mans, for instance, in 1842 warned the Pope that to prohibit the practise of contraception would weaken the power of the Church in France. It was only in December, 1930, that the Pope finally slammed the door upon "toleration" in this matter and restored the sacrament of marriage to an unambiguous material significance.

The Roman Catholic Church thus remains as a body the most

practical, the least "spiritualized," of all the main sects of Christianity. It confronts its adherents with a definite way of living which in this respect at least is in plain antagonism to modern ideas. It has launched upon a deliberate struggle to deflect education from modern ends. Roman Catholics have now no choice but to obey, or to disobey and lie about it (which the confessional makes difficult) or to leave the Church.

In Moscow I have been told there is a Museum of Religion of a bitterly polemical type. But it is possible to imagine a Museum of Comparative Religion void of all polemical suggestion that would bring together in a very illuminating way the altars, rituals, symbols, costumes and prescribed types of building of all the world's creeds from Rome to Hayti and from Tibet to Yucatan. We should trace how Persia, ancient Etruria, Hellenic Alexandria, have contributed to the temples of to-day. There could be gramophone records of music, of revivalist preaching and chants, working models of genuflexions and prostrations, and all the instruments and methods of purification, mortification, and penance. All these things a museum could show, but no museum can recapture the hopes, the ecstasies and despairs, the passions of devotion, the abasement and the ennoblement of minds, of which these things are the sounds and hulls and instruments. Throughout the ages ten thousand million souls have been lit and have flamed upward, consoled and exalted by religion.

A myriad religious activities are in progress as this page is read, and our panorama of all that occupies mankind would not be complete without them. At Benares fakirs and saints are doing the strangest things, sitting cross-legged, their arms limp, their palms upward, squinting at the tips of their own noses in a meditative ecstasy, lying on beds of spikes, maintaining incredible attitudes; yellow-robed, shaven-headed men are tending the wind-driven praying wheels of Tibet; there are pilgrimages afoot in every quarter of the globe, chantings, kneeling, sacrifices. At Altotting, in Bavaria, on nearly every day in the year there are men and women on their knees dragging heavy wooden crucifixes round the Chapel of the Black Virgin. Wherever you are, there are probably men and women fasting and praying within a few miles of you. There is exhortation going on at this moment in cathedrals, in great public halls, in little plain chapels, at the street corners, in forest clearings.

All this religious doing is as much a part of the world of work and wealth as the beating of foundry hammers and the clatter of looms. It may be withdrawn a little from the main stream of production and distribution and consumption, but it draws its impetus from the same sources, and it moves forward together with the rest of the living flood. It reacts upon production, consumption, buying and selling, population and practically all the material concerns of life.

Statistics, such as they are, suggest that the current of these ceremonies and devotions has dwindled relatively to the main stream of life in the past century or so. It is difficult to ascertain what proportion of the world's population is now under vows, consecrated to a religious life. There do not seem to be any statistics to show the increase or decrease of the monastic and conventual life. The maximum, so far as Christendom goes, is believed to have occurred in the thirteenth century. Nor are there figures to show the waxing or waning of Buddhist monasticism. The Christian churches complain of diminished attendances of the laity. The churches open their doors for service, the church bells peal, but the swelling torrent of modern life seems to heed these invitations less and less.

Perhaps the most vital contemporary religion—as we have defined religion—is embodied in the disciplines of the Communist party. It is vital in the fact that it is still in continuous contact with conduct. It is elaborately protected against "spiritualization" by an insistent dogmatic materialism. It admits no significance for life whatever except here and now. The Communist prides himself upon this implacable materialism. He, at least, he is resolved, will not fall away from the intense practicality which all other religions have so conspicuously lost.

If he does fall away in the future, it will be in the name not of spirituality but of strategy and tactics. He may *reculer pour mieux sauter*, and then never return for the leap. Christianity

AN UNPRECEDENTED UNIVERSITY BUILDING

THE new college building in the Civic Centre at Pittsburgh, housing the University of Pittsburgh.

MODERN UNIVERSITY SCENERY

THE stadium and part of the college buildings of Harvard College, photographed from the air. The group of buildings just above the stadium include the Harvard School of Business Administration and the new dormitories. The older college buildings are at the left, beyond the scope of this picture.

started with a community of goods which it presently became convenient to disregard. The sense of this danger of "weakening off" haunts the Communist world and produces, just as it has produced in other religions, a heavy stressing of orthodoxy. The religion is fighting hard for great ends, and there is a heavy strategical disadvantage in any modifications of doctrine in the face of the "enemy." It fears criticism for exactly the same reason that the military type fears criticism, because it weakens discipline and breaks the fighting front.

Communism clings to orthodoxy, the true and only faith, and already there have been heresy hunts in the Communist body. There is a sort of Inquisition into the sincerity of professed believers and servants, and there has been a panic lest the faith be betrayed. Eminent officials are accused; they are subjected to rigorous enquiries, they confess and submit gratefully to discipline. If the Five Year Plan falls short, it will be through conspiracies and sabotage, for it is contrary to the creed that the Five Year Plan should fail through any inherent defect. For the edification of the weaker brethren there are now prophets and saints, Marx and Lenin to begin with, whose intelligence and character must no longer be questioned, whose every utterance was divine. And there is even a mystical communism, affecting the art and literature of Moscow profoundly, whose aim is self-identification with "the Proletarian." "The Proletarian" is a superhuman entity with whom the devout Marxist seeks and attains spiritual communion. The individuality of the worshipper is merged therein. From the Proletarian springs "Prolet-art," for example, among the first fruits of the new spirit. It is art without individuality. Proletarian thought, proletarian science, proletarian conduct have, it is believed by the devout Communist, strange and novel superiorities of their own.

Already Fülop-Miller in the *Spirit and Face of Bolshevism* has initiated the study of these developments. The comparative theologian will find close and interesting analogies between these aspects of Communism and Christian and Moslem mysticism.

From our present point of view Communism is only the latest and not the last of the world religions. We may foretell, but it is difficult to anticipate, others. One guess may be permitted here. Communism may be the last wave of dogmatic religion. It seems probable to the writer that the development of religion in the future may differ in one important respect from the way in which all religions, up to and including Communism, have arisen in the past. In the future there may be a religious organization without a Founder or an initial inalterable Teaching.

All religions hitherto have begun with extreme definition; with the assumption that the final truth was now revealed. That was on all fours with the mental dispositions of the ages of tradition. But just as nowadays all sciences are consciously progressive, working towards more truth but never attaining absolute truth, so modern religion may become also a continually progressive thing. Do not modern conditions indeed necessitate such a new type of religious approach? Our world is now launched upon a perpetual investigation and innovation, and its ideal of education is no longer the establishment of a static ideology, but the creation of a receptive and coöperative alertness. For that no fixed inalterable teaching will suffice.

All those forms of mental service we have considered in our study of the priestly persona, that have escaped one by one, as we have said, from the original comprehensiveness of religion, need now to be brought back into a common understanding. They left organized and formulated religion behind very largely because of its inflexibility. They left it high and dry and flowed out into the world. So that the world has become more and more scattered in its ideals and aims. Education, law, finance, research, literature, all begotten by the priestly tradition, have ceased now to have even ceremonial relations with organized religion. Liberal minds conceive education nowadays as divested of any existing religious form. Nevertheless, we realize the necessity of some more comprehensive teaching that shall restore the declining unity of human motives. If we cannot teach imperatives we have to teach aims. We have to restore unifying power to education. We seek a new education to achieve the synthesis of the new world community.

But if we are seeking to frame out a new education in view

of the new ways of living that open before us, we are thereby and at the same time starting religion anew.

§ 4. *Universities*

Just as the forms and methods of the new economic organization of mankind spring from the social order of the Atlantic civilizations, so the types of educational method that now prevail and spread over the earth are mainly the fruits of Western Christendom. The two things have gone together. In the educational museum of the future, the young Moslim shrilly learning the Koran by rote, the Chinese student toiling to recognize and shape one complex character after another and acquiring a miscellany of phrase and information in the process, will be found in side galleries leading nowhere. The main aisle will carry us from the schools of Rome through the schools of mediæval and modern Europe to the world education of to-day.

Latin education under the Empire had separated itself very widely from religion. Religion had passed into one of its most attenuated phases, and the recognized worship of the gods was being supplemented by that variety of cults, Neoplatonism, Isis worship, Mithraism, primitive Christianity, and so forth, out of which orthodox Catholicism arose at last triumphant. The school and the pedagogue had practically nothing to do with these religious developments. Formal education concerned itself with the teaching of Greek and Latin and with rhetoric, and it was restricted to a limited class. What ideology the young received came to them from the world about them. There was no religious doctrine in formal education. There was not, therefore, as Cloudesley Brereton points out very clearly in his excellent article in the current Encyclopædia Britannica, any violent conflict between ascendent Christianity and the pagan schools. They were taken over by the Christian synthesis.

The dark ages of barbaric disorder and social confusion in Europe attenuated but did not break the Latin educational tradition. The curriculum of the schools that emerge in the ninth and tenth centuries is recognizably the same as that of the schools of the second century B. C. plus an ideology—to wit doctrinal Christianity—and minus any Greek learning. The Latin language, some Latin literature, logical reasoning, an astrological astronomy, rudimentary (and quite bookish) science, counting and a little computation and vocal music, constituted the substantial equipment of an educated man. And even this much education did not extend far beyond the organized clergy.

From such schools, with the restoration of social order in the eleventh and twelfth centuries, there presently arose those distinctive centralizing organs of the European educational systems, the universities. They were developed in close relation to the Church and monasticism; their organization was essentially monastic. Salerno stands out as an exception. It arose in the tolerant atmosphere of tenth century Sicily, where Moslim Christian and Jew could meet and exchange ideas, and it was primarily a school of medicine. Its growth was fostered by that pioneer rebel against the Papacy, the Emperor Frederick II. The others were aggregates of scholars, aggregates growing out of local schools, as learning spread and the increasing social stability made law more important and a knowledge of law desirable.

The teachers and scholars in these expanding schools organized for mutual assistance in guilds under an elected rector. The typical university was, to begin with, a teachers' and students' association. It was not created by a ruling authority. At first the students lodged haphazard, but later came residential colleges. The method of teaching was chiefly by lecture and notebook. At these concentrations, law, bookish medicine and theology were studied, and at a lower level was the preparatory "arts" course for those insufficiently prepared for the major studies. The "arts" were Latin, logic, rhetoric, stale book-science, music, descriptive astronomy and a little summing. The arts student graduated B. A. and, if he meant to teach, M. A. The teaching in all faculties was the teaching of tradition.

"The methods of instruction," says Mr. Cloudesley Brereton, in the article already cited, "—by lecture, or commentary on received texts; and by disputation, in which the scholars acquired dexterity in the use of the knowledge they had absorbed—were in harmony with this conception, and were undoubtedly thoroughly well suited to the requirements of an age in which the ideal of human thought was not discovery, but order, and in which knowledge was regarded as a set of established propositions, the work of reason being to harmonize these propositions in subordination to the authoritative doctrines of the Church."

The growth of the universities of this pattern throughout Europe was accompanied by a development of local schools preparing for the "arts" course. These, represented in England by the public schools and grammar schools, made no attempt to educate the general population. They simply prepared aspirants for the three great professions and supplied instruction in the "elements" and a smattering of learning for the sons of prosperous people. By the thirteenth century the formal education of Europe was firmly established upon these lines, and the essentially traditional universities had secured a controlling grip upon educational organization that endures to this day. Some reading and summing leaked out beyond the established schools, men and women learnt to write their names and so on, and an outline of Christian ideology was imparted to nearly everybody in the community by the priest, who used the painted walls of his church and its carved decorations as a picture book for the illiterate.

But this organization leading up to the clerical universities was not the only medium for the transmission of knowledge and ideas in the Middle Ages. By its side there were other educational processes going on, sometimes waxing and sometimes waning in relative importance. The rich and powerful employed private tutors for their children. There was an education of the castle as well as an education of the schools. The young gentleman began as page and learnt equestrian and military science; he learnt estate management; he was trained in instrumental music, versification and good manners. In the presence of the dingy erudite he carried himself with pride. He rarely went near a university to learn. His crowning graduation was foreign travel.

In the fifteenth century, the increase in the number of intelligent gentlemen was making this other line of education more and more important. They were reading and thinking. The education of the universities was fading, just as in the preceding section we have described religion as fading. It was failing to cover the realities of life. It was like a small cloak shrinking to the dimensions of a handkerchief on a growing body. The drive towards trade expansion and exploration in the fifteenth century and most of the intellectual stir of the time were not coming through the universities at all.

The acceptance of Greek and of a study of the Greek and Latin literatures for their own sakes, were forced upon the universities through the influence of the merchant princes of Italy, the princes of Germany and the sumptuous ecclesiastics of Rome. Tradition fought against these innovations. The convulsion of the Reformation saw a great decline in the entire university-school organization, and more especially in the Protestant countries. Education retreated for a time to the gentleman's library and study. It was the counter reformation under the Jesuits that salvaged the schools and universities of the Catholic countries and set a pattern for the Anglican public school.

The attempt to reorganize education in the seventeenth century would make a long history. Oxford and Cambridge counted their students by hundreds then, where once they had counted thousands. Severe religious tests excluded the Catholic and the Nonconformist from these centres. The intellectual thrust of the new times was embodied in such new institutions as the Scientific Academies whose development we have already discussed in Chapter II, § 5. The most rigorous and energetic of the Protestant sects evolved their own teaching institutions. Max Weber in his *Protestant Ethic and the Spirit of Capitalism* shows how closely the religious revivalism of the time, the "new life" of the Calvinists in particular, was associated in spirit with the business methods that are now grouped together under the name of Capitalism. It was not simply a religious break-away that occurred. It was an educational break-away. It was equally a break-away from the faded clerical tradition of the time embodied in the universities. In our analysis of social motives we have pointed out some of the results of this detachment of the entrepreneur from the clerical tradition. The "uneducated" man really had an advantage at that time over the "educated" in his boldness of initiative and in his closer grip upon reality. He had no use for "book learning" emasculated by generations of "scholars." That he had certain moral deficiencies was not so apparent and interfered not at all with his crude success in that industrial revolution which preceded the mechanical.

It would be too long and subtle an undertaking to tell here how the European university-school system after its ebb towards the middle of the seventeenth century came back again to its present formal predominance in educational organization. This recovery has been made by a series of adaptive abandonments. Conspicuous among these has been the extensive abandonment of religious restrictions bringing the Nonconformist and the Jew, as well as in Protestant countries the exiled Roman Catholic, back to the depopulated lecture rooms.

This was only one aspect of a still profounder abandonment: the abandonment of the idea that the chief function of a university is to preserve traditional learning. Reluctantly but steadily during the last two centuries the idea of intellectual progress has been accepted. "Scholarship" has ceased to rule the teacher's world. Side by side with the older disciplines the gymnastics of mathematics arose. The astronomy of the telescope followed mathematics into these centres. Then, as the nineteenth century ripened, the experimental sciences won their way to academic protection and encouragement. We have noted the fashion in which this came about in Chapter II, § 5. Now the universities of the world are conscientiously progressive. No man or woman of powerful intellectual initiative need despair nowadays of at least posthumous recognition by these chastened and reinvigorated institutions.

And as an aspect of this renascence the universities have taken up exterior teaching also—before it was too late. They have just prevented the development of a school system independent of them, planned on novel lines to meet new needs.

One may doubt whether this has been altogether a fortunate thing for the community. By great but measured concessions to the more formidable forces of our time they have brought the whole system of secondary education under their sway. The popular State schools that have spread about the world since the need of at least an elementary universal education has been recognized, came into existence largely beyond their purview, but they are gradually bringing these also into relationship by means of a scholarship ladder and the infiltration of the ranks of teachers and inspectors with their graduates. If they have really begotten very little of modern education they have at least now enormously adopted it. New educational institutions have been shaped to their pattern. The new great University of London and scores of other modern educational centres throughout the civilized world, recall the more venerable institutions in a hundred particulars. They even ape their antiquated costumes and ceremonies; they imitate their "degrees" and courses.

With a difference. Imagine the encounter of a bright young modern-spirited girl in traditional doctor's cap and scarlet robes, dedicated by a scholarship at the London School of Economics to, let us say, "sociological research," with a learned doctor, robe, hood, and cap essentially the same, a monster of erudition, a great bag of quotations, a mighty "scholar" resuscitated from the dignified mental repletion of seventeenth-century Oxford. On the one hand we should have an effect of masquerading impertinence, on the other, I fear, apoplexy.

The universities of Christendom have survived because of the enormous concessions they have made, because of their sedulous propitiation of the strong and successful; they have spread all over the world with the general Europeanization of the world; but it is permissible to question whether they and the conceptions of education they embody are destined to any very prolonged predominance over the intellectual processes of mankind.

In spite of all their apparent modernization the universities have never yet discovered how to lead a community. They have a timidity in their hearts; they would rather propitiate than dominate. They have simply substituted the tradition of yesterday for inalterable tradition to·save themselves. They have almost come up to date, and they have been carried on prosperously by a hurrying and not too critical world. But they will always be by their very nature, by their instinct for following power instead of·exercising it, not quite up to date. It is difficult to imagine how they can ever get beyond yesterday. With their fundamental hieratic prepossessions, their degrees and examinations, their curricula and direction of study, they must always remain organizations for the confirmation and transmission of what has already been accepted in the unorganized world of free intelligence. They cannot handle knowledge in this fashion until it is more or less traditionalized. They may be of service in stereotyping ideas for general distribution, but they can neither monopolize nor control the spontaneous directive processes of human thought. These last, in a world where there are no longer any educational limitations to class or type, must play freely through the general intellectual community.

The university in its origin and essence is the culmination of a great system of classrooms in which teachers talk and exercises are done. But is it necessary now that the classroom should extend up to the adult level? For the more or less systematized teaching of the elements and for the establishment of a common ideology the gathering of very young people into classrooms may still be desirable. This we will examine in a later section. But the present fashion of sending young men and women of from seventeen to twenty-two or three to universities for a modernized "arts" degree may give way very rapidly before a clearer conception of education.

The recovery of the universities from their decadence in the eighteenth century was due very largely to the growth of new social types, keenly aware of their educational deficiencies, but by no means clear about the education they needed. The primitive entrepreneur despised book learning, literature, science. His successor demanded education as he demanded a standing among the gentry.

The old universities were distended and reanimated by the

requirements of these people. Rich men, stirred by creative impulses, founded new ones in the naïve persuasion that any learning was good knowledge. We have devoted a brief section already to the civilization of the entrepreneur (Chapter VIII, § 5). The wealth won by innovation bowed down in the halls of tradition and founded new halls. But as its intelligence grew it became critical, and then it was that the old universities began to affect that air and complexion of youth and achieved that remarkable rejuvenation we are dealing with now. The more fashionable became in effect concerns for the flattering of the prosperous old and the entertainment of the prosperous young. The classroom is at last only the venerable nucleus for institutions essentially modern, a formal centre for the playing fields, the boating, the picnicking, the making of helpful friendships, the amateur music, the amateur dramatic societies, the gay, fantastic ragging. Learning indeed is still pursued in real earnest, but only by a despised minority. These are like those persistent mystics attached to various religions who are understood to save all the sinners of the world by their unseen and unheeded exercises and mortifications.

The newer and less wealthy foundations to the best of their ability have imitated the pattern set them by the older ones. If they cannot be as meretricious as their great exemplars, they are at any rate as gay and sporting as their means and circumstances permit. The idea of training and breaking in people to disinterested service which was the sustaining idea of the mediæval university has evaporated altogether from the universities of to-day. They are an unstable rebirth, clad in the garments and buildings of ancient institutions. They impart no intelligible ideology because that would "arouse controversy." Modern universities are the last places in the world for controversy. They are imposingly frivolous. They flourish and are indicted.

Nowadays the intelligent rich are becoming more circumspect in their endowments and more careful with their sons. They endow special research institutions, and they begin to think out special courses of training for their own boys and girls. In many matters the fashion set by the rich to-day is taken up by the ordinarily prosperous classes to-morrow and becomes the general usage of the day after. This may be the case in education. The break-up of the universities may be at hand in their very phase of maximum expansion. The undergraduate body may melt away quite suddenly, dispersing to forms of work and training of a more specialized and continuous sort, and with that the university properly speaking, that immense obsolescent educational gesture, that miscellaneous great gathering of students and teachers, will achieve a culminating gala of sport and splendour —and cease.

For "research universities" and "post-graduate universities" are clearly a contradiction in terms; they are something new. We are not writing of them here. We are not writing of the working, thinking and innovating minority which is found in nearly every university in the world. The original university knew no more of research than it did of athleticism. It taught, and you learnt, and when you had learnt everything you were a "doctor," and its task was done.

An encyclopædia of work and wealth might supply us here with a mass of statistics about university and college funds and attendances throughout the world. They would be impressive, but useless for the ends we have in view, and so would be lists of various types of continuation schools, technical schools and the like. Classification and nomenclature have still to be brought into line with reality in the field of education. What is called a college here may be classed as a school there; the schools in one country may be doing the "arts" work of the universities in another. All comparisons between the educational level of one country and that of another are unsound, and most of them very irritating to the country which appears at a disadvantage.

More interesting would be that part of the Museum of Education containing pictures and plans of university layout and a display of the architecture and sanitation of existing universities, from Oxford's dreaming spires to the single great skyscraper of forty stories designed to hold the entire University of Pittsburgh. The Museum of Education would have to assemble great masses of detail and range widely, to make its presentation complete. There might be gramophone records of the discourses of typical university lecturers and studies of actual laboratory instruction, and there would certainly be a display of the use of the talking film as a substitute for anatomical and other scientific demonstrations. A picturesque side section would display the peculiar costumes that students wear, the spatterdashes of Lisbon, the corps caps of Germany and the red gowns of Glasgow, and a complete collection of academic robes, hoods and decorations.

A large and striking range of the museum galleries would be devoted to university sports and the rôle of scholarly athleticism in relation to the sporting world. All the present abundance of university sport surged up out of the unpretending relaxations of the mediæval student at a quite recent date. It became conspicuous about the middle of the nineteenth century, and it has since played a large part in advertising and popularizing the modernized university. The training of athletes is now a recognized function of universities, a function that would have shocked Roger Ascham beyond measure. For to the tutor of Queen Elizabeth all sports but archery were "vile."

The Oxford and Cambridge boat race rowed every spring at Putney must not be forgotten in the story of university athleticism. It marked the first public display and popularization of the university as a sporting centre. The first inter-university boat race was as early as 1828, though it did not become a regular public function until later. Since then, as we have told in Chapter XIV, § 3, the expansion of the play side of the universities has been—magnificent. In America the faculties have frankly adopted sport as a main business of a university; the sports coach is as important as any other professor, and the sporting side is supposed to develop the distinctive qualities of American public life in their highest manifestation. Great stadia are a feature of all the wealthier American universities —that of Stanford University is capable of holding 88,000 people. But we have already described these developments and noted the claims made on their behalf.

The whole effect of this mélange of bright activities, youthful exuberance and picturesque tradition, this exhibition of schools and universities, would, I think, be indeed one of rapid and spontaneous development but also one of imperfect adjustment, of much energy misdirected, aiming awry or aiming not at all at the realization through mental training of the vast possibilities of man's present attainment.

§ 5. *Education Outside the Classroom*

In the preceding short history of formal education it has been made clear that never at any time since reading and writing began has formal education been the whole of education. This is a very important distinction on which we would lay the utmost stress. People nowadays have a habit of associating education with the classroom, the professor and the schoolmaster. But the professor and schoolmaster are no more inseparable from education than the galley slave or the mule are inseparable from transport. They are just the operators of one way of education. They are connected with education, but it is not an essential connection. Great intelligent communities have carried on without them. Hellas knew of no schools, as we understand schools to-day, and we have noted how the universities seemed to be fading out in the sixteenth and seventeenth centuries.

Not only has the intellectual process of mankind gone on steadily far beyond the boundaries of professional intellectual activities, whenever there were security and leisure, but also there has always been more or less informal transmission and communication of the results of this free, extra-mural thinking to the general body of mentally active people. The advent of the printed book and the diffusion of reading, the newspaper and the popular press have progressively increased this external educational work, and now such new devices as the cinema and broadcasting are carrying the informal diffusion of fact and ideas still further.

The proportion of stuff in the mind of the "educated" man and woman of to-day, which is of school or college origin, to the stuff that has come to them from extra scholastic sources, is enormously less to-day than it would have been in the case of their social equivalents a century ago. Turn out the mind of a bachelor of arts to-day and see how much his school and university have given him. A little store of Latin, rusting through disuse, a scrap or so of Greek, a very imperfect knowledge of one or two foreign languages and literatures, the views of various learned gentlemen on his own language and literature, scraps of ten-year-old science, the incomplete foundations of mathematical computation, and some "period" history.

But a word here about that "period" history. If so many of us had not experienced it, few would believe it possible. It is partly like heavy stale gossip about incredible individuals, partly like trying to get interested in the litigation of unknown people in a remote country, and partly like watching a university don playing soldiers on his study floor. (How he loves his "Decisive Battles of the World"!) The murder or execution of one or another of the more tiresome characters in the story comes as an all too rare relief. A certain feverish liveliness is sought by grossly patriotic appeals. In the growing citizen's childhood, home, governesses, playfellows, friends and a world beflagged, have conspired to distend to the utmost his natural disposition towards tribal partisanship. The "period" historian whenever possible plays upon this predisposition, because by giving a certain pseudo-personal flavour to his narrative he hopes to redeem its essential dreariness. He incites his students to say "we." "We," it seems, were the Royalists or the Puritans or the Balts or the Medici or the Knights of Malta. "We" conquered India; "we" defeated the French; "we" crossed the plains to the Pacific and bested the Spanish. In this mouldering paste of corrupting facts dates are set like pebbles on an unappetizing cake. They are for production under examination in evidence that the stuff has been swallowed. Such is academic history to this day. Happily this is not now any large part of the mental content of a modern man. It fades and lies forgotten after his last "exam." Beyond that, and with no vital connection with it, he has a score of skills he has acquired, and a whole universe of ideas, in which this poor little old "education" of his lies like a worm-eaten nut that has been dropped by chance into a salad.

Now here, in these after-school and out-of-school acquisitions, is a large and still uncharted region for the sociological observer. We have no orderly account, no working classification of the actual educational influences that play over the minds of girls and boys and adolescents in the world to-day. They are various, unequal, good and evil, unpremeditated as educational influences, and mostly quite accidental. They are controlled in the feeblest way. There are certain censorships, the contracted vestiges of far more extensive restrictions in the past. Everywhere there still exists a standard of sexual decency maintained by the law, that is justified wholly and solely by educational considerations. Youth must not be stimulated prematurely: that is the generally accepted idea; it is good for social growth to delay and minimize sexual adolescence. Conceptions of stimulation vary widely, but that we cannot discuss here; the general agreement against deliberate and even careless stimulation is undeniable. Apart from these legal restraints there is scarcely any screen now between the young and the relatively immense conflict of suggestions, the information, the appeals that rain upon them from the world beyond the schoolmaster's collection of exhibits. The illustrated newspapers, books, magazines, the cinema and a multitude of shows, an immense clangour of advertisement, build up a vision of the round world in their minds infinitely more vivid than the instruction of the schoolroom. Discussion of a hundred urgent questions, from birth control to tariff reform and from military service to immortality, is forbidden nowhere except in the academic preparation for life. Within the schoolhouse, at least, the orthodox religious formulas are treated with infinite solicitude, and only examiners may ask questions about them. School is no longer an enlargement but a withdrawal. It is like an embanked canal running far out into the lake of adult life and keeping the current needlessly apart from the waters with which it must ultimately mix.

Moreover, it has to be noted that the "educated" man whose mental content we are considering is still actively learning. There again we have a remarkable change that has happened to us by swift yet almost imperceptible degrees. The old order was permeated with the idea that for every rank of life there was a definite, sufficient, once-for-all education. You graduated, and the task was over. You learnt, and you stopped learning and worked out the consequences. But now we never stop learning. We add to our ideas, we modify and replace them daily. The process of informal education that begins directly a child opens its eyes upon the world proceeds crescendo throughout its entire life. Schools and universities are losing their importance because, so far as ideas and information go, the whole community is now in fact its own school. It is an undisciplined, ill-planned school, if you will, but it is vocal, explanatory and directive as no community has ever been before.

Let us attempt a brief survey of what this ultra-scholastic education consists and of the nature and quality of its principal media. Three main things it gives the citizen. In the first place he gets News, that is to say a constant development, correction and elaboration of his view of the world about him. History is written and revised under his nose. The things he knew before are recalled to him, brightened, emphasized, added to. He gets fresh intimations of human character and conduct; he learns of discoveries and inventions; daily, geography unfolds itself anew before him, and particularly the human side of geography. Map, diagram and picture, in newspaper and in the increasing multitude of ephemeral books about contemporary things, informed him and inform him, and now the cinema and the radio increase the service. He makes the tour of the world in an armchair.

On the whole, it is sound stuff he gets. We have traced the sordid origins of the newspaper, we have noted how the spirit of propaganda and the influence of the advertiser can deflect and censor particular streaks of news; nevertheless, the bulk of trustworthy statement that gets through is very great. A newspaper cannot lie comprehensively; its lies are no good to it unless it is generally credible, and every propaganda from its very nature goes on in the teeth of counter propaganda. Concealment is special and occasional. Newspaper history is far more

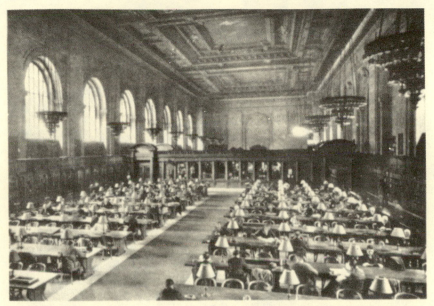

I WING GALLOWAY.

THE MIND OF THE WORLD: A CELL OF ITS BRAIN

THE main reading room of the largest free public library in the world,
that in New York. It has been estimated that two out of every three
persons using the library do so for research in business or science.

THE MIND OF THE WORLD: ITS NERVE AND BRAIN TISSUE

ONE of the huge machines which is used for the high-speed production of book and magazine paper. The pulp enters one end of the machine in a solution containing over 95 per cent water, and issues as a finished sheet from the rolls at the left.

veracious than the dogmas of some biassed pedagogue unchecked in his classroom. So far as libel goes there is law, even in the United States, faint but pursuing.

No doubt the modern newspaper has found retailing the unimportant and exciting, more to its advantage than studiously balanced statement. But how far newspapers, even if they are conducted on absolutely mercenary lines, can venture to be trivial depends upon the general moral and intellectual atmosphere. Even our most tawdry and sensational prints retain the affectation of a certain dignity. The common man may be a fool in a hurry, readier to laugh or marvel than learn, but he is not an absolute fool, he takes thought occasionally, and his apologists can point to a fairly steady improvement in the quality of the world's news service in the last hundred years. More and better news gets now to more people than it ever did before.

It would need a specialist who was a very subtle psychologist to expound all the mysteries and complications of a journalist's honour. But the most base, overbearing, energetic and subtle of newspaper proprietors will still find himself with intractable material between himself and the public he would hoodwink and control. And for the other side of the medal, the honest realization of his duties as well as his opportunities, is his sure and certain way to wealth, influence and the conspicuous and splendid service of mankind.

The second educational thing that the ordinary man gets from the ultra-scholastic educational influences of the time is a constant revision and extension of his general ideas. He need not go, as the Greek had to do, to the Agora to hear of some new thing; all about him is the Agora, the Forum. The increase of public discussion in the last decade or so is one of the most remarkable of contemporary phenomena. The character of the newspaper has changed completely with regard to opinion. There was a time when there was about as much free thinking in the column of a newspaper as there is in Little Bethel. The editor did the thinking, with his staff well under control; he told his readers what they thought about things, and if the strain became too great they changed their paper. If anyone objected to the pronouncements of the paper they could write a letter on the chance of its being printed, without pay, in the "Correspondence." But within the past quarter century, it dawned upon various newspaper directors that it would attract quite a number of the curious and arouse very little resentment among the faithful if they opened their columns to heterodox views, provided these were properly disavowed in an editorial note. This ventilation of opinion has developed very rapidly. It was a draw; it made the paper exciting in a new direction. The philosophers, religious teachers, radicals, and scientific men were very reasonable about fees, and these debates cost far less than, for example, sending special correspondents and commissioners to investigate the latest murder. The usage was established very rapidly, and now it would be difficult to abandon it. For the ordinary man wants to have his views discussed and reanimated just as he wants to know and to vivify his knowledge. The note of interrogation which is born in the nature of every human being has been released.

The newspaper changes continually. In the early nineteenth century, when printing was a comparatively primitive business, newspapers were largely the creation of "great journalists," and their influence was relatively much greater than their capital value. Their mentality was of more importance than their machinery. But they reached only to the middle class. The masses had no newspaper at all. Like every other social concern, the newspaper has experienced the "change of scale" of our period. The change reached it late because it was first necessary that the elementary education of the working masses should prepare a public to justify large-scale production. That wider public only became effective in the eighties and nineties of last century. Then came, first the mechanization, and then the popularization, of the "new" newspaper. The mechanical advances that made the printing house of a modern newspaper a great factory of costly and beautiful machines, not simply printing but folding and counting and packing, made newspapers huge business enterprises demanding an immense initial outlay of capital. The traditions of the old type of journalist proprietor were all against a ready adaptation to the new requirements. Because of this the newspaper passed very largely into the hands and is still in the hands of highly individualized entrepreneurs, much more akin in their character to the ordinary financial adventurer than the older type of newspaper owner.

The contemporary press is a new thing and not a real continuation of the nineteenth-century press—even when old periodicals have been made over to the new methods. It is still very largely dominated by the commercialized development of the peasant persona. It is in the first phase of industrialization. Its conscientiousness about the quality of its goods and the use of flavour, colour, diluents, and substitutes is at about the same level as that of the jam trade noted in our chapter on Food. There the new press follows behind other great industrial organizations, such as the steel or chemical industry, which are for the most part passing from individual to group ownership and control, coming under the "service" mentality of the official and paying a close regard to the quality and purity of their products.

Some great periodicals indeed are now owned and directed by special organizations; the *Christian Science Monitor,* the property of a sect, is a very attractive and trustworthy daily, and the London *Times* has become a quasi-public institution whose ownership is controlled by a body of trustees designed to save it from falling under merely profiteering influences. But these periodicals are exceptions to current conditions.

It is possible that a movement towards responsibility in the newspaper world may be developing behind the scenes similar to that which has made banking and insurance semi-official and public-minded. Much will certainly happen to change the newspaper in the days before us. If it becomes semi-official and responsible-minded, its trustworthiness may increase at the expense of its liveliness, and it may cease either to discuss boldly or to entertain. There may be a definite split and distinction between the responsible papers we shall buy and trust and the irresponsible papers we shall buy to entertain, excite or irritate us. Or Opinion, after its present rush into the newspaper columns, may presently find the editors growing restrictive, interfering or stingy, and resort to the intermittent instead of the periodical press, to pamphlets and special periodicals. We want the news every morning, but it may be to the taste of many of us to have our arguments by the week or occasionally, for us to take up when we are so disposed. What concerns us here is whether the common man is likely to get as good news or better in the future than he does now and whether there is likely to be any diminution of his present free access to every sort of opinion about every possible subject. There is little or no indication of any reversal of the general advance in these matters.

In imaginative works about the future, the writers are apt to abolish the newspaper altogether and represent the news and so forth as being distributed entirely by wireless, cinemas and the like ultra-modern devices. But it may be doubted whether such contrivances will ever do more than act as supplements and stimulants to the reading of books and newspapers. For all these other things you must go to an appointed place or listen at an appointed time. You cannot choose your programme or consider your own convenience. But the book and newspaper, with an almost canine fidelity, follow you meekly everywhere and brighten up when you turn to them, at any hour.

Within their limitations and on account of certain advantages of presentation the newer media are extraordinarily helpful accessories in the general task of informing and quickening men's minds. In Great Britain the distribution of sound by radio is the monopoly of the British Broadcasting Corporation, and there have been some very lively contests at the headquarters of the organization between the educationists and the entertainers. These struggles are very illuminating when the educational value of these new media is under discussion. The B. B. C. has made a great feature of talks by the most stimulating thinkers in the world. Keenly appreciated by many hearers, these talks are bitterly denounced by others, who want light music and facetiæ all the time, and who do not wish to have their guiding ideas loosened or modified insidiously. The Roman Catholic hierarchy wishes to confine the discussion of theology and the deeper things of life to qualified specialists, which it naturally identifies with the Roman Catholic hierarchy. The war rages with varying fortunes, and the educational light of the B. B. C. flares and wanes. Possibly it may be blown out altogether.

The educational film is equally a part of a programme and equally subject to suppression, if a majority, or even a truculent minority, objects. And always there are the limitations of a set time and place for each item.

Listening-in and the cinema, so far as they are educational at all, seem likely to supply only high lights in education, and tend less to sate curiosity than to send men and women back with quickened appetites to the printed word. In the immediate future, as in the recent past, the press seems likely to be the main medium of news and the principal forum for popular discussion, and the editorial journalist, whether he likes it or not, one of the most important agents in the education of the world.

News and the forum; these are the first and second things that the shows, noises and newspapers of our contemporary world bring to the normal man. But, as we have already suggested in the Introduction of this work, his mind has been rather stimulated than satisfied by the incoherent masses of news that come to it, and the battles of thought, propaganda and persuasion that go on round and about himself. He wants to know in a more orderly fashion. He asks for education—adult education—long before education goes out to find him. In response to this demand, a considerable and increasing mass of published matter has developed which is neither trivial nor original, which summarizes what is known in this or that wide field of reality and puts it forth in a plain, assimilable, trustworthy fashion. This present work with its associates, the *Outline of History* and the *Science of Life,* and various collateral works, is a sample of this new literature of information. Other works of the same character will occur to the reader. So far such enterprises have had to be produced upon strictly commercial lines, and they have many of the characteristic defects of a production for profit.

But the need for such comprehensive digests for ordinary intelligent people is so manifest that in due time these pioneer attempts to state a complete modern ideology are bound to be replaced by sounder and more authoritative successors.

Besides these "outlines" and "summaries," which give a mental framework and stand-by, there is and there has been now for half a century a steady production of informative books in series, by various firms of publishers. There seems to be an insatiable market for little books that will give, or appear to give, the latest results of modern research and discussion in this department or that, in an assimilable form. More often than not they are written by eminent specialists and are generally years in advance of the textbooks used in our schools.

This literature of information is only one aspect of the way in which the demand for after-school education has outrun the supply. We have to put beside it also the spectacle of the classroom, abandoning school and university, so to speak, and starting off across country, in pursuit of adults still eager to learn but unable to afford the time and money needed for residence at an educational centre. At the proper time, school and university missed these people, and now they are learning in a pseudoacademic manner from extension teachers. So we get also in a loose coöperation with those educational Ishmaelites we have noted, "Adult Education," a sincere attempt of the university to recover this lost clientele. We find, for example, a British Institute of Adult Education, and a World Association for Adult Education, active in developing the organization of the ordinary man's after-school thought and reading.

By Adult Education here is meant, of course, real post-school education and not merely the belated teaching of the "elements" to totally uneducated grown-up people such as is going on now in Russia and Anatolia. Adult Education is a rapidly expanding movement. It is not a substitute for general reading, but its value in directing, steadying, confirming and disciplining such reading must be very great.

The English universities (since Oxford initiated the movement in 1907), working in association with the Board of Education, developed Tutorial Classes, of which in 1925 there were 500 with 12,000 students. All these students were volunteers, with no immediate mercenary reward in view. The classes have usually a weekly hour's lecture throughout the winter followed by an hour's discussion, and the student undertakes to follow the course for three years, and to read and to do written work for it. Similar activities are to be found in most intellectually living countries. *An Adventure in Working Class Education,* by Albert Mansbridge, who is the chairman of the World Association for Adult Education, gives the spirit and intention of, and fuller particulars about, this type of educational enterprise, which is after all, considerable as it is in itself, merely one intimation of the wide hunger for real knowledge and mental disciplines in the contemporary world.

It is interesting to contrast the Workers' Educational Association, which is a frank attempt to shepherd back this widespread appetite for self-education into the university fold, with what is called the Labour College movement. The Workers' Educational Association was a development of the University Extension movement, and although, in response to the demand of many of its working-class students in the industrial centres, the classes carried on under its auspices often deal with economics, history and the social sciences, it has always tried to stress the importance of bringing general culture—in the quite orthodox sense—into working-class life. It would teach about Italian art or Gothic architecture with extreme readiness. The Labour College movement (formerly the Plebs League) is on the contrary frankly and aggressively independent of both academic organization and inspiration. It claims to be a spontaneous expression of the need felt by manual workers themselves—miners, railwaymen, engineers, building workers—for an education based on an attitude critical of the existing social order, and it concentrates primarily on such subjects as will fit its students to think and act politically. To which my friend Professor Carr-Saunders adds, on reading these proofs, that the Labour Colleges claim freedom in one form in order to abandon it in another. They teach the religion of Marx. They are theological colleges.

§ 6. *Mental Training*

So far our account of the world's formal education amounts very largely to a summary of insufficiencies and to a compensatory display of the very extensive and growing system of activities outside it and independent of it, which now supply the bulk of the material of a contemporary ideology. We have shown how, concurrently with this shrinkage of the primary rôles of school and college, these bodies have taken on a secondary function in the organization of athleticism. We have shown them, indeed, as diverting rather than directing energy. But is this a condemnation of formal education? Is it a glorification of press and show as the only education needed? By no means. It is indeed a very grave criticism of the existing organs of general education throughout the world, as a stocktaking encyclopædia would have to display them. But the criticism is that they fail to supply the formal education they should supply: not that a formal education is unwanted. To-day still there is everywhere a clear distinction in people's minds between an "educated" and an "uneducated" man, and to the nature of that difference we will now give our attention.

In our analysis of the personas operative in our world we have stressed the rôle played in the progressive development of society by what we have called the "educated" or priestly type. The essential fact about that type, as we have defined it for the purposes of this book, is that its dominating motive is service as distinguished from the peasant's motive of gain by toil and the nomad's motive of gain by gallant violence. The gist indeed of our study of the working of the human ant-hill has been to accentuate the primary importance of this educated element as priest, administrator, lawyer, in keeping the coöperations going, and to show how the conception of conscientious service has ruled professional medicine and law, saturated the official classes, and passed over to the professional scientific and technical worker and even to the man of letters and the artist of to-day. We have pointed out again and again how the grade of social organization possible at any time or in any country is dependent upon the educational level of a community and we have maintained throughout that our hope of our racial future— our sole reason for hope—lies in the extension of this "educated" quality to the whole of mankind.

Our gravamen therefore is not against formal education, but against the existing organs of formal education, because they are insufficient and beside the mark. Our study of the present "faded" state of religion is manifestly associated with this exposure of the inadequacy of deliberate education. Formal education to-day is also in a faded phase. We have shown how immensely exterior forces now supplement the schools so far as knowledge and suggestion go, but that substitution of newspaper, book and cinema for the classroom lesson does not in any way abolish the need for a drilling, ordering and invigoration of the minds subjected to this tumultuous invasion. Rather it intensifies that need. The establishment, confirmation and diffusion of the spirit of service are more than ever necessary in the presence of this stupendous froth of knowledge and ideas.

A certain moral disinterestedness is not the only characteristic we evoke when we speak of an "educated" man. We also imply a certain mental power and fastidiousness. Through the ages, a proper use of language has been a main objective in education. This world-wide contemporary education, deriving from the European schools, has, even in its weariest, most decadent phases, set itself to that end. The attempt to make language an instrument of precision and to keep thinking lucid and exact, has never been altogether relaxed. For all the informative-suggestive uproar of our time there is very little training to be got outside school and university in the exactitudes of mathematics. Our complaint is that there is not enough within those institutions. It is our gravest accusation against present-day universities that they will now graduate men and women who speak and write inexactly, have no framework of general ideas, and think no better than labourers who have left school at twelve or thirteen. It is the most damning charge that can be brought against them.

So that for our complete encyclopædia of Work and Wealth,

in addition to that broad review of the visible apparatus of education we have made in the preceding sections, there must be a more difficult and profounder study. We have to go into the precise details of the mental processes involved. How is language taught, its grammatical and its logical use? Language is far less important as a means of talking about things than as a means of thinking about things, but we use it now almost entirely as a means of talking about things. What might be done with human minds in sharpening and tempering this instrument, and what is done? Do any real exercises in thought survive at all in an ordinary education? How are they supplied? How can they be supplied? Mathematical studies can be a fine exercise in precision. How far are they used in that way? But they do not cover the whole field of thought; they do not quicken the observation nor strengthen the judgment. We have roundly asserted (in Chapter II, § 2) that the world to-day suffers greatly from the shelving of the discussion between Realism and Nominalism at the Renascence. To that we return. The issue between the one and the many is an issue of perennial importance—and our alleged education does not even raise it. There can be no fine thought or fine understanding widespread throughout the community until that has been understood and remedied.

Everyone has heard that Plato and Aristotle were exceedingly wise men and that our world is infinitely in their debt. And everybody knows that Plato wrote divers dialogues that are understood to have a beauty no modern writing can rival. (Everyone should try a dialogue or so in translation.) And these two were associated with a certain Socrates who so irritated the public of his time by insisting upon clear thinking so far as he understood it, that he was obliged to drink an infusion of hemlock and die. But how many people in a cinema theatre know *why* or want to know why we are so profoundly in debt to Plato and Aristotle and what these unparalleled people were talking about so continuously in their academy? If it was unimportant, the Academy ought to be forgotten by this time, and if it was important, the gist of its teaching ought to have got by now to the ears of all the men and women in the cinema theatre.

These Greek philosophers were, in fact, opening out that same debate between the one and the many, the species and the individual, which also exercised the schoolmen. It has never been altogether dropped, but it goes on now in other forms. Modern biology has had to rediscover and revive these fundamental exercises in its examination of the nature of individuality, and modern physics in its rediscovery of the uniqueness of "events." There is no lack of material nor of means of approach to these mind-sharpening issues, but the truth about our present education is that they are not even approached. Even the university honours-man with pretensions to philosophy is not put through these disciplines at all effectively. Directly the old issues appear in modern dress, he seems unprepared for them. Nothing is more amazing to the enquiring and intelligent humble in the pursuit of understanding than the realization of the intellectual sloppiness and defensiveness of the academic dignitary.

I believe that an exhaustive enquiry into the intellectual training that is going on in our world to-day would reveal an amazing deficiency of sound, thorough instruction in the processes and dangers of thinking. There is a certain amount of logical training in Catholic seminaries, but to judge from contemporary controversies it is of the thirteenth-century Realist type. Contemporary thinking, alas! outside those circles "comes by nature." One may go through school and college to-day and never once be reproached for a foolish generalization, an unjustifiable inference, an unsound conclusion. We ought to have experts everywhere, like food and drink inspectors, exposing the torrent of invalidity in the newspapers and public utterances of the day. But few people are sufficiently keen on lucidity to follow such exposures. The public would be restive. It would say these experts were splitting hairs, that they were highbrows; they would be bawled down by loud journalists. We pick up good or bad habits of thinking as luck and our natural brightness may determine. In thought and statement we are all untrained amateurs. A very large part of contemporary discussion is spent

in misunderstandings due to our universal intellectual slovenli-
ness.

And it is not simply that we are untrained amateurs; we are
also conceited amateurs. We resent correction. We *like* the rich
confused stuff in our minds. When we hear a thing repeated
twenty times with emphasis we believe it. It would trouble us
not to believe it. It does not trouble us in the least that it should
be entirely incompatible with some other equally emphatic belief
we have adopted. We have not had that sort of training. We
need it badly. At present a few adult classes in logic and methods
of reasoning are all we have in the world to set against the
undisciplined confusions of modern thought.

§ 7. *Education for the Modern Progressive Community*

After this résumé of the world's education to-day we can turn
to its objectives and consider the actual needs of the nineteen
hundred-odd million human beings who are being drawn together,
dangerously and with infinite complication and difficulty, by the
forces of mechanical invention into one great economic community.

Suppose we allow ourselves a brief respite from the crowded
assemblage of fact and imagine we have a free hand to plan an
education for all the world. We have studied education in the
preceding sections, faint but pursuing, toiling along behind the
disappearance of distance, the acceleration of communications,
the mechanical revolution of the world, to preserve understanding and a proper spirit in our human coöperations. Let us now
imagine the schoolmaster not kicked along by powers beyond his
control, but coming to meet and assist them. What would that
new, helpful education give, and what would be the machinery
it would use?

First let us plan out what it would give and what it would
impose upon the normal human persona.

The foundations of education are laid in early infancy. The
psychological work of the past thirty years has brought out the
immense importance to the adult of his infantile impressions.

It is by them that the foundations of his character are laid, and his dispositions established. By the time the young human being goes to school, he has already gone far either along the road of adapting himself happily to the requirements of civilization or towards failure, towards the establishment of those instabilities whose consequences we consider in the last section of this chapter. Pre-school education in a civilized world will be based upon a scientific knowledge of children's minds. That is not a thing of to-morrow. For it presupposes parents not only educated in a general sense but equipped for their task with a certain definite body of training and information—information which can hardly be considered accessible at present. To attain it one must still wade through a mass of highly technical psychological literature, fiercely polemical in character and made particularly repugnant to the ordinary mind by its lack of grace and literary dexterity. And even when that literature is read the enquirer will find that what he is studying is the treatment of abnormality rather than the needs of the normal child. The normal child, however, is also being studied—a few courageous schoolmasters here and there are actively experimenting in the treatment of more normal types. It becomes manifest that a great proportion of later recalcitrance, inadequacy, dullness, irresponsibility and actual physical illness is due to the mishandling, with the best intentions, of children's minds. For the pre-school education of the days ahead we may reasonably hope for a body of principles simple and clear enough to be understood and applied by men and women who are not specialists. Modern methods of dissemination will make that body of principles part of the mental equipment of the entire population. And through the application of these principles the mass of the children of the future will arrive at their formal education with free and balanced minds. To that formal education, to the schooling of the modern state, as it should be, we will now proceed.

To begin this we require universal elementary teaching. That use of language which is picked up from the circle of folks immediately around a child must be made finer and fuller and extended to reading, writing and calculation. How that can best be taught is a highly technical question. It can be done, educationists assure us, much more swiftly and efficiently than it is usually done. And they tell us too that every normal child can learn to draw. An educational world net, by the bye, would also be very convenient in noting and doing what is possible to correct various physical defects (of eyes, ears, teeth and so forth) and hereditary taints. That is not education, but a good thing that can be very conveniently saddled upon an educational institution. Moreover, there is a phase somewhere between five and sixteen when children are most apt to learn foreign languages and, with modern methods and means (gramophones, the radio lesson, etc.), it would not be any very great additional burthen on the educational machine to give every child a sound and practical knowledge of at least one of the great world languages, English, French, German, Spanish, Russian, in addition to its mother tongue. The possibility of one of these languages becoming so widely understood as to serve as a world lingua franca is not very remote.

Need children go to school continuously for a number of years for these elements? This is a question for the expert. But there is a widespread persuasion now that classroom work should be intensive and restricted to brief periods. Children should go into a bright, well lit and well ventilated classroom only when they are fresh and alert; they should meet keen, active and highly competent teachers, and the teaching and learning alike should be vigorous and direct. One should go into a classroom as one goes onto a tennis court, for brisk, continuous action. In a classroom one should work *hard*. Learning is a special exertion. The future world citizen cannot acquire too early the idea that effort is required in learning. If schools are to be used as places where the young are to spend whole days and long periods of time, they must have rooms other than classrooms; they must have rest rooms and playrooms and playgrounds where the activities are not intense. Here the less specific factors of the educational process come into play. Here is where the youngster acquires a regard for others, civility, sociability and a habit of reciprocal and coöperative action. Here is where the impulse to make, to draw, to write and invent is given scope and satisfaction. The rôle of the teacher here is to be supervisor and helper; encouraging tactfully, restraining bad conduct, but compelling not at all.

For this primary stage of education, large, beautiful, healthy schools are required throughout the world with a proper equipment, toys, books, apparatus, the gramophone, the demonstration cinema. Music and singing will play a large part in this schooling phase. The productive energy of the world is now fully able to provide all this for every child on earth. If you would know why this is not done now, go back to Chapter IX again and read what has been told about Hetty Green, Lowenstein, and the Great Slump of 1930–31. Read too of Sir Basil Zaharoff in Chapter XII and of the paradox of overproduction in Chapter XI. We cannot afford this manifestly necessary education, although all the material is ready and the workers stand idle. That is the absurd truth, the idiotic truth, of our situation. When the world has found its way to collective buying, the weaving of this planetary net of schools will be its first concern.

Next, using perhaps those same school buildings, the children of the new age will be learning to think. Logic should not be separated from grammatical teaching, and both should be associated with an acute attention to precise meaning. The boy or girl should be accustomed to use language like a rapier, should despise a clumsiness in inference as if it were a foul in a game. The classes should collect blunders, disingenuous statements and false conclusions from public discussion. They should botanize for errors and bring the precious finds to the classroom for dissection. They will also go as far as their willingness and aptitudes will take them in the exact and rigid reasoning processes of mathematics. And they will learn of the growth of knowledge and the methods of the scientific investigator with his measurements, his experiments, and his controls. They will do some exemplary scientific work at this stage, not for the sake of knowledge but as mental exercise. The discussion of theories and generalizations will be more important here than the accumulation of facts. Far more important than scientific knowledge is scientific method. This much, and watchfully directed bodily exercise, is surely all that there need to be in the universal primary education of mankind.

But this is merely equipment and the sharpening of the human instrument. Next follows the socially more important part of the task of education, the establishment of a persona which will lead to the service of the race and protect the individual from social mischief, economic offenses, political delusions, frustrations, disappointments and evil conduct towards others. A picture of the world and of the ways of the world in relation to the self, and what is honourable and right for the self, has to be imposed upon the growing mind. The foundations of its ideology have to be laid.

Now, as we have made perfectly clear in § 6, the school alone can contribute only a small part of a contemporary ideology. That grows and changes day by day under the thousandfold impacts of reality. But we are speaking here of certain foundation ideas upon which this living and developing fabric can be poised. First there is the idea of man's history as one whole. A child has to be guarded against early infection by picturesque, false, and short-sighted national traditions. The effectual exorcism for that sort of thing is the plain, straightforward teaching of human history as one progressive adventure in which all races have helped and all have sinned. Picture and book, story and lecture, cinema and school museum must converge upon that rational presentation of man's collective life. And secondly the citizen of the world must have a sound conception of the evolution of life and its nature, that is, he must have learnt elementary biology thoroughly. Thirdly he must learn geography and the economic layout of the world as one coöperative field of enterprise. These are the three pillars of a modern ideology, the three branches of knowledge which constitute that "New Education," of which I have already written something in my Introduction. This is the essential instructional material for a modern world vision. All the rest is training and equipment.

Here we will not expand the suggestions already made in the chapter on Housing, that the primitive "home" in which a

THE LINKING OF SCIENCE AND INDUSTRY

THE cold testing of motors in a refrigerating chamber in the Physical Laboratory of a great automobile plant in Detroit.

SCIENCE AND INDUSTRY

CHEMICAL research laboratory in a great industrial plant. It is research of this sort, carried on at great expense by various manufacturers, which has almost done away with the old-time inventor and has made many of the greatest strides in recent scientific development possible.

swarm of children, servants and poor relations centre upon father and mother has already broken up for a great majority of the European peoples and given way to new social units. All prosperous people in the advanced communities entrust their children to nurses, tutors and governesses, whenever they can, and send them away to preparatory schools; the continuous contact of parent and child does not seem to be either desirable or desired. In the case of the small family there is also a considerable educational advantage in associating children with their equals in strength and age. All this points to the ordinary general school as having a third function as the modern form of "home." In many cases it may be a boarding school; or in a town or village it may be a day home. In the happier world-state to which we look forward, the struggle of various "faded" religious organizations to capture and control as many schools as possible in order to preserve the distinctive "atmosphere," the graceful legends and misleading assurances of this or that cult, will, we presume, have died away.

The "elements," a foreign language or so, directed opportunities for artistic "play," mental training and the elementary knowledge of history, biology and social relations necessary as a basis for a modern ideology: this is really as much as the general school need give a human being.

I do not know how far it may be possible or desirable to control some of this general education by examinations. That is a question for the sociological educationist. Maybe the common citizen of the future will have to pass a leaving examination before he sets about his special adventure in life. Maybe he will have to pass a matriculation test before he embarks upon various definite callings. Or it may be found that the compulsion of these tests is not required.

But from the end of the school stage onward—which ought to be completed at latest in the middle teens—I can see no use for any further general education in school. Everything necessary for a common mental foundation will be there. The ordinary "arts" course in our older universities to-day is merely a wasteful prolongation of puerility.

In Chapter XII, at the end of § 6, we have noted a suggestion made long ago by Professor William James that everyone should do a year or so of compulsory service for the State. We may refer to that suggestion again here. Such a term of service might do very much to strengthen the sense of citizenship in the individual. We shall return to that idea when we deal with certain difficulties in the staffing of public institutions in § 10.

After, or concurrently with, the closing years of the general school course in the middle teens, specialization will begin. But special and technical instruction is not a task for the upper forms of general schools where the stabilizing, standardizing, unstimulating scholastic mentality is bound to prevail, but for schools carefully planned to achieve the particular end in view and in close contact with real activities. The adolescent citizen will take up his or her technical (or professional) education, and that may or may not be combined with actual productive work. In Chapter VII, § 6, we pointed out how the organizations of great industrial enterprises are becoming interlocked with technical schools, and how continuation schools supplying scientific instruction can carry on through the whole career of a worker and keep his knowledge up-to-date and effective. For the worker ceases now to be a *hand;* he is chemist in a thousand forms, he is electrician, he is engineer, he is artist. The various sorts of scientific investigator for which the coming order will have an insatiable demand, the medical man, the cultivator of plants and animals, the sociologist, policeman and lawyer, the architect and local administrator, the industrial organizer, the statistician and banker, and all the multitudinous variations of the active citizen, will follow their special trainings from the general school onward and the nature of those trainings, the methods of qualification and graduation, will vary as endlessly as the occupation. Training will be given where it is most conveniently given. Educational vacations, when workers from one region of the world may visit the museums and hold conferences with those of another, inter-professional gatherings when, for example, the student-practitioners of medicine may meet lawyers and sociologists, may play a very important part in this lifelong educational process.

But though the common citizen will have done with the general school and turned to specialized work and study by the time he is adolescent, he will not have done with general education. He will now be carrying it on—or the world about him will be carrying it on—through all those multifarious agencies of suggestion and information to which we have referred in § 6. He will go on being educated until he dies.

We have touched upon those agencies outside the classrooms and their development at various points in this work. We have glanced at current developments of book and newspaper and their new educational auxiliaries. We are describing the present and not imagining the future in this survey, and so we will refrain from any Utopian speculations about the educational community of the years to come, the community that will be in itself educational. How can one mind foretell where thousands of minds of the liveliest sort are inventing, contriving, trying, and judging new methods of presentation, distribution and stimulus? But we may at least go so far as to anticipate that the information and suggestions that will beat upon the minds of our grandchildren will be far less confused and confusing, unequal and casual, than those amidst which our own generation lives. In this chapter, thus far, we have noted an immense amount of incoherent learning in progress; a clamour of statement, misstatement and counterstatement; summaries of knowledge read by perhaps one man in a hundred and counted great successes, and innumerable series of little books and radio talks, flying, hit or miss, through the mental atmosphere. It is possible that the presentation of reality to the mind of the ordinary man may presently become much less haphazard, much more orderly and deliberate. There may be a systematic ordering and drawing together of human thought and knowledge. To that possibility we will now address ourselves. It is a possibility all too little apprehended at the present time.

8. *The Rôle of an Encyclopædia in a Progressive Civilization*

The importance of the encyclopædia as a necessary educational organ and the possibilities and probabilities of considerable developments of the encyclopædic idea are still very imperfectly understood. For some centuries a limited number of men have been aware of the importance of a general summary of thought and knowledge which will serve as the basis for common understandings between specialists and for the ideology of education, and so become a guiding centre for the intellectual activities of mankind. But the mass of the public is still quite heedless of this need. It takes its knowledge as it takes its milk, without enquiring how it came to the door.

Attempts to get ideas and knowledge together for general use were made in the classical world, and the peculiarities of the Chinese writing made encyclopædic lexicons a natural development of Chinese learning. The great Chinese encyclopædias, however, are something different from our current idea of an encyclopædia; they are collections of extracts from the classics rather than summaries of knowledge, and most of them were overwhelmingly vast. Condensation and simplification are Western tendencies. I do not know why it should be so, but the Chinese seem to have a real preference for elaboration, in their games, in their art, in their life; they have nothing like the Western aptitude for short cuts. A failure to simplify writing is probably, as the *Outline of History* explains, the main reason for the Western advantage over China to-day. Even to-day the Chinese find themselves unable to send telegrams in their own language because it has no alphabet adapted to the purpose. The various Chinese literary and scientific collections, for that is really what they should be called—the Yung Lo assemblage ran to 22,937 volumes—date from the tenth to the seventeenth century and they are not really equivalent to our modern European encyclopædias at all. We mention them because the reader is sure to have heard of them, simply to note that they are beside our present discussion.

The first important movement towards encyclopædism—which, however, did not actually produce an encyclopædia—was due largely to the initiatives of Aristotle. Perhaps he was one of the first of men to be altogether possessed and directed by the passion for assembling and ordering knowledge. To him we must ascribe Alexander's foundation of the Museum at Alexandria with its great library and its book-copying organization. It was plainly modelled on the pattern of the Lyceum at Athens, which also was dedicated to the Muses, and had a library, maps and possibly other assembled material. (And, says Mr. Ernest Barker, it had its college dinners and even its own plate.) This home of the Muses at Alexandria was much more like the encyclopædic world-organization we shall presently foreshadow than any mediæval university. The *Outline of History* tells of its achievements and its decline. Latin culture produced nothing to compare with the Hellenic initiative at Alexandria, but it can claim at least to have produced the first encyclopædic book, Pliny's *Natural History*.

Manifestly while hand-copying was the only means of multiplying a work, an encyclopædia was a thing of very limited effect. The bigger, more comprehensive it was, the more impossible it was to distribute it to many people. It was a rarity for the erudite, and not an educational instrument. It was easier for the student to go to the knowledge at the museum or the university than for the knowledge to place itself at the disposal of the student in book form. It was only with the onset of printing on paper from movable type that the thing we call an encyclopædia to-day became a practical possibility.

First came "dictionaries" with long explicit articles. John Harris, the first secretary of the Royal Society, produced a Universal Dictionary of Arts and Sciences in 1704 and Zedler's Universal Lexicon in 64 volumes (Leipzig, 1732–50) was a great and comprehensive work. The Encyclopædia Britannica lists a number of parallel undertakings. It was the genius of Diderot (1713–84) which first revealed the power and importance latent in these great gatherings of fact and theory. Comenius, the Bohemian educationist, had, however, anticipated his idea of a synthesis of current knowledge in a pamphlet published at Oxford in 1637 (*Conatum Comenianorum Praeludia*), but he was unable to carry out his scheme. Diderot was invoked to revise and rearrange the translation of an English work, Chambers' Cyclopædia (of the Arts and Sciences), and it is clear that the light of a great opportunity dawned upon him as he struggled with this task. He proposed to the bookseller who had brought it to him to scrap the English original entirely and embark upon an altogether bolder, more comprehensive undertaking. He had definite ideas and much enthusiasm, and he won a considerable amount of support among the liberal spirits of his time.

His scheme was plainly to make his encyclopædia the substantial basis of a modernized ideology, gather together the accumulating criticism of tradition and established usage, and organize the new and growing knowledge of the age into an effective instrument for social, political and religious reconstruction. His Encyclopédie was something new; the Encyclopédistes constituted a definite movement towards a new education and a new social life. The first volume was issued in 1751. It was only as the subsequent volumes appeared that the full force of his design became apparent. The story of its production is a complicated and stormy one. The work was held up after the second volume appeared in 1752, as a danger to religion and the King's authority, but after a delay of a year its resumption was permitted. In 1759 the still incomplete Encyclopédie was formally suppressed and its sale forbidden. It was continued furtively and in fear of the police. The last volume of letterpress was published in 1765, and the final volume of plates only reached the subscribers in 1772. The work was distributed secretly in Paris and Versailles. Altogether 4,250 people subscribed to it: a formidable body of opinion for that time. The later volumes were emasculated by the cowardice and treachery of the printer Lebreton. He had the articles set up in type exactly as the authors sent them in, and when the final proofs had been corrected by Diderot, "he and his foreman, hastily, secretly and by night . . . cut out whatever seemed to them daring, or likely to give offence, mutilated most of the best articles without any regard to the consecutiveness of what was left, and burnt the manuscript. . . ."* Diderot knew nothing of what was going on until he saw the printed book. What an amazing, embittering, heartbreaking experience it must have been for him to turn from page to page and find clear statement and crucial argument, blunted, weakened, made absurd!

So, crippled, damaged, uneven, the first encyclopædia of power came into the world. Defective as it was, it was of cardinal importance in the great intellectual movements of the time. There was enough left to get through to men's imaginations. Its influence in giving an ideological content to the first French Revolution was immense. It radiated far beyond France; it released minds and steadied progressive thought everywhere where men read books; it set a pattern for all kindred enterprises—in this respect at least, that henceforth they treated ideas historically and recognized diversity of opinion.

The first edition of the Encyclopædia Britannica appeared in 1768 onward, and its very title shows its indebtedness to and its competition with its French predecessor. The ideology was conservative and patriotic, and the dedication to a supplement to the third edition, in 1800, refers to the Encyclopédie as a "pestiferous work." But the likeness to the parent increased with each edition and compensated for this ungracious repudiation. It is against nature that a comprehensive survey of reality should be reactionary. In 1812 we hear a very different note; we find general introductions being planned to show the progress of science since Bacon, similar to "the excellent discourse prefixed by D'Alembert to the French Encyclopédie." The breadth and power of each new edition increased. It is a question whether the ninth (with supplements, the tenth) or the eleventh (with successive supplements, the twelfth and the thirteenth) edition is to be counted the better and more influential. Both were widely distributed by modern methods of marketing and still constitute a sort of intellectual backbone for the body of

*Encyclopædia Britannica: Article, *Encyclopædia*.

English speaking and writing, for teachers, preachers, journalists, authors and intelligent people generally.

The article in the fourteenth edition to which we are indebted for these present facts gives a résumé of the other leading encyclopædias that have served the Atlantic world since our age of organized knowledge commenced. The Conversations Lexicon of Brockhaus is the chief among these, but there is scarcely a European language now without a reasonably good encyclopædia. The contemporary French mind has been moulded to a very remarkable extent by the dictionaries and encyclopædias initiated by Pierre Larousse. There is a pre-revolutionary Russian encyclopædia based on Brockhaus and a Communist Bolshaya Sovietskaya Entsiklopediya is now said to be in hand. That should prove an exceptionally interesting production. The Jesuits have produced a Catholic Encyclopædia of their own which is also very characteristic in its spirit and quality.

But if Diderot could return to this world, learn the vast potentialities of our age, and sense our present intellectual atmosphere, I doubt if he would be content with the current phase of "encyclopædization," widespread though it is. Encyclopædias have multiplied and spread considerably, but the mechanical structure of our world and our economic and social organization have developed out of all proportion to their increase. The modern encyclopædia should bear the same relation to the Encyclopédie or the early Encyclopædia Britannica that a transcontinental railway engine bears to Cugnot's steam road car. But does it do so? Let us take, for example, the current edition (the fourteenth) of the Encyclopædia Britannica as the last achievement in this great movement towards a guiding synthesis of human knowledge and ask whether it is not capable of further very great invigoration and development.

We are criticizing a fairly good thing here to which indeed we are manifestly indebted, and when we criticize, it is not to say that the work is bad but to suggest that it has not fully realized the measure of contemporary necessity. You will find in it some magnificent articles to stir the creative imagination, the article upon architecture, for example. It is full of the stimulating statement of concrete achievements and possibilities. I repeat it is impossible for any encyclopædia to be truly reactionary. Such articles as the one on pottery and porcelain are marvels of illustration and copious information. But they are out of proportion. Full justice is done to the actual wealth and vigour of our times. But when it comes to a question of directive general ideas such as the idea of property, or the creative possibilities of financial or political reorganization, it is mute or unstimulating; it speaks with an uncertain mind. For the most part, and in its preface and general scheme, it seems to assume political institutions and financial methods that even the man in the street is questioning. And one discovers odd gaps. I wanted some particulars about the enquiry into the labour atrocities of Putumayo and its outcome, and I could find nothing. Nor is there a word about Sanderson of Oundle, most original and stimulating of British schoolmasters. This latest compilation is to say the least of it lacking in just that stirring sense of a better ordering of things at hand, ours for the effort of realization, which was the heroic quality, the essential and power-giving quality, of Diderot's great endeavour. And indeed, in his Preface, Mr. J. L. Garvin, the editor, frankly abandons the *Encyclopédiste* ambition. The world, he says, has become so multitudinous, so overwhelming that a directive synthesis is impossible. It is as if a general had failed to conceive a plan of campaign and ordered his army very eloquently to advance in all directions. It is a diffusion, not a synthesis. He had great difficulties in his task, one can understand. Perhaps his hands were not altogether free. But his encyclopædia, in its abandonment of synthesis, is a reversion to the "cyclopædias" and universal dictionaries that existed before the days of Diderot, rather than an advance beyond its predecessors. It is an all too characteristic product of our time. It is multitudinous, defective and discursive in just this present phase of the world's history when the need for directive general concepts, gripped firmly and held steadfastly, is the supreme need of our race.

But impermanence is the lot of all encyclopædias, and though the Britannica, after some decades of virtuous excitement, shows now these marks of advanced maturity, of "middle-aged spread," that is no reason for supposing that the spirit of Diderot is dead, or that this impulse towards comprehensive intellectual coördination, which has been going on through the past two centuries as if it were a natural necessity for the human mind, will not continue. Perhaps the days when the making and issuing of encyclopædias could be regarded as legitimate business enterprises are drawing to an end, and our world is near realizing that the assembling and presentation of knowledge and ideas, of ideological material, that is, should become a primary function of the educational community.

The encyclopædia of the future may conceivably be prepared and kept by an endowed organization employing thousands of workers permanently, spending and recovering millions of pounds yearly, mediating between the original thinker, the scientific investigator, the statistician, the creative worker and the reporter of realities on the one hand and the general intelligence of the public on the other. But such an organization would outgrow in scale and influence alike any single university that exists, and it would inevitably tend to take the place of the loose-knit university system of the world in the concentration of research and thought and the direction of the general education of mankind.

The World Encyclopædia organization as we are here conceiving it would reach down to direct the ideological side of human education. But it could scarcely come into existence without on the other hand creating organic relations with the main statistical activities of the world. It would almost inevitably develop a centralized system of world statistics in direct relation to its needs. It would have its Year Book volumes. So it would be a natural collaborator with Lubin's pioneer Institute in Rome for an annual world census of cultivation and staple production generally. Moreover, it would be a natural nucleus about which specific researches could cluster very conveniently, and it could undertake with advantage that systematic indexing, abstracting and exchange of research publications, to which Madame Curie has directed the attention of the International Institute of Intellectual Coöperation. At present the old universities, in spite of their encumbrance with tradition, sport, entertainment and the belated unspecialized education of backward young men and women, are the natural recipients of endowments for research, because they still seem to be the only possible agents in the matter. An encyclopædia organization, reviving on a modern scale the high ambitions of the Alexandria Museum, would change all that. It would become the logical nucleus of the world's research universities and post-graduate studies. It would be the central Museum of a world, Hellenized anew after the long twilight of Latin predominance.

In another direction one sees this convenient centre annexing or duplicating the League of Nations' registry of treaties and organizing a world digest of laws.

How far this establishment of an encyclopædia as a recognized central organ in the mental life of mankind may be attainable by a transformation of university activities, by the formation of special societies and groups of learned, wealthy and influential people, by inspired feats of publication, and by state action, I will not venture to speculate; nor how closely it may be associated with a world system of informative and demonstrative museums. Nor do I know how closely it will be linked with the research laboratories, experimental farms and reserves and statistical bureaus of the advancing world. But the need for it and the existence of forces making for it are undeniable. And whatever other functions it had, its main function would be to irradiate the ideological teaching of every common school in the world.

If no great catastrophe arrests or delays the present prosperous advance of our race, the coming of a world encyclopædia is a matter—it may be—only of decades. It is an enterprise that the League of Nations' Institute of Intellectual Coöperation might very well consider. That body, given the necessary organizing ability, is in a position of exceptional advantage to bring together large groups of publishers, writers and universities for such an associated production. And we can prophesy with considerable assurance that so soon as it comes into existence this culminating Encyclopædia will be made available in all the chief languages (the Conversations Lexicon of Brockhaus, with wide variations of title and considerable local adaptation, has gone into most of them already), and that it will be undergoing constant revision and reprinting. This suggests the desirability of considerable detachability and interchangeability between its parts. A faint prevision of the rows of volumes of this coming encyclopædia is evoked by these considerations. We can even foretell some probable details of arrangement. Many of the earlier encyclopædias did not have numbered pages—perhaps in view of possible insertions—and it may be desirable at any rate not to have numbered volumes. There seems little reason for retaining the alphabetical arrangement of the whole book. It might be divided into main sections which could be lettered and there could be one or more numbered volumes under each letter. Then any section could be revised independently and its one or two volumes replaced by three or four without disturbing the general arrangement. Within a section there might be a retention of the convenient system of major articles and alphabetically arranged minor articles characteristic of the Britannica.

To speculate in this fashion about the form in which a world encyclopædia may presently appear falls very properly into our present design. We may even make an anticipatory summary of the arrangement and contents of the work. Such a summary is not in the least irrelevant to our enterprise, for it enables us to make a survey of all contemporary knowledge and all contemporary ideas, and so evoke another set of figures to add to our grand ensemble of human activities, which would be otherwise difficult to introduce. There are the men and women, more men as yet than women, who are engaged in original thought. They are the men and women who know best, the men and women who think and express best, the sources. What sort of people are they?

For the most part they will have to be presented sitting at well-lit writing tables and desks in conveniently appointed apartments lined with books. They read, they make notes, the pen scratches over the paper, some perhaps dictate to stenographers, and within easy reach of many of them are typists with their typewriters, the first step towards print, towards stereo plates and the roaring presses that will bring the new idea, the novel suggestion, the illuminating comment into the common mental life. One sheet of manuscript follows another, and presently the day's work or the night's work is done and pinned together.

The rooms of these individuals are sometimes in the dignified colleges of universities, sometimes in carefully sought country retreats, sometimes in the quieter streets of great towns. An increasing number work in laboratories now, and in the reserved rooms of the ever extending museums of our time. The laboratories may be of the largest or smallest type, elaborate with the most extraordinary apparatus, or simple with some little object rendering its secret under examination. Others of these intellectual workers watch in observatories or scrutinize the stellar photographs observatories have made under their directions. Many of these men and women who are "sources" explore now and excavate with teams of trained workers, amidst Arctic severities or under a tropical sun. Then back they come with their finds, to explain, write up what they have done, compare and discuss.

These fundamental people are not very gregarious as a rule; they have not much time to spare for small talk; but they have their sociable moments and may even ventilate their preoccupations by two's and three's or in little groups, or you may find them assembled in attentive roomfuls while one of them reads a paper and ideas are interchanged. Some are negligently dressed and distraught in their bearing, but for the most part they look fairly well cared for and have little or nothing to mark them off from the ordinary bourgeoisie. You may pass Mr. Einstein, who upset all our ideas of space and movement, carrying his violin in the streets of Berlin and take him for nothing but a smiling fiddler on his way to a recital; you may dine with the Royal Society, and it looks remarkably like the company at an ordinary city dinner. In the more inaccessible parts of the sunny East we are given to understand that beautiful sages of manifest and immediately recognizable sagacity, meditate profoundly in propitious attitudes amidst their adoring disciples. Little that is worth while comes through to us from them, and until it does, it is to those other scattered, busy, unposed, unpretentious and often quite obscure-looking Westerners, that we must ascribe the essential living thought of the world. Altogether their actual thinking is physically a very unobtrusive series of activities. A single shipyard at work makes more noise than all the original thought of the world put together.

But generally these individuals we have termed the "sources" are not in direct communication with the general mind. They will contribute to the World Encyclopædia, no doubt, and they will in their own sphere of interest exercise powers of revision and criticism of its contents, but much even of that work of explanation and correlation can be done by their student associates as well or even better than they can do it themselves. But such a vigorous and original thinker as Professor T. H. Huxley (Darwin's Huxley) found the delivery of a course of elementary lectures or the occasional production of a textbook a very illuminating and beneficial exercise for himself because it obliged him to put his abbreviated technical thoughts into plain and simple language. There are endless pitfalls in technicality, and many temptations to retire from the general intelligence into a cloud where one's proceedings can no longer be checked.

Between the original "sources" and the common thought of the world there intervenes a much more abundant and almost as various a multitude of busy individuals. There are interpreters, would-be interpreters and mis-interpreters. There are also the sham sages, the presumptious, conceited and ambitious among the intellectual workers. Some serve a useful purpose, some sting and stimulate and some obstruct and corrupt. In all the big centres of population are great libraries, as, for example, the British Museum library, and thither converge daily a swarm of preoccupied individuals, with portfolios and notebooks. Some of these may be original workers of importance, "sources" themselves. Most of them are of the transmitting, intervening, checking categories. Manifestly this present work you are reading falls into this mediatory grade of transmission. And from these we pass on to such types as the specially qualified interviewer consulting the savant for the press. He brings us to scientific and technical journalism, a little world in itself, still very under-developed, and so to all these popular means of diffusion we have already discussed. One of the most useful and unpretending of transmission organs is that weekly paper *Nature,* which serves for intellectual exchanges, as far as science goes, throughout the whole English-speaking, English-reading world. A World Encyclopædia kept sedulously in direct contact with as many as possible of these fundamental minds we have considered would be of enormous value in steadying, controlling and informing this secondary network of transmission, correlation and interpretation.

And if we think of all these primary intellectual activities on which the progress of the world depends, gathered together and summarized into a World Encyclopædia, what are the main sections of that work likely to be? Let us sketch a provisional answer to that question.

Manifestly the opening section would have to be an account of the philosophies of the world, compared critically and searchingly in an Introduction. Then, in separate articles, there would be accounts of the main systems of philosophy with their variants and the lives of the chief philosophers. There would have to be a history of philosophies and of the development of general ideas. There would be an account of logic, of what used to be called "significs," the values of language. Philosophical and comparative philology would be dealt with, for we are approaching a time when a real history of languages becomes possible, and a study of grammar and idiom in relation to turns and habits of thought. Then would come the origins and development of writing. Number and the mathematical exploitation of form and conceptions of space and time would follow, and an account of mathematical signs and symbols and their relation to realities. A history, classification and analysis of fallacies and of superstitions and prevalent errors arising out of the incautious use of symbols would seem to be indicated. This would constitute the opening section.

From it there would probably branch off a section devoted to specific languages and the literary cultures associated with them, and a third section would deal with the detailed development of pure mathematics.

The fourth section would be a compendium of pure physics, chemistry and astronomy, the whole of what is still best called "material science." Biographies of the men who have built up this body of science would be given, and a history of its development.

Next would come a fifth section—the general science of life and a great series of articles devoted to the forms of life. Biographies of biologists and a history of biological science would be added.

From this fifth section there might branch off a sixth. Health and medicine would be dealt with in this, mental health as well as bodily health, and with that might come an account of sport, exercise and pastimes.

Then in a seventh section there would be a fuller treatment of human biology and the general history of mankind. The history of exploration would form a subsection of this.

The histories of various peoples and political systems, e. g. Greek and Roman history, would make an eighth section, and here would come a political Atlas and general biography, the stories of outstanding men and women, except the artists and men of science whose lives will be treated elsewhere.

The ninth section would deal with education, religion and ethics treated objectively and historically, the science and art of education, the laws of conduct and the treatment of crime.

Then two huge parallel sections would give a double-barrelled treatment of economic life, one from the point of view of production and industrial organization, and the other from the points of view of distribution and finance. Here the principles and laws of property would be dealt with and here would come an economic geography and Atlas of the world. These really constitute that as yet imaginary *Science of Work and Wealth* which has served so useful a purpose in easing the burthen of detail in this work.

The twelfth section of our World Encyclopædia would stand somewhat apart in spirit from the rest of the enterprise, and it would deal with beauty. It would be devoted to the æsthetic concepts and accomplishments of our race, with music, with every form of art, with poetry and all that can be called creative literature. In it æsthetic criticism would pursue its wild, incalculable, unstandardized career, mystically distributing praise and blame. Here would come the lives and critical studies of the work of poets and artists of every kind; the history of the drama; of opera; architecture considered as cultural expression; the high mystery of the Novel, as it was understood by Henry James. And here the multiplying new resources of artistry, the cinema, radio, gramophone and the like, of which the mechanical and financial sides would have been considered elsewhere, would be treated from the point of view of their æsthetic possibilities. The artist in his studio, the composer in his music room and all the multitude who invent and write down their inventions, have hardly figured as yet in our world panorama, and even now we can give them but a passing sentence or so. They are an efflorescence, a lovely and purifying efflorescence on life. And still more of an efflorescence is that vastly greater multitude of painters who cannot paint, of sculptors who leave us colder than their marble, of musicians who have but to approach a piano to put us to insincerely apologetic flight, and of an endlessly brawling, posturing, insulting, lusciously appreciating swarm of people— for the most part of small independent means—who write, talk, fight and bore about art. All this clamorous obscurity we glance at under the lower edge of this twelfth section of our World Encyclopædia, contemplate ambiguously for a moment and dismiss.

With that twelfth volume the great survey of human wisdom and initiatives would be complete. Then would come a dictionary index, with brief definitions for use as a dictionary, and the fullest index references to the encyclopædia. Good indexing is absolutely essential to an efficient encyclopædia. Every section should be indexed, every main article should have an index and a full bibliography, and in addition there should be this comprehensive general dictionary index, a section in itself.

Manifestly this is a much completer enterprise than any encyclopædia hitherto attempted. But then the resources of our world are vastly greater than they were in the days of Diderot and the first Encyclopædia Britannica. It would indeed do little more than bring those gallant pioneer essays properly up to date and scale. It would need as much money to bring it into existence as would launch a modern battleship. Are there no anti-Zaharoffs to bring back money to these better uses? And when it was launched it would need half a million pounds a year at least to keep it under constant revision. It would maintain as large a permanent staff as all the faculties of three or four great universities and unless it sold by the million sets it would not possibly *pay*. It would probably have to be a stupendously endowed enterprise. Yet in relation to Diderot's achievement it would be in no greater proportion than a modern liner is to the little sailing ships that lay in the Downs waiting for a change in the wind a century and a half ago.

And consider its certain effects. It would become the central ganglion, as it were, of the collective human brain. It would keep the thought of the world in a perpetual lively interchange. It would be the living source of a true *Outline of History,* instead of the poor sketch the world buys to-day, of a lucid *Science of Life,* of an understandable summary of the business of the world. It would sustain the common ideology of mankind. It would be the world organ of our correlated activities. And after all, at its most magnificent, if it used some thousands of men continually, it would not cost a tithe of the money spent upon such aimless, excessively dangerous extravagances as the French army which may never fight, or the American fleet, or the British fleet, or the militant forces the Germans are now endeavouring to restore.

§ 9. *Open Conspiracy*

And now that this great spectacle of human toil and effort rises to its culmination a crowning question becomes manifest.

Wherein does true sovereignty reside? What is ruling and directing this millionfold diversity of activity towards its objective of synthesis order and power?

It is clear that existing governments do not really govern. We have shown how provisional and sometimes how obstructive and dangerous are these formal governments of our time. Their origin was combative. They drift by an inherited necessity towards war. They are not really governing any more than our formal educational organizations are really educating, or our religious bodies really inspiring and shaping human lives.

The world needs a world government to supplement, control or supersede these traditional governments, a recasting of its schools to meet the needs of a new education, and a formulation of modern religious feeling that will free us from the entangling rags of ancient superstitions. And the strange thing is that in spite of the conscious and unconscious resistance of governments, schools and religious bodies, and the whole machinery of mental and material direction, in spite of the absence of any real progressive organization of the world, mankind does move forwards towards that new world, has moved indeed with increasing rapidity for the past two centuries, and still struggles with gathering vigour and effect against the restraints of the past. What is the power that sustains this forward urge? What is it that inspires so many of us with the hope of presently making an end to war and of so marshalling our present confusions as to achieve a world of justice, health, achievement and happiness such as life has never known before?

In our analysis of the social motives of humanity, we have already found some intimations of an answer. We have drawn attention to the peculiar effect, the almost paradoxical effect, of the priestly training in turning minds to the scrutiny and revision of tradition. Men can be broken in to all sorts of submissions but the last thing you can break in is thinking. Every system of shams, every system once living that has become unreal, carries with it that ferment of skepticism. In spite of profit and advantage, in spite of the universal longing for peace and comfort, there is a disposition—it is as deep almost as an instinct—for truth, at work in us all. But that is not the only strain that is making for the revision of our world. The nomad, the autocrat, has never come into civilization submissively. He may not be a noble creature—*Homo sapiens* is not as yet a noble animal— but he has pride. His tradition is all against suppressions and smothered whispers. Tell the truth though the heavens fall, is the heroic phrasing of it.

And further, man has brought down from his arboreal ancestry, an unsleeping curiosity, an incessant disposition to experiment and invent.

Now these various sources of unrest have worked together, altogether unconsciously, to frame out this new world civilization that dawns upon us amidst the institutions and traditions of the old. The critical man, the inventive man, the adventurous and outspoken man, have worked together for consequences greater than they knew. When Stephenson watched his "Active" pull out the first passenger train upon the Stockton & Darlington Railway, it did not dawn upon him that this puffing and hissing contraption was destined to ensure the unity of the United States and make every frontier in Europe too tight. When Franklin flew his kite on a thundery day and drew sparks from the key at the end of his string, he had no idea that he was one small link in the huge chain of thought and realizations that was to throw a mantle of instant intelligence about the whole world. One step of curious enquiry, one act of simple mental integrity, multiplied a millionfold, has made the possibilities and opportunities of to-day. Behind these more recent and more successful innovators are others, more tragic and heroic. These are the men who told the truth as they conceived it about the heavens, though the churchmen of the time and all the established powers thundered together against them; there is Socrates drinking his hemlock because his genius had forced him to quicken the minds of the young.

Before that unpremeditated convergence of criticism, enquiry, suggestions, experiment and outspoken denial, the traditional order has become unreal in our minds to-day, and a new way of living opens before us. All that innovating, subversive activity was an unconscious conspiracy to evoke a new world.

But latterly that once unconscious conspiracy has been developing an awareness of itself, at first dimly but now more clearly. For a century and a half, at least, the idea of a conscious handling of the future of humanity has been establishing itself in our minds. Man finding knowledge and power growing in his hands and his range of possibilities increasing continually, has gone on to the obvious next step of putting his knowledge in order and making his attainment of yet more knowledge and yet more power, purposive and systematic. For that new apprehension we have made Diderot, with his poor burked and mangled and persecuted Encyclopédie, our symbol. We would put him against his monarch, making the latter, with his preposterous robes and ceremonies, his pretentious magnificence, his infinite self-complacency, his "foreign policy," his diplomatists, his mistresses and his piety, the very crown and embodiment of vulgar tradition. Who at that time would have imagined that Diderot would be alive to-day, a power and an inspiration, and his gorgeous sovereign as gone and happily gone out of human admiration and imitation as Nero or Cambyses before him.

With Diderot at last, that hitherto unconscious conspiracy for progress began to know itself for what it was. The nineteenth century was the century of liberalism, of the undermining of privilege and restriction. Progress came to be regarded as a necessary, rather than a merely possible, good. Lord Tennyson was the laureate not only of progress but of that limited reactionary little lady, Queen Victoria; and he reconciled the two without a qualm by presenting her as a veritable queen of light and guidance. Since he felt the world must surely "broaden down from precedent to precedent," how could she be anything but that? It was only a limited number of people who realized the finer truth that the secular development of a world civilization is not inevitable, but the outcome of constant effort and critical vigilance. Progress went on in that age of good fortune as though it went on by itself. It was the catastrophe of the Great War which has recalled us to the fact that the malignant possibilities of tradition had also been enhanced amidst the accumulated opportunities of that prolific awakening century which revealed to man all that he might hope and dare. After the Great War the impulse towards planned effort, towards the timely repudiation of obsolete institutions and towards educational reorganization has grown exceedingly. And it still grows. The word "plan" grows upon us. The Five Year Plan is only the first of many such plans to come.

To-day it is impossible to estimate how far human affairs are still drifting by hazard and material forces, and how far conscious scientific construction is making head against the adverse elements, within us and without, that would turn us back to outworn methods and racial recession. Our review of human affairs has been a display of almost unqualified growth under the influence of what we have just styled the "unconscious conspiracy" of original thought and innovation and experiment. But throughout we have had to note defects and waste in the working of this developing ant-hill for which no inevitable compensations appear, and dangers that have grown at least as vigorously as the rest of men's concerns. We have had at every step to qualify the confident effortless progressivism of the nineteenth century. The nineteenth century was a run of luck for mankind, a gust of good fortune, that may never recur. We see now plainly that we live in a world advancing still—but advancing dangerously and stumbling as it advances. We have shown political and financial science and method, lagging behind mechanical invention, and education faltering at its task. It seems that we can no longer rely upon the successful working of that "unconscious conspiracy" alone, to carry our intricate politico-economic system through the great dangers and stresses, so manifestly ahead, so rapidly drawing near. There is a quickening sense of this need for more concerted action, that is to say, for a new way of living, if the promise of humanity is to be fulfilled.

What are the activities to which men and women should now address and adjust their lives? They are, we shall find, activities that cannot be done by isolated men in out-of-the-way places or by energetic groups working for partial ends and heedless of the general drift of things. Railways could be spread by such groups—the governments of the time and the bulk of men scarcely heeding the network that grew about them and their planet—telegraphs, automobile and aëroplane could arrive without asking for any general consent. But the organization of a world peace can come into existence only through the previous acquiescence of at least all the chief governments in the world. That change must come about in a different fashion from the preceding changes. Men must be brought to a common mind in the matter, and that can be done only by the concerted efforts of a great number of influential and devoted people organizing propaganda and action. They must know themselves and each other, for that action to be effectual. There must be a Five Year Plan or a Ten Year Plan for all the world to understand if world pacification and disarmament are to be achieved. And similarly the readjustment of our cash-credit arrangements whose entanglements promise to strangle our growing prosperity, must be a world-wide, conscious undertaking to which governments must assent. You cannot introduce a new economic method in New Jersey or Denmark while the rest of the world abstains. The failure of a score of hopeful Utopian experiments in the nineteenth century demonstrated that. Concerted action by numbers of energetic men in all the great communities can alone meet this occasion. The world must have a plan like a banner that all men may follow, if the tariff walls are to crumble out of sight and a new money serve all the planet. Both these great tasks, the political and the economic, which mankind must perform or perish, are associated with and dependent on a concurrent world-wide renewal of education, which must equally be planned and carried out in the light of day. Restraint of population too must be world-wide.

We are forced therefore towards the conclusion that the phase of the "unconscious conspiracy" is drawing to its end, and that the further stages in the development of the new order of human life have to be achieved only through a world-wide movement conscious of itself.

Elsewhere I have used the term "open conspiracy" to express

such a movement of men of ability and understanding towards world-wide concerted effort. As I conceive it, "open conspiracy" is not in itself the name of a defined project, but a term to accentuate and to help people to the realization of this present need for conscious and stated creative coöperations. It is something already going on; the unconscious conspiracy of effort and circumstance in the past becomes open conspiracy by imperceptible degrees, as the necessity for combined effort becomes plain and its recognition outspoken. All political, economic, and social service that is free and unhampered by patriotic limitations is open conspiracy. All biological work is that, all physical science and all straightforward industrial innovation, in so far as it sets no limits to its inferences and makes an unrestrained communication of its results and suggestions to the whole world. All these forces will gain enormously in effectiveness by common protection and support, one for the other, and by a clear formulation of their common end.

As I conceive it this open conspiracy of the educated is dawning now. Unless I misread the signs of the time it should grow articulate and spread very rapidly through the world's educational organizations. It should find a response and expression in literature and art. It should quicken the imaginations of financial and industrial directors and organizers, and it should bring them into understanding relation with the civil services of the world's governments. It should become the dominating idea of an increasing multitude of active personalities. In our Chapter XII, § 13, the problem of world unity was discussed, and it was shown how pressing and probable great world commissions for world planning in such fields as disarmament and international trade have become. These must bring to a head, into a common constellation of activities, just such elements as I have indicated here as the formative threads of this open conspiracy. The open conspiracy is not a remote utopian project; it is something very probable, almost actual, close at hand.

In this idea of a concerted world-wide effort to sustain and continue the progress of the past two centuries, we have surely just that criterion of the value of conduct, that indication of an end for our activities, that the decay of the old faiths and explanations has deprived us of. We have the call for a new type of devotion and the indications for a new system of disciplines. We have indeed, at the practical level at which all this book is written—for life in space and time—the working elements of a new religion. But it is a religion that emerges, without founder or dogma or any finality, from the factors of social effort and desire that have been fostered and elaborated in the mind of man, by and throughout his developing social life. If man is to continue and still progress, it can only be by such a direct and simple apprehension of his world of work and achievement.

If the line of thought pursued in this book is sound, then what is here called open conspiracy is the practical form modern religion must assume, and the aim of modern education, as we have unfolded it here, must be to make every possible man and woman in the world an open conspirator.

§ 10. *The Recalcitrant*

In the preceding section we have ventured in criticism and forecast far beyond our enterprise of presentation. Let us return now to some very hard and serious realities in the shadow of the human community with which our enumeration of human life schemes must conclude.

The community breaks in the individual by education, and sometimes that education involves disciplines of some severity. Education passes by insensible degrees into adult government, into the public control of conduct, into the infliction of restraints, pains, and penalties. There is no gap, no real dividing line between education proper and the prevention and punishment of crime; they are two aspects of one thing.*

Let us consider what crime is, in the light of contemporary knowledge. Man at the level of *Sinanthropus* probably had no more conception of crime and sin than any other animal. He

---

*A good recent work on the repression or cure of the recalcitrant is Dr. Pailthorpe's *What We Put in Prison,* published by the London Association for the Scientific Treatment of Criminals.

had still to begin to be broken in to organized social life. He was like a dog which will commit incest, murder another dog, steal a bone—without feeling a stain upon its character. He may have had a certain awe of his master or his assembled fellows, as a dog has. We can only guess about that. We have stated the broad facts of the prehistoric process of breaking-in of *Homo* in our Chapter I telling how Man became an economic animal. Restraint was imposed upon him by taboos. He was brought to restrain his sexual impulses by the incest taboo, and to respect property by the tabooing of this object or that to all but its owner. He had to restrict his impulse to violence. There is no instinct, psychologists tell us, against murder, robbery, theft or incest. There is no natural inherent virtue. Virtue is an artificial thing, an achievement, which is why we praise it to one another. A system of inhibitions is built up in our minds from our earliest days against these society-destroying impulses. For most of us, this system of inhibitions is sufficiently strong, under normal conditions, to keep us out of mischief. But it helps almost all of us to know that behind these acquired dispositions of ours is the law, with its pains and penalties.

So long as our moral education holds, and reasonable social circumstances and our good fortune keep us out of temptation, we do not release the potential murderer or robber within us, but there he is, nevertheless. Our ideologies, our conception of ourselves and our world, keep him out of sight even of our introspection. But whenever a murderer goes to be hanged, "there but for the grace of God" go the reader and the writer.

There was a fashion some years ago for denying this fairly evident truth. An Italian psychologist, Cesare Lombroso, produced a book, *L'Uomo Delinquente,* in which he declared that for the most part criminals had distinctive physical traits, "criminal" ears, thumbs and so forth. This idea carried out to its proper conclusion would enable us to hang our murderers on anthropometric grounds before they killed anyone. He modified his views later, but that qualification was less exciting "news" and did not get the same publicity. After his book on criminals Lombroso published a book in which he attempted to show that men of genius are defectives and akin to the insane. As everybody who writes believes himself or herself to be a genius, this gave Lombroso what literary circles call a "bad press," and his reputation collapsed. But his views have been more convincingly disposed of by Dr. Goring (*The English Convict,* 1913) who has shown that there is no distinctive physical or mental criminal type. Dr. Kischway (Encyclopædia Britannica, under Criminology) questions the latter half of Dr. Goring's conclusion, namely that there is no mental difference. The truth of the matter may lie in the fact that though there is no innate criminal quality there are probably certain distinctive qualities in the ideology established in the mind which resorts to crime. There may be unstable types in which a criminal ideology is established with facility. Professor Burt lays stress on this in his *Young Delinquent.* The practical distinction of innate and acquired qualities may be a difficult one. There are certainly criminal types of persona.

We return to our assumption that crimes and offenses are artificial, they are restrictions imposed upon the normal "natural man" in order that the community may exist and work. There is no real difference in anything but degree between the man who outrages and robs his aunt, the man who deliberately drives an automobile round a corner on the wrong side of the road in order to get a thrill, the man who pulls a railway communication cord without proper excuse, and the man who uses a cleaned-up postage stamp over again. Each is giving way to his own impulses regardless of conventions established for the general good. The right or wrong of what they do is relative to society; there is no absolute right or wrong. A certain sanctity has been imposed upon the lives of aunts and the defacement of postage stamps, and the offender has refused to respect it. The social organization cannot afford to ignore this disregard. The artificial nature of crime becomes very plain when we consider such an offense as forgery. The precise imitation of a bank note or of a private signature on a cheque is made a serious offence in order to keep our cash and credit systems in working order. Otherwise it would be merely an elegant accomplishment. As a magistrate I have committed forgers for trial without feeling the slightest moral disapproval of them. There was a case came before the Folkestone bench: A prosperous gipsy woman bought a horse and almost immediately went mad; her nephew, who worked with her, took her cheque book and signed her name to pay for the horse. In perfect good faith. He did not even try to imitate her signature. What could have been more straightforward? How many women suddenly left penniless by a husband's insanity must have been disposed to do likewise? But the law has never been able to devise special arrangements for such hard cases, and so "forger" is established in our minds side by side with "robber" and "murderer" as a specially tainted being.

Crime, then, is that much of recalcitrance to the established processes and regulations, laws and by-laws of the social organization, which is punishable by law, and our best way of approaching it is by some preliminary considerations about recalcitrance in general. Why do people suddenly or of set habit and disposition refuse to "play the game" and disorganize the social operations about them?

This is a question that can be addressed in precisely the same terms to a school disciplinarian. The problem of order in society is one with the problem of order in the school. The latter is only the former in an earlier and simpler phase. The educationist's discipline is merely the prelude to the policeman and the criminal law. His science, which has advanced immensely in the last century, tells him to get just as much of right conduct as possible into the persona, to build up continually by example and precept, encouragement and disapproval, the suggestion that this is "done" and that is "not done." As far as possible he avoids reasoning about things; there is less friction if a type of act is established as being in itself "right" or "wrong." Telling the truth, avoiding and objecting to cruelty, playing fair, can all be put into a mind as handsome and creditable things by a competent teacher without any discussion at all. One of his most important disciplinary forces, is "the tone of the school." Individual ideas float on ideas generally prevalent. The preservation of the tone of the school is his constant solicitude. He resorts nowadays to compulsion and punishment only when the equipment of the persona is inadequate. But the youngsters over whom he rules are not passive wax for his moulding. His example and precept must be a consistent system in itself and consistent also with the general conception of the world that is developing in the developing mind. Suggest that one must be brave and independent, and some of the subordinations you are imposing may take on a timid look; suggest that one must be loyal and you raise perplexing issues between the chum in trouble and the law. The schoolmaster has to discriminate between individuals. Some are more vigorously egotistical than others, some are reserved and secretive. The former sort are apt to clamour for justice and consideration, exclusively directed to themselves. They are excitable; they flare up and rebel easily. They are dramatic. They clamour for popular approval or defy it. The subtle ones make their private reservations about right and wrong.

The school is already dealing in miniature with the two chief types of recalcitrant. The former is the open recalcitrant, the rebel, the violent breaker of rules, the type which needs open suppression, and the latter is the incredulous sneak, who accepts outwardly all the conventions of the community for the advantage of contravening them while others do not do so. But these two main classes by no means exhaust the disciplinary problems of the schoolmaster. There are exceptional types which seem to have an inherent mental twist against the restraints of social life, they are extravagantly egoistic and fail to "adjust," or they are dull and brutish and cannot establish or cannot sustain the necessary nervous connections. These are the mentally unstable and defective. The schoolmaster rejects the more marked individuals of this group; they must go to special institutions for such special compensatory or curative treatment as may be possible. Already across the crowd of normal educable youth in a school fall the shadows of rebellion, crime, defectiveness and lunacy. These shadows darken but do not change in their essential forms as we pass up to adult life.

The schoolmaster has got a certain proportion of the new

generation morally educated. In no case, however, will he have suppressed the primordial human being altogether. The adolescent he turns out as one of his successes, is still an egotist, but now with his anti-social impulses sufficiently minimized to remain ineffective or altogether latent throughout life. He wants sincerely to be a good citizen. He would be a good citizen because of his education, were there no law, no policeman, no jail. But that is the more perfect product in the educationist's output. Of such is the Kingdom of Heaven—and the Utopia of the anarchist. A number, probably a larger number, are sufficiently tamed and well disposed to refrain from anti-social behaviour while there is a reasonable prospect of detection, unpopularity and punishment. Finally there are those who will give trouble anyhow, the recalcitrants and the "mental cases."

The proportion of the recalcitrants to the rest of the population will vary enormously with the social atmosphere, which is the adult equivalent of the schoolmaster's "tone of the school." Where the community is saturated with common understandings, where the law and social usage are but little questioned and in harmony with the prevailing temperament, recalcitrants may fall to a very low percentage of the community. We get what is called a law-abiding community. A generally accepted law is what is called a "just" law, and the administration in a justly organized community can carry on its work with an air of righteousness and justice. Everyone helps and nobody hinders.

Where, on the other hand, the law is widely vexatious in any respect, as, for instance, Prohibition is vexatious in the United States of America; where there is a mixed population or an alien government with a consequent conflict of ideals and the suspicion of partiality; or where economic stresses fall unequally, the essential artificiality of right and wrong becomes apparent, the administration loses moral prestige and the proportion of recalcitrants rises. As recalcitrance rises the administration necessarily becomes more and more repressive. A community with a large proportion of recalcitrants is parallel to a school of which the tone has degenerated through mismanagement or has still to be raised to a high level, and which is consequently "out of hand." Punishment has to be vivid and unsparing, the forces of law and order vigorously aggressive.

We have shown that in the past education was a much more violent breaking-in than it is to-day. The modern teacher has a subtlety, gentleness and success of which no previous age ever dreamt. The treatment of social recalcitrance has undergone and is still undergoing a parallel amelioration.

The methods adopted in the past to maintain the health of the social body, to educate the community to seemly coöperation, make a terrible chapter in the history of mankind. The main purpose of all punishment is exemplary. The plain logical thing to do therefore, it seemed, was to exhibit the punishment to the crowd and make it as impressive as possible. "Do likewise and so it shall be with you," said the lawgiver. A kind of moral rage was excited in the struggling ruler by the breach of social rules, he lost his beneficence, and so the idea of teaching and reforming the malefactor himself played only a secondary rôle in the affair. The welfare of the wretch had passed out of consideration. What the ruler had to do was to demonstrate that he had got the better of the wretch and not the wretch of him.

In the old-fashioned education, birchings and floggings, the wearing of the foolscap and standing in painful attitudes, were inflicted if possible in the presence of the whole school for the benefit of all. The same publicity characterized the penal code. The stocks were still a common discipline a century and a half ago; the cangue was used in China within the lifetime of most of us—I am not sure that it is entirely disused even now; the seventeenth-century pillory, where exposure in discomfort was often combined with the mutilation of ears or nose, carried an inscription defining the offense committed. Executions were public festivals. Our projected Educational Museum must needs have its chamber of horrors, accessible only to those of a stout stomach, in which we shall pass from the more familiar instruments of school discipline to apparatus for the most terrifying executions. All these things played their part in the social education of man, the heavy-handed breaking-in of the past.

It is with a note of apology nowadays that one even mentions torture, but the world-wide use of torture before the days of Voltaire and the French Revolution, had a certain illuminating justification. There was a remarkable objection to putting a malefactor to death until he confessed his crime. He was tortured to produce a confession. Nothing could bring out more plainly the fundamentally pedagogic attitude of criminal law. It was not simply avenging an outrage upon society. The victim was being *taught* in spite of himself. If he died contumacious, he had not learnt his lesson, and, so far as he was concerned, the ruler had suffered defeat.

For obvious reasons the punishment of crime in primitive communities has always been summary, killing or beating or hurting in some way. Before the Middle Ages imprisonment was not widely used as a punishment, and prisons were simply mews for persons awaiting trial or execution. Sir Basil Thomson (whose *Story of Dartmoor* is well worth reading) ascribes our modern use of imprisonment to the influence of monastic Christianity, which regards solitude as a great help to penitence. Monks were among the first to be punished by imprisonment, and the aim in their cases was quite definitely educational. The oubliettes, dungeons and so forth of the mediæval castle were rather guest chambers for people the lord of the castle disliked and wished to treat as disagreeably as possible, than places of punitive restraint; they may have been persuasive in some cases, but they were not penal. They were revengeful. Such prisons as the Bastille in Paris or the Tower of London were essentially places of detention, and it was only after the First French Revolution that the legal sentence of imprisonment came into effect in France to replace a variety of brutal summary penalties. Under the vanished monarchy, French law had been almost as bloody as the English, which still in the first two decades of the nineteenth century hung men, women and children for thefts of a greater value than forty shillings. (But before the Revolution there were prisons for women and minor offenders in Holland and in 1703 Pope Clement XI built a special prison for youthful offenders.)

Throughout the ages the practise of selling recalcitrants into slavery and using them for mines, galleys and other excessive forms of labour has appealed very strongly to economical governments. It was a favourite expedient of the British in the provision of cheap labour for their earlier colonies. In Defoe's *Moll Flanders* transportation to the West Indies is highly commended as a way of starting life anew. In Soviet Russia, it is said, engineers and other skilled workers are charged with sabotage, sentenced to death, and then have their sentences commuted to so many years of unpaid work. But through a large part of the modern world now, except for capital sentences and the brutalities of army training, the only physical punishment inflicted is imprisonment.*

The use of prisons for convicted criminals was a distinct step forward from the public cruelties inflicted upon the recalcitrant in earlier times. Partly it may have been due, as Sir Basil seems to suggest, to the Christian idea of reforming the sinner, but mainly it was a product of the increasing decency and civilization of the world, which so quickened sympathy for those who might be condemned that witnesses would not come forward to give evidence nor juries, with the dire penalties of the time in view, convict. Severity defeated itself, and the offender went scot free. The public sufferings of the condemned advertised the atrociousness of the law. In the eighteenth century in Britain, though the yearly massacre of criminals was counted by the thousand, the annual depredations upon property lying in the Thames, says Sir Basil, amounted to half a million sterling, and no mail coach out of London was safe without an armed escort.

The prisons of the new régime of comparative mercy that followed the French Revolution were not indeed very wholesome places for repentance. They had to be improvised by authorities with not too much money to spend, and often with little sympathy for the new ideas. The intention of the law, no doubt, has always been something in the way of a rigorously clean little cell, a hard bed, simple, barely adequate food, cheerless exercise and meditation. Or labour upon quarries or public

---

*In 1920 flogging for certain types of robbery with violence was restored to the British penal code.

buildings conducted austerely in an edifying spirit. But these things are easier to launch than to keep in order. The trouble in all prisons throughout the world is at bottom the same double-headed trouble—expense and the staff. It is a trouble that also affects mental homes and lunatic asylums, which we may therefore bring into the picture very conveniently here. It is almost impossible to say where responsible recalcitrance ends and irresponsible recalcitrance begins. The taxpayer, the press, protest at the "pampering" of offenders, and there is a widespread feeling that their treatment should be below the lowest standard of life outside. There is a similar jealous objection that a mental asylum should not be a "palace."

It is the greatest tragedy of lunacy that the afflicted speedily become unendurably tiresome even to their intimate friends and close relations; so that they have few champions except a few philanthropic specialists. Both classes of establishment therefore are very subject to the economizing "axe." During the war the lunatics of Europe had a very bad time; in nearly every belligerent country they were half starved. Prisons and mental homes alike are by their very nature secret places, secluded from casual inspection. And the difficulty in getting an adequate staff of a suitable quality is very great. The ordinary warder or asylum attendant is not highly paid, and few people would undertake the work, unless for religious reasons, who could find equally well paid employment outside. A prison governorship is not regarded as a great prize. Economy understaffs and makes the work more exacting. The demands for patience and self-control in dealing with recalcitrants under restraint are enormous, and the normal lunatic, not simply from lack of understanding, but often because of an inherent maliciousness, can be incredibly vexatious.

All this leads, not indeed to tragic and horrifying events, but to a régime of petty tyrannies, illegal beatings, spiteful deprivations and misery. Most warders and attendants, when one meets them, are manifestly honest and worthy people; the community certainly gets its money's worth from this class; but they are bothered from morning to night, teased and overstrained. The monotony of a prison must be dreadful for all who have to keep it in a going state. The prisons of the world, rest assured, are cold, hard and needy places; the mental homes and asylums are full of wretchedness. In neither category are they, as yet, the organizations for cure, reform and adaptation they might well become.

One very dreadful result of the understaffing of mental homes is the reluctance these establishments frequently display in releasing the almost sane, once they are brought into the institution. Because, you see, the almost sane are so manageable comparatively and they can "help with the others." This is a clear and natural outcome of the instinctive abandonment and essential parsimony with which these unfortunates are treated.

As far as possible the insane and feeble-minded are given work to do that will keep their minds moving in tolerable paths. They follow various industries in the institutions provided for them; they work in the open air inside the high walls of the asylum grounds. There is no absolute difference between ordinary sane and law-abiding people, criminals, lunatics and the feeble-minded; there are only differences of degree. They feel as we do; if they do not act as we do, they act after the same fashion, with the same sort of mental sequences—at least, until their disease has gone on for some time. The criminal guides himself by a persona that permits him to do forbidden things more readily then the normal citizen. The lunatic's moods and interpretations fluctuate as ours do, but more widely and convulsively. He has impulse systems that get the better of him more completely than our impulse systems; his attempts to rationalize his world into harmony with the demands of his egotism are more extravagant than ours. We all comfort ourselves by delusions about our charm, our value, our ability, but he becomes God, or the King of the World, or the "mysterious European," or the Napoleon of the press. As far as he can he acts accordingly. The bulk of asylum patients may all have been curable at an early stage; there is no insane *type* any more than there is any criminal type; at most there is an excessive excitability which may soon, with advancing medical science, be quite controllable by glandular treatment; and in every asylum there are certainly men and women who were originally quite balanced but whose minds have been overwhelmed by some adverse chance too great to square with their general view of existence. Whether it is inherent or the result of misfortune, a defective or a mis-shapen and untrustworthy persona is what the alienist has to deal with. The picture within is wrong. The ideology is at issue with society. It is an incurable discordance rather than a delib-erate recalcitrance that takes these afflicted individuals out of the world. It is not that they will not, but that they can no longer will.

The visitor to a modern mental home feels the distress of it only by degrees. His first impression is one of space, light and cheerfulness. He sees tennis courts and cricket fields; men work-ing in gardens, people promenading and talking. He scarcely heeds the high wall that closes it all in from the world. He enters the building and finds people sitting about reading news-papers, talking, smoking. Then he notes as he goes from floor to floor the sound of keys being turned. And he begins to re-mark a certain listlessness here or a smouldering excitement there. He finds patients sitting inert, or muttering to them-selves, or repeating some phrase or some movement mechani-cally and endlessly. They are doing very much as we do when we are greatly strained and troubled. They have been forced into uncongenial associations; they bore one another fright-fully and increase each other's malady.

By comparison the appearance of a jail is dark and gloomy. The inmates are under a closer discipline and more obviously subjugated. They sit in separate cells doing some daily task, or they sit still. The peeping visitor speculates about what is going on in that cropped averted head. Does that particular criminal think he was justified? Was he treated fairly? The law has got him now, but next time will he get away with it? There is little or nothing in cell or exercising yard to cause a rebirth to a braver, more generous system of ideas. There is little to restore confidence in one's fellow men.

Since the days of Jeremy Bentham there has been a steady movement towards the development of the reformatory type of prison for at least young offenders, in spite of many financial and administrative obstacles. Borstal in Kent was the germ of the new methods so far as Britain is concerned. The Borstal idea is essentially adolescent reëducation, on the principle of better late than never. It deals with young criminals between the ages of sixteen and twenty-three. They have grown up, it is assumed, in a bad environment; they have got false ideas, a bad ideology, a warped persona, and that has to be set right before it is fixed forever. So they are treated with an austere kindliness, set to learn useful trades, encouraged to play social games that evoke the concepts of team-play and fair-play, and released under supervision to start the world anew. The method is so far successful that of 6,000 cases observed, two thirds have never troubled the law again.

But it has to be noted that the Borstal prisons, of which there are now four in England, are not *cheap* prisons to run, and that they demand a certain very special enthusiasm on the part of governor, house master and staff. That one can get for one pioneer prison, for four prisons even, amidst the stir and hope of a new movement. But how far can the methods be extended before the strain on the supply of devoted officials becomes excessive? People like Mr. Alec Patterson, the Prisons Commissioner for the Borstal Institutions, Sir Wemyss Grant Wilson who founded the After Care work, and Miss Lillian Barker of the girls' Borstal, do not grow on every family tree.

The name of Thomas Mott Osborne is closely associated with the parallel movement in America to make the prison educational. He trained himself in the matter by undergoing a term of voluntary imprisonment at Auburn, New York. Under him, the New York State Prison at Sing Sing was the scene of some very remarkable and successful experiments in social rehabilitation. The punitive factor was reduced to a minimum. He even introduced a form of convict self-government known as the "mutual welfare league." But note that I write with caution; I write "under him." Lately (1930) there has been grave trouble in Sing Sing. The celebrated Juvenile Court of Judge Lindsay in

Denver also was a one-man court, a self-embodiment rather than an autonomous machine.

In these cases, as in all such cases, the directive personality in a prison seems to be the supremely important thing. Good educational prisons are still exceptional prisons. They have not been made into machines with replaceable parts, and perhaps that will never be possible. It needs only a little relaxation of guidance for them to lose their educational quality and lapse into irritation and unhappiness. The same is true of the lunatic asylum and the mental hospital. The relation of warder and prisoner, or attendant and defective, is normally one of restraint and resistance, and so it is always close to the keen edge of exasperation. The history of reform in both these types of human institution from the days of John Howard and Beccaria onward, is a history of indignant and devoted personalities. Such reformers capture the imaginations of authorities and helpers and force up the tone of the business—for a time. But the normal, healthy human mind, with an instinctive economy of effort and feeling, turns itself away from the fate of the recalcitrant and ill-adjusted. It is a special job for a special type, which responds to what religious people speak of as a "call."

What hope have we then that this painful substratum of social life may be mitigated or reduced to nothing in the future? Will the world solve this problem of personal management and staffing? To what may we look for a steady and if necessary an increased supply of service?

Our first hope lies in the schools of the future and in the general educational atmosphere of the community. These will fail to establish the law-sustaining persona with a smaller and smaller percentage of the young. They will be cutting off the criminal supply at the source.

And there may be a further interception of possible criminals with defective personas at the leaving school stage. The juvenile prison at Wandsworth is interesting in this respect. Young persons under remand are put through the same sort of examination as we have mentioned in Chapter VII, §6, our account of the London Institute of Industrial Psychology. A very material proportion of young criminals commit offenses because they are misfits and unhappy in the calling chosen for them. The juvenile prison affords every facility for a change over to congenial and satisfying jobs. Here again is another preventive force to diminish the load upon the prison at least, if not upon the mental retreat.*

Next, to keep down the criminal load there is the deterrent force of efficient policing. It is a proved and tested maxim of the criminologist that the surer the conviction of the offender, the less likely he is to offend. Light but inevitable punishments are far more effective than uncertain heavy ones. Sentences can be reduced therefore with every improvement in policing, and there will be fewer people in prison, and they will be there for shorter terms.

Turn now to the mental home, and here again there is a reasonable hope of a great reduction in the number of cases. Actual lunacy, as we have remarked already, may soon become much more curable if taken in time than it is at present; it is to begin with a disorder of the thoughts associated with a misbehaviour of the endocrinal glands, both controllable things. The psychoanalyst may come to the help of the family doctor, and the standard of medical education may be raised very greatly in this field. The load upon asylums may also be lightened presently by the sterilization of mental defectives (discussed in Chapter X, §6).

While the load is thus being reduced, it may be possible to supplement and improve the staffing of both series of institutions very considerably. There is the possibility of a reinvigorated moral education and a revival of the religious spirit among the young. I have already noted in two places (Chapter XII, §7, and in this chapter, §7) William James's suggestion of a year

---

*A good summary of Children's Courts throughout the world is given in W. Clarke Hall's book with that title. This has ample references to the general literature of the subject. Professor Cyril Burt's *Young Delinquent* is a fuller treatment of this most interesting borderland between normal education and police restraint. Apart from the interest of the subject itself, these books introduce the reader to a very cheering and inspiring group of inspectors and court officials, sterling good people that one is the better for knowing about.

or so of universal public service for all the young people in the community. A certain proportion of these, carefully selected by a scientific testing of character and intelligence, would find an ennobling use in the responsibilities of prison and asylum work.

There is also another and perhaps even more valuable element in the population that could be brought to bear upon both prison and asylum. That is the student who proposes to specialize as a doctor and in particular as a mental doctor, or as a lawyer, educationist or practising teacher. We have already commented (Chapter VIII, § 7) on the remarkable general ignorance of solicitors. In no class of men is an acute sense of the defects and dangers of human impulse more necessary than in these modern successors of the father confessor of the past. The lawyer in training also might well supplement his law studies with a year or so of practical work among the extremer cases of impulse, defect and recalcitrance. There is a strong case for impressing the law student for this work. When we take into consideration all these possibilities of improved and scientific staffing on the one hand and of restricted supply on the other, the ultimate complete civilization of both prison and mental seclusion ceases to appear an impossible dream and takes on the character of a finite and solvable problem. But their ultimate abolition is a remoter issue altogether.

And now, with a sigh of relief, let us turn our backs upon those museum galleries of past and present restraint and repression we have had to conjure up, with their models of prisons and cells, their effigies in convict clothing, their handcuffs, stretchers and straitjackets, their frightful disciplines and intimidations, and all that depressing but unavoidable display of human frustration, and let us turn our subject about and ask, "What is recalcitrance?" What, that is, are the things society considers it desirable and justifiable to insist upon in its individuals, and what are the tendencies it must restrain or suppress if individuals will not or cannot do so?

In the past, through the clumsiness of the current conceptions of social relationships, a great number of acts and attitudes were regarded as inimical to social well-being which we, with our broader outlook, know to be matters of indifference. Ceremonial negligences, the questioning of received opinions, disregard of various obsolete taboos, alchemy, magic practises, witchcraft, heresy, the eating of forbidden things, unorthodox fashions of life and behaviour, were supposed to offend the Higher Powers so gravely as to bring misfortune on the community. Accordingly, such acts were prosecuted and punished, often very cruelly. We speak of these things as "persecutions," but from the point of view of the persecutor they were as much crimes as murder or theft or forgery. They awakened the same horror and the same vindictive passion in the well disposed. To this day, in those darker corners of the earth where savage life still lingers, there are sacrifices to avert disaster, but in most of our world there are now no involuntary offences and no propitiatory sacrifices, and there has been an immense release of thought and act from the narrower, fear-haunted ideology of the past.

Every new phase in social development must create new offenses and supersede old ones. The progressive organization of world unity will, for example, abolish the offenses of smuggling and espionage. You will be able to take anything anywhere, look at anything, and tell anybody what you have seen. On the other hand, a modern state may suddenly bring new spheres of activity within the criminal code. Before the war the brewing, sale and delivery of beer was as honourable an occupation in New York as it is still in London. By a constitutional amendment this has been changed in the United States against the will and conscience of great numbers of hitherto decent people, and as a consequence of this and of a pedantic deliberation, and possibly a certain venality, in the machinery of the law, a new and formidable criminal organization has been evoked in that country. The attempt to control a particular detail of conduct in a community accustomed to great freedom of personal initiative was manifestly entirely unscientific. The voters in that democratic country should have been educated to a clearer idea of what a law can and cannot do. The ante-war saloon was no doubt a very great social and political nuisance, but its impatient, crude suppression has replaced it by far greater evils and done a very deep injury to the American morale.

The Soviet Republic, in its attempt to replace a mediæval autocracy by a scientifically organized collectivist state, has had to revise its code of right and wrong in the most drastic fashion. It had for instance to make an offense of "speculation," punishable in the case of members of the Communist party by death. Speculation was simply buying to sell again at a profit instead of buying for use. Every shopkeeper and every pedlar became a criminal. A more vaguely defined offense, "economic sabotage," has also been pursued with implacable fury. "Economic sabotage" seems to be failing, "with intent," to get the very best result out of every machine or organization of which one is in control. Indeed, a whole series of offenses has been created in defense of the Soviet régime. What the rest of the world would call political opposition has become stark treason in Russia. To point out defects in the Five Year Plan or suggest coöperation with capitalist Europe is a crime.

Never have the definitions of right and wrong fluctuated so wildly as they do to-day. They change and are bound to change with every attempt to adjust our overstrained and dislocated economic, political and social ideologies to the vast new needs of the time. In this comprehensive statement and analysis of human coöperations we have attempted, it is made plain that in all existing political and commercial systems there are the gravest defects and dangers. They are undergoing adjustment amidst great stresses. It has been impossible to describe them without condemning their past and foreshadowing the future. The so-called Capitalist System is not in being, it is continually becoming. But to forecast developments is to forecast new methods of dealing and new rules of conduct, and that is to open up a new list of offenses.

We advance into no anarchist paradise. Progress is only possible through repression. For example, we have traced lightly but sufficiently the growth of the armament industry in the last half century. We have seen how the conduct of a small number of energetic individuals pursuing profits on entirely legal and permissible lines, has already contributed to a monstrous destruction of human life, happiness and material. Largely that was possible because incitement to war, whether secret or public, in school or press, is not a criminal offense. But now at least it ought to be a criminal offense, if the Kellogg Pact means anything at all. Incitement to general murder ought to be brought into line with incitement to murder specific individuals. And the speculative manufacture of arms by private individuals so that their purchase can be forced upon reluctant governments, and the public sale of lethal weapons, are manifestly much more socially injurious and should be made at least as criminal as brewing or the sale of cocaine has been made in the United States of America. Both indeed would be extremely easy to suppress were there the will for it.

Moreover, we have shown how badly, and at present how ominously, the system of production for profit with its current methods of credit, works. It is clear it has to be changed and made to work in a new spirit if we are to avoid a catastrophe. By successive replacements at this point and that, production for use and large measures of collective buying have to supersede profit production and the incoherent direction of the unorganized purchaser. And in personal conduct the spirit of service, and service as a criterion of moral quality, have to be brought in to modify the deliberate and admitted self-seeking that rules our economic life to-day. These developments involve a correlated adjustment of instruction and the law. The persona has to be set in certain new directions by education, and the criminal law has to confirm that bias.

There is need of a sustained, continuing scrutiny of the methods of banking, the manipulation of money and credit, the permissible devices of trading, the financing of enterprises. There is need of a progressive modification of the law in association with this scrutiny. Our economic life has to be brought more and more into harmony with the concept of collective effort for the common welfare to avert the disaster the tradition of chaotic competition, the legacy of the peasant, and the predatory nomad will otherwise bring upon us all. The fierce and drastic suppressions of economic recalcitrance in Russia are violent beyond any necessity of the Atlantic communities, but it is plain that since, under the compulsion of new dangers and stresses, all the world, and not Russia alone, struggles towards more highly organized mutual service, a more deliberate, parallel restraint upon anti-social individual enterprise becomes inevitable in the non-Communist communities also.

The aim of this work throughout is to translate the abstract ideas of economics and sociology into terms of concrete human beings, and there need be no apology offered for an attempt to present "anti-social individual enterprise" in the form of living types. What manner of man and woman, what sort of persona, does that phrase "anti-social individual enterprise" convey?

I would suggest that the type of crime this age will find most difficult to deal with is not the rough, overt recalcitrance of former times. So much of that as still gets past preventive education can be dealt with by competent police methods. The comparative abundance of violent crimes in the United States is a temporary phase, due to short-sighted repressive legislation and an ill-organized police system; both of which disadvantages one may count upon the American people to overcome. In the rest of the world, as school, reformatory, police integrity, and efficiency advance, the open recalcitrants diminish. But on the other hand, in certain types of crime, in the possibility of undetected hidden crimes and in acts, plainly antisocial but not yet definitely made criminal, it is not so easy to congratulate ourselves. The police organization plays a long and difficult game against, for example, the intelligent poisoner. The law finds itself in constant perplexity about the intricate cheat. Sir Basil Thomson found most of his "old lags" at the convict prison of Dartmoor men of poor education and inferior mental quality. The proportion of educated cheats and middle class criminals who come into jail seemed to him unaccountably small, in view of all the cheating and overreaching that was going on in the world outside.

From America comes a sobriquet I find attractive, "Smart Alec." I propose to use it here. It raises in my mind a figure of just the qualities I have in view. Smart Alec is a sharp lad, who retains the peasant persona, polished to an extreme brightness, in spite of all the modern educational forces that may have been brought to bear upon him. For some reason of innate quality or faulty suggestion, the ideas of honour, service, frankness, and truth do not "take" with him. He professes to accept them, but within they have no hold on him. His persona is pervaded by the persuasion that he is "not a fool." Fools take these things as fundamental, but not he. He has ends of his own, private standards of what is desirable. These ends may be the gratifications of sense or vanity or the secret triumphs of advantage and avarice. An immense vanity and a profound secret self-reliance are in his make-up. He does not trust. Even with those he values and cares for, he does not give himself away, or he does so by some lapse into boasting. From this angle it is that Smart Alec comes into the game of life.

(I write of Smart Alec to economize my third personal pronouns. There are Smart Alexandras—with certain differences of aim and method; it may be, as abundant.)

He comes into the game of life with the idea not of serving, but of beating the community, and the community, so far as it is wisely guarded, sets itself to defeat and if possible "save the soul" of Smart Alec. All up and down the scale of misdemeanour and punishment we find Smart Alec being found out, and how many Smart Alecs are never found out we cannot estimate. Some are caught cheating in school, and some are caught cheating at games. They get a check, and perhaps they mend their ways. But the abler or more fortunate Smart Alec has a finer discretion and does not cheat too crudely. He studies the weaknesses of his masters and wins good marks with a minimum of exertion. He plays his games according to the rules. His companions say that he plays for his own hand, but playing for one's own hand is not yet scheduled as an offense. He watches his averages and gets through his examinations. He pushes out into the world alert for opportunity.

Where is there most opportunity? That may vary with the circumstances in which he is launched, with his special aptitudes, with his general intelligence. He may choose a trade or a profession. Law has had some brilliant, unscrupulous successes to fire the imagination of an ambitious youngster. A political career, particularly for a smart and smartly bold lawyer, offers a way to prominence and many glittering prizes. A lawyer may do many things a layman dare not do. He knows the law better and within limits, if men denounce him, he can trust to the instinct of professional solidarity. There are some good prizes in the Church, too, and less competition than there was in former days. But industry, commerce and especially financial organization, beckon to Smart Alec with both hands.

There at present he finds his richest field. There is an amazing tolerance in finance for the man who plays for himself alone. Boldness with property ceases to be heroic in the business man's imagination only when it comes into the dock. Some of the older banks may distrust youthful brilliance and lay snares for its feet, but the prevailing standards of the financial world still blend the traditions of peasant and raider. In Chapter X we have exposed all this region of human activities to the light of a careful analysis and shown what a danger its unplanned looseness of play is to the whole human organization. The task of its adjustment would still be enormously difficult if everyone concerned in it were giving himself unreservedly to assist. But nothing of the sort is going on. Smart Alec meets one at every twist and turn, ready to oppose everything that will embarrass him, alert to snatch and take advantage. He stretches the poor old law to the utmost and cheats a little when it is likely to inconvenience him. He has his confederates in the legislature; his friends who own and direct newspapers; Smart Alecs likewise.

The man of good-will, as we call him, himself by no means perfect, thinks and plans to save and serve the civilization that in his mind has come to be something more significant than himself. He is part of that once unconscious conspiracy that now becomes conscious, the conspiracy of constructive service to sustain and continue civilization. He has no ambition to flare across the heavens as the richest man in the world. He has his own conception of satisfaction and his less obvious and deeper standards of success and failure. He is an official, or a man of science,

or a lawyer with an enlightened sense of honour, a teacher, or he
may be many other serviceable things. His wealth, his power, so
far as that depends on wealth, and his knack of getting, may be,
man for man, almost incalculably inferior to that of any of the
more flagrantly successful Smart Alecs, but there is this on his
side and on the side of civilization, that he is capable of wider
and wider coöperations, while Smart Alec is by his very nature
an individualist, playing for his own skin. Smart Alec does this
and that and one Smart Alec skins another Smart Alec, Smart
Alecs are cannibals among themselves, the gross, limited and
ignorant crowd thrusts stupidly this way or that or lapses into
collective inertia, but the open conspiracy will go on more and
more steadfastly doing the same system of things, working
toward a more and more clearly defined objective.

Between Smart Alec and the conscientious, devoted, all too
pedagogic makers of order and progress, the limited, instinctive
traditional life of the multitude blunders along, at once protected
and entangled, in a fabric of laws and methods that is still manifestly casual, unstable and incalculable. The multitude is
ignorant, and Smart Alec can lie to it convincingly and bril-
liantly; he can fool its dim impulses to do right and turn them
against his toiling pursuers. Its loyalties are dull and strong, attached to decaying idols and superseded necessities, but Smart
Alec will champion and defend and utilize the honoured tradition, the ancient institution, and reward and advance himself
with all the picturesque honours it can confer. Or some devitalized religion spreads its attractive endowments about the
world for Smart Alec to seize upon and sustain. He is to be
found playing the rôle of the enthusiastic Nationalist, the acute
Protectionist, for of all systems of opportunity for the alert,
war and war preparation are the greatest. A staff uniform becomes him well. In the trenches and tortures of warfare men may
come to see Smart Alec plainly, in a blaze of revelation, but
there is no going back for them then; he is well out of range.
And now that Smart Alec has been so busy with our currencies
and prices that this swarming world of work and wealth hangs
dangerously on the verge of panic and despair, the Smart Alecs

continue their reckless manœuvres, sell to keep the depression going and buy at bedrock prices, traverse every effort to unify the incoherence of a divided economic front, and bid fair to accomplish the ruin of our civilization. Then, amidst the discomforts of a brigand world, Smart Alec, with his gains mysteriously gone and his comforts and indulgences shattered beyond recovery, will adjust himself knowingly and briskly to new occasions.

Unless we of the open conspiracy who hunt him incessantly can net him tightly enough to save our world from his exploits.

These are the fundamental sides of the internal conflict of the human community as we see them to-day. Education, law, an advancing psychology, and social science have the brute, the dull and the defective well in hand. That much may be counted as done. The broad task now is a vast and difficult political and economic reconstruction of the world's affairs, with Smart Alec as the main recalcitrant. Law, like a living, self-repairing net, seeks for him. The mind of the race in literature and social psychology sustains a perpetually closer criticism of motive and conduct and so exposes and pursues him. Continually the modern community, thoughtfully, steadfastly, powerfully, must be anticipating, circumventing, defeating, and, as may be necessary, punishing Smart Alec. For Smart Alec is now the chief enemy of mankind. He is the antagonist and betrayer of open conspiracy; his rôle is to prevent the salvaging of civilization. We have to fight him in the whole world about us. We have to fight him by school, by art and literature and law. We have to meet and fight him in our daily transactions. We have to fight him in ourselves.

And conversely, Smart Alec is rarely if ever found—how shall I put it?—in a state of chemical purity, a hundred per cent Smart Alec. Nearly always, if not always, his private self, his persona, will have been infected with some qualities of a wider, less personal scope. He has a conscience. There are moments when the Smartest Alec sees himself for what he is.

If, in space and time, but outside of and above our world of work and wealth altogether, some commanding intelligence could survey and appraise it in its simplest form, the whole spectacle of our activities, our desires, our efforts, and our defeats would appear as one continuing struggle between the creative synthetic will and thought of the human mind on one hand, and the subtle, endlessly various self-centred recalcitrance of the individual man on the other.

CHAPTER THE SIXTEENTH

THE OUTLOOK OF MANKIND

§ 1. *The Next Phase Latent in the Present Situation.*
§ 2. *Uncertainties in the Human Outlook.*
§ 3. *Hope and Courage Are Inevitable.*

CHAPTER THE SIXTEENTH

THE OUTLOOK OF MANKIND

§ 1. *The Next Phase Latent in the Present Situation*

WE HAVE now completed our general account of this little world of men, our survey of the activities and interaction of the one thousand nine hundred million souls who make up the human garment of our globe. We have shown how things are with that film of life to-day. We have shown how it stirs and carries on. We have ranged from the financial adventurer in his aëroplane to the miner hacking at the seam, and from the work girl in the atelier, and the peasant bent down to his soil, to the film star and the military commander; clerks and machine minders, stokers and cabmen, the parson in the pulpit, and the fur trapper in the snow have all figured in the reckoning. We have noted, if only by mere indicative gestures, a hundred culs-de-sac and out-of-the-way corners, the prisoner in his cell, the burglar "at work," the lunatic under treatment, the religious ascetic wrung with prayer, the noiseless jungle savage. It is the main masses that have chiefly held our attention; it is the broad realities we have examined. So human beings live, so they work, so hating and loving and bickering and bargaining they serve and depend upon one another and pass away.

What has evolved this multitude? What has woven this magic network of aid and service between them? That has been asked and in a manner answered here. Example, imitation, teaching, intricate educational processes. It is a psychological net. Why has this world of ours so many corrupting kinks and morbid developments, so many parasites, rebels and betrayers? Because of the imperfections of its educational adaptations. The web is not perfectly woven. To crown our work we turned to the teachers,

preachers, writers, innovators, propagandists and all that miscellany of people who keep ideas alive and operative and weave
new conceptions of action and new threads of relationship into
the dispersed millions of our kind. We showed their retarda-
tions and their difficulties. They are always a little behind the
mechanical drift of things, as the upthrust of a wave is behind its
crest.

This planetary ant-hill of interrelated living creatures is
changing as the reader turns these pages. It never pauses in its
changes. In the past minute about twelve human beings have
been born upon this globe as it spins steadily through space, from
day to night and from night to day, born each with a blank new
brain, upon which the first writing has already begun: those first
impressions, those foundations of dim experience which will be
built at length into a unique, unprecedented persona with all the
intricate reactions of self-conscious, self-directive individual life.
And in the last minute—unless there has been some exceptional
catastrophe—some ten human beings have died, taking with
them, each one of them, a world.

Many of those so recently dead, dying while the last few paragraphs were read, were quite young creatures, some just born;
but most of them carried with them out of the impulses of mankind, unforgettable memories, obstinate prepossessions, life-worn
traditions, obsolete skills and responses, unteachable determina-
tions. Over the teeming minds of the young play the suggestions, traditions, examples, preachments and reasonings of our
newer time. These minds in their turn are going on to hope and
desire, struggle and consume, suppress disagreeable facts and
exaggerate pleasant ones, embrace self-protective delusions, conduct themselves according to their lights and so act their parts.
They too will be shaped and set and hardened, but not exactly as
their predecessors were. The pattern is always changing. Work
goes on day by day about the planet, and wealth is gathered and
spent. The threads interweave, and the pattern passes into new
shapes and new promises. In the end these others also will pass
away. Man is forever dying and forever being born, and it is
impossible to tell of what is, without passing on forthwith to the

only aspect that gives the present significance and reality, the things that now arise out of the things that are.

§ 2. *Uncertainties in the Human Outlook*

Let us before we conclude devote a section to the possibility that this human adventure will fail. We have no guarantee whatever against many sorts of cosmic disaster. There is the risk, an infinitesimal but real risk, of meteoric bodies hurtling through our system, bodies so large and coming so near to us as to destroy our planet as a home for life. So remote is such a mischance that Sir James Jeans can dismiss it as negligible. If the lot falls against us in spite of the odds, there is nothing more to be said or done. Fate will end the story.

But other sinister possibilities, less catastrophic but in the end as decisive, are not so easily dismissed. We still know very little of the secular changes of climate, and it is conceivable that in quite a few years, in a hundred thousand or a thousand thousand, that is to say, this planet may be returning to a phase of widespread glaciation, or temperature may be rising to universal tropical and ultra-tropical conditions. Within the sun, for all we know, explosive forces are brewing—or on our earth itself—to heat or chill or shatter. Or again, if steady urgencies of upheaval and disturbance are not still astir under the feet of our race, the rains and rivers and waves will presently wear down our mountains and hills and flatten out our lands until one monotonous landscape of plains of exhausted soil and swamps and lagoons of tepid water has replaced the familiar scenery of our time. Or if these terrestrial tensions increase, our race will pass into a period of volcanic violence and earthquakes, forces from within breaking loose to thrust up new mountain chains and giving fresh directions to wind and sea current, and the conditions of life may become extreme and diversified beyond adjustment.

Here plainly we are still under the sway of the Fates. Presently we may be able to foretell; later we may even control such fluctuations, but certainly the sun and planets and our little globe have their own motions and changes regardless of our needs and desires. The cards as they are played are being swept up for a fresh deal. The hand our race must play to-morrow may be very different from the hand we play to-day. There are no fixed conditions to human life, and if this new-born world community of ours is to go on through vast periods of time, man will have to be forever guessing new riddles. Will he be able to get so far with his science as to map out at length in their due order all the coming throws of the planetary roulette? Or get a mastery of the wheel? There will have to be an encyclopædia of knowledge for such feats as that, vaster than anything we can dream of to-day. There will have to be a mightier sort of man, very marvellously educated, and perhaps by virtue of an advancing science of eugenics innately better, to do things on that scale.

Such are the difficulties and problems for our descendants, that must slowly develop themselves age by age, even if they solve the riddles of our present civilization. But will mankind ever solve these immediate problems? There was recently published a very suggestive and amusing book by Olaf Stapledon, *First and Last Men*. It is an imaginary history upon an astronomical scale of the future of humanity, a grimly cheerful mixture of biology, burlesque, and satire. He sees our present species blundering through some further great wars and unified at last under American rule into one world state, a world state of a harshly plutocratic type which undergoes an entirely incredible moral and intellectual degeneration and ends in a new Dark Age. *Homo sapiens* is then practically exterminated by a catastrophe he has himself provoked, and only a few individuals survive obscurely to become the progenitors of two species of *Homo* who presently increase and come into conflict. The remoter speculations of Mr. Stapledon about the succession of the latter Hominidae and their final extinction, vivid and amusing though they are, and stimulating as they will prove to those unversed in biological and cosmological possibilities, need not be discussed here. But the nearer issues he broaches, do pose very disturbingly the considerable probability of a failure in our contemporary civilization to anticipate and prevent fresh world warfare and an economic crash. I see that possible economic crash nearer and larger and more important than he does, as a greater menace, indeed, than the militant nationalism from which it arises. But I believe in human sanity more than he does, I believe that that widely diffused will and understanding which I have termed "open conspiracy" may be strong enough to carry the race through the economic stresses ahead of us, and to delay, minimize and finally repulse the onset of war.

There has been a great quickening of the general intelligence about political and economic life in recent years, and the man of action and the man of thought have been drawn nearer together. There may be some dark chapters in human history still to be written, and provisional governments and a mightier Judge Lynch may figure in the drama. The forces that will carry on, develop and realize the abounding promise of our present civilization are by no means sure of victory; they may experience huge and tragic setbacks; but the balance of probability seems to be largely in their favour. If they win out, it will be men of our own kind, better, according to our present values, but men still—not beings specifically different and beyond our sympathy—who with a whole planet organized for the conflict, will face those greater problems, the long-period problems of terrestrial and cosmic changes which advance upon us behind the skirmishing dangers of to-day.

But nothing is certain. Men may breed and bicker too long, be overtaken by some swift universal epidemic they have had no time to arrest, perish of a phosphorous famine, or be destroyed by some war machine they have had the ability to invent but not the intelligence to control. In the Mesozoic Age great reptiles multiplied and dominated the earth, and suddenly they passed away. In the Miocene flourished countless varieties of huge mammals, now altogether extinguished. Why should we suppose that we are specially favoured items in the spectacle of existence? Millions of us are wearied, chased about, heartbroken, wounded and killed, for no evident good, in war; millions are destroyed by accidents without apparent reason or justice; beasts of prey in India and Africa slay and eat their thousands of "man the master" every year; millions die in unalleviated pain through a multitude of cruel diseases. Is there any difference in quality between one single case of a dear human being killed by cancer and the murder of a world? It is simply a difference of numbers and scale. If the universe can kill a child unjustly, so it can kill a race or a planet unjustly. If so many individual lives end tragically, why should not the whole species end tragically?

We may say, "It shall not," but what weight have such words?

§ 3. Hope and Courage Are Inevitable

What have we to put into the scale against this presentation of the whole human adventure, as nothing better than a freak of chance, flung up in the incomprehensible play of forces forever outside our understanding, and destined to be reversed as casually and wiped out of being altogether?

So far as our powers and knowledge go, we have nothing. We are forced back upon something more fundamental in us than knowledge or reason; the innate inevitable faith in itself that every healthy conscious being must necessarily possess. "Where there is life," says the old proverb, "there is hope." A creature with no faith in itself will die and pass out of the reckoning, leaving the world to those whose faith remains. We are unable to believe that the universe that has evoked the will to live in us can be without will. We can no more believe the universe insane by our measure of sanity and altogether indifferent to our urgencies than we can prove it sane.

But the pessimist also can prove nothing. He argues that the antagonists are very strong; he does not show they are invincible. He reminds us that we are not insured against this or that gloomy mischance. But there is no inevitability about any of these gloomy mischances. The unknown is full of possible surprises for mankind. There is no more probability of these surprises being dreadful than there is of their being delightful. The chances are strictly even. When everything has gone into either scale, there still remains this fact to tilt the balance in our favour; that here we are with courage in us.

What is the culminating effect of a survey of history, of the science of life, and of existing conditions? It is an effect of steadily accelerated growth in power, range, and understanding. All these things lead up to us—and how could they seem to do otherwise? Progress continues in spite of every human fear and folly. Men are borne along through space and time regardless of themselves, as if to the awakening greatness of Man.

Why should we not believe that amidst the stars ahead of us the world-state will be won, and that long ages of progressive civilization, ages of accumulating life and power open out before our kind? And though that is the present frame of our vision, why should we suppose that any end has been set to the growth and advancement of our race while the time garment still wraps about it and veils its eyes? For our history is just a story in space and time, and to its very last moment it must remain adventure. We have no ultimate measure of life's potentialities, no reason for supposing that what seems to us to be insurmountable obstacles will not dissolve to nothing before an ever increasing knowledge and resourcefulness. Our vision is limited indeed, but not by any fated and assured end. Even these ingenious paradoxes by which space and time merge into one another and all our absolutes and infinities dissolve away have no quality of finality about them. One feels there is more to be said; much still to be thought out. They challenge; they do not capture and convince. Our most fundamental ideas are provisional ideas, no doubt, but as yet there is nothing to replace them. Ten thousand or ten million years from now will still be ten thousand or ten million years from now. So far and beyond, this adventure may continue and our race survive. The impenetrable clouds that bound our life at last in every direction may hide innumerable trials and dangers, but there are no conclusive limitations even in their deepest shadows, and there are times and seasons, there are moods of exaltation—moments, as it were, of revelation—when the whole universe about us seems bright with the presence of as yet unimaginable things.

THE END

INDEX

INDEX

A

Abir, the, Company, and Congo atrocities, 301.

Abélard, Pierre (1079–1142), fixed decisively scholastic manner of philosophizing, 75.

Abolition, of distance, 4, 135; of toil, 117.

Academia dei Lincei, Galileo a member of, 91 .

Académie des Sciences, 91.

Academia Naturæ Curiosorum of Madrid (1657), 91.

Academia Secretorum Naturæ of Naples (1590), 91.

Academy of Athens, and first effort for new view of life, 8.

"Acceptable substitute" in adulteration, 190 sqq.

Accuracy of work, great improvement since time of James Watt, 129.

Acousticon plaster, 231.

Acquisitive Society, Tawney, 349.

Acton, Lord, quoted, 6.

Adams, Charles Francis and Henry, *High Finance in the Sixties,* 481.

Adams, Professor Romanzo, 736.

Administrators' persona scrutinizea, 345.

Adult education, 12, 820, 826.

Adulteration, "acceptable substitute" in, 190 sqq.; 189.

Adventure in Working Class Education, An; Albert Mansbridge, 827.

Advertisement, history of, 248 sqq.; media in, 250; story of cigarette, 250.

Advertisement matter on money, 382.

Advertising and Selling, H. L. Hollingsworth, 249.

Advertising, Its Use and Abuse, Sir C. F. Higham, 249.

Aërial archæology, 158 sq.

Aërial beam, 167.

Aërial photography, 158.

Aëroplane quickly developed after automobile, 155 sqq.

Aëroplane "dope," 102.

Africa and Some World Problems, General Smuts, 739.

African Association, International, for promoting civilization, commerce and humane purposes, 297.

After Care work, and social rehabilitation, 873.

Age of, fossil power, 123; toil, 117; tradition, 117 sqq..

"Age" of oil, 149.

Aggressive nationalism in schools, 8; nomad, 340.

Agricultural operations by oil engine, 184.

Agriculture, "electrification" of, 183; for immediate consumption, 184; for marketing, 184; in evolution, 48; in New Zealand, 207; in "Soviet Russia," 205.

Air, compressed, 140.

Airplane, quickly developed after the automobile, 155 sq.

Airplane "dope," 102.

Air routes, lighting, 236.

Airships, development of, 156 sq.

Air transportation, development of, 157.

Airway, and the New Road, 154.

A la Conquête de la Richesse, Lewinsohn, Richard, 457, 464.

Alchemists, Arabian, the elements, 84.

Alchemy, and iatro chemistry, 80.

Alcock and Brown, 155.

Alexandria, Museum at, 89.

Allan, Mr. A. P., 29.

Allen, Devere, *The Fight for Peace* (1931), 614, 690.

Altotting, Bavaria, 803.

Aluminium, 99.

Amalgamated Clothing Workers' Union, 270.

Amanuenses, 374.